*Between Damnation
Priests and Merchants ... - ...*

In 1997 the Canadian constitution was amended to remove the
denominational rights of Newfoundland churches regarding education, erasing the last vestiges of a uniquely organized society. Until
the 1950s and 1960s Newfoundland had been characterized by
an electoral map drawn to denominational specifications, cabinet
and civil-service positions allocated on a per capita sectarian basis,
and government expenditures divided according to denominational
proportions of the total population.

While some scholars have focused on various aspects of the
denominational origins of the education system, and others have
revealed the influence of religion on the electoral results of the
pre-1864 period, the complete story has never been told. In *Between
Damnation and Starvation* John Greene presents for the first time
a far-reaching analysis of the origins and evolution of developments
in both religion and politics in Newfoundland. He reveals the full
details of political struggles, presenting them against the background of the historical evolution of churches in the century prior
to the granting of representative institutions.

Between Damnation and Starvation provides a comprehensive
treatment of a complex subject, taking into account the social,
economic, and political developments of the entire period.

JOHN P. GREENE is a writer and researcher living in Newfoundland.

McGILL-QUEEN'S STUDIES IN THE HISTORY OF RELIGION

Volumes in this series have been supported by the Jackman Foundation of Toronto.

SERIES TWO   In memory of George Rawlyk
Donald Harman Akenson, Editor

Between Damnation and Starvation

Priests and Merchants in Newfoundland Politics, 1745–1855

JOHN P. GREENE

McGill-Queen's University Press
Montreal & Kingston • London • Ithaca

© McGill-Queen's University Press 1999
ISBN 0-7735-1880-0 (cloth)
ISBN 0-7735-2195-X (paper)

Legal deposit fourth quarter 1999
Bibliothèque nationale du Québec

Printed in Canada on acid-free paper
First paperback edition 2000

This book was first published with the help of a grant
from the Humanities and Social Sciences Federation of
Canada, using funds provided by the Social Sciences
and Humanities Research Council of Canada.

McGill-Queen's University Press acknowledges the
support of the Government of Canada through the
Book Publishing Industry Development Program
(BPIDP) for its activities. We also acknowledge the
support of the Canada Council for the Arts for our
publishing program.

Canadian Cataloguing in Publication Data

Greene, John P.
    Between damnation and starvation: priests and
    merchants in Newfoundland politics, 1745–1855
    (McGill-Queen's studies in the history of religion)
    Includes bibliographical references and index.
    ISBN 0-7735-1880-0 (bnd)
    ISBN 0-7735-2195-X (pbk)
    1. Church and state – Newfoundland – History – 19th
    century. 2. Newfoundland – Politics and government –
    1763–1855. I. Title. II. Series.
    FC2172.G74 1999   971.8'01   C99-900907-9
    F1123.G74 1999

Typeset in New Baskerville 10/12
by Caractéra inc., Quebec City

To Sheila

land. His idea would never work, Coster maintained, because the lack of intellectual stimulation in the Newfoundland outports would cause the clerics to die of boredom. Besides, Coster felt, controlling salaried clerics would simply provide an opportunity for Cochrane to exert too much control over the church. And, for Coster, that control might smack too much of latitudinarian or evangelistic principles.[52] Nevertheless, Cochrane pursued the idea. When Bishop Inglis of Nova Scotia came to tour the Newfoundland section of his diocese in the spring of 1827, the governor initiated extensive discussions about an organized plan of action. On the advice of Coster, the bishop drew up a nine-point program for submission to the British government. It included: government assistance in building churches; government support for eight additional clergy; appointment of clergy to accompany the judges on circuit; fixing of parish boundaries by the governor and Colonial Office; appropriation of church glebes throughout the colony; government securing of title to land belonging to the church; licensing, by the governor, of laymen to marry; government support for schools; and creation by the government of a classical school.[53]

Inglis's program would have been appealing to many in the mid-eighteenth century; but by the second decade of the nineteenth century, such ideas were a chilling reminder that Inglis and his followers were deeply out of touch with the social and political reality of the times. By 1825 it was widely accepted in British politics that colonial governments should no longer depend on the home government for maintenance but should henceforward pay their own way.[54] This independence had spread to dominate attitudes towards the colonial churches as well, with the British government now wanting to rid itself of the burden of supporting the Church of England overseas. Consequently, the British had instructed the governor of Nova Scotia in 1826 to look to the local land-granting system as a source of revenue for the church.[55] In the previous year, the same advice had been given to the governor of New Brunswick;[56] and in Upper Canada, where the Constitution Act of 1791 had expressly reserved lands for that purpose, a political crisis had developed over church competition for public lands.

In Newfoundland, a colony completely dominated by the cod fishery and one where the poor quality of the soil and the shortness of the growing season necessitated the importation of all foodstuffs, the British government was unable to support the church out of local lands. But the Colonial Office had alternative plans for Newfoundland, and so it doomed Inglis's ideas by silently passing them on to the Treasury Department. The Colonial Office plans had arisen from the grass roots in Newfoundland itself, right under the nose of the

Anglican bishop and in a field that was destined to become the principal battleground of the churches: education.

In the debate about saving the Church of England from the Methodists and the Catholics, a number of rural clerics had long suggested education. Those were the same clerics who recognized that, because they had lost most of the Avalon to the Catholics, the coming struggle would be concentrated in the area comprising Conception Bay and northwards and the Burin peninsula and westwards. The real battle was between the Anglicans and the Methodists.

The Reverend John Leigh, writing from Twillingate in 1817, reported that the dissenters were doing their utmost to ridicule the established church and that the best way to counteract it was to instruct the young.[57] From Trinity in 1821, the Reverend Aubrey Spencer reported that Methodism was increasing in large degree because "of the religious education of childhood."[58] He wrote again in the same year to emphasise the importance of education in getting people away from Methodism and back to the established church. In 1822 the Reverend William Bullock, complaining that even the SPG school at Trinity had been taken over by Methodist teachers, urged the Society leaders in London to fire them.[59]

For more than a hundred years before Cochrane arrived in Newfoundland, the SPG had been founding day schools.[60] But, since the burden of providing missionaries alone had proven to be beyond the Society's capacity, for some time it had been reducing its education department. In fact, the SPG was now in the process of salary retrenchment for their catechists and lay readers. Besides, the church in Newfoundland was now facing an internal split. Those clerics and lay people who were possessed of a more missionary spirit were extremely unhappy with the existing state of the established church in the colony. They were the types who, like Dr George Skelton of Trinity in 1819, believed that their church had unfortunately "long shook hands with the Church of Rome." The lack of clergy, the poor quality of the missionaries, the greed of the fishermen, the rapacity of the merchants, and the zeal of the Methodists and papists were all advanced as reasons for the decline of the Church of England. But Skelton advanced an additional reason that struck a responsive chord among many discontented Anglicans. He claimed that the established church had become too lethargic and lazy because of its too close alliance and dependence on the state. It had lost its crusading spirit because too many clergy were like the Reverend John Clinch, who was not only the resident missionary in the town of Trinity but also "doctor, apothecary, accoucheur, naval officer, collector of Greenwich hospital duties, magistrate, surrogate, and collector and controller of the customs." Thus, Skelton concluded, the adherents of that Church were members "in outward form only."[61] A revival was required to return the church to the basics of true religion. Many Anglicans in England and Ireland had already arrived at the same conclusion.

The period following the end of the Napoleonic Wars had witnessed the heightening of liberalizing attitudes in British politics.[62] By the mid-1820s the tide was running against church establishment even in England, and the surging O'Connell movement in Ireland tended to destabilize traditional attitudes towards all existing church policies. Many of the leading Anglican clerics believed that their beloved church was in a state of siege. The archbishop of Dublin, James Whateley, warned that the church in Ireland was "on the eve of foundering" and the church in England would follow suit "unless very strong and speedy measures" could be adopted.[63] The English church responded to the challenge by undertaking an evangelical crusade to strengthen the Irish church and convert the Irish.[64] At the same time, it wished to extend this evangelical effort to Newfoundland. Several SPG teachers in Newfoundland had already come to that same conclusion. One teacher who performed the church services on Sundays and preached evangelical principles conducted school along the same lines. When his more conservative, high church supervisor in St John's complained, the teacher responded by calling his congregation together for a vote. The majority vote received, the congregation went, church property and all, over to the Methodists.[65] It thus became clear that the evangelical revival could be misdirected and needed strong leadership from within the established church.

Nevertheless, Newfoundland evangelicals strongly believed that their movement was the way to reform the Anglican church. Among their firmest supporters in St John's were a wealthy fish merchant, Samuel Codner, and a Royal Engineer lieutenant, Richard Vicars. Both Codner and Vicars were natives of the English west country and members of the evangelical movement then sweeping the British Isles. By the early 1820s the evangelicals were in control of the Colonial Office, and their leading lay supporter was none other than the third Earl of Liverpool, the prime minister of the United Kingdom of Great Britain and Ireland.[66]

In October 1821 the Earl of Liverpool was guest speaker at a meeting of the British and Foreign Bible Society. Speaking of the necessity of supporting the established church in the colonies, especially in the field of education, the prime minister appealed to his audience to suggest a remedy. Listening to him at the time, along with Earl Bathurst, secretary of the Colonial Office, were Samuel Codner and Richard Vicars. Having discussed possible ways of meeting Liverpool's challenge,

Codner and Vicars, at a public meeting on 30 June 1823, founded the Newfoundland Society for Educating the Poor.[67] This society shortly hired and trained two teachers, and by 1824 it had opened in St John's the first school in what was destined to be a chain of twenty such schools throughout Newfoundland. In 1827 Lord Bathurst of the Colonial Office, while referring without comment to the Treasury Department the nine-point program of Bishop Inglis, pointedly ordered the Newfoundland governor to afford every facility in his power "to the extension of the operations of this Society" within the government.[68] Almost immediately on receipt of that dispatch, Governor Cochrane enrolled himself with the prime minister of the United Kingdom as vice-patron of the Newfoundland School Society (NSS).

One of the most immediate and more pronounced effects of the NSS in St John's was to excite the alarm and jealousy of the Roman Catholics.[69] Their children had long been attending the St John's Charity School, an interdenominational institution founded on the impetus of Governor Erasmus Gower in 1802. While its teachers were all Protestant, its education had been conducted along liberal principles, reserving religious instruction to those pupils whose parents wished to remove them for that purpose. The Roman Catholic bishop and his priests in St John's sat on the Charity School's board of directors and the leading Catholic gentlemen in the town subscribed to its coffers.

The presence of the new school after 1824 caused serious anxiety in some Catholic quarters, especially since the Charity School began to lose ground and some Catholic parents enrolled their children in the rival institution. The Benevolent Irish Society (BIS), an interdenominational and charitable body, met in 1825 to discuss the most effectual means of providing for the education of its indigent poor.[70] Some Catholic members were content with the present situation, but the BIS president, Patrick Morris, argued that the Newfoundland School Society was far from satisfactory and that parents sent their children there with great reluctance. He felt that there were not enough schools to meet the increasing needs of the expanding population of St John's. Besides, he was concerned about the breaching of "liberal principles" by the NSS and wanted a school where all denominations could send their children without fear of proselytism. Only in this way, he believed, could they preserve amity and avoid the religious discord which had rent asunder other communities. Morris had his way and in 1826 the BIS opened its now famous interdenominational Orphan Asylum School, in which the teaching of religion was expressly forbidden.

But perhaps it was political jealousy as much as anything else that had aroused Morris's alarm. As an up-and-coming middle-class merchant with Irish and Roman Catholic roots, Morris had for several years been involved in the struggle for constitutional reform in the colony.[71] In Ireland he had immersed himself in the emancipation struggle, becoming a member of Daniel O' Connell's Catholic Association. Throughout the south of Ireland Morris helped heighten the Catholic rights agitation, the chief target of which was the infamous anti-Catholic, Liverpool administration in London. The leading members of that government and its backbench MPs were the founding organizers of the Newfoundland School Society. When, at an annual meeting of this society in 1826, remarks were made about the backwardness of Newfoundland, Morris launched bitter attacks on the NSS in Irish and Newfoundland newspapers. As the emancipation struggle intensified throughout the British Isles, numerous clashes between the O'Connell-Morris party and the officers of the NSS occurred. The leading officers of that organization in the British Isles joined the ultra-Tory, right-wing, extremist group that fought to the end against Catholic emancipation. In Ireland the hated and despised anti-Catholic Henry Goulbourn, the second most important man in the Irish government, became a vice-president of the NSS in 1827. For O'Connell, Morris, and the British liberals, the removal of Goulbourn was necessary before Catholics achieved equality, and they made him a target for the Newfoundland Reformers. In 1828 the treasurer of the NSS, John Wells, MP, declared at an anti-Catholic public meeting that he would fight for Protestant ascendancy "up to his knees in blood."[72] Such was the atmosphere in which Roman Catholics waged their campaign against the NSS, a campaign that persisted long after the emancipation struggle had been won in 1829.

Roman Catholic distrust of the NSS was marked by a similar distrust on the part of the leading Anglican clergy. Their parent organization in London, the SPG, warned the Reverend Bullock of Trinity in 1824 against too close an alliance with the evangelically minded NSS. Bullock profusely apologized for any countenance he had mistakenly given to that organization and began to distance himself immediately from it. The Reverend George Coster tried unsuccessfully in 1826 to prevent the NSS from founding a school in Bonavista. Its masters, he declared, are all of "evangelical principles" and he had great fears for the future of the established church. The Methodists, he stated, were steadily gaining ground especially because of the NSS schools. To add to his fears, he was becoming annoyingly discouraged because of a distinct lack of overt support from a "conciliatory and liberal" government. In this and other matters, he complained, "the Methodists have cocked their tails and flung up their heels at us."[73]

Coster, and others of like sympathy, took up the subject with Bishop Inglis on the latter's arrival for an episcopal visitation in 1827. Having surveyed the scene on a first-hand basis, Inglis condemned the NSS schools in no uncertain terms. They are of a "fanatical character," he declared, "set on foot by the Calvinistic party from whom the Masters are selected though they all attend the Church of England."[74] What was required, the colony's high Anglican clergy concluded, were schools that were more closely connected with the church establishment, schools in which the principles of the established church would be the main focus. Coster urged them all to remember that "it's easier to prevent mischief than to remedy it" and the Anglicans should therefore place the emphasis on those parts of Newfoundland that were still mainly Protestant.[75] A viable strategy, it met with the unanimous approval of the bishop and his supporting clergy. But what kind of program would secure the hundreds of Protestant coves and harbours strung out along thousands of miles of shoreline north of St John's and west of Placentia Bay? What sort of program would succeed where the established church and its SPG schools had had such failures over the past seventy-five years? Coster had the answer – it was the "National System," also known as "Dr. Bell's" system.

The "National system" referred to the schools in England of the National Society for Promoting the Education of the Poor in the Principles of the Established Church Throughout England and Wales.[76] These schools had been established to rival the Lancastrian schools that were supported by the evangelicals and non-conformists. What was most appealing to the archbishop of Canterbury and his supporters was that the National schools taught the principles and doctrines of the established church to all pupils. Dr Andrew Bell, one of the church's more popular teachers, had pioneered in India a new teaching technique that saved money and helped overcome the teacher shortage. Known also as the "monitorial system," it consisted of enlisting the more mature students in the service of teaching the younger ones. A comprehensive, but definitive, curricular program that could easily be mastered with repetition was devised. Those Monitors were then employed teaching other monitors and students so that larger and larger enrolments could be accommodated in the same school.

The monitorial system was implemented in St John's Charity School during the school year of 1827–28. Initially, it made some headway against the NSS schools. But Inglis and his supporters received a major setback when their overall program, submitted to the Colonial Office later that year, did not receive the expected financial support from the British government. To add to the problem, the government decided instead to back the rival NSS. When Governor Cochrane placed his support behind that body, it quickly regained what it had lost. By the early 1830s, the end was in sight for the Charity School and the National System in Newfoundland.

Contributing perhaps more than anything else to these failures on the part of the Church of England was the fact that Newfoundlanders seemed to prefer the evangelical brand of Christianity. This had been made clear in 1830 at Portugal Cove, where, as earlier recounted, Archdeacon Edward Wix[77] watched in despair as an Anglican congregation bolted from the church of England to the arms of the Methodists.[78] The Reverend Charles Shreve from Harbour Grace reported in 1833 on the same propensity on the part of Anglicans of that town and Carbonear. Wix, in a mixture of anger and frustration, lashed out at his own clergy. Impatiently declaring that he could not convince all his ministers to withdraw their pupils from the NSS schools for religious instruction, he complained: "Our Clergy ... too readily yield the ground for the sake of peace."[79] Therein lay the revealing admission of yet another problem that hampered his campaign against the NSS – too many of his clergy were of the evangelical stamp. Wix seemed to have belatedly realized that fact and in the fall of 1831 installed a system of monitoring the preaching of all his clergy so as to weed out those not strictly adhering to the teachings of the established church. On all those clergy who were willing to cooperate he urged the necessity of starting a Sunday school to combat the NSS's insidious influence on their own faithful. When Bullock, of Trinity, implemented the plan the Society schoolmaster there threatened his pupils that, if they went to Bullock on Sundays, they should not come to him on weekdays. When Bullock complained to the parent body in London, the local teacher denied the charge; at this point Bullock had several parents give sworn statements in his defence, initiating a public quarrel that split the community in two. Governor Thomas Cochrane, along with the Trinity member in the new House of Assembly, John B. Garland, and the chief Justice of the colony, R.A. Tucker, were all drawn into the fight. With the assistance of the latter two public figures, the governor arranged a compromise that restored the peace and quiet.[80] But it was a peace and quiet that left the status quo intact, and the advantage remained with the NSS. Bullock wrote Wix to warn him that the Wesleyans were out for a fight and "we must gird ourselves for the combat."[81] He urged Wix to call a meeting of all the clergy in an effort to deal with the problem. The Reverend Charles Blackman[82] supported Bullock and announced his intention of founding a new school in St John's in 1834. Blackman, who possessed an M.A., swore that with his educational attainments the school would be sure to succeed.

Coinciding with Blackman's announcement of a new, more conforming, Anglican school was the founding of a new, very special, and

much celebrated Roman Catholic school in St John's. Believing that
the NSS had been established for the purposes of converting Roman
Catholics,[83] the new Catholic bishop, Michael Anthony Fleming, had
recruited an order of Irish Presentation Nuns to teach Catholic youth.
With much fanfare they landed at the St John's waterfront in September 1833 and within a month Fleming had presided over the opening
of their new school. That development signalled significant changes
in the attitudes of the Roman Catholic Church in Newfoundland. It
also heralded a potential conflict over education between the Roman
Catholics, on the one hand, and their former Protstant allies, on the
other, as well as within the Catholic community itself. No wonder the
Chief Justice Richard Alexander Tucker felt "fearful of what might
happen,"[84] while Governor Cochrane and his officials sensed the
presence of a dark cloud hanging over the colony. They awaited with
bated breath to discover how much of a departure from the traditional
Roman Catholic policy in Newfoundland would be made by the new
Catholic bishop.

   In the post-1820 period, therefore, competition between the
churches had been translated into rivalry over education. This development had deep roots in the Protestant community going back to
the middle of the eighteenth century. The struggle between evangelical and non-evangelical Protestants had effectively sectarianized the
education debate by the early 1830s with both sides establishing their
own schools. Through all of this, the Roman Catholic Church had
mainly been an observer. Then, as new leadership appeared in the
person of Bishop Fleming, that church also followed the lead of the
other denominations in founding church schools.

3 Bishop Fleming and Newfoundland Catholicism, 1829–37

Governor Thomas Cochrane must have approached the 1830s decade with a great deal of anxiety. Internal divisions rent the church he supported, and Methodists were bitterly complaining of high Anglican actions. Compounding Cochrane's fears were two political movements for change that built up momentum in the 1820s: one, in England, held as its goal Catholic emancipation, and the other, in Newfoundland, aimed for constitutional change. Together, these movements held out the possibility of Irish Catholics becoming involved in the political process. More than ever before in Newfoundland, there was anxiety over how the Roman Catholic Church might behave. Already there were worrisome signs that there might be a departure in policy from that exercised in the previous decades.

The year 1829 was a fateful one for Newfoundland's Roman Catholics. That April, the Catholic emancipation bill was passed by the British Parliament. The once obnoxious, odious, and infamous oaths that had prevented Roman Catholics from serving in Parliament or occupying positions in the upper levels of government service were removed. Throughout the British Isles there was great rejoicing, but nothing exceeded the joyful excitement which greeted the news in Newfoundland.

The Protestant *Public Ledger*, a supporter of emancipation, had carried verbatim accounts of debates on the bill in the British Parliament. When news arrived in early May of its final passage, the Congregationalist editor declared that it was "humiliating to think that such an act of justice took so long."[1] On May 7 the *Newfoundlander* first broke the news in St John's to an anxiously awaiting Roman Catholic public; its editor declared that there was great jubilation and gratitude throughout the colony. The Roman Catholic bishop, Thomas Scallan, declared 21 May as a day of public thanksgiving for the blessings conferred by the legislation. The Benevolent Irish Society convened a special meeting to lay plans for a parade through the capital involving all citizens in the celebrations.

In St John's huge parades soon wound their way around the circumference of the town, their ultimate destination being the Roman Catholic church where Bishop Scallan and his priests performed a Mass of thanksgiving. The Reverend Michael Anthony Fleming preached an impressive sermon characterized by "sentiments purely loyal and patriotic" and he concluded by leading the congregation in three cheers for the King, Peel, and "as many as their lungs could permit for O'Connell."[2] After Mass the parades continued, with banners waving, colours flying, and drums beating; guns fired all round the town, cannons roared from both sides of the harbour, while ships in the stream and merchants on shore displayed their colours. Celebrations continued throughout the night.

Harbour Grace declared 25 May as its own day of public thanksgiving, and celebrations continued throughout May and early June in Carbonear, Bay Roberts, Port de Grave, and other towns in the colony. At Harbour Grace, celebrations commenced with a huge bonfire fuelled by twenty barrels of pitch and tar; parades arrayed with fife, drums, and streamers meandered through the streets; ships and mercantile establishments were adorned with colour. Fort Duckworth fired volleys of salutes, and night became like day with lighted homes and decorated buildings.

Detailed, biweekly reports of such celebrations were carried in all the St John's and Conception Bay newspapers. The way was now cleared, it seemed, for Roman Catholics to take their places as equal citizens side by side with the Protestants and for Bishop Scallan to assume his seat at the Council table in company with the Anglican bishop, John Inglis. But Governor Cochrane, despite his initial readiness to accommodate Roman Catholics, then hesitated.[3] It was a fateful hesitation, for it initiated a series of Roman Catholic complaints that would eventually culminate with Cochrane's unceremonious dismissal five years later.

As we have seen, on arriving in Newfoundland in the fall of 1825, Cochrane had shown an eagerness to unburden the Roman Catholics from their disabilities; in constructing the first colonial council, he nominated three Catholics for membership therein.[4] Cochrane had hoped that the British government would allow him to suspend the infamous anti-Catholic oaths, as had been done sixty-five years earlier in the captured French-Catholic colony of Quebec. When the same exception was not made for Newfoundland, Cochrane expressed his disappointment, saying that with such heavy immigration from Ireland he expected Roman Catholics soon to be in a majority in the colony. However, with the successful conclusion of the emancipation struggle, Cochrane made no attempt to submit Roman Catholic names for appointment to his Council. Instead, he looked for a delay, asking the law officers of the crown whether or not the legislation applied to Newfoundland. They replied in the negative and advised him that, in order to remove political disabilities from the Catholics of Newfoundland, entirely new vice-regal instructions would have to be issued by the king.[5] Although Cochrane officially supported Catholic emancipation in his report of this legal advice to the home government, he took no steps whatever to mollify the effects of such bad news in Newfoundland. When news of the law officers' opinion leaked out, there was bitter shock among the Catholics, followed by sincere hurt and dismay that soon gave way to bitter anger. As rumours swirled, several Catholics formed a committee and convened a public meeting of Roman Catholics for 17 December 1829. There, amidst loud expressions of indignation and regret, they read the governor's reply to their previous request for information. Before answering their courteous and reasonable demand, Cochrane condescendingly lectured them for their audacity in calling "a Roman Catholic" meeting. That course was "calculated to disturb the harmony which has long existed between the various religions" and was sure to cause trouble by "exciting the ignorant" among them.[6] Then he officially dropped the bad news – Roman Catholics in Newfoundland were not yet emancipated. Eight leading Roman Catholics in the church and community addressed the meeting on the subject of religion and political liberty, and all reports referred to the perfect peace and orderliness of the proceedings.[7] The gathering passed resolutions to petition the British Parliament for relief and made plans for another such meeting on 28 December at the Roman Catholic church. Then they dispersed with cheers for all the ladies present at "the largest meeting ever held in Newfoundland" and for the Roman Catholic bishop. The subsequent meeting adopted the resolutions and commissioned Patrick Morris to convey them personally to Daniel O'Connell for presentation in the British House of Commons. It was the spring of 1830 before Morris heard a favourable response and late May before the news reached Newfoundland. Thus, it took more than a year after the

passing of the Emancipation Act before the Catholics of Newfoundland were told that they would be placed on the same political footing
as their co-religionists in the British Isles.

In the meantime, agitation that had commenced for a local house
of assembly quickened after Catholic emancipation had been granted.
In an attempt to block British acquiescence to Newfoundland's
demand for representative institutions, Governor Cochrane argued
that the colony was too primitive to sustain a local parliament.[8] He
suggested instead the formation of an enlarged council for which he
submitted the names of fourteen principal inhabitants. Most were
prominent merchants; not one was a Roman Catholic.

What had happened to Governor Cochrane's determination to give
justice to the Roman Catholics? Where was his idealism of 1825, when
he had attempted to place three Catholics in his Council to forestall
any disharmony or sectarian grievance? What had caused such a shift
in his policy to the extent that he was willing to include three Catholics
out of thirteen in 1825 but in 1831 not one out of fourteen? Certainly
his Newfoundland experience had contributed in large part to his
change of view.

Perhaps the decisive factor related to the altered circumstances in
the salt-cod industry. The previous few years had witnessed the beginning of deterioration in the fishing industry. From the mid-1820s
onward, production in the fishery grew only marginally[9] while population increased at an alarming rate, more than 40 per cent in the
period from 1820 to 1827. There were disturbing signs abroad as well.
Norway had entered some of Newfoundland's traditional markets, fish
prices were falling, and there were indications of rising tariffs in
Portugal and Spain. These were especially worrisome trends since
Newfoundland's export trade in cod went to foreign markets instead
of British Empire destinations. Mercantile interests engaged in the
production and export of salt cod were especially vulnerable for they
were dependent on the British government to manage foreign competition and tariffs.[10] Those merchants favoured by Cochrane for
Council seats were all involved in that branch of the trade; and, as the
momentum for an elected house of assembly increased, they could
not help but be reminded that the focus of decision making had now
shifted to St John's. The fact that the laws governing the production
of salt cod in Newfoundland were now in a state of flux complicated
their problems and there was a widespread diversity of opinion on
how those laws could best be adjusted.[11] There were worrisome signs,
too, of greater political cohesion on the part of the Irish population
which, if allowed to come to fruition, would seriously threaten the
power of government officials and the mercantile elite. It was there-

fore natural for those same merchants to attempt to solidify their position in the face of impending political and economic changes. But there were other reasons as well for Cochrane's change of view.

Thomas Cochrane, as we have seen, arrived in 1825 in a colony that had become a battleground between the rival churches. So intense was the battle that Cochrane himself was soon conscripted on behalf of one of the combatants. Hard upon his assumption of office came a continual barrage of demands reflecting different points of view in the church that he supported. Soon he was giving as much attention to serving the interests of the established church as administering the Newfoundland government. Cochrane, of course, did not have to be convinced of the importance of the Church of England, for in England, Ireland, and Wales that church was officially established. The governor shared the prevailing view that the best way to develop good citizens and supporters of the constitution was by cementing the ties between the people and their clergy. By 1826 he was convinced that there was a greater necessity in Newfoundland for this policy than anywhere else for these "ignorant" people were "easily led off by those who possess their confidence."[12] Cochrane was not only personally a "latitudinarian" leaning to the support of the evangelical wing of his church – the prevailing trend in Newfoundland – but his superiors in the Colonial Office in London were of the same stamp and told him in no uncertain terms whom he should support.

In addition, the intensification of the Catholic emancipation struggle at home and in Newfoundland coincided with Cochrane's assumption of the governorship of the colony. Although he personally and privately supported Roman Catholic relief, his support arose from his perceived need to placate troublesome Catholics rather than from a commitment to tolerance. In England, Parliament had finally passed the Emancipation Act of 1829 on account of a perceived fear of an impending rebellion in Ireland. The legacy bequeathed was not one that earned any lasting Catholic gratitude for the British government.[13] This was especially so in Newfoundland because there the final, long-awaited boon was delayed for more than a year on legal technicalities by Governor Cochrane and the judges. That move proved extremely frustrating to Catholic leaders who, it appears, would have opted for more radical and aggressive agitation had not their desires been dampened by the Roman Catholic bishop, Thomas Scallan, and his conservative friends.

Scallan had been pursuing the traditional, conciliatory policy inaugurated by O'Donnel, the founder of the Roman Catholic Church in Newfoundland. In fact, there is evidence that Scallan gave to that policy a hue peculiarly of his own stamp.[14] Through his exceeding graciousness and deference to the British government, the military, the magistrates, the business community, and all Protestants, Scallan posthumously earned the gratitude of British officials. The Reverend F.H. Carrington, Anglican rector in St John's, referred to him as his "much valued and esteemed friend"[15] and years after his death a Protestant governor fondly recalled his memory.[16] In fact, Scallan's own episcopal successors censured him for "being too yielding in his endeavours to please and propitiate his Protestant friends."[17] Nevertheless, while Scallan received full credit from the governor for his calming policies and demeanour, he failed to earn thereby any trust for his Roman Catholic flock. Cochrane's officials continually filled the governor's ears with exaggerated reports of the rebellious tendencies of Newfoundland's Catholics. Converts to the Roman Catholic Church, they warned, were becoming "aliens to their God and to their country."[18] The ignorant Catholics of Newfoundland, he was told, could not distinguish between spiritual and temporal authority and their priests therefore secured "absolute control." In Newfoundland, as in England and Ireland, that control was considered a threat to the British constitution. Even during the rather meek protest of December 1829 over the delay of Catholic relief, with Bishop Scallan still humbly eating at his table, Cochrane could only express deep regret that "an R.C. meeting" had been called.[19] And Chief Justice Tucker nervously wrote the governor to say that he was fearful of what might happen.[20] Of what were they afraid? What was wrong with a Roman Catholic meeting? Were they just plain and simple bigots? In fact, their assessment of the political situation arose from a full knowledge both of the British constitution and of the circumstances of Newfoundland society.

In the British system, power, as both Cochrane and Tucker knew full well, was the sole preserve of an elite of upper-class landlords who exercised their prerogatives through a bicameral legislature. While the House of Lords was a thoroughly appointive body, the House of Commons did, at least instrumentally, possess an elective characteristic. Tenants, on landlord property, were permitted in open voting to select their landlord's representative, a procedure not complained of as long as landlords got the man they approved.[21] Most often, however, as enclosure of farms had driven huge numbers of tenants off the land, representatives were chosen by only a handful of tenants or appointed by the landlord himself. In cases where, through enclosure, landowners had amassed huge areas of the country, they frequently controlled several seats in the Commons and often sold them to the highest bidder. The process of filling up the Commons was regularly referred to as the rights of property, and any interference with this right occasioned loud complaints. To give an example, if tenants were

Roman Catholic and voted according to religion, the right of property, perhaps the most sacred right in the British constitution, would be in jeopardy. That was the threat posed to the British system by O'Conell's organization in Ireland and by the Roman Catholic Reformer, Patrick Morris, in Newfoundland.

Cochrane, as well as authorities in England and Ireland, was fearful of any hint of Catholic union, and the political value to the Newfoundland government of the services of a bishop like Scallan increased with the imminence of religious agitation. Once emancipation had occurred, it became more of a necessity to rely on Scallan, for whom profuse praises emanated from all quarters. When he died on 29 May 1830, the grieving was unparalleled in the community.[22] Marching in his funeral procession were seven thousand people, including the clergy of all the Protestant denominations. Shops were closed. Ships in the harbour flew their flags at half-mast. The Protestant *Ledger* carried two separate reports of a man "adorned with the brightest virtues" and eulogized Scallan as a man of greatness, goodness, wisdom, charity, tolerance, and duty. "Never died a man in this country," declared the Protestant Winton, "more universally beloved and revered" than Scallan.[23]

Praise for Scallan was a backhanded way of telling the Catholic Church what kind of bishop was favoured by the British. It also signified what kind of bishop they did not want because Catholics were expected to conform in a certain specified manner. In Newfoundland, Catholics were supposed to be quiet, and nothing pleased the governors more than to describe their condition in those terms.[24] Being quiet meant that Catholics should not commence a political agitation but should wait for relief to be duly granted. If the aggrieved became impatient, then the British system forced them to follow a clearly defined route for redress, the privilege of the British parliamentary system: it was the custom to act for change upon receipt of the usual petition. Some principal gentleman, or gentlemen, upon request from a previously approved and prearranged public meeting, would present a humble petition to the governor, whose consent to receive it had been ascertained in advance. It had to be framed in a specified manner to show proper deference to the king, and the governor reserved the right to decide whether or not to send it home. If redress was not granted, the aggrieved had to submit with resignation or try again. In Ireland, Daniel O'Connell had refused to be content with this system and began something radically new; he held huge public meetings, often in the open air.[25] The British government recognized that tactic as a distinct revolutionary threat to their system of controlling demands for change and repeatedly confronted O'Connell with legal challenges that spuriously sought to confine him either to the courtroom or, preferably, to the jailhouse. In Newfoundland, requests for public meetings on the most innocuous matters had to be forwarded to the sheriff, who could then grant them without prior approval from the governor; for meetings related to issues of greater sgnificance, the governor's consent was required.

The wisdom of Scallan's policy, for which Cochrane felt so thankful, was based on the bishop's success at controlling Catholic protests and preventing agitation of any kind, especially that based on religion. But underlying official approval of Bishop Scallan and his predecessors was the implied threat that, if Roman Catholics did not behave in the expected manner, they would immediately be labelled as troublemakers. Newfoundland governors seemed perennially to consider the Irish Catholics as existing permanently in a state of suspended animation. Perhaps that was justifiable considering that appointments of Catholic bishops were entirely outside the governors' control; in fact, the most anxious time for a British governor was always that following the death of one bishop and preceding the installation of his successor. Thus, the basic message conveyed by the near-universal praise heaped on the late Bishop Scallan in 1830 was that Roman Catholics should be given another bishop of the same political temperament. Indeed, official anxiety was then more intense than ever because Scallan had died barely a year after Catholic emancipation had been granted. His successor, Michael Anthony Fleming, gave Cochrane little time to fret for he almost immediately repudiated the traditional policy of his predecessors. From now on, he soon informed everyone, Roman Catholics would not simply beg for their rightful place in Newfoundland society but would demand it as a right.

Fleming had been born in Carrick-on-Suir, Tipperary,[26] in 1792 and at the age of sixteen had joined the Franciscan monastery in Wexford where he received the habit from its superior, Thomas Scallan, the future bishop of Newfoundland. That was the very same bishop who would later recruit the young novice for the Newfoundland mission. Ordained in 1815, Fleming was apprenticed to his uncle, Father Martin Fleming, in his home parish of Carrick where he served until 1823 when he accepted the invitation of Bishop Scallan to assume the duties of a curate in St John's. There young Fleming soon gained a reputation as a man of great strength. The physical exertions that he displayed during religious parades or stations of the cross taxed the endurance of all parishioners. In constructing the great cathedral which stands today in his memory in St John's, Fleming astounded the labourers, stonemasons, and carpenters alike as he joined in the work. They could only stand by in awe as he pitched himself into the heaviest pushing, lifting, and hauling. He created a sensation when, in an effort to acquire stone for the church, he built himself a crude shed on a small island in Conception Bay and spent several months there performing by hand not only the most menial but the most difficult of tasks. His devoted followers feared for his health on the island as he faced several months of the harshest of weather on a rather meagre diet. "As for himself," said a Presentation nun, "he appears not to care for anything in this world."[27] That same vigour was shown in his clerical work. The zeal with which he carried on his private prayers and public religious devotions became legendary. For example, on New Year's Day, 1834, Bishop Fleming sang two High Masses one after the other, a chore that likely took more than two hours. Following the second Mass he called the Presentation nuns to the front of the altar and led them in a renewal of their vows. Then he honoured them with a sermon of approximately one hour's duration. His reputation reached right to the doors of the Vatican, where the pope came to regard him as an outstandingly pious and holy man. Perhaps it was that zeal which led his former superior, Thomas Scallan, to select him for the Newfoundland mission.

Although Fleming had been six years in Newfoundland and fourteen years a priest before assuming the leadership of the Newfoundland church, he had given little public hint in St John's of the policy he was to pursue. Given his background, however, it should not have been a total surprise that he harboured views contrary to prevailing church policy in Newfoundland and Ireland. His formative years occurred against a background of failed hopes for Catholic emancipation in Ireland and of the efforts of young lawyer, Daniel O'Connell, to change the direction of the Irish Catholic representative body, the Catholic Committee.

When Fleming was a boy, the church was still engaged in sort of a tenuous alliance with the British government, one that owed its origins to political developments in late-eighteenth-century Ireland.[28] Following the Seven Years War (1756–1763) the Irish Roman Catholic Church had moved towards an accommodation with the British government in order to accomplish a relaxation of the penal laws and to secure a legitimate role for itself in Irish life. The British government responded positively for a number of reasons, so that by the end of the century they had removed all but some political restrictions on Roman Catholics. In 1795 they even took the unprecedented step of partially endowing Maynooth, a new Roman Catholic seminary for the training of clergy. The result was the emergence in Ireland of a Roman Catholic Church loyal to the British government and dominated by "Castle" bishops who supported the British link to the extent they condemned the rebellion of 1798 and gave effectual support to the parliamentary union of 1800. Pursuant to the union, the Irish church raised the possibility of a British-government endowment for all Roman Catholic clergy and opened negotiations towards according a British government veto over clerical appointments to Irish sees.[29]

In 1813 the proposal was placed before the British House of Commons, but in Ireland Daniel O'Connell created a sensation when he urged all his countrymen to reject it. O'Connell split the Catholic Committee over the veto and in the strongest terms condemned all clergy who dared to support it. He issued a challenge to all Irishmen to rise up and force their Catholic Church to change its policy. Joining O'Connell in the struggle against the church's official position was the Reverend Richard Hayes, a seminarian instructor whose star pupil at that time was none other than Michael Anthony Fleming. Hayes carried the fight right to the foot of the papal throne, remonstrating with the pontiff to rescind his support for a proposal he had previously approved. O'Connell and Hayes were crowned with success and a new era in Irish politics began. Their thinking was based on the premise that the Irish Catholic Church should remain free and independent of British control. For O'Connell, also, there was the opportunity to use religion as a rallying cry and a basis for a campaign for emancipation without conditions.

It seems that the struggle led by O'Connell and Hayes had a long-lasting impact on young Fleming's life. He remained an ardent admirer and close friend of Hayes, continuing to correspond with him even after the bishop of Ferns had suspended him for his contentious preaching.[30] Fleming was destined to carry from Ireland to Newfoundland the indelible marks left by the anti-veto campaign and the philosophy behind that strategy was destined to dominate his church policy in Newfoundland. When he left Ireland for Newfoundland in 1822, therefore, he harboured views contrary to those entertained by the great majority of his brother clergy at home.

After the veto crisis, O'Connell established the Catholic Association, through which, over the next few years, he would entirely transform the church hierarchy's attitudes. The Irish Roman Catholic church would shortly become an independent and formidable power bloc in British politics to the extent of severely limiting any independent political action in Ireland on the part of either Dublin Castle or Westminster. Fleming was destined to transform the Newfoundland Catholic Church into a similarly formidable power bloc. In Ireland such a feat was accomplished largely through lay efforts and from the bottom up, but in Newfoundland it became a top-down operation. In that sense, the Fleming revolution in Newfoundland was unprecedented.

Fleming was possessed of a deep-seated fear and suspicion of the British-Protestant government and for that reason, apparently, he unreservedly opposed a British government veto for Irish episcopal appointments. For the same reason he felt contemptuous of the "Castle" church which he found on his arrival in the colony. As soon as he assumed the leadership of that church, he announced a complete break with the policies of his predecessors and began to build an independent church based on popular support beholden to no one except Rome and the common fishermen. Even before he was officially installed as bishop, he took unprecedented steps to declare independence for the Catholic clergy in Newfoundland. After he had unsuccessfully remonstrated with the governor over the obligation to pay marriage fees, Fleming announced that the Roman Catholic clergy in this colony would never remit such fees again.[31] He then informed the Anglican rector, who was obliged to collect burial fees: "I consider it the most penal act of injustice that could be imposed on any denomination of Christians to compel them to pay to a clergyman of a different persuasion a fee for the interment of their dead."[32] In that way he stopped the burial fees as well.

It was symbolic of Fleming's position as ruler-in-waiting that he played the key role of preaching the sermon at the Mass of celebration on the occasion of Catholic emancipation; and it should have been a harbinger of things to come when, right in the middle of Mass, he took the unprecedented step of leading the congregation in cheers for Daniel O'Connell.[33] Just a few weeks before his episcopal ordination, the guiding hand of the new bishop-elect could be detected behind the first Catholic meetings called to protest the delay of emancipation. These meetings had exceedingly worried the governor and had led to an expression of fear on the part of the chief justice. Fleming, however, showed no reluctance about fighting for political equality; he considered the struggle for equality just as much his duty as religious instruction. While visiting Ireland in 1830 to recruit priests, Fleming made a special trip to the Colonial Office in London to press for emancipation of the Newfoundland Catholics.[34]

But, for the British authorities, the greatest shock was to come in March 1831. Then, in a speech in Ireland, Fleming toasted his native land, blaming all its economic and social ills on "the system of misrule by which Ireland was governed." He extolled O'Connell as one who had done more for the liberty and prosperity of Ireland "than any other man that has appeared since the invasion," and in a declaration that the British government must have considered verging on treason, Fleming urged all Irishmen everywhere to rise up and demand repeal of the union.[35] Fleming and O'Connell had become impatient with the British government for Catholics had waited more than thirty years for the fulfillment of a promise solemnly made on emancipation. In the case of Newfoundland, while the act abolishing Catholic disabilities had passed the British Parliament in April 1829, the commission authorizing the governor to give effectual relief did not arrive in Newfoundland until the spring of 1832. So it was that Newfoundland Catholics had to wait three full years for the opportunity to enjoy privileges given to all other Catholics in the British empire in 1829. In 1832 the grateful Roman Catholic bishop publicly thanked and congratulated the governor and the British authorities for emancipating Newfoundland Catholics. But although the obnoxious oaths that had prevented Catholics from serving in high places had been removed, there still remained another oath which Bishop Fleming considered an insult to Catholics. That was the oath requiring Catholics to "renounce, reject and abjure the opinion that Princes excommunicated by the Pope and Council, or any authority of the See of Rome or by any authority whatsoever, may be deposed or murdered by their subjects."

Fleming shot off a public letter to the *Newfoundlander* condemning such a declaration as an embarrassment to all Catholics and saying that he felt abashed to have such an oath administered in the presence of Protestants.[36] There was not a single Catholic left in Europe who would not subscribe to it, he said, because it was perfectly compatible with Catholic doctrine. Catholics, he pointed out, owe no allegiance to the pope. William IV was king and a Catholic subject's only temporal allegiance was due to him. But, while Fleming swore his loyalty to the throne, he continued to be guided by his innate suspicions of the Protestant British governments in St John's and London.

Fleming was so adamant about keeping the governments, British and colonial, at arms length that he remained contemptuous of the subservience shown by his predecessors.[37] He sarcastically dismissed claims that the British government had encouraged O'Donel to found the Roman Catholic Church in Newfoundland, and he insinuated instead that the British government was in fact dependent on the church to keep the colony loyal and prevent its following the route taken by the Americans. It was a such a necessity, Fleming believed, that led the British government to grant religious toleration in the first place – not from any genuine desire to aid the Roman Catholic Church. The church in Newfoundland owed the government nothing. Indeed, Fleming blamed the government and his own episcopal predecessors for the sorry state of Newfoundland society: "It is not to be wondered at that religion should have made comparatively little advance during the incumbency of the three prelates who preceded me in the Episcopal chair of Newfoundland."[38]

Fleming's attitude to government was soon made clear when he rejected the salary that had been paid to earlier Catholic bishops.[39] Later, when charges were made against him by members of his own church, he indignantly repudiated the interference of the British Colonial Office when it attempted to get an explanation.[40] He considered the Colonial Office's inquiries as an encroachment on his spiritual authority and replied that he answered only to Rome. Still later, when the subject arose of re-organizing the church in the British North American colonies, including Newfoundland, under the jurisdiction of Quebec, Fleming wrote a strong letter to Rome regarding the "impropriety of separating Newfoundland from a connexion with any other save that of Rome."[41] That particular course, he said, he adopted for one paramount reason: "The fact that my confidence in a portion of the hierarchy that have so often given the clearest evidence of their being under the immediate control of the Protestant British government is by no means fixed and this dependence is likely in my mind to continue as long as they owe so large a portion of their revenue to British Protestant bounty while their aggrandisement on the other hand by placing all the North American colonies under their spiritual control would have the effect of strengthening their claim upon that government for even an accession of pay."[42]

Fleming, who had no intention of being beholden to anybody but the pope, served notice of his independence from government by initiating steps to cement his control atop the church in Newfoundland. His suspicions of Protestants were parallelled by a marked refusal to allow lay people any participation in church governance whatsoever. He believed that the laity "should be kept entirely at bay for once a lay control was admitted in small things the evil would grow progressively until the Prelate or the Priest who at first shirked the trouble next was startled at the interference of Laymen led on by their own acts then alarmed at their dictation are eventually crushed beneath a monstrous power of their own creation."[43]

Fleming was convinced that the disorders then afflicting the church in Ireland, Gibraltar, Nova Scotia, and the United States stemmed from the same cause, namely, allowing lay people to take charge of the church temporalities. Those practices, he warned Bishop William Walsh of Halifax, "are calculated to shake the whole fabric of the church to its core."[44] Under Fleming's predecessors in Newfoundland, a committee of laymen apparently had full charge of raising and expending all building revenues as well as purchasing all supplies for the church and clergy.[45] "I could never understand," Fleming told the pope, "how bishops or clergymen could consent to this degradation."[46] While still a curate he had attempted unsuccessfully to put an end to that abuse, and, as soon as he was consecrated bishop, he fired the lay committee and assumed total charge of its affairs. It appears that two of the more prominent fired laymen were Patrick Kough,[47] a government contractor, Timothy Hogan,[48] a St John's shopkeeper and president of the BIS. They made their opposition to Fleming a public matter by opposing the involvement of the bishop and the church in politics.[49] In doing so, they identified themselves with the conservative, pro-government, pro-mercantile party in the 1832–33 elections, giving their outright support to the government newspapers that continually launched bitter verbal assaults upon the Roman Catholic Church and its clergy. Beginning in 1834 Fleming and his supporters worked to oust Hogan from the presidency of the BIS. By 1835 all offices in that body were in the hands of Fleming's backers,[50] and by 1836 Hogan, Kough, and their knot of defenders had been squeezed out of the BIS and forced to hold their own rump celebration of St Patrick's Day. When they attempted to return to the fold in 1837 for the regular annual festivities honouring St Patrick, they were humiliated by the majority and forced to apologize.

In the meantime, Fleming's clerical assistants in St John's labelled those Catholics behind Kough and Hogan as bad or Orange Catholics, alias "Mad-Dog" Catholics.[51] Their names were read from the altar and posted at the back of the church with warnings that they should be proscribed. In a number of notorious instances they were refused the sacraments of the church. At the same time, Fleming was busy recruiting clergy from Ireland to assist him in Newfoundland. For that purpose he journeyed to Ireland, taking care to select each priest personally.[52] It was crucial, he believed, to surround himself with the right kind of priests, perfectly loyal ones on whom he could always depend. About priestly loyalty, he stated: "Perseverance alone is necessary whereby you can gradually gather around you a body of Priests pious, prudent and faithful in whom you can confide."[53] Fleming believed that goal to be a necessity in view of the fact that in Newfoundland a hostile British government and a core of disaffected lay people surrounded the church. He warned the bishop of Halifax: "Be cautious of the clergymen around you. There is a circle of busy lay people round every discontented or jealous Priest whom you will always find treacherous, and the Protestant and the Government Party will all the time be lookers on chuckling at the distraction likely to arise."

Fleming experienced the open opposition of only one priest the Reverend Timothy Browne,[54] who had been his competitor for the episcopal office and whose service he inherited from Bishop Scallan. Though Fleming was careful not to condemn Browne publicly, the latter quit the colony in disgust in 1840 upon realizing that Fleming's supporters in politics and the church had recruited his own parishioners.

Coincident with the solidification of his power within the church and among the laity, Bishop Fleming undertook a massive building campaign, including a cathedral that was destined on its completion to be one of the largest churches in all of North America. This focused the church's attention more than anything else on the necessity of an adequate fund-raising program. Fleming was fond of saying that his subsistence would depend entirely upon what his flock in their generosity decided to give him. That was no different from the experience of his three predecessors, O'Donel, Lambert, and Scallan.[55] Yet there were problems with the actual collecting of the subscriptions which the Catholic fishermen and servants were willing to give. Merchants controlled the accounts of the fishermen and a considerable portion of the trade was in truck.[56] Thus, the merchant had the final say as to whether or not a particular account would be deducted in favour of a particular clergyman. Here, the Methodists apparently suffered the greatest grievance for they complained that the merchants were favouring the Catholics and the Anglicans. One Wesleyan preacher, George Ellidge, complained about the lack of merchant patronage to Methodists and described plainly how the system worked. He said that merchants wanted to "receive all and pay all" and demanded of fishermen that they "give the whole catch of your fish to me before you pay either Parson, Doctor or Shoemaker."[57] Ellidge explained that, if a planter had dealings with an agent for one hundred pounds and could only pay ninety, the parson's ten shillings would be among the ten pounds unpaid. When, at the close of a voyage, the year's accounts were settled, it was in the power of the agent to say in respect of a request for church subscriptions that "his account is not settled" or "I'll see when he settles his accounts." Later, when the planter had taken his winter supplies on credit, the agent would say that "he's in debt, he cannot pay." One had therefore to be in special favour with the merchants in order to have deductions made for a church account.

O'Donel, Lambert, and Scallan were indeed held in special favour by the merchants and the governor, which in large part explained their deference to the British Protestant authorities in Newfoundland. In recommending his successor, O'Donel told the pope that the person selected must be one who could retain the long-standing favour of the Newfoundland merchants upon whom our "whole precarious and poor subsistence depends."[58] Earlier, in writing the archbishop of Dublin for more priests, O'Donel had said that the only way a priest could make a good living in Bonavista and Trinity bays was by "living on good terms with the English merchants."[59] If Fleming wanted to depend on fishermen-servant subscriptions, it meant that he might have to be as dependent on the mercantile authorities as O'Donel,

Lambert, or Scallan had been. But that was not a palatable alternative to Fleming, who soon entirely repudiated any such dependence on the merchants. Through the columns of the *Newfoundlander* he made a grandiose announcement that the merchants' financial power over the church in Newfoundland should forthwith cease. He thundered: "I despise such support. My subsistence, and that of my clergy, depend on the generous and voluntary contributions of my flock and I shall never DURING THE REMAINDER OF MY LIFE, place myself or them under what may be considered obligations to Bookkeepers for woe to my church and to my people, if they, or I, depended on such protection."[60] Hence, he announced, "the fishermen and shoremen will, in future pay to myself what they can afford."

As laudable as this sounded, there yet remained the problem of physically collecting the donations. In the beginning it appears that Fleming resolved on the institution of a program of fish collections during the season when the fishermen were curing their fish. It meant that each parish priest would have to avail himself of the services of a boat on a continuing basis from about mid-August to October. That was required for the purpose of collecting dried fish from each parishioner in order to ship it to the priest's own account with the merchant or his agent. Few records remain in the form of company-account books to show the effects of this program. But those that do survive prove that in some instances the program was successful while in others it was a total failure. The ledgers and account books of the old mercantile firms of the Slades and Cox's, both headquartered at Fogo, to provide the only detailed information on fishermen's accounts in the eighteenth and nineteenth centuries. Those records reveal that by 1837 Father Joseph Michael Bergin,[61] a devoted supporter of Bishop Fleming and the parish priest of Tilting on Fogo Island, had instituted a fish-collection service in his parish for the construction of churches in Tilting, Joe Batt's Arm, and Fogo.[62] By 1841 Bergin was annually shipping substantial quantities of fish sufficient to enable him to complete his building program. But his parish extended well beyond the confines of Fogo Island, embracing the entire coastline as well as all the islands situated in Notre Dame Bay between Cape Freels and Cape St John.[63] There is no evidence to suggest that he was able to inaugurate a fish collection service throughout his entire parish; the nature of the program was such as to render it a physical impossibility. Bergin was successful at Tilting Harbour because he lived in the midst of successful planters, all of whom were devoted Irish Roman Catholics who in one day could make a circuit of the entire little harbour for the purpose of collecting and shipping the fish. In Joe Batt's Arm, only an hour's walk away, he found a successful planter and schooner owner, Henry Starks, who was able and willing to collect the fish for him. Fogo harbour, also only a few hour's walk from his base in Tilting, was well within his range of supervision in the fish-curing months of August and September.

Bergin's practice at Tilting can well stand as a model for the record of other clergymen in cooperating with Bishop Fleming's policy. Parish priests eager to cooperate with Fleming could well institute the fish-collection program in their immediate areas; however, they would find it an impossibility to extend it to all the harbours and coves. Newfoundland had too extensive a coastline for the church to raise money in such a fashion in the shortened days of the short fish-curing season. Fleming himself, it appears, depended initially on the good graces of an unmarried schooner-owner-planter, Patrick Brawders, from Bergin's Tilting.[64] Brawders, a devoted political supporter of Bergin, lent his services and the use of his schooner to Father Edward Troy and Bishop Fleming in collecting fish around the eastern Avalon. But that service had to be discontinued when Brawders absconded in the face of a trial for perjury in 1837. Thereafter, it appears, Fleming had a boat built expressly for fish collection; and, although the program continued on an ad hoc basis, it was not the panacea that he had expected at the beginning. On numerous occasions the bishop complained of being absolutely strapped for cash;[65] consequently, he found himself having to institute supplementary methods of raising sufficient revenue.

One of these methods was a regular household visitation by parish priests for the exactment of what was known as the customary yearly dues. The docile flock, of which Fleming so often spoke, would have found such an approach difficult to refuse and it consequently led to a number of abuses. One of those was the reading from the altar of the names of those who did not pay and the writing of these names on placards located at the back of the church or in the churchyard. While the names of Fleming's political opponents appeared on the lists as well, there was a tendency to identify those who could not pay with those who refused such payments. The result was that complaints became public and the opposition press used the issue as another political tool with which to attack Fleming.[66] The complaints against Bishop Fleming and his clergy were lodged with the governor, the Colonial Office, and the Vatican.[67] A local Anglican priest privately observed that the Roman Catholic priests earned their livelihood in the following way: "Enslaving the minds of the people with the grossest superstition, so that almost any evil would be overlooked in their flocks sooner than a neglect or non-payment of the customary dues."[68]

Even if this were an exaggerated view, there was some truth to it. Indeed, by 1841 Fleming himself had resolved on an improvement to the system. In that year he initiated the founding of a society for the actual collection of the dues on a weekly basis. That would lighten the burden on the lower classes, who naturally found it oppressive to give all the dues required in a lump sum. Even Fleming's opponent, the *Newfoundlander*, congratulated him on the excellence of the plan.[69] Yet this did not eliminate the problems involved in collecting donations from the fishermen of Newfoundland. Clergy of all denominations complained of trying to subsist off the voluntary contributions of an impoverished class which was locked into the infamous credit and truck system. Even for those who were willing to pay, there was the insurmountable problem of finding cash when their accounts were entirely in fish and supplies.

Nothing if not ingenious, however, Fleming soon discovered among the fishermen a hardy class of men with ready cash in hand willing to blaze new frontiers whether on the land or on sea. These were the sealers, whose unique place in Newfoundland's history has recently been analysed in a comprehensive study.[70] By the time Fleming had assumed leadership of the Newfoundland church, most of the sealers on the Catholic Avalon were recent arrivals from areas within only a short radius of the bishop's own birthplace in Kilkenny. As sealers they were a landless, property-less class and the true frontiersmen of nineteenth-century Newfoundland society. Fleming stood forth immediately as the champion of their homeland. He appealed to them as one of them, as an Irishman. He proved his Irishness by building an Irish church organization with Irish priests and Irish nuns. He stood out as the most conspicuous admirer of O'Connell and advertised this fact in the local press by placing his name at the head of the O'Connell tribute, as the fundraising campaign in support of O'Connell's campaign was called.[71] When sealers went on strike in Conception Bay in early 1832, Fleming publicly identified with their grievances and defended their protest on the basis that they were Irishmen asserting their rights.[72] His repudiation of mercantile support for the church and his assertion that the church he led would be a church of the ordinary people struck a responsive chord among the sealers.

Fleming and his clergy preached sermons aimed directly at the sealers, and when the latter congregated in St John's each spring for the annual hunt, Father Troy led their parades through the streets of the capital. The spring sealers' collections (sealers, unlike fishermen, were paid in cash) were considered crucial towards the bishop's building program; the sealing captains or schooner owners assiduously performed these collections at the end of each voyage.[73] Upon completion of the cathedral in 1855, Bishop John Mullock, Fleming's successor, looked back on the struggle for its construction that had begun in the mid-1830s with Fleming's quest for land. He recalled:

"Nothing seems so eloquent as the reading of the sealer's subscription list to this work, upon their return in the spring of each year from their perilous voyage."[74]

Nothing contributed more, perhaps, to Fleming's solidarity with the sealer-fishermen than the fact that he pitched himself physically into the actual work by performing even the most menial of tasks. He showed the way by not expecting even the most common labourer to perform tasks that he himself was not prepared to do. "It is true," he admitted, "that I set the example."[75] He further pointed out that he considered it "more than ever necessary to appear at the head of my flock." He boasted to Rome that the Catholic people of Newfoundland were possessed of such extraordinary zeal and solidarity that they gave free labour to the church to the value of many thousands of pounds.[76] And when the famous cathedral was completed in 1855, Bishop Mullock toasted it as a monument to Bishop Fleming and declared it belonged to all the Catholic people of Newfoundland.

But the cathedral, immense as it was, was only one part of Fleming's enormous building program. For at the same time as his cathedral was going up in St John's, Fleming built churches in Torbay, Portugal Cove, and Petty Harbour; two enormous convents in St John's, one of which was surmounted by a tower fifty feet high; and, to top it all off, a school in the capital as well. These physical structures, of course, all assisted in forging an identity for all Roman Catholics. To enhance the actual presence of the buildings, the cathedral and its adjacent convent buildings were erected on the most conspicuous promontory in the settled area of St John's, so that, even as they do today, they tended to dominate the town's landscape. Fleming was well aware of the value of the churches, a value that went beyond their being places of worship and devotion. "I was always of the opinion," he said, "that the cultivation of the arts operates much to elevate men's minds." He knew of no art better calculated to excite the best feelings of the heart, he continued, "than that which raises around us noble structures particularly to the service of God."[77] Fleming could look around him and see the fruits of his efforts – filled churches and a zealous flock. He had no compunction about bragging of his policy and achievements in Newfoundland when he reported to the Vatican.

The main elements of Fleming's approach – a suspicion of lay people, a commitment to securing the church's freedom from interference by a Protestant state, and an emphasis on building a local, independent church staffed by an obedient clergy and answering only to Rome – were put into practice in other jurisdictions and have been categorized as ultramontane.[78] The description fits Fleming's approach, too, and indeed the same can be said of other aspects of his policy.

One of the more prominent features of ultramontanism was the extension of the influence of religious orders. Fleming brought two orders of nuns from Ireland to Newfoundland, the Sisters of the Presentation and the Sisters of Mercy. Both were eventually to extend their work to all geographic regions of the colony. Fleming also recruited the Franciscan friars to establish schools, the first being built in St John's in 1848.[79] Religious societies were still another feature of ultramontanism, and, here again, Fleming fit the pattern: he introduced a Christian Doctrine Society and a Catholic Total Abstinence and Benefit Society.

Perhaps the most prominent characteristic of the Irish ultramontane church, as it emerged later under Cardinal Paul Cullen, was the emphasis given to clerically controlled education. Fleming said that, as soon as he arrived in Newfoundland and studied the state of society, he came to the conclusion that the greatest need of all was that of education. "And to this end," he said in 1834, "were all my efforts directed since my elevation to the prelacy."[80] As a curate Fleming made an early attempt to introduce religious education into the BIS school but was rebuffed.[81] Upon inheriting the episcopal mantle, however, he renewed the struggle and succeeded in carrying his point against the BIS leadership. Fleming was alarmed by the proselytizing efforts of the Newfoundland School Society and by sounds of the struggle emerging between the evangelicals and their opponents in the Protestant community. Catholics had hitherto been attending Protestant schools on the basis of what were known as principles of liberality. That meant that all children would be guarded from religious proselytism by rival denominations. The BIS had resisted Fleming's attempts to inculcate religion in their schools because apparently it wanted to maintain its tradition of appealing to all sections of the community by excluding the teaching of religion entirely from the school and even the school grounds. But what was happening in the Protestant community could not be ignored. The BIS, too, was nervous of the operational plans of the NSS.[82] As events drifted towards a climax in the contest between the sectarian and non-sectarian forces in education, word was received of the grant of representative institutions. And the campaign for seats in the new House of Assembly became an opportunity for all sects and their representatives to advance their own interests.

The emancipation of Newfoundland's Catholics had coincided with the advent of new leadership in the colony's Catholic Church. That leadership set about immediately constructing a church based on Irish Catholic solidarity, minimization of lay and particularly Protestant government influence, clerical control, and obedient priests closely supervised under episcopal direction. These developments, in turn, overlapped with an evangelical revival in the Protestant community and created an intellectual climate conducive to inter-church conflicts. The first electoral campaigns in the colony's history supplied an opportunity for politicians and political parties to exploit those circumstances.

4 Religion and Politics, 1832–36

While Bishop Fleming had been busy planning his moves against the lay people and recruiting nuns for the implementation of his educational plans in 1831–32, the evangelicals in the Protestant community were quarrelling over educational plans of their own. Both struggles took place against a background of constitutional reform, for early in 1832 Governor Thomas Cochrane received instructions to summon Newfoundland's first House of Assembly.

The new constitution called for a two-house legislature consisting of an appointed upper house, styled the Legislative Council and an elected lower chamber. The former, which would also serve as an executive council, originally consisted of seven members and was appointed by the crown upon nomination by the governor. The lower house, styled the House of Assembly, was to consist of fifteen members elected from nine districts representing the coast of Newfoundland excluding the French Shore (part of the coast on which France was given a right of fishery by the Treaty of Utrecht of 1713 and which it retained until 1904; see map 2). Every male British subject of the age of twenty-one or over was qualified to vote for the new Assembly provided he occupied a dwelling house as owner or tenant for one year preceding the election. And every such elector was entitled to become a candidate for the new Assembly provided he had resided in the colony for at least two years preceding such election. Returning officers were told that the election must be held between 25 September and 8 December 1832, at which time the elector's choices were to be made in open voting.

For several years before Newfoundland's first general election, the O'Connell movement in Ireland had been acquiring support in Newfoundland. Prominent Irish leaders throughout the Avalon peninsula were members of O'Connell's catholic association and subscriptions were regularly remitted across the ocean to its coffers. On the eve of the 1832 general election, therefore, it seemed entirely likely that the Roman Catholic clergy and the name of O'Connell would be drawn into the political conflicts.

By September, campaigns were in full swing throughout the colony for seats in the new fifteen-member Assembly.[1] In St John's, where three seats were at stake, at least eleven candidates offered themselves to the constituency. Among the most prominent were W.B. Row,[2] an English expatriate lawyer; William Thomas,[3] an English expatriate businessman; Patrick Kough, the Irish builder, government contractor, and BIS notable; William Carson, the Scottish doctor and long-time Newfoundland Reformer; and John Kent, auctioneer and commission merchant of Waterford.

As a supporter of the Church of England, the lawyer W.B. Row ran into difficulty at the outset. He faced a repeated barrage of charges that he secretly supported a government plot to use public moneys for the benefit of the Church of England. Though he issued public denials in the press, it was to no avail. The anti-Anglican campaign against Row was so strong that rumours were circulated to the effect that he intended to introduce tithes. In a constituency such as St John's, with its large Roman Catholic majority, such a charge spelled political disaster. In spite of a published second denial, he was forced to withdraw from the campaign after only two days of polling. But his withdrawal did nothing to lessen the influence of religion in the campaign.

Of all the candidacies, John Kent's generated the greatest controversy. Though only twenty-six years of age, Kent had received a solid classical education. His speeches and addresses revealed an extensive vocabulary, and he quickly achieved a distinguished reputation as a brilliant orator, fluent in French as well as in English. Kent's candidacy was shortly the talk of the town. Although well-recognized liberal and conservative ideas appeared sprinkled throughout the addresses of the several candidates, it was upon Kent that the conservative interests centred their main attacks. Kent, condemned as an upstart, resented as too young, and deemed to be too inexperienced and unqualified, was discounted as a candidate lacking influence in the community. Perhaps some of these charges might have had some merit. There is evidence to indicate that Patrick Morris had expected to be nominated by his nephew John Kent; but taking advantage of his uncle's absence in Ireland, Kent had nominated himself instead. Nevertheless, Kent's conservative opponents committed a tactical error by laying too heavy a hand on the young candidate; their bitter, concentrated attacks soon began to generate a sympathy vote for Kent. Invitations flooded in from around the colony affirming support for him and requesting his candidacy in their own district.

However, Kent stuck to St John's, spearheading a vigorous, energetic campaign among the populace in efforts to foment a class war in his own favour. His obvious success particularly rankled the conservative journalist of the *Public Ledger,* Henry Winton, who ran a lead article defaming Kent. "Beware of impostors," Winton warned in reference to Kent, adding, "We never thought that he had any substantial claims either to the character of a scholar or a gentleman." Then, in condemning Kent's recent address to the public, Winton stated, "We shall ... be permitted seriously to inquire whether he be not on the verge of becoming a fit subject for a lunatic asylum."[4] This first recorded public personal attack in a Newfoundland political campaign opened the floodgates to the gutter politics which was to distinguish nineteenth- and twentieth-century politics in Newfoundland. Four days later, before Kent had the opportunity of replying, Winton again used his *Public Ledger* to castigate Kent further and to immerse himself even more thoroughly in the personal campaign he had inaugurated. But this time he introduced religion and used the name of Bishop Fleming, who was called on to witness his charges. This tactic was also to have a long life, for religious sectarianism, like ad hominem vitriol, would characterise much of Newfoundland's succeeding political history.

In the political address that had given rise to Winton's lunacy charge, John Kent had rhetorically asked, "To what does Mr. Winton object?" and proceeded forthwith to answer.[5] His reply was the perfect example of unchecked political drivel delivered amidst hot emotional intensity. "Mr. Winton's objection to me proceeds from something more obnoxious than my youth," began Kent's reply to his own question. He then completed what was initially a serious, non-partisan, non-personal statement with a bombastic outburst: "I will not be the first to call up vernacular prejudice, but I will distinctly state that there is a party here whose objection is not to my youth nor my want of affluence, and who, if I were an imbecile, would elect me. They do not wish that a person as humble as I should come between the wind and their nobility."

Winton seized upon that final remark to inflict serious political damage upon his adversary. "What!" declared Winton, "does this man possess an influence sufficiently powerful to command the return of an idiot to our local Parliament!"[6] Winton's clever political repartee tended to prove that Kent was just such a person as Winton had averred. In fact, Winton's rejoinders were so devastating that, in the days following, rumours swirled about Kent's withdrawal from the campaign. Clearly Kent was in serious need of damage control. Fortunately for him, he was provided with an escape route by Winton's own tendency to unnecessary verbiage. Rhetorically asking, "Upon what influence does Mr. Kent rely?" Winton had answered by hinting at religion and declaring that Kent had insulted both Protestants and Catholics. "Sure we are," he challenged the Roman Catholic community, "that Bishop Fleming will not tolerate such conduct nor permit it to be tolerated by a member of his flock. If Kent does indeed possess that influence, he concluded, then, "he is a highly dangerous political character."[7] The problem that now faced the reform campaigners was what could be done to rescue Kent from possible defeat. One possibility was for Bishop Fleming himself to become involved in the campaign and give full backing to Kent. Fleming could base his excuse for doing so on the fact that the *Public Ledger* had already dragged in his name and that of his religion and he was thus obliged to respond in one way or another. To remain silent would risk his being tarred with guilt-by-complicity in everything Kent had said, would lend credence to Winton's charges, and would possibly bring about Kent's defeat.

Kent's defeat was not a palatable prospect for Fleming. An O'Connellite reformer and personal friend of the bishop, Kent was the lone Catholic in the campaign with whom the Roman Catholic bishop had any direct influence or control. Of the remaining Catholics in the contest, the only one of any particular distinction was Patrick Kough, standard bearer of the conservative interest and servant of the upper-class merchants. As a prominent government contractor, Kough had been garnering substantial support from the Irish populace. To replace Kent with a more suitable candidate was by then impossible; the only credible alternative, Patrick Morris, had been absent since early summer on an extended business trip to Ireland. To risk Kent's defeat would thus be a blow not only to Fleming himself but also to the local O'Connell movement and the whole Reform campaign. As the nephew of Patrick Morris, Kent had stood by his uncle's side throughout the battle for a local Assembly and had played a subsidiary, though important, role to both Carson and to Morris. Throughout the present campaign Kent had stood as the standard-bearer of O'Connell by circulating posters and handbills declaring himself to be "the O'Connell of Newfoundland" while the name of Bishop Fleming prominently headed the O'Connell tribute in each issue of the weekly and biweekly newspapers. Thus, a Kent defeat would be a considerable setback to the whole movement.

If, on the other hand, Fleming simply chastised Winton, deprecated the use of sectarian tactics, and warned all candidates to have a just regard for religious harmony, then it would be interpreted as an official notice that Kent was on his own. Being no help to Kent, it would also provide an opportunity to any Catholic, Kough for instance, to use the same religious leverage with impunity and by so doing not only help defeat Kent but perhaps imperil other Reform candidates as well. Besides, a refusal to confront directly Winton's charge that anyone with Catholic influence was "a highly dangerous political character" was not an agreeable option for a bishop who had resolved to "raise the character of Catholicity." Besides, Kent had portrayed himself as the Irish champion, the O'Connell of Newfoundland; and Fleming had already thrust himself forth as a leader desiring Irish solidarity. If Irish Catholics could be united politically around such expatriates of their own as John Kent, it would contribute immensely to the bishop's program of building a church free of government and mercantile influence. At the same time, some of those lay people who had opposed his episcopal policies were running on the conservative ticket, their strategy also being to appeal to the Irish Catholics and their goal being the defeat of John Kent. Given the complex political situation, Bishop Fleming flung himself entirely into the campaign; and his notoriously controversial reply to Henry Winton became the signal for his parish priests to take to the hustings.

Addressing his reply to the editor of the *Newfoundlander*, Bishop Fleming objected to the unjustifiable manner in which Henry Winton had brought up his name and that of his clergy. He spoke of his own good conduct "for nearly ten years past in this country" and strongly took exception to the insinuation that, if Kent was supported by the Roman Catholic bishop, then "he is a highly dangerous political character." Fleming rhetorically demanded: "Does my Episcopal character deprive me of my rights as a citizen? That's the old cry of ascendancy fears and is confined to only a few who aspire to exclusive honours and privileges. We must champion the poor for they have always stood by us." The bishop therefore recommended to the electors the names of John Kent, William Carson, and William Thomas.[8]

The next day Winton replied with a personal attack on Bishop Fleming. In a leader addressed in large print "TO THE RT. REVEREND DR. FLEMING," he charged: "You have stooped to prostitute your sacred calling ... You have been guilty of as gross and wilful a misrepresentation of our sentiments as the mind of a Jesuit could possibly conceive."[9] But, instead of defending his views and trying to clear up the misrepresentations, Winton with these statements inaugurated a series of biweekly articles and letters strongly attacking the Irish populace and the Roman Catholic clergy.[10] The usual fist fighting then so common among the lower class in Newfoundland and the personal assaults and ruffian attacks normally occurring in the St John's streets and taverns were blamed on the supporters of John Kent, while all the respectable inhabitants were said to support Kough and the Conservatives. More than 99 per cent of those on poor relief, the *Ledger* charged, were Irish Roman Catholics. Winton openly doubted "whether English institutions were suitable to the Irish" and moaned, "Who could have imagined that the baneful influence of Priestcraft"[11] would have arisen here in Newfoundland! The suffrage was too wide, wailed the *Ledger*, for most Roman Catholics were not free to cast votes. That, Winton concluded, would throw the control of the House of Assembly into the hands of the Roman Catholic bishop. The *Ledger* had ignited an anti-Catholic campaign that was destined to continue with little variation for decades thereafter.

Kent's supporters responded with a mass meeting of Roman Catholics in St John's where the numerous speakers praised Bishop Fleming and denounced Henry Winton and the *Public Ledger*. Addresses to the bishop were moved and adopted, and committees of delegations were appointed to present them. All such proceedings became the opportunity for large numbers of supporters to come together with music and streaming banners. In a public, open-air ceremony, Bishop Fleming received the addresses and made another speech favouring Kent, Carson, and Thomas and praising the Catholic clergy. Catholics in Harbour Grace, Carbonear, Brigus, and other centres with substantial Catholic populations followed the same procedures. All meetings were held in the open air to allow for the largest possible crowds to gather. In the case of Harbour Grace and the other towns outside St John's, the deputations that were appointed travelled all the way to the capital, where their delivery of the addresses to the bishop occasioned more public meetings and open-air celebrations. Both the addresses and Bishop Fleming's replies were then submitted for publication in the *Newfoundlander*.

As a consequence, the Reform campaign soon took on the character of a Protestant-Catholic struggle with at least the Catholic clergy in St John's and the Anglican clergy in Bonavista both taking to the hustings. But, while Reverend Coster's campaign on behalf of the Conservative interest in Bonavista generated little public interest, Bishop Fleming's involvement led to his becoming the main target for all the Conservatives and Protestant merchants in St John's and Conception Bay. Because these merchants recognized the ultimate impact of a religious campaign among the Irish Catholics on the largely Catholic Avalon, all political guns were levelled at Bishop Fleming. Understanding that, as a result of Kough's candidacy, the Catholic community was divided and that among Fleming's own clergy there was opposition as well, the Conservatives hoped that their attacks on the bishop would render him a liability to the Catholic Church in Newfoundland.

Perhaps this tactic had its desired effect, for the bishop gradually lessened his involvement towards the close of the campaign. In the end, the Catholic Kough was elected in direct opposition to Fleming's wishes.[12] Perhaps the greatest cause for anxiety on the part of the bishop, however, came from a St John's Fish Company bookkeeper who pointedly warned Fleming that the campaign against the Protestant merchants would leave his pocketbook empty. For years, as we have seen, the custom in the fishery had been that financial support for clergy of all churches depended on the cooperation of the merchants. Upon receipt of fish from the fishermen, the merchants normally "stopped," or set aside, a certain designated quantity in favour of a clergyman assigned by the seller. That fish was then credited to the account of the clergyman in question. Though the system had worked well for the Catholic Church in the days of O'Donel, Lambert, and Scallan, its inherent risks became clear in the 1832 election. A certain bookkeeper warned Bishop Fleming in the midst of the campaign: "Charity is the cream of goodness. And perhaps the hint won't be squandered if I tell you that the change in your Reverence's ideas … has abated their ardour for 'stopping.'"[13] Fleming rose to the challenge and condemned the bookkeeper while indignantly repudiating the idea of his church's dependence on any fish merchants. But the message of the incident was plain to the bishop, who in succeeding years was forced to institute a fund-raising system involving his own fish-collection service which dealt directly with the fishermen.

Governor Cochrane was delighted with the campaign against the bishop, who seemed so badly beaten in the election as to be finished with politics.[14] Fleming himself, however, denied any attempt at religious exclusiveness and deliberately chose to support two Protestants, William Carson and William Thomas. Those selections were made in such a manner as to represent all three ethnic groups in St John's: Kent representing the Irish; Thomas, the English; and Carson, the Scottish. Fleming's hopes were somewhat dashed for the results in St John's demonstrated a more marked denominational character than he had anticipated. His nominees Kent and Thomas were able to head the poll, and the Roman Catholic Kough was able to draw off enough support from his coreligionists to defeat the Protestant William

Carson on the last day by fifteen votes. Kough's success, nevertheless, did not prevent him from complaining about the illegitimate influence which had been used against him by Bishop Fleming and the clergy as they worked to elect Carson.

The *Public Ledger* was much more pointed in its post-election post mortem. It regretted the religious compromise in Conception Bay, a compromise that allowed two Roman Catholic, lower middle-class "dealers" (traders or merchants) to be returned to the House of Assembly. Winton condemned the folly of electing politicians on the basis of religion. The Conception Bay electors have proceeded on a false premise, he declared: "Instead of a coalition between two Catholics and two Protestants there should have been something like a coalition of the people to return four of the most honest and able men among them and have left their religion to themselves."[15] In other words, if religion had been left out of the campaign, four upper-class merchants could have been elected for Conception Bay. But Winton need not have been so pessimistic. At least nine out of the fifteen members elected belonged to the merchant class while only five could be categorized with certainty as middle-class men. As for the denominational character of the house, the Protestant districts had elected all Protestants. The only exception was Conception Bay, where a prior agreement had shared the four seats equally between the Catholics and Protestants. In the majority Catholic districts, three Protestants had been elected: one in St John's and one each in Placentia–St Mary's and Ferryland, giving the Protestants a total of ten members in the fifteen-member house. But the Reformers fared worse than either class or religion. Apart from the quiet, low-key alliance of the so-called St John's Reformer William Thomas with John Kent and William Carson, only two other candidates, the Roman Catholics Peter Brown[16] and James Power[17] of Conception Bay had publicly allied themselves with the Reform leaders. On 1 January 1833, then, the Reformers met a decidedly Protestant, Conservative House of Assembly dominated by the mercantile interests.

For Cochrane and his Anglican supporters, the first election had been a triumph. Ten out of the fifteen members elected gave at least nominal allegiance to their beloved Protestant denomination. That was positively reassuring to Cochrane who had entertained grave doubts about how an elected Assembly might behave, especially as regards the colony's revenues and expenditures. The British government's intention to raise more revenue from the Newfoundland trade had alarmed the principal merchants and had given added impetus to the Reformers' campaign for a local Assembly. The government's policy, however, encouraged Cochrane, who secretly hoped to guide a portion of the increased revenues towards support of the ecclesiastical establishment.[18] His plan became public knowledge when an October 1830 issue of the *Newfoundlander* loudly objected to taxes destined for the benefit of the Church of England. The plan was "fraught with evil consequences," said the *Newfoundlander*, and "not a man in Newfoundland would publicly support it."[19] The *Newfoundlander*'s exposure of Cochrane's scheme may have been an important reason why so many Roman Catholics and dissenters were prominent in the campaign for representative government. On Cochrane's part, it undoubtedly was a factor in his attempts to prevent the British government from granting representative institutions to the colony. He had enlisted the support of his attorney general, the Anglican James Simms, in drawing up reasons an Assembly should not be granted to Newfoundland.[20] They received the assistance of James Stephen, a high-ranking official in the Colonial Office in London, but their efforts were unavailing. Counteracting the Reform movement then sweeping the British Isles was an insurmountable task for Cochrane. The granting of an Assembly to Newfoundland was as much the result of political pressures in Britain as a concession to any local campaign.

The 1832 campaign nust have alarmed Cochrane, for it witnessed both Bishop Fleming on the hustings and the governor's friend and supporter William Row being forced to withdraw by an anti-Anglican campaign. But the new house that resulted from the elections alleviated the governor's fears. He was thrilled with the quality of the Assembly and was profuse in his praise for Newfoundland's election campaign.[21] Cochrane took particular pleasure in telling the Colonial Office that the Roman Catholic bishop became involved in the campaign only to suffer a humiliating defeat. For a man who feared Catholic meetings and loathed troublesome bishops, that thought was an abiding consolation. Just as cheering was the fact that William Carson, the man Cochrane despised most of all in Newfoundland, had been beaten.

Cochrane had assumed office in 1825 with an ingrained and fervent antipathy to Carson, whom he described as "a thorn in the side of every Governor since his arrival"[22] in the colony in 1808. He privately told the Colonial Office that Carson, who was on his personal payroll as district surgeon, was old and useless as a doctor and his patients had no confidence in him. Cochrane stated that he retained Carson on his payroll to keep him quiet. This worked for a while, but Carson eventually detected the slight and quit the governor's service. Cochrane believed that Carson then began to plot against him as a result of the governor's opposition to a House of Assembly. Thus, Cochrane's pleasure at Carson's defeat must have been all the more intense.

But Carson's despair at his own defeat was as intense as Cochrane's pleasure. Carson had lost the chance to obtain a seat in the Assembly, where he had hoped to be appointed to the speakership; in addition, he had vacated his medical practice in his son's favour. Now, at sixty-two years of age, Carson faced an uncertain future. In 1808 Carson had become the first voice for modern constitutional reform in Newfoundland.[23] He had rebelled against the arbitrary rule of the military-naval governors and lashed out at the abuse of power in every sector of Newfoundland society. Every program from roads and bridges to imperial affairs fell subject to his intense scrutiny. Both the local and imperial governments were made to feel the full weight of his indignation at misgovernment in those spheres. By 1824 he and Patrick Morris, who had joined his crusade in the previous decade, had accomplished some small measure of success when the British government finally conceded colonial status. Not content with that constitutional change, Carson and Morris stepped up their campaign for representative government and were joined by John Kent, William Thomas, and several other prominent St John's merchants. By 1830 Carson was the universally acknowledged leader of the Newfoundland Reformers; and when an elected Assembly was granted in 1832, it was widely assumed that he would become a sitting member for St John's. His defeat came as a severe shock, and he bitterly accused both Kent and Kough of cheating at the polls.

Yet Carson had carried on a listless and complacent campaign for his Assembly seat. Confident that he could ride to victory on the coattails of his long-standing reputation, he seemed content to finish out his days above party matters and openly campaigned for the speaker's job.[24] He was nominated at the polls by an upper-class merchant who had assisted the representative government, and was supported by the middle-class Joseph Shea, whose family owned the *Newfoundlander*, a paper that had consistently refused to engage in local party politics. With Bishop Fleming's support, Carson thus seems to have been convinced of his appeal to all classes; and his confidence in victory precluded his carrying on the aggressive campaign which he belatedly learned was such a necessity. In contrast, Kent and Kough campaigned extensively and aggressively among the populace, deliberately appealing to Irish Catholics.

The third candidate on the Kent-Carson ticket, William Thomas, was an upper-class merchant who employed large numbers of male and female labourers in his extensive farming enterprise. As an Anglican with Bishop Fleming's backing, he could lay claim to Protestant and Catholic votes and appeal to all classes of society as a Reform candidate. Carson, on the other hand, had since 1808 alienated considerable segments of the population. His anti-government pamphlets had antagonized not only governors but also that class of government officials whom Kent had castigated as the "Executive Party." Moreover, Carson's liberal, reform-minded views, combined with his campaign for farming as an alternative to the fishery, must have irritated large blocks of the upper-class fishing interests too. On still another front, Carson's attacks on the exclusiveness of the Anglican establishment could not have endeared him to the voters of that persuasion either; furthermore, just before the 1832 campaign, he engaged in a controversial, public row with the Reverend Edward Wix, the leading Anglican cleric in the colony.[25] By the time the campaign had begun, it should have been clear to Carson that his hopes for success rested almost entirely with the Irish Catholic populace.

Perhaps the system of open voting, whereby the candidate was required to bring forth his support in tallies of ten, militated against a man of Carson's age and habits. In a fairly extensive geographical district like the St John's of 1832, traversing the area from Petty Harbour to Pouch Cove to line up supporters and lead them to the polls required substantial endurance. Carson, like all candidates, must have further suffered from the fact that, it being the first election ever, he was inexperienced at coordinating efforts for such an event. But most telling of all in Carson's defeat was the nature of his alliance with Bishop Fleming.

The bishop had been initially forced into the campaign to defend his own character, to promote Catholic rights, and to assist his friend and co-religionist, John Kent. Once he had fired his first political salvos, Fleming became a target for anti-Catholic attacks from which he found little hope of retreat. Trapped, he threw himself more deliberately into the campaign and led his St John's priests directly onto the hustings. In order to deflect some of the anti-Catholic charges, he went to great pains in supporting Kent, Carson, and Thomas to point out that he was supporting three religions and three nationalities. But Patrick Kough, who had personally targeted Carson for defeat, went to Bishop Fleming to affirm his own religious loyalty and protest the bishop's opposition.[26] With a respectable delegation of Catholic merchants and shopkeepers in his wake, Kough demanded an explanation for the bishop's hostility. Fleming informed Kough that there was no ill will and that, if Kough coalesced with Kent, he would drop Carson and be pleased to support Kent, Thomas, and Kough instead. When Kough refused, Bishop Fleming declared there was no deal; whereupon Kough and his delegation threatened that, if the bishop appeared on the hustings once again, they would openly rebel and make a complete separation. Kough had substantial support from the Catholic community, whose leaders were a respectable group.

Fleming, awed by the threat, retired from the contest. Then, in the last few crucial days, Kough and his supporters beat Carson. Carson, apparently, with an exaggerated notion of his own personal stature in the community, failed to realize that Kough's exploitation of the Irish Catholic vote directly threatened his candidacy. It was only by his bitter loss that Carson learned his most important lesson in practical politics.

From the vantage point of December 1832, William Carson's future looked abysmally dim. He had failed to gain an Assembly seat, had lost the speaker's job, and at sixty-two was considered an old man by the standards of that time. Since his whole life had been given to the struggle for Reform, retiring in such disgrace was not an acceptable alternative to him. He resolved to give what he had left to the Reform movement. In conducting his own election post-mortem, he could not fail to see that while there had been Reform candidates, there really had not been any Reform campaign. Each of the Reformers had conducted an individual campaign in relative isolation; in fact, they had even fallen into the trap of criticizing each other. Kent had conducted his own campaign, which increasingly became more and more a purely personal one as the days wore on; and Carson himself, eager to get the speaker's job, had taken particular pains to inform the electorate that his was an individual solicitation entirely.[27] Even William Thomas, the other Reform candidate publicly supported by Bishop Fleming, had warned that he would not ally himself to anybody.[28]

The sorry state of the Reform movement was borne out by the events of the first session of the new House of Assembly, which convened on 1 January 1833. Kent, the acknowledged leader of the Opposition, was only twenty-six years old; thoroughly inexperienced, he was unable to command the respect of his fellow members, all of whom were his senior. The only two other members, Brown and Power from Conception Bay, willing to identify themselves unconditionally with the Opposition were so weak and ineffectual during that first year that they could only force three recorded divisions throughout the entire session. If Reform was to go anywhere, it would have to regroup outside as well as inside the house, act in consort, and find a unifying cause.

Nevertheless, the prospects for the future were not entirely bleak. The relatively young and energetic Bishop Fleming had demonstrated a willingness to engage in the campaign on behalf of Reform and was positively eager to champion Catholic equality. In Conception Bay a Roman Catholic campaign had succeeded in electing two Catholic Reformers in a majority Protestant riding. A Catholic rights campaign with the active support of the bishop and priests might secure for

Reform in the next election the six seats in the Roman Catholic districts of St John's, Placentia–St Mary's, and Ferryland. With the two seats in Conception Bay, Reformers could then take control of the House of Assembly with a slim majority of eight to seven. The likelihood of such a turn of events increased each week on account of the campaign waged by the Protestant newspapers, especially the *Public Ledger.*

Although Cochrane thought that Fleming was finished with politics after Kough's victory, it is almost impossible to think that the governor failed to see the gathering storm in view of the campaign of the *Ledger* and the *Times.*[29] Kough kept up a running war against Carson as if the election campaign had never ended, and the *Ledger* refused to let go of its anti-Irish, anti-Catholic rhetoric. In fact, the paper intensified its efforts to link Irish Catholics with rowdyism, ruffianism, violence, intimidation, disorder, murder; in short, Irish Catholics were seen to show a general unfitness for a British way of life. Typical of its journalistic efforts was an article on 15 January 1833 entitled "Wild Sports of the West of Ireland." These sports, according to the *Ledger,* were ruffianism, horse stealing, fighting, and throwing paving stones at respectable Englishmen. "Do you go out to dinner?" the writer asked; if you do, he said, "calculate on being fired at when returning." There followed a long series of articles throughout the winter and spring on troubles and disturbances in Ireland. On 8 February 1833 a *London Times* article titled "Administration of Justice in Ireland" received large play in the *Ledger.* It purported to show that Ireland "lags behind the spirit of her laws, even of those which to Englishmen are most invaluable, and requires for the protection of life and property some fiercer guardians than the Habeas Corpus Act and the trial by jury." The conclusion was that laws could not be administered in Catholic Ireland, where opposition to law was "so systematic and instinctive."

But most insulting of all to Irish Catholics was an anti-nun article of 19 March 1833 entitled "Taking the Veil." The article detailed a reputed Irish Catholic ceremony in which a young woman entered the convent. "There is an extreme eagerness in the Catholics who profess celibacy," reported the onlooker, "to decoy young persons into toils from which they themselves cannot escape." The ceremony was described in minute detail to evoke the readers' pity for a woman who had no wish to join but who had been resolutely forced to do so by her cajoling parents and conspiring pastor. The welcoming smiles of her fellow sisters were referred to as "the treacherous smiles" of her "fellow prisoners" and the heartbreaking ending to the article was that "she lives still in a state approaching to madness, and death alone can break her chains."

Incessant attacks against Irish Catholics heightened sectarian jealousies to the point of irrational intensity. The Roman Catholic bishop and his clergy were dismayed that the *Public Ledger* was rewarded on a biweekly basis with substantial patronage from the office of the governor. The ordinary Catholic must have been more puzzled than dismayed, for no public response was forthcoming from the otherwise erudite and pugilistic Fleming and the Catholic *Newfoundlander* was similarly silent on the *Times-Ledger* attacks. The Sheas of the *Newfoundlander*, however, had always ignored local politics, opting instead for the larger imperial sphere so as better to ensure, their enemies said, a just share of that necessary patronage from all sectors of society. Then, again, the Sheas had been intimate friends and supporters of Bishop Scallan and apparently had opposed all mixing of religion with politics. Obviously it was for those reasons that they had refused the columns of the *Newfoundlander* in 1832 to Bishop Fleming because his communication was allegedly of too inflammatory a nature.[30] This peculiar circumstance played right into the hands of William Carson. Deprived of his chance to sit in the Assembly and looking round for a political role he could play in his declining years, Carson remembered the activity that had made his political reputation in the first place – writing. But there was no outlet at that time for pamphlets or letters advancing Catholic reform sentiments. The columns of the *Ledger*, *Times*, and *Newfoundlander* would be barred to either Carson or any Roman Catholic liberal agitator. Thus, on 15 July 1833, William Carson came out with the first issue of the now legendary *Newfoundland Patriot*.

Under Carson, the *Patriot* soon staked out its ground as the foremost champion of all the aggrieved within the colony. Governor Cochrane, his officials, and all those favoured with their patronage soon felt the heat from Carson's bitter pen as he repeatedly vented his spleen for the contempt they had shown him. Carson depicted Cochrane and his Council as a tyrannical clique monopolizing all government offices for themselves and their families while fattening themselves on the people's money. Such assaults became even more embittered after Cochrane's firing of Carson in early 1834 from his last and long-held government office as district surgeon. Besides attacking the civil officers of government, Carson focused his fire on the quasi-established Church of England. He made every effort to champion all dissenters as well as Roman Catholics, and he deliberately instigated a bitter press debate with the Church of England archdeacon, the Reverend Edward Wix, almost immediately as the *Patriot* took to the streets.

Above all, Carson launched a ceaseless attack on what he termed the fish monopolists, the St John's-based and English west country firms which had traditionally dominated the Newfoundland fishery to the exclusion of any non-trade-related activity. That strategy permitted Carson to appeal to the Scots and Irish against the English monopolists, to the outport people against St John's domination, and especially to the merchant-farmers and agriculturists against the exclusively fish-oriented merchants. He even republished in the *Patriot* his old, dated tracts of nearly twenty-five-years' standing promoting the cause of colonization. They were published in the midst of his Assembly campaign as if they were as relevant as when he had first brought them forward. Soon Scots and Irish, Protestant dissenters and Roman Catholics, merchant-farmers and outport spokesmen were flocking to his cause. Carson attributed his success in this regard to the fact that his 1832 defeat had been due to his failure to align himself with others who had grievances in common with himself. He rejoiced now that he had found the alliances that would transform the Reform cause into a potent political force in Newfoundland.

Another factor accounts for Carson's political revival. Carson and the group of men who responded most positively to his appeal belonged to that middle class which for several years had been bearing the brunt of hard times in the fishery. The post-1825 period was marked by diminishing returns in the fishery. In particular the decade of the 1830s was one of depression in the trade owing to a combination of factors.[31] The five years following 1830, for example, saw the production of salt cod drop 20 per cent below the levels of the five years previous to 1830. The decline occurred against the backdrop of an ever-expanding population, one that was annually increasing at a rate of approximately 25 per cent by the time that Carson came out with the *Patriot*. This combination of decreasing fish production and increasing population placed a severe burden on the newly emerged but still vulnerable Newfoundland middle class. None, perhaps, was more adversely affected than the fabled planter, the backbone of that class. Anxiety was further deepened by the fact that the British laws governing the internal operations of the Newfoundland fishery had lapsed by 1832; and it fell to the new House of Assembly in St John's to define the future shape of fishery in the colony. In the face of an assertive mercantile, St John's-led elite then reinforcing its power in the governor's Council, the middle class, and most of all the planters, must have contemplated the future shape of legislation with a great degree of uncertainty. It was therefore natural for them, as a class under siege, to gaze round for allies in efforts to acquire the support of the fisherman-servant class so necessary in capturing control of the Assembly. Carson's blatant attempts, through the *Patriot* and on the hustings, to parade himself as the champion of the Roman Catholic

Church, although appearing as madness to his Protestant opponents, possessed much more of method than they were willing to admit. Even his initial moves in the by-election campaign in 1833 proved that he had discovered the driving force right from the outset.

The *Patriot* was not long in coming to the defence of Bishop Fleming, the Catholic Church, Catholic priests and nuns, and Catholicism in general. That defence occasioned counter-defences of Protestantism on the part of the *Ledger* and the *Times.* Soon the entire colony was awash in a sea of recriminations, charges, and countercharges against all religions. While it was ironic that in the sectarian war the leading Catholic protagonist was a Protestant, that fact was lost in the intensity of the insults hurled back and forth. In fact, Carson so closely identified himself with the Roman Catholic Church that, having purchased a carriage from Bishop Fleming, he drove around town in the conveyance to the end of his days completely indifferent to the large gilded mitre emblazoned on its panels. Thus, at the very moment when Carson was at the lowest point in his twenty-five-year political career to date, he found a jump spring that rejuvenated him once again. He launched himself on a new political career and within a few short months his name was dominating all political discussions in the colony. The *Newfoundlander*, the *Times*, and the *Public Ledger* combined in a ceaseless attack upon Carson while they opened their columns to anonymous letter-writers intent on his personal political destruction. In the private despatches of the governor, Carson was damned once again as the demon who had resurrected the discord that Cochrane believed had gone to sleep.[32]

Then, just a few days after he had issued his first *Patriot*, Carson received the surprise of his political life. In a classic case of political blundering, Governor Cochrane appointed two sitting Assembly members to the Council, one of whom was William Thomas. The latter's vacated seat necessitated a by-election in St John's which was destined to be a critical turning point in the history of Newfoundland politics. Cochrane, it turned out, had simply made an incorrect assessment of the political picture of the period. He had convinced himself that Bishop Fleming's foray into politics had been an isolated occurrence not likely to be repeated. More important, interpreting Kough's victory as a significant defeat for Fleming, Cochrane was strongly convinced that the bishop would henceforward confine his energies to the ecclesiastical field. As for William Thomas, he had been extremely aggressive in his own political interests and had no hesitation in pressing the governor for favours, especially for a Council seat. The other member appointed to the Council, John B. Garland of Trinity, had been speaker of the house and was a close ally of Cochrane, especially in support of the Newfoundland School Society. Cochrane's opening up a seat in Trinity to replace Garland was also an opportunity to provide an Assembly seat for William B. Row, a close friend who had suffered a stinging defeat in the Irish Catholic district of St John's in the election of 1832. This time, Row would be victorious. As for Carson, who had practically abandoned all hope of ever sitting in the House of Assembly, Thomas's appointment was a God-given deliverance and he was immediately on the campaign trail with Bishop Fleming by his side.[33]

It seems that Carson had learned the lessons of 1832 extremely well for his campaign in the St John's riding revolved around praise for Bishop Fleming and his clergy interspersed with the occasional attack on Anglican exclusiveness. The Protestant newspapers in Conception Bay and St John's responded too with intensified attacks on both Roman Catholic priests and Carson's efforts to label his opponents as "priest-catchers."[34] Carson's Conservative opponent was Timothy Hogan, a prominent Roman Catholic shopkeeper who belonged to the Patrick Kough party – the party that had beaten Carson the previous year. Fleming was extremely worried that the Kough forces had attracted a considerable number of Irish Catholic votes by campaigning against Fleming's support for two Protestants. Recognizing that this attempt to divide the Irish Catholic vote was not only a clever ruse but also a very real threat, Fleming stepped up the campaign in favour of Carson. At Sunday morning Mass the bishop told his congregation that Carson was their man and that Hogan was inimical to the interests of the Catholic Church in Newfoundland. The priests, especially Father Troy,[35] followed Fleming's example and preached against Hogan.

The campaign became extremely bitter and noisy as thousands jostled each other in the streets day and night, shouting and screaming. Carson, meanwhile, took advantage of the official church endorsement to organize a Catholic boycott of Hogan's store. With such huge crowds milling in the streets in support of Carson, hardly anyone dared go near Hogan's store for days, let alone venture inside the shop. Hogan, his business in danger of complete ruin, capitulated in early December and published a withdrawal notice that was personally insulting to Bishop Fleming. "A Reverend Gentleman has announced from the sacred altar," stated Hogan, "that it would promote the interests of religion to elect my opponent and has thundered forth in prophetic anathemas that he would cause grass to grow before the doors of those who would vote contrary." While Hogan sincerely regretted having to withdraw, he knew that the die was cast for "the will of a Reverend Gentleman must be considered as the test of ... choice in a Representative."[36] That submission prompted further personal attacks on Fleming and Fathers Patrick Ward[37] and Edward Troy by Henry Winton of the *Ledger*. Huge crowds gathered in the streets, ostensibly to celebrate Carson's victory but primarily to shout threats at Winton and their political enemies. By nightfall on 25 December the crowds had swelled and a heightened sense of excitement filled the air. Generously lubricated with more than sufficient quantities of Christmas spirits, the adult men enjoyed the shouting, cheering, singing, youngsters' fights, and snowball throwing. Suddenly someone struck Winton's house with a snowball, and a continual barrage of snowballs ensued. The terrified Winton ran to the magistrates, imploring help from the military. The order was given for the troops to disperse the crowd. At first sight the soldiers were hooted, jeered, and pelted with snowballs. They promptly fixed bayonets and repeatedly charged the crowd. Dozens were wounded and the retreating injured people were spilling their blood all over the white snow.

Someone, sensing the great danger to the lives of all, ran to the bishop's palace. Fleming soon arrived on the scene with Father Troy and, gaining the first convenient promontory, the bishop quickly attracted the attention of the mob. He condemned Winton's anti-Catholic attacks and expressed pain at the governor's support of them by his patronage of the *Ledger*. The bishop then made a succession of soothing remarks in an effort to gain control of the situation. He urged the retreat of the soldiers on condition that he would guarantee the peace. As the troops withdrew, Fleming urged everyone to make a solemn promise to immediately return to their homes. Afterwards, he and Father Troy remained behind to tend to the wounded.

The next day Bishop Fleming responded to a summons from Government House, where Cochrane received him most cordially and expressed his revulsion at the abusive press in the capital.[38] Neither he nor any of his officials, Cochrane assured Fleming, interfered in any way in local party politics. Bishop Fleming was pleasantly surprised and thanked Cochrane but pointed out that it was the unnecessary introduction of the military among a peaceful, innocent Christmas gathering that outraged him most of all. In order to retain the bishop's sympathy, Cochrane said that the introduction of the troops was an act in which he had not participated, that the magistrates had done it independently, and that he had learned of it in the same manner as Fleming. Moreover, Cochrane said that Fleming could be assured that the governor had the interests of Roman Catholics as close to his heart as those of any other group. Fleming was happy and departed very much appreciative of Cochrane's stand.

In spite of what he had just said to Fleming, Cochrane immediately sat down and wrote an urgent appeal to the Colonial Office for an increase in the garrison. Although Cochrane would later attribute the 1833 disturbances to the vicious press attacks on the Catholic clergy,[39] he now told the British government that the Catholic priests had been the main instigators of the trouble. Because the franchise was so wide and the bulk of the populace was Roman Catholic, the result had been, Cochrane explained, "to throw the representation in their hands and as they equal in bigotry and subservience to the Priesthood the very worst part of the most disturbed district in Ireland – ultimately into those of their Clergy who, it is much to be lamented, have taken a most active part in the politics of the place." Bishop Fleming, he said, had turned the local Roman Catholic church into "a political club-house" and had threatened to excommunicate anyone who dared to do business with his political opponents. The priests, he said, have resorted to every means imaginable to arouse a "too dependent and submissive flock"[40] and directly instigated the physical attacks on Winton and his house. If it were not for the military, Cochrane judged, Winton and his family would have all been murdered.

Cochrane might have been able to continue pursuing his double-dealing for some time longer had Carson not wanted to press the advantage he now spotted as a result of Bishop Fleming's report on his meeting with the governor. To gain ground, Carson called a public meeting for the afternoon of the next day. There, amidst great throngs of people and jubilant cheering, he praised the bishop and his clergy, whom he had arranged to have standing by his side. Then he asked Fleming to give an account of his meeting with Cochrane. With high praise for the governor, Fleming reported verbatim what Cochrane had said, that he condemned the abusive press and that he had had no participation in the decision to call out the military. In that context it appeared that the governor was condemning the *Ledger* and siding with the *Patriot* while at the same time implying that the magistrates must take the blame for calling out the troops.

If Cochrane had not filled his reports to Britain with so many denunciations of Roman Catholics, he might have had some room to manœuvre and develop a compromise. But he had burned his bridges behind him and was now left with no alternative but to repudiate Bishop Fleming.[41] Cochrane's subsequent announcement to that effect delighted the Protestant community and drove a permanent wedge between the governor on one side and the whole Catholic Church and its supporters on the other. From that day forward the Roman Catholics of Newfoundland considered Cochrane as their prime public enemy.

William Carson was riding the crest of a wave of popularity when the New Year broke in 1834 and soon had occasion to place another laurel in his cap, to the great dismay of Governor Cochrane. Carson's new victory was the acquisition of the outright support of Robert Pack,[42] a Protestant member of the Assembly from Conception Bay and sitting colleague of the Reformers Brown and Power. In the 1833 session Pack had displayed a tendency to vote with Kent, and they both found common ground in the debate over a Wesleyan marriage bill.[43] Newfoundland Methodists had petitioned the house for an Act to place their clergy on the same footing as the Anglicans and Roman Catholics with regard to the celebration of marriage. The bill was adamantly opposed by the Anglican archdeacon for Newfoundland, the Reverend Edward Wix, but John Kent just as adamantly supported it. The Wesleyans held the balance of power between Anglicans and Catholics in two districts electing five members. Kent milked the opportunity for all it was worth and presented an extensive petition from Bishop Fleming in its favour. The bishop said that he wanted to draw the attention of the house "to the painful condition to which ... the Dissenters of this country are subjected" by reason of the marriage law. He went on to say that the Methodists were subjected to a cere-mony that was "unjust, unchristian, and intolerant, and in direct violation of the fundamental principles of the Constitution." He knew from experience, he said, the grievance of having religious and civil liberty barred. Therefore, he stated, "he should deem himself unwor-thy of that freedom ... he now enjoys, could he for a moment be insensible to the hardships of his Dissenting brethren, or hesitate to seek ... the same share of liberty for them." Fleming entreated the house to extend a measure of peace to all religious bodies, describing the marriage bill as "a measure which will conciliate the affections and gratitude of so extensive and respectable a portion of His Majesty's subjects, and also ... effectually consolidate ... all classes of Chris-tians."[44]

Kent made much of the petition, and over half a century later Catholics were still bragging of the part Fleming had played in helping the Wesleyans. But Robert Pack was just as eager to cater to the Wesleyans. Although he had originated from a Wesleyan family in the west of England,[45] some of his contemporaries reported him an Angli-can while he, himself, declared that he was of no particular religion. Pack, however, did have a common cause with the Wesleyans, who had been having serious difficulties with the big merchants, especially in Conception Bay. Methodists considered the credit system on which the fishery operated as "harmful and destructive to morality and reli-gion,"[46] and, in practical terms, they complained that they did not receive sufficient cooperation from the merchants in collecting their dues from fishermen's accounts. Those were the same merchants, agents of transatlantic firms, with whom the Carbonear merchant Robert Pack was in competition. Pack contributed handsomely to the Wesleyan Methodist Missionary Society and, whatever his religion, Wesleyans considered him their "greatest friend in Conception Bay."[47] William Carson felt that he was in a good position to exploit merchant-Wesleyan rivalries and carried on a campaign aimed directly at the Wesleyans.

Himself a Protestant and variously regarded as a Socinian, Unitarian, Presbyterian, or sceptic, Carson never publicly disclosed his personal religion. But what he did disclose, and that very frequently, was his aversion to the Church of England. At every possible opportunity, the *Patriot* insulted that religious body and promoted the Wesleyans, Presbyterians, and dissenters. Throughout his election campaigns of 1832–33, Carson published several anonymous letters signed "Dissenters" supporting his candidacy, and by January 1834 he had acquired Robert Pack's unconditional support for a run at the speakership.

When the house opened on 29 January 1834, John Kent demanded the support of the Roman Catholic member from Placentia–St Mary's, Roger Sweetman,[48] on the grounds of religion and the necessity of defending the Catholic Church against government-supported attacks.[49] Sweetman delivered his vote, much to the delight of Kent, with the result that the Reformers had six solid votes in the battle for the speakership. Because of the impossibility of winter travel during that period in Newfoundland's history, two Tory members from the outlying districts far from the capital were unable to make the journey to St John's. The end result was not in Carson's favour, but it was a close thing: Carson lost the speakership to Thomas Bennett by only one vote. Waiting in the wings to read his throne speech, Thomas Cochrane must have been alarmed at the dramatic change from last session. He knew that he would be in for a political war when he read the following lines on the post-election disorders: "Recent events in this town of a tumultuary and discreditable description have shown the necessity of a small and well-appointed militia, to aid the civil Magistrates in suppressing lawless and illegal assemblages, and in defeating the mischievous in their designs upon the lives and properties of His Majesty's subjects."[50] Those words seemed harmless enough to many but not to John Kent, who, soon after the governor had withdrawn, denounced them as "foul calumnies against the character of the people … principally directed against the Catholics."[51]

Peter Brown, in supporting Kent, said that the domestic enemies were those who tried to "lessen the influence of the priesthood over the people." They therefore directed all their efforts over the first several days of the session towards embarrassing the governor by amending the address in reply to make it appear that the governor had been duped by Tory magistrates in needlessly calling out the military. They forced at least seven different recorded divisions in that debate, all such efforts creating a 6–6 tie and thus forcing the speaker to cast a tie-breaker to save the governor from serious embarrassment.

Cochrane was disturbed by the Reformers' show of strength and told the British government that "not a member from the other side could absent himself for a moment."[52] Carson, just as much aware of the Reformers' strength as was Cochrane, realized that control of the house was within reach if the seats of some of their hated opponents on the Government benches could be vacated.[53] First Carson and Kent led an attack on John Martin, the member from Placentia–St Mary's, claiming that he had no right to sit in the Assembly. They argued that, as an agent of a British firm, Martin did not own the house in which he lived and was thereby unqualified to sit as a member. They resolved to vacate his seat on that ground, but the resolution was lost when the speaker cast his vote on a 6–6 tie. Carson and Kent next sought to eject Charles Cozens, a Conception Bay member, on the ground that he had become insolvent. But after a stormy debate, they failed once again by the same margin. Undaunted, they petitioned the British government to order Cozen's seat vacated on the ground that it was contrary to British law for such a member to sit as a representative.

In the meantime, Carson and Kent focused their strategy on getting rid of Newman Hoyles, member for Fortune Bay: they claimed that Hoyles, having accepted the office of Colonial Treasurer, should vacate his seat and face his constituents in a by-election. It was symbolic of the extent to which party divisions had become so hardened and definitive that the resolution to get rid of Hoyles came from none other than William Carson, the man whom Hoyles had nominated for a seat in the legislature at the 1832 election. After an exchange of some bitter words between the two, Hoyles declared that if he were thrown out he would somehow find a way to have Carson treated similarly. Once again, Carson was defeated by the casting vote of the speaker. But the Carson gang was not stuck for strategies. Aiming to hold an election as early as possible, they brought in a bill to dissolve the house after the 1835 session. Failing once again in the same manner, they began to organize public meetings throughout the colony to frame petitions requesting the governor to dissolve the Assembly and hold a general election.[54] The petitions were drawn up by Patrick Morris and William Carson and sent around the colony to all the Roman Catholic parish Priests for signatures. On 14 March, having collected several thousand names, they held a large open-air meeting in St John's to organize a parade to Government House for presentation of the petitions. Cochrane referred them to the Colonial Office with the comment that most of the names were fictitious. Somewhat inconsistently, he later told the Colonial Office that "not one name" on the petition "was free from the influence of Bishop Fleming or his Party."[55]

Neither Carson nor Morris nor any of the Reformers had deluded themselves into thinking that a dissolution would be granted, but their efforts both inside and outside the house had served to focus the attention of the populace on their political and economic grievances. However, it was at least two years before an election, and so the problem that beset them was maintaining the feverish excitement of the first few months of 1834 in the absence of a clear political victory. To add insult to injury, in April Cochrane fired Carson from his position as district surgeon and gave that place to Dr Edward Kielly,[56] a political opponent whom Carson despised.[57] In an effort to save his professional reputation, Carson wrote Cochrane for an explanation of the reasons for his dismissal. He expressed surprise especially in view of the fact that the supply committee of which he was chair had assumed that existing officeholders would retain their posts. In a vengeful attempt to embarrass Carson, Cochrane made the letter public before the house; and in a dishonest effort to embarrass his nemesis further, the governor suggested to the Assembly that the letter was an affront to their privileges. By the casting vote of the speaker the house carried a resolution embodying Cochrane's view; whereupon, hurt and embarrassed, Carson and his supporters withdrew and initiated a boycott of the house for the remainder of the session. But Carson took out his spite on Cochrane by having the *Patriot* present a series of anonymous articles supporting the views of "Junius" who had written an attack on the governor which was so damning that Cochrane first thought it better ignored.[58] Yet he soon changed his mind. Giving notice of court action, Cochrane wrote the *Patriot* and demanded to know the author. Reformers and their Catholic supporters were jubilant when the author appeared in public print in the next issue of the *Patriot*. It was none other than the Reverend Edward Troy.[59] Reformers and the entire Catholic community believed Cochrane to be checkmated; instead, the governor, bitter with prejudice against Fleming, told the Colonial Office that Troy was too ignorant to have written such a piece and affirmed his belief that the bishop was behind it.[60] Thus, Catholics were stunned when he went to the Supreme Court and took out a writ against Troy. But, before he could complete his action, the Colonial Office, learning of the deep divisions engendered by the Cochrane-Carson-Fleming confrontations, recalled the governor in disgrace.[61] Father Troy had the last laugh. He ascended the pulpit on the Sunday morning previous to Cochrane's departure and urged his congregation to give the governor a good send-off.[62] The Catholics did not disappoint their priest, lining the roadways and the dock in the thousands to jeer and hoot the Cochranes as they embarked for England. Once safely on board the ship, the intensely embarrassed Cochrane gave vent to his feelings and denounced the two culprits mainly responsible for his disgraceful exit – William Carson and John Kent. Needless to say, the Reformers and Catholics in general were in a celebratory mood and showed it in November with more than enthusiastic displays of welcome for the new governor, Henry Prescott.[63]

The triumph of getting rid of Cochrane plus the joy of acquiring a new governor ought to have momentarily checked the political conflicts. Indeed, Prescott tried to appease Catholics by discontinuing the suit against Father Troy. However, no lull occurred in the Newfoundland political storm. Since his arrival in the past year, the new chief justice, Henry John Boulton,[64] had gradually taken the political initiative away from the governor and the elected Tories and soon became the acknowledged leader of the anti-Catholic forces in the colony.

Staunchly and stubbornly conservative, and possessed of an irascible temperament given to fits of oratorical denunciations, Boulton had been attorney general of Upper Canada until a succession of serious confrontations with Reform leaders led to his dismissal.[65] His subsequent appointment as chief justice of the Newfoundland Supreme Court was due perhaps more to a desire to remove him from the Upper Canadian political scene than to a recognition of his talents. A later nineteenth-century historian would label him narrow-minded, inhospitable, and personally mean,[66] and a contemporary councillor termed him imprudent in offering his opinions when they were better left unsaid. "Dominant in his dispositions and habits," Attorney General James Simms told Cochrane of Boulton, "he is uncompromising on all subjects, great and small, cares or feels nothing in regard to the feelings, situations, or relations of other persons." Simms further observed that Boulton was "too fond of the right to pursue the expedient."[67]

As chief justice of Newfoundland, Boulton became president of the Legislative Council and also the chief adviser to the government by virtue of the fact that the same Legislative Council also sat as the governor's executive. Boulton arrived in the midst of a by-election where William Carson, known as the William Lyon Mackenzie of Newfoundland, was fighting for a seat in the Assembly. Destiny would soon place Boulton and Carson in direct opposition. Their respective political positions would have been enough to guarantee a political clash; however, Boulton's family background rendered such a clash inevitable long before the two houses even had a chance to meet. Boulton was married to a Roman Catholic, and his wife, Eliza, soon let it be known that she had nothing but contempt for the legalistic and formalistic religion on which most Catholics then so much depended.[68] Eliza Boulton, perhaps one hundred and fifty years ahead of her time, refused to be churched after giving birth, did not do her Easter duty, and scoffed at the foolishness of holy water. To make a bad situation worse, she became almost immediately upon arrival in the colony the friend and sentimental supporter of Patrick Kough, chief enemy of Bishop Fleming and implacable opponent of William Carson and the Reformers. After the by-election campaign of 1833, it was widely and credibly reported that Eliza Boulton had been the chief source for the reports of the sermons of Bishop Fleming and Father Troy and that she had complained to Rome on that account. As a result, Bishop Fleming had felt constrained to write Rome in his own defence and labelled Eliza Boulton as one of the "Liberaux" or "Liberal Catholics"[69] – a term that was then throughout Western Europe a byword for rebellious Catholics. In St John's, Catholics were aghast that Eliza Boulton had the audacity to go to church every Sunday morning in spite of the strong feelings running against her on the part of the people and clergy alike.

In the Legislative Council in January 1834, Boulton soon took effectual control over the other councillors and assumed to himself, as president, unjustified rights and privileges for which the British government later reprimanded him. When he presided over his first Supreme Court term in early January 1834, he startled everyone with an announcement that he had changed the system for empanelling juries by enlarging the right of challenge. Catholics had heretofore expressed their displeasure at the jury system, since it had been restricted to merchants and principal gentlemen. With so few co-religionists in that category, Catholics in the past nine years had been badly underrepresented on all the juries called and now were worried that the jury system might become even more exclusive. Ostensibly, Boulton's move was made in order to ensure the selection of the most qualified jurors, but in actual practice the small clique of Tory lawyers challenged the Catholics to such an extent that for the numerous trials of 1834 only two Roman Catholics survived as jurymen throughout the term.[70]

The Catholic clergy and their representatives charged that Boulton's action amounted to a deliberate anti-Catholic plot, and their suspicions increased with the debate over admission of a Catholic lawyer to practise at the bar. Not only was the small knot of nine lawyers then constituting the Law Society exclusively Protestant, but each member was a well-known Tory supporter. Since the Catholic clergy and the *Patriot* were embroiled in a number of libel suits, either as plaintiff or defendant, it was considered imperative to have a Catholic lawyer at the bar. For that purpose Fleming had recruited from Ireland John Valentine Nugent, who arrived in the summer of 1833. Following Nugent's arrival, Fleming met with Boulton about the lawyer's admission to the bar.[71] Fleming was given to understand there would be no problem, but Boulton completed the court ceremonies at the January 1834 opening and proceeded immediately to trial without even mentioning Nugent's name.

At the first opportunity, Nugent approached the bench and enquired if Boulton had forgotten to sanction his admission. He could not have done that, Boulton informed him, for he had not had a petition from him. True, admitted Nugent; for it had been Fleming who had petitioned on his behalf. But Nugent was thunderstruck; he knew immediately that Boulton intended to place every obstacle in his path. Forthwith Nugent drew up the petition in the usual style and presented it personally in open court as decreed. Boulton, who had the sole power under the court's charter of regulating the admission of barristers and attorneys, dismayed Nugent with the statement that consultation with existing lawyers would determine if there were enough business to warrant an addition to their ranks. Naturally, the existing Tory clique had no desire whatever to admit a person of Nugent's stamp; Nugent already was reliably rumoured to be the letter-writer for Father Troy and author of numerous anonymous letters and articles in the *Patriot* attacking the Conservatives. They therefore turned him down. Boulton washed his hands of the whole affair, and a Roman Catholic was thus denied entrance to the Law Society and the bar. Both the bar and the bench remained exclusively Protestant, and Catholic grievances against the entire system of Government began gradually to shift from the governor to Boulton. The campaign against Boulton accelerated in the spring following the celebrated murder trial of Catherine Snow and by September 1834 occupied centre stage.

Catherine Snow, a Roman Catholic from Conception Bay, had been arrested along with two men for the murder of her husband, John Snow, whose body was never found.[72] The two males were convicted of murder; Catherine, with being an accessory before the fact; and all three were sentenced to be hanged. The *Patriot*, as usual, took the anti-Boulton side in an effort to embarrass him. But this time it had a good case. The jury that convicted Snow and the two men had, said Carson, been improperly summoned because of an illegal appointment to deputy sheriff, a position forbidden by the Supreme Court's charter. Carson argued also that the verdict could be quashed on the technicality that the victim's body had never been found and that the only evidence against Snow was the statement of her co-defendants, evidence Boulton had ordered the jury to ignore.

The talk about town was that Carson had the better argument, but there was no sense of urgency to act on the subject of Snow's reprieve for, upon disclosure that Snow was pregnant, her sentence was respited by the judge until she had delivered. As a result, sympathy grew in favour of Snow and reached a climax when her seven little children were brought to St John's and personally placed under the guardianship of Bishop Fleming. It was generally believed that Snow's life would be saved. However, Bishop Fleming and all her supporters were profoundly dismayed when, immediately after her deliverance of a child, Catherine Snow was summoned to court by Chief Justice Boulton and given one week's notice of hanging. The community was in a deep state of shock, and Bishop Fleming and Father Troy began a series of frantic efforts to save her life. The record shows that Boulton, having given credence to rumours that she could be saved by petition, dragged his feet on the matter and did not fully cooperate with Troy on that fateful weekend prior to her execution.[73] Father Troy claimed he was just putting the finishing touches on her petition to the governor on Monday morning when he learned – to his great amazement and sorrow – that Boulton had advanced her execution date by two hours and she was already dead. The Catholic community was deeply saddened. The sight of Snow's body and the eight little children engendered intense bitter feelings towards Boulton. Every opportunity was taken to malign and attack him as a devilish hanging judge bent on persecuting Catholics.

But the event that precipitated Boulton, more than anything else, to the centre of the political stage was his behaviour at the regular annual meeting of the Charity School in August 1834. This event occurred subsequent to an important educational announcement by the governor.

Cochrane, an official supporter of the Newfoundland School Society, announced early in 1834 that the long-standing government grant to the St John's Charity School was to be discontinued.[74] He used the argument that, since the other schools received no Newfoundland government money, he considered it unfair that one should be singled out for favour. He further argued that to make grants for education was the task of the newly formed House of Assembly. While his arguments were reasonable, the withdrawal of the grant can plausibly be regarded as a clever, backhanded strategy in favour of the NSS. While

Inglis, Wix, and their supporters endured a dramatic setback as a result of the loss of their only government education grant in Newfoundland, the new chief justice delivered the fatal blow.

For thirty-two years the public had met each year to hear the annual report of the St John's Charity School. These meetings had usually been routine, humdrum affairs of reading the financial reports, announcing statistics on the students in the school, and passing flowery resolutions of profuse thanks and praise to all the leading clergy and gentlemen involved. But the meeting that took place on 23 August 1834 was far from routine.[75] The Charity School had been a popular institution in the community at large. Although the education it offered was entirely secular, every denomination had the opportunity to remove their students for specific religious instruction if they so desired. Roman Catholics had taken advantage of that rule for decades. They were shocked, therefore, by the proceedings during the later stages of the August 1834 meeting. The governor's secretary, E.B. Brenton, and Chief Justice Boulton both rose to put forward their evangelical education program. They advanced a motion to unite the school with those of the NSS. Catholics protested, but the motion was carried unanimously on the part of all the Protestants at the meeting.

In order to give effect to the motion uniting the schools, Brenton moved that a committee be appointed. Boulton, William Thomas, T.B. Job,[76] C.F. Bennett,[77] Newman Hoyles,[78] John Dunscomb,[79] James Crowdy,[80] and Colonel William Haly[81] would constitute the committee.[82] In view of the fact that not one Roman Catholic was named to the committee, a person identified only as a gentleman rose to protest. Pointing out that Roman Catholics had always attended the Charity School and that since 1802 Roman Catholic clergy had sat on its governing board, this person charged that Brenton's motion was an invidious attack upon the Roman Catholic Church. Brenton attempted a defence, but he was absolved from all responsibility by the chairman of the meeting, Boulton, who strode to the podium and began an extensive oration on education, Protestants, Catholics, and religion in general; his speech turned the meeting into chaos and soon set the entire community ablaze with public outpourings of sectarian invective.

Boulton began by declaring that the Roman Catholic clergy had no intention, in future, of countenancing the Charity School in any way. He gave as his authority a private interview he had had with Bishop Fleming. Whether his report of the private conversation was as correct as he claimed was destined to be debated for more than a decade. Nevertheless, the public was enormously surprised to hear of a departure from a policy that had been in operation for over thirty years. Boulton did not stop with reporting Bishop Fleming's conversation, however, but proceeded to comment on the general relations between Protestants and Roman Catholics. It would be worse than idle, he said, for the committee to be governed by the thought that Catholics and Protestants could be educated together. "It was impossible to amalgamate them," he declared, "they may as well attempt to blend oil and vinegar or bring the two poles together." Anticipating that he would be charged with inflaming sectarian passions, Boulton declared that he would make no apologies to anyone. He shouted, "If the whole Catholic hierarchy were present, I would state the same thing – I would not be influenced by them, either in my mind or in my purse – I would do it in the very heart of Spain."[83]

Roman Catholics were stung by what was destined to go down in history as Boulton's oil-and-vinegar speech and interpreted his purse reference as an imputation that financial support of their church was provided under duress and that Catholic minds were, therefore, enslaved by their clergy. As for Bishop Fleming, in a letter to the *Newfoundland Patriot*, he described Boulton's speech as an impertinent, bitter personal attack upon himself and his priests. Fleming charged that Boulton had deliberately twisted what he, the bishop, had said about mixed education and then used that deliberate misinterpretation as the basis for an attack upon Fleming's church. "I objected," said the bishop, "to an unauthorized version of the Bible being placed in the hands of Catholics, and to the desecration of that sacred volume by having it thumbed as a school book."[84] He reminded everyone of the beneficent support that the Roman Catholics had consistently given to the Charity School since its founding in 1802. Because after 1827 that school had been assimilated to the model of the National System, with closer ties to the Church of England, Fleming on coming to the episcopacy in 1829 took advantage of the school's liberal principles to remove Catholics for separate religious instruction. It was those liberal principles, he charged, that had now been destroyed by the single-handed action of the chief justice. In closing, he attributed "the most rancorously illiberal" sentiments to Henry John Boulton.

Of all the statements made by Fleming, the one that rankled most of all was the charge of illiberality against Boulton. The leading figures of Newfoundland society had always given a great deal of lip-service to the theme of liberality. To the governor, liberality was of utmost importance as a curtain to conceal the festering sores beneath the veneer of Newfoundland society. Because he had always felt it was his special duty in administering the colony to smooth things over, "to keep up society, to placate the opposition,"[85] he was fond of holding an extraordinarily high number of social gatherings at Government House. These gatherings consisted of guest lunches, dinners, and even breakfasts at which he patronized the leading people in politics, business, and the church. He ran up such high expense bills at those meetings that he was reprimanded by the Colonial Office and became subject to budget restrictions by the British Treasury Department. Implicit in that policy of liberality, however, was the assumption that any person indiscreet enough to peel away the veneer and publicly state the truth would be held in universal opprobrium and regarded as an outcast.

Immediately following Fleming's letter, supporters of the chief justice rushed to his defence, attacking the bishop and laying the charge of illiberality at his feet instead. Supporters of Fleming launched a counter-attack on Boulton. While the latter, as president of the new Legislative Council, had speedily incurred the wrath of all liberal politicians, as he had done in Upper Canada, politicians on opposite sides of the political spectrum joined the debate over who was really the most illiberal person, Fleming or Boulton. The Conservative, Protestant *Times* defended the character of the chief justice while its sister newspaper, the *Public Ledger*, attacked Bishop Fleming and opened its columns to correspondents who attacked Roman Catholic attitudes to the Bible. The Liberal, Catholic *Patriot* replied with an attack upon the *Ledger*'s Henry Winton. "The worst trait in the character of this bloodhound," screamed the *Patriot*, "is that he labours incessantly to sever the link which binds the people to their spiritual instructors."[86] Early in 1835 the Reformers appealed to the Privy Council in London for Boulton's dismissal. Prominent among the charges against him were that he had used all his influence "to plunder the people of a Charitable institution founded in the year 1802," and that he had publicly declared "that Catholic must essentially be opposed to Protestant, and Protestant to Catholic."[87]

Political controversy, especially in Newfoundland, has always tended to create its own momentum. Those who led the protracted debate over illiberality in 1834–35 were more or less seeking to escape their own responsibility. No matter how strongly they protested, nor how bitterly they complained, the fact could not be concealed that sectarian education, under a shroud of liberality, had been in existence for decades. Even in pre-colonial times, the struggle between the Methodists and the Anglicans had partly revolved around the instruction given in schools,[88] and later the evangelical revival in the Church of England had pointedly focused its attention on the specific manner of teaching the Scriptures in schools.[89] In any event, the most immediate result of the Boulton-Fleming quarrel was to force Archdeacon Edward Wix, to choose sides between evangelical Anglicans in his own church and the idolatrous papists under Bishop Fleming. That was not much of a choice for Wix who came down hard on the Roman Catholics by issuing a charge of illiberality[90] against Fleming. The ultimate outcome of the dispute was to unite the Anglicans and the debate soon resolved itself into a quarrel over denominational education. As Fleming had already established a nun's school for Roman Catholic girls and had placed Catholic, clerically controlled education high on his agenda, Boulton was only really making public that which had been operating privately for some years past.

By 1835 the clergy of all denominations were begging government for financial assistance for their respective schools, and Governor Prescott felt constrained to reply. In early January 1836, the throne speech announced that an education act would be laid before the legislature. The new act met with unanimous approval and, as well as making grants for the existing schools in St John's, legislated public money for the support of new schools to be established by governor-appointed school boards in all the electoral districts of the colony. The potentially vexing question of making rules and by-laws for the actual operation of those schools was reserved, subject to the governor's approval, to the individual boards, and the tackling of that task soon became the battleground for the rival denominations.

St John's, having received its warrant of appointment on the same day it was gazetted, led the way in convening board meetings. By early July it had completed its program of drawing up rules and by-laws which were soon recommended to the rest of the colony as the example to follow in regard to religious instruction. Its seventh rule, which received the unanimous concurrence of a mixed board of Anglicans, Methodists, Congregationalists, and Roman Catholics, read as follows: "That all ministers of Religion shall have power to visit the schools under the control of this Board, and from time to time to withdraw the pupils of their respective communions for the purpose of imparting to them Religious Instruction; for which every facility shall be afforded by the teachers; but no minister shall be permitted to impart any such instruction in the School."[91] From such a pronouncement it can be understood that the new schools were to be strictly non-sectarian and the teaching of religion expressly forbidden, as in the National Schools of Ireland set up five years earlier by an act of the British Parliament.[92]

Identical rules were put into place in all the districts with Roman Catholic majorities. But in the Protestant districts no such spirit prevailed. The Conception Bay board met at Harbour Grace on 8 August and conducted its proceedings with unanimity on ten of the twelve rules proposed.[93] Then the Anglican cleric, the Reverend Charles Blackman, and his co-religionist John Stark[94] moved for separate education in separate schools for Roman Catholics, Methodists, and Episcopalians. Blackman, a high church Anglican, who for years had supported Wix and the National Society, feared the influence of the evangelicals and the Methodists. His tactic was directed at getting as much educational control as possible for the Church of England and distancing himself from the supporters of the NSS. But his motion was roundly defeated by a combination of his Protestant opponents and the Roman Catholics. The latter argued that the legislature had no intention of voting public monies "to engender religious distinctions in the pupils," a position earlier confirmed by the debate in the House of Assembly on the act in question. They also cited the precedent set in early July by the St John's board, when Bishop Fleming had spurned separate education. But the precedent that had the strongest bearing on their conduct was that set in Ireland in 1831; there, the Roman Catholic Church had opted for combined, non-sectarian education and this had been sanctioned by the British Parliament as well.

Anglican Robert Prowse[95] now moved what appeared to Stark and Blackman to be more or less a compromise measure in rule eleven: that "the authorized version of the Holy Scriptures, without note or comment, be added to the books already proposed and adopted by this Board and that an hour, either before or after regular school hours, be appropriated for the reading of such by the children of the parents who may desire it; and that after such time the Scriptures shall be removed from the School Room."

Boulton and his evangelical supporters in the Church of England and the NSS had long supported this strategy, which combined all Protestants for scriptural education. It was also the program supported by the British and Foreign School Society and its Methodist and evangelical supporters in England. Initiative on the part of Catholic parents would be required in order to prevent Catholic students from attending those Bible classes, a course of action that had been pursued only intermittently in England and Ireland. Prowse's manoeuvre, then, held the promise of evangelizing Roman Catholics. That undoubtedly was a prospect that appealed to Methodists and Anglicans alike. As well, Boulton's supporters in the Harbour Grace meeting had rejected separate education for the same reasons that led Boulton and others in 1834 to unite the St John's Charity School with the NSS. While Boulton had declared, at that time, the futility of trying to unite Protestants and Catholics for educational purposes, the action by the Conception Bay board would perhaps force most of the Catholics to withdraw and leave the Protestants in majority control. Prowse's motion met with united opposition from the Catholics, on the same ground on which they had opposed Stark's original resolution. Two Protestants who supported the liberal cause of non-sectarian education supported the Catholics and the board was split right down the middle. But the motion was carried with the casting vote of the Anglican chairman, the Reverend John Burt.

As soon as Governor Prescott received the board's report, he immediately observed that "as the authorized version of the Scriptures is alone to be used, the benefit of it must be confined to Protestant children" and suggested, instead, that the board adopt the seventh rule of the board for the district of St John's.[96] Prescott was, perhaps, attempting to avoid a too-close identification with either side for fear of being drawn into the raging political controversy. He was painfully aware of the potential for local colonial politics to destroy gubernatorial careers, especially in view of what had only recently happened to his immediate predecessor, Thomas Cochrane. Prescott volunteered his personal opinion that the Bible ought to be confined to Protestant children, a perfectly neutral position in that no one, either in Conception Bay or St John's, had come out in support of that particular stand. Secondly, he suggested as a compromise that the rules of the St John's board be adopted in Conception Bay. The wisdom of that manœuvre was based on the fact that it had received the backing of the heads of the three major denominations at the recent St John's board meetings. Prescott seemed to have chosen safe political territory by neither opposing Bible teaching, which would have alienated most Protestants in Conception Bay, nor lending his backing to the Boulton-inspired resolution of Robert Prowse, which would have totally alienated the Catholic Church and its supporters. Besides, neither the Protestants nor the Catholics in Conception Bay were unanimous on the subject of religious education, and those divisions tended to widen as the controversy continued unresolved. Since Prescott could not have been able to predict which opinion would ultimately prevail, his stands in favour of Bible teaching for Protestants and in support of Bishop Fleming's position in St John's may not have been the safest politically but perhaps were the most sensible of the alternatives advanced to date.

The Harbour Grace board convened a special meeting to consider Prescott's communication, and the former supporters of the eleventh rule spoke of their determination to continue to use their Bible in the schools. The Roman Catholics moved that the controversial rule be replaced, according to the governor's suggestion, with the seventh rule of St John's, a move that resulted in a 5–5 tie. The chairman, the Reverend John Burt, then declared that the original rule, which had been carried by a majority, would remain unaltered; whereupon two of the Roman Catholic members – Peter Brown, Assembly member for Conception Bay, and Father Charles Dalton,[97] parish priest of Harbour Grace – withdrew from the meeting. They immediately lodged a further protest with the governor demanding that he withhold his assent from a measure that "will have a tendency, if carried into effect, of depriving the Catholic children of this District of the benefit of an elementary education,"[98] which the legislature intended should be given to all without religious distinctions. When the governor complied with their request and ordered the Conception Bay board to expunge the eleventh rule,[99] it refused and continued to enforce its own rules,[100] prompting the Catholics to organize a boycott of the school. The consequences, then, of the board's actions were that public monies were withheld and Catholics were denied schooling.

Back in the capital, meanwhile, the Catholic *Patriot* had objected strenuously on 9 July to the denominational composition of the boards. While the act had ordained for each district thirteen-member boards, including the resident senior clergyman, it left to the governor the option of appointing a total of ninety-four members. The *Patriot* correctly pointed out that, out of that ninety-four members, Governor Prescott had appointed only ten Roman Catholics. Even in Ferryland district, a riding more than 95 per cent Roman Catholic, only three of the thirteen board members were Roman Catholic. This was an inauspicious beginning for Prescott and one not calculated to earn the confidence of Roman Catholics.

One might wonder why the Protestant members in the Roman Catholic districts chose a route so different from their co-religionists in Conception Bay. In the predominantly Catholic districts, the Protestants may have considered it thoroughly impractical to press for either sectarian or mixed-Protestant, Bible education. With the Roman Catholics having already announced their preference for the Irish National System, the Conception Bay approach would at best have initiated a pointless squabble that could have led to no practical results for the Protestants. At worst it could have antagonized the Catholics to the point where the latter would force the boards to be reconstituted so as to conform to the majority denominational pattern in their districts. Such a scenario would place in jeopardy the education of the minority Protestant population, a cause already perceived to be threatened. The Anglicans, both high and low, had several years previously chosen the Methodists as their main rivals and had opted to focus their efforts on the northern bays. Perhaps it was for this reason that they refused to precipitate a struggle with the majority Catholic population of the Avalon peninsula. Methodists, on the other hand, had always been the most fervent anti-Catholics both in Newfoundland and in England. Traditionally, they had opposed any state-run system of education because such a system would be dominated by the established Church of England and also because state payment for teaching the authorized version of the Bible could lead only to requests to teach the Roman Catholic Bible too.[101] From such a prospect Methodists had always recoiled in horror. Perhaps it was for these reasons that Methodists supported, in all the Roman Catholic districts, the Irish National System of education so favoured by Roman Catholics as well. Because of the Methodist support, Catholics were found to be conciliatory when the Protestant-controlled boards met in the Catholic districts.

Such was the equanimity with which the Protestants began their work on the St John's board that they unanimously refused to continue on the ground that the board was illegally constituted without Bishop Fleming. Governor Prescott apparently had made a genuine but highly unfortunate mistake. Using his knowledge of the established Church in England as his yardstick for making decisions regarding the Roman Catholic Church in Newfoundland, he had placed on the school board for St John's the Reverend Father Troy instead of the Roman Catholic bishop. He soon realized his error and appointed a new board, with Fleming on it. But by the time this remedial action had been taken, Father Troy had fired some telling, political shots at the governor. Echoing the Catholic *Patriot*'s declaration that Fleming and the church had been insulted, Troy wrote the board Chairman Frederick Carrington, charging that the bishop's omission was "a gratuitous indignity upon the Catholic clergy and the Roman Catholics."[102] Prescott was so taken aback that he wrote for advice to the Colonial Office, which told him that the only possible thing to do was to accuse Troy of misconstruing the governor's action.[103]

The crisis soon passed, and the St John's board did its work amicably until news of the Conception Bay crisis broke upon the capital. Three days after the first school board meeting in Harbour Grace, the *Patriot* condemned the Conception Bay rules as Boulton's oil-and-vinegar policy. It followed up with a campaign in favour of the Irish National System but opposed to the use of the Bible in Newfoundland schools. The movers of the Scripture resolution in the Conception Bay board were personally criticized and objetions were levelled against the Bible being "doubled down in dogs-ears and thumbed by brainless and thoughtless and wayward school urchins as a common and ordinary school book." If the eleventh rule were not rescinded, said the *Patriot*, education would become a humbug.[104] Throughout August and September, the *Patriot* carried verbatim accounts of the dispute in Conception Bay and charged on 10 September that the crisis had been occasioned by one party "looking to establish an ascendancy by banishing from the schools the children of Roman Catholics, as well as Roman Catholic teachers."

Meanwhile, the Protestant *Public Ledger* praised Boulton's oil-and-vinegar policy and championed separate education for Protestants and Catholics in the Protestant districts.[105] The *Ledger* maintained a steady campaign against the Catholic clergy and opened its columns to the leading Protestant clerics, politicians, and merchants who wrote anonymously against the interference of the Roman Catholic Curch in educational matters. Friar Fleming, the pejorative nickname for the Roman Catholic bishop, was attacked as "an oily-tongued bigot and a sanctimonious bigot." People writing under the pseudonyms Arcanum, Z, and Pro Bono Publico urged all Protestants to protest to the governor about the Fleming's behaviour towards the Conception Bay board. Writer Z complained that Protestants were being denied their just British rights and summoned his co-religionists to rally round "the holiest of all causes." He added a warning: "Be this your watchword, No Bible-no schools."[106]

The Presbyterian *Times* gave strong support to the *Ledger*'s campaign against Bishop Fleming, his clergy, Daniel O'Connell, the Catholic liberals, and the *Patriot*. But in the midst of its anti-Catholic campaign the *Times* paused on 14 September to praise the St John's board's seventh rule on religion. "The liberality by which its regulations were formed," said the *Times*, "puts them all above any suspicion to proselytise." The *Times* seemed to contradict itself by praising the rules of both the St John's and Conception Bay boards. However, Conception Bay had a majority of Protestants, the *Times* pointed out, while St John's had a majority of Catholics. The paper's consistency lay in the fact that it supported majority rule in both places.

While the Education Act was an attempt at centralized state education for the colony, as far as board appointments and public monies were concerned, the actual operation of the schools was the responsibility of the regional authorities. In the northern bays, that meant Protestant control. One would expect that, if Protestant majorities meant Protestant control, then Catholic majorities, as in St John's, Ferryland, and Placentia–St Mary's, should mean Catholic control. If such distribution was possible, it is puzzling why those districts should be content with secular education. For Bishop Fleming, secular education meant secular education by secular teachers.[107] Religious education was a thing apart. What St John's seventh rule had done was to separate religious education entirely from the secular education given in the schools and reserve it for the Catholic pastor whose proper province it was believed to be.

But there was a practical as well as a theological reason for the Roman Catholic bishop's support of St John's seventh rule. Bishop Fleming was not confident that the church could find in Newfoundland secular teachers competent enough to teach religion. His attitude is not surprising given that the various Protestant congregations and the several religious societies had been, since the previous century, recruiting their teachers from the British Isles. The same was true of the clergy, with none of the Protestant or Catholic clerics being a native Newfoundlander. Fleming himself had to campaign for almost four years before he was able to recruit Irish nuns to start a girls' school in St John's. Another decade would elapse before he could recruit enough to start a second school. Therefore, one would think that – if the Protestant boards adopted St John's seventh rule – the Catholic program would be complete. The *Times*, in fact, made that very point; and, in an attempt to compromise, the Harbour Grace board convened a special meeting and passed the seventh rule, a move supported by the lone Catholic who attended.[108] But this action was sufficient neither for the Catholic liberal politicians nor for Bishop Fleming and his clergy, who had desired the rescinding of the rule regarding the use of the authorized version of the Bible altogether. Catholics wished, instead, to pursue a centralized, consistent policy on education for the whole colony.

There were additional reasons for catholic opposition to state Bible teaching, as revealed by the disputes in the Trinity and Bonavista Bay boards. The Trinity Bay board met in July and adopted religion rules identical to those subsequently adopted in Conception Bay.[109] But the governor, perhaps through lack of vigilance and also perhaps because of the unanimity in the Trinity board, accepted the rules and did not realize his error until the political storm broke over the same rules in Conception Bay. Then he advised the Trinity Bay board to expunge its rule relating to the authorized version of the Bible and adopt in its place the seventh rule of the St John's board.[110] In doing so Prescott was trying to enforce the colony-wide system of secular education approved by the majority in the House of Assembly and, as demonstrated by the votes on the St John's board, supported by the heads of all denominations. Because of the delay occasioned in St John's by the Troy-Carrington dispute, Governor Prescott had approved the Trinity Bay rules before the St John's issue had come to a vote. Consequently, in August he had to undo in Trinity what he had done in July, suffering the inevitable loss in credibility that came as a result of his having to make an about-face. Soon Catholics as well as Protestants were calling down wrath upon his head.

Generally, Prescott and the Roman Catholics had stood together since the beginning of the educational dispute, but the governor's wavering over the issue in the Trinity Bay board worried the Catholics. They and their supporters had exploited the Conception Bay dispute as an opportunity to pressure the governor to apply the St John's rules across the colony indiscriminately. Such pressure had forced Prescott to apply the rule in Trinity Bay, but the force of the arguments against him there eventually induced him to attempt a compromise. Skelton, the Trinity Board chairman, called Prescott's attention to the preponderance of Protestants in the district, to the unanimity in the board debates, and to the incontestable argument that "to keep those sacred deposits of truth and knowledge out of sight in twelve schools, because a few Roman Catholic children may attend them, is surely too great a concession to make. Such a concession would be a sacrifice of principle – a sacrifice which no Protestant would require a Roman Catholic to make under a change of circumstances; and which, therefore, no Protestant is bound to concede to a Roman Catholic."[111] Prescott admitted the strength of the arguments and told Skelton privately that he was in personal agreement with him. Therefore, Prescott attempted another compromise – that, if Catholics in the district did not complain, then he would allow the rules to stand. Luckily for the governor, the Trinity board could not accept that condition, and so Prescott enforced the same rules in Trinity Bay as in St John's, with the result that the Trinity board rejected his interference entirely. The governor replied by withholding the funds.

Besides the governor's dalliance with unapproved rules, there was another aspect to the Trinity Bay dispute that disturbed St John's Catholic leaders. Specifically, in contrast to other areas of the colony, there was a singular lack of protest from Roman Catholics in Trinity Bay. Indeed, there is some evidence that there were Roman Catholics in the Trinity district who were content to send their children to schools where the Bible was being taught.[112] It was a worrisome sign that became much more pronounced as the dispute in Bonavista Bay gathered momentum.

In Bonavista, the board met, made all the provisions necessary for opening schools, and adopted the textbooks in use by the Newfoundland School Society.[113] The governor happily approved the board's rules and reminded it that the books used should not be repugnant to the tenets of any sect whatsoever. When he noticed that the board had made no rule with regard to religion, Prescott suggested the adoption of the seventh rule of the St John's board, a suggestion which the Bonavista Bay Board subsequently accepted. To that date all decisions of the Bonavista Bay board had been made in an atmosphere of amity and unanimity even though there were several Roman Catholics on the board, including Father Nicholas Devereux,[114] the Roman Catholic parish priest of King's Cove. But on 4 October 1836 a letter signed "Catholicus" from Bonavista appeared in the *Public Ledger*, condemning the board for not having adopted the books of the Irish National System. The next day the governor informed the board that, if its textbook rule meant the authorized version of the Bible, he would have to withhold his assent. The board was shocked. In Bonavista Bay, it informed the governor, there had never been any quarrel with Roman Catholics over the use of the Bible in school. Catholic parents had for years sent their children to schools of the Newfoundland School Society without complaint and the Roman Catholic members had approved all of the board's recent decisions. Apart from the protest of Catholicus, there had been no disagreement; not even the Catholic parish priest on the board had signified any displeasure. The Bonavista board repudiated the interference of the governor.

For Bishop Fleming and his supporters in St John's, the willingness of outport Catholics to attend such schools aroused their greatest fears. Their campaign for non-sectarian education was designed as much to protect the faith of Roman Catholics such as those in Bonavista Bay as to preserve clerical control over religious teaching. In this respect they had allies in the Protestant clergy on the largely Roman Catholic Avalon, who were similarly concerned about the faith of the minority Protestant population in that region. It appeared, then, that as the distance from St John's increased so did the frustration of St John's leaders as they attempted to impose a state system of education. More and more it became as much a regional as a sectarian conflict.

Peter Brown, Assembly member for Conception Bay and school board member in that district, had resolved to tackle this aspect of the problem as soon as the house opened in 1837. On 26 August 1837 Brown brought in an amendment to the Education Act appointing new boards in the disputed districts. This amendment banned the use of any book to which any religious denomination objected.[115] It passed all three readings in less than a week and on 6 September went to the Legislative Council, where it ran headlong into the opposition of the uncompromising anti-Catholic Henry John Boulton.[116] Under Boulton's insistence, the Council expunged all sections relating to sectarian books and the appointment of new boards. It inserted instead a provision allowing boards to use any book they pleased "provided that no child be required to use any book objected to by parents or guardians of such a child." Thus, the Boards of Conception, Trinity, and Bona-vista bays would continue to teach the Bible to all students until some parent objected, after which objection the child's remaining in the class would become strictly a voluntary matter. The Assembly refused to deal with the Council's amendments, resolving that the upper house had destroyed the principle of the Bill. There followed a series of conferences between the Council and Assembly, with both sides advancing the arguments that for a year had graced or disgraced the pages of the various newspapers. The Council repeatedly declared its determination to stand by its amendments, and the Assembly responded in kind. Finally, Boulton lost his patience and refused to receive any more messages from the Assembly on education.

The Education Bill was only one of the more than twenty bills that had been blocked by the upper house that year. The impasse had arisen mainly as the result of the emergence of a cohesive Reform Party having secured control of the House of Assembly following the general electons of 1837. The triumph of Reform had many causes but the gradual emergence of sectarianism was surely the most impor-tant. Sectarianism had played but a minor role at the general elections of 1832. William Carson, however, became convinced that it had not been used effectively by the Reformers. In the following years Carson accentuated the sectarian factor to suit his political interests little suspecting that its inborn tendencies might rage out of control. Over time, the debates over the jury issue, Nugent's attempt's to enrol at the bar, and the Catherine Snow murder trial had become so intense that by 1836 the sectarian issue threatened to override all others. It tended to mask the achievements of William Carson, who had engi-neered the construction of a broad-based coalition of middle- and lower-class, St John's and outport, interests to challenge upper-class domination. Then the Bible battle broke and from this time forward political conflict in the colony was pre-eminently sectarian religious conflict.

5 The Catholic Crusade, 1836–38

H.J. Boulton had been removed from Upper Canada because of his intransigence in the political struggle there. It was Newfoundland's ill luck that a change in Colonial Office personnel led not to his political oblivion but to his transfer to St John's as chief justice. In spite of heading Newfoundland's Supreme Court, he became a central figure in the colony's political debate and was destined to play a key role in the general elections of 1836–37. To the Reformers seeking control of the House of Assembly, Boulton was a godsend. His penchance for controversial decisions along with his extremist positions on cases allied to Cathoic grievances allowed him to be portrayed as the anti-Catholic devil. But, while focusing a campaign around the sense of Catholic hurt carried enormous appeal on the Catholic Avalon, there were dangerous shoals ahead for a political party flirting with sectarianism as its main campaign tool.

Carson and his successor as editor of the *Patriot*, Robert John Parsons, made every effort to keep alive the sectarian education debate initiated by Boulton in 1834. One writer using the name Brutus, in several issues of the *Patriot*, charged Boulton with having started all the discord and bigotry; the writer asserted that Boulton was the evil genius behind the authorities' action in calling out the military on several occasions in the past year. His speech at the Charity School meeting was labelled as "a wanton, an indecent, a gratuitous insult"[1] to all Roman Catholics in Newfoundland. In its editorial section, the *Patriot* declared that Boulton was "ill-fitted" to deal with Bishop Fleming and that he should have steered away from the "sectarian cabal."

"Instead," said the *Patriot*, Boulton had "incautiously and indiscreetly put himself forward as the rallying point, the very nucleus of the Protestant Party."[2]

In the last Assembly session before the general election Carson and Kent had initiated efforts to have Boulton impeached before the Privy Council in London. Unable to muster enough votes to establish an inquiry into Boulton's conduct, Carson and Kent began to organize outside the house to petition Britain for the chief justice's removal. They were helped immensely in arousing public agitation by Boulton's writ against the *Patriot* for the article "Stick A Pin Here." Parsons had accepted responsibility for the sarcastic, libellous piece concerning "the beneficial effects of hanging."[3] Boulton sued Parsons for libel, and, as judge and jury, he heard the case against himself by himself. He convicted Parsons, fined him heavily, and sent him to jail to do hard labour for three months. That sentence further added to the Catholic sense of grievance against Boulton.

After several successive attempts to enrol Nugent at the bar had failed, Reformers had attempted to repeal the Law Society Incorporation Act in order to make it easier for Nugent to join. The Tories gave the act the six months' hoist, following which Reformers began a public campaign to petition the governor for the specific purpose of admitting Nugent to the bar. It was while Reformers and their Catholic supporters were busy organizing petitions favouring Nugent's cause and attacking Boulton that the latter proceeded against Parsons. Parsons now became the hero of the hour, and Catholic priests became actively involved in the campaign to secure signatures on the anti-Boulton petition.

The petition against Boulton was so successful that he felt constrained to cross the Atlantic in his own defence. But the voyage did not help his cause since the British government found that he had acted improperly in the Parsons case; it ordered the fine repaid and Parsons freed.[4] Huge parades greeted Parsons's release; he was feted, wined, dined, and toasted at a public breakfast where Boulton was just as much pilloried as Parsons was praised. Feelings began to run so high against Boulton that he felt his family was unsafe. The governor was forced to post guards around the courthouse in the daytime for the judge's protection and around his house at night for the safety of his family. Boulton and his family henceforward refused to go outdoors except in the daytime, and the Reverend Edward Wix kept a loaded pistol handy at all times. The editor of the *Public Ledger*, Henry Winton, who continued an incessant attack upon Bishop Fleming and his priests, was attacked in broad daylight by a gang of masked men who brutally mutilated him by cutting off his ears.[5] Governor Prescott blamed the gruesome incident on Bishop Fleming and his clergy and told the Colonial Office that Newfoundland society was in "a state of great ferment."[6] Incredibly, neither Prescott nor any other of the authorities in Newfoundland made the least attempt at conciliation to cool down that ferment and prevent an explosion. Instead they aided and abetted incidents of violence and unrest.

Boulton had hardly returned from his failed mission to London when the Roman Catholics of Newfoundland were startled with the electrifying news that Father James Duffy, the Roman Catholic parish priest of St Mary's, had been arrested and charged with burning a merchant's flake.[7] The arrest and subsequent charges were made by none other than the sitting Tory member for that district, John W. Martin, who was also magistrate for the district and chief clerk to the firm that owned the flake in question. When Boulton learned of the charges, he immediately ordered Duffy brought to St John's for trial. Catholics protested vigorously at the injustice of not hearing the case in the southern circuit court at St Mary's and at the severe hardships inflicted on Duffy by requiring him to take such an extensive overland winter journey to St John's.

Since Duffy's backers in St Mary's refused cooperation, the colonial brig, with several constables on board, was sent to St Mary's to arrest his co-defendants and subpoena witnesses. They arrived at night but were afraid to go ashore on account of the menacing presence of huge crowds that roamed the seashore all night long. When day broke they landed a constable, who attempted to go through the crowd to arrest one man. But the constable was attacked and beaten; the brig forced to leave. The next day they tried again by landing Constable R. Butt, who went straight to John Martin's house. There, Martin summoned his clerk, William Burke, of whom Butt demanded directions to the home of one of the accused. Burke, flatly refusing to give the information, was fired on the spot by Martin. Burke departed and soon everyone in St Mary's was milling around Martin's house threatening to kill the first man who tried to arrest anyone. Butt hastily retreated aboard ship. The next day the captain himself thought he would try his luck. He landed alone and went to subpoena John Roach as a witness. Roach grabbed his sealing gun, stuck it in the captain's face, and vowed to fire if the captain did not leave the house immediately. The captain beat a hasty retreat. The next day, 15 December, they made one last attempt. Two constables went on shore and tried to arrest Thomas Murray, but a crowd appeared and gave the two constables such a severe beating that they were lucky to escape with their lives. The brig returned to St John's, where Martin told the court that it was useless to attempt getting witnesses from St Mary's. The people in St Mary's, Martin reported, were so organized and determined that they had set up a system of light signals in the event of a night attack so that everyone along the coast could be summoned to their defence.

Duffy's case was postponed to the following year and in February 1836 the British government ordered a man-of-war to proceed to St Mary's. In the meantime Father Duffy had petitioned Boulton for a Catholic lawyer to act in his defence.[8] When Boulton denied the request, petitions flooded in from Roman Catholics around the colony demanding that Duffy be allowed the privilege of a Catholic lawyer to defend himself. Patrick Morris and some friends relayed to Boulton the Catholic petitions from Conception Bay, to which Boulton replied in such a personally insulting manner that he was later reprimanded by the British government. The Newfoundland government and all its Tory supporters, nevertheless, supported his anti-Catholic campaign. The *Ledger* chastised the court for even daring to entertain the petition for a Catholic lawyer. "It's preposterous," declared the *Ledger*, "that they dared to petition for a Catholic lawyer and object to a Protestant Judge and Jury."[9] Hostility had reached such a height that, in revenge, John Kent charged John W. Martin with having poisoned a well at St Mary's, a charge later thrown out by the grand jury.

In the 1836 House of Assembly, in what was to be the last session before a general election, the two parties lost all semblance of respect for each other. What was proposed by one was greeted by the other with the six-months' hoist; what the other put forward was rebuked in kind. The Tory majority, with its tight party discipline, checkmated every Reform attempt to pass a favourable bill. Only one subject received bipartisan support. That was the Education Act on which both houses agreed – primarily because the operational details were left out of the bill and assigned to the regional boards provided by the act. Shortly after it received royal assent, the real educational struggle began and the debate over the Bible became the signal for the Catholic priests and their liberal supporters to take to the campaign trail.

In July 1836, in the midst of discussions over the Duffy trial and just as the St John's and Conception Bay school boards commenced to draw up rules for their respective schools, the head of the Roman Catholic church in the colony departed for England to commence high-level negotiations with the British Colonial Office relating to his grand cathedral. As he took his leave, it must have been supremely comforting for him to contemplate the successes of the previous few years. The Protestant journals had played right into his hands with their anti-Catholic, anti-Irish attacks; and the consequence had been the creation of an Irish Catholic solidarity that would have been just a pipe dream in the days of Bishop Scallan. As Fleming looked round at the throng gathered to see him off, he beamed with obvious delight.[10] All space as far as the eye could see was jammed with a solid phalanx of Irish Catholics – men, women, and children. The long-standing and bitter attack upon the church, he told the assembled multitude, "was an index of their success." The crowd roared its approval, perhaps as much for the implied wish that those attacks continue as for the efforts of their religious leader.

During the long transatlantic passage and his extended stay in a foreign land, Fleming became extremely worried about what his supporters might be doing behind his back. Already, there had been charges that some of his priests had overstepped the normal boundaries of their proper sacerdotal duties. He complained that they did not keep him informed of what was going on back home. In a communication burning with anxiety, Fleming warned Father Troy: "Should an election take place before my return, I hope that you will not interfere in any public manner with it."[11] But, while Fleming remained safely out of reach on the opposite side of the Atlantic, his St John's priests were soon as much involved in the general election as if they themselves were the candidates.

As noted earlier, Father Troy fired the first shot in the election campaign of 1836 by taking advantage of a technical error made by the governor in not appointing Bishop Fleming to the St John's school board. Even though Troy himself had received the appointment in the bishop's stead, Troy claimed that it was a deliberate attempt by Governor Prescott to insult Bishop Fleming. As well, Father Troy pointed out, the bishop and the Roman Catholic Church in general were gravely offended that the appointments were published in a journal "infamously notorious for its false and malignant libels"[12] upon the Roman Catholic Church. Troy was referring to the *Public Ledger,* whose campaign against priests in politics played right into the hands of the Carson-Kent Reformers. Although the governor was quite puzzled at the intensity of Troy's interpretation of the vice-regal error,[13] the *Ledger,* which did not pretend to be so naive, declared that Troy's fulminations were simply a ruse to stir up the lower orders for the campaign ahead.[14] And, even though the governor corrected his mistake by immediately replacing Troy with Bishop Fleming, the *Patriot* maintained that it was still insulting that Father Troy was not permitted to continue on the board. Thus, for the *Patriot,* the principal issue in the election campaign of 1836 was the authorities' assault on the honour of the Catholic Church and clergy. When Carson, Kent, and Patrick Morris took to the streets as the Reform candidates in St John's, they had a bevy of Roman Catholic priests by their side.[15]

On Sunday, 23 October 1836, Fathers Troy and Ward led a parade through the streets of the capital on behalf of the three Reform candidates. Three other priests, accompanied by five hundred people, marched with colours flying, drums beating, and fiddles playing. Troy, riding in the lead position on horseback, drew up his mount in front of the doors of those Roman Catholics identified as opposed to the Carson team and now commonly referred to as Mad-Dog Catholics. He then led the crowd in unison with a chorus of groaning and "baaing." When they passed the doors of those known to be supporters, they called their names, beat the drums, played the fiddles; all cheered and roared as loudly as their lungs could stand. The town's Protestants, who had historically a respect for the Sabbath far surpassing that held by the Roman Catholics, were scandalized by the flagrant breach of Sunday observance. But they were outraged beyond patience when, in passing the Anglican and Methodist churches in late afternoon, the paraders with tumultuous din interrupted and prevented the continuance of the services. The next day the Protestants had warrants issued for the arrest of Fathers Troy and Ward, the three candidates, and fourteen others for unlawful assembly and violation of the Sabbath. The charges against the two priests helped lend credence to Reform claims that the Catholic Church in Newfoundland was under siege.

In St John's district the priests and their candidates were then able to remind their co-religionists of the necessity of defending the Catholic Church against the deliberate encroachment of its enemies – those who ruled Newfoundland. The *Patriot* continued to give everyone a blow-by-blow account of the struggle over the Bible in the Protestant districts, pointing out that a certain class of Protestants was foiling attempts to give schooling to all.[16]

In the days following the arrests, Carson, Kent, and Morris whipped into a frenzy the thousands of people – men, women, and children – who milled into the streets looking for excitement. The people were led to believe that the very existence of the Catholic Church in Newfoundland was at stake and that the judges, lawyers, police constables, and military were all behind the conspiracy. Carson was reported to have said that he had ordered a thousand pickets, while Morris advised the mob to lash the Tories with the boughs tied to the ends of the sticks they carried and "if that didn't work to use the other end." Kent, in a burst of unrestrained braggadocio, declared that "if the Military were called out they would burn St John's to the ground."[17]

Wild statements such as those by Kent and Morris were all accepted literally by the Tories and used as political ammunition. Their charges, filed with the governor, alleged that violence was deliberately planned and that he, therefore, should call out the military. Prescott was reluctant to do so for fear that, under such intense pressure from a mob of several thousand jeering, stone-throwing people, some soldier might lose face and fire. One could not predict the full ramifications from such an unfortunate occurrence. Prescott shrank from the task for several days. But there was a second reason that Prescott was reluctant to call out the troops – the possible political repercussions. The Catholics and the Carson-Kent party would use it as a campaign tactic with the home government to effect the governor's removal, and Prescott could not forget that the same fate had befallen his predecessor over just such an incident in the 1833 by-election. At the same time, the marching crowds were inclined to swallow verbatim what their leaders said and, using the campaign oratory as their excuse, took advantage of every opportunity to attack their Tory opponents. Catholics marched from house to house and, where they could not identify a supporter, with insults and threats challenged the inhabitants to come forward.

The three Tory candidates tried to avoid a confrontation by restraining their supporters from taking to the streets. They postponed the opening of a committee room until 10 November, the latest possible moment in the campaign, just four days before the commencement of polling. No sooner had they opened the committee room than it was forthwith thrashed by the mob while, some reports had it, Fathers Troy and Ward looked on. The Tory candidates – Kough, Nicholas Gill, and James Grieve – then redoubled their efforts to have the military called out. Prescott finally relented. Several hundred soldiers marched up Water Street with weapons poised, but the sight only served to attract to the scene more people – women and children included. Thousands lined both sides of the street to hoot and jeer the soldiers while the three Reform candidates, accompanied by Fathers Troy and Ward, enjoyed conspicuous positions on the side-lines. When it looked as if the soldiers would break ranks and fire, Troy leaped onto the street in front of the officer commanding the troops and began a spirited conversation with him. They reached a compromise whereby Troy would disperse the crowd to their homes if the soldiers were withdrawn. The danger passed for the moment. When darkness fell that night, huge crowds roamed the streets and thrashed the homes of those who had been rash enough to sign the Tory requisitions. Windows were smashed, doors were broken down, and homes were pelted with rocks. Darkness made it impossible to effect any arrests, and only sun-up brought a quiet end to the devastation.

What had started out in July as a Catholic-Protestant campaign in St John's had, by 10 November, become almost exclusively a Catholic-Catholic feud. The split in the Catholic community that had first appeared in the 1832 general election had widened considerably during the Carson by-election campaign in the fall of 1833. In March 1836 it took a new and more menacing turn as the Benevolent Irish Society made plans for its usual annual observance of St Patrick's Day.[18] Drs Edward Kielly and Joseph Shea, Patrick Kough, and Timothy Hogan led a revolt against the Morris-Kent majority faction in the BIS, walked out of the meeting, and ultimately held their own St Patrick's Day dinner. Governor Prescott, Chief Justice Boulton, and Major Robert Law, commandant of the troops, graced the banquet with their presence, made speeches defending their politics, and blamed all the political troubles on the Fleming-inspired priests.

When the Morris-Kent section met on St Patrick's Day, Bishop Fleming led off the event with a major speech on the issue of the clergy in politics. The bishop's reasoned, dispassionate defence of priests in politics was based on their rights as British subjects. It was a perfectly defensible position and the Fleming-supported banquet would have had by far the better part of the debate had it ended there. But after Fleming sat down, speaker after speaker rose to attack the Kielly-Kough faction on the grounds of religion and morality. As Mad-Dog or Orange Catholics who lacked the courage to join another religion, they were neither real Irishmen nor real Catholics.[19]

The hurt felt by the BIS was all the greater for the split in the organization came on the thirtieth anniversary of its founding. Father Troy had advertized the BIS event and appealed for a large turnout. At the next Sunday Mass the priests read out the names of those who had attended the Kielly-Kough function and warned the congregation to have nothing to do with them or their families. Fathers Thomas Waldron and Troy refused communion to wives and family members of several of those who had attended. Others were denied baptism and, in several notorious incidents, funerals. One Catholic corpse was abandoned in the streets because the priests refused to attend the person on the grounds that he had been a Mad Dog. Anglicans finally took pity on his family and buried him in their own churchyard.

Incidents such as these were signals to the Catholic mob that Mad Dogs could be attacked with impunity. Acting on this knowledge, soon after the 1836 election campaign began, huge gangs roamed the streets searching for opportunities to attack their Catholic enemies. Except for Gill and Grieve, the two Protestant candidates on Kough's ticket, Protestants had largely abandoned the field to the Roman Catholics by the time the campaign was under way.

On Sunday morning, 13 November, the day before polling commenced, the Roman Catholic priests committed what was perhaps the worst abuse of their office to date. As Father Edward Troy emerged from the sacristy to celebrate Mass, he shot a sidelong glance at the congregation and instantly halted so that a deafening silence ran through the densely crowded church. "What!" he roared, "do I see a Mad Dog amongst our congregation?"[20] He was referring to Michael Scanlan, who was sitting near the front of the church with his wife and family. Scanlan, a Roman Catholic layman, was a well-known campaigner for Patrick Kough and the Conservative party. Troy immediately ran to the altar rails and screamed that he would never say mass with a Mad Dog present. He demanded that Scanlan leave immediately, but Scanlan refused. Then, in the eyes of Catholics, Scanlan committed an unpardonable offence by shouting back at Troy from his pew and beginning a speech in his own defence. Troy, incensed, threw off his vestments, ran through the aisle at Scanlan and physically attacked him in the middle of the church. The priest was soon ably assisted by several of his parishioners who dragged Scanlan down the aisle and out the door. The Reverend J.M. Bergin, a Dubliner, at the time parish priest of Tilting in the Twillingate-Fogo district, ferreted out the remaining Mad Dogs and ejected them from the church. Schooner owner Patrick Brawders, who had transported Bergin from Tilting so that Bergin could take part in the St John's campaign, performed yeoman service in throwing people out of the church but he roughed up Michael Scanlan's wife so badly that she had him arrested for assault causing bodily harm. The church emptied quickly so that people could witness the beatings outside. But then Father Bergin stepped in because he feared, it was said, that Scanlan would be killed. He ordered the Mad Dogs to their homes and the remainder of the congregation inside to hear Mass. There, Father Troy preached on the necessity of all good Catholics turning up at the hustings in the morning to support their religion and put down the Mad Dogs.

On election day the Catholics did not disappoint Father Troy but turned up in the thousands to cheer Kent, Morris, and Carson. With ear-shattering tumult they made it impossible for anyone but their own candidates to be heard. When Tory supporters complained, they were surrounded and beaten by the mob. The fighting continued for hours; and although 140 special constables were sworn in and sent to the scene, they were utterly helpless in their attempts to restore order. Those who attempted to make arrests were attacked, had their staffs confiscated, and were beaten with their own weapons. Kough, Gill, and Grieve resigned the contest, leaving Morris, Kent, and Carson the winners by acclamation.

But the defeated candidates succeeded in their efforts to have the troops march on Water Street. As soon as Father Troy spied the soldiers marching with fixed bayonets, he realized that their game plan was to take as many prisoners as possible and lay charges for riotous assembly. With the assistance of the other five priests attending the hustings that day, Troy soon had the crowd all running for home. Within minutes the streets were deserted, and the Royal Newfoundland companies had only one prisoner. When night fell, the crowds returned to the streets to go from door to door thrashing the houses of the Mad Dogs they had seen on the hustings. Darkness, stone throwing, and mud slinging foiled the soldiers' attempts to take prisoners by the bayonet. The entire capital reverberated with a continuous chorus of people shouting, screaming, and crying, as well as groaning from injuries. The night scene was characterized by the sounds of shattering glass, splintering doors, and running soldiers. Sun-up brought quiet to a scene of devastation throughout the town. Streets were deserted and tired soldiers held only eleven prisoners. But there was jubilation in the Carson-Kent camp; they had won three seats in the House of Assembly.

In Conception Bay, where Protestants were in the majority, the campaign became much more of a Catholic-Protestant struggle than in St John's. There, the contest took place against the backdrop of school board meetings seriously split over Bible resolutions. The prime movers of those resolutions were board members Thomas Ridley[21] and Robert Prowse, who were the Tory standard-bearers for the district and whose campaign aimed at uniting Protestants in their own political interests. The remaining lay Protestant member opposing the Catholic position was John Stark, who would probably have been a candidate too had he not held the several official positions of clerk of the northern circuit court, commissioner of probates, district coroner, registrar of deeds, commissioner of education, commissioner of roads, and stipendiary magistrate. Instead he became co-chairman of Ridley's election committee and in that capacity played a leading role. The House of Assembly subsequently investigated Stark for gross impropriety.[22]

The campaign centred on Catholic efforts to keep the Bible away from Protestants, who were urged to vote only for those who supported Ridley's position. That cause was strengthened by the fact that the two leading lay Catholics on the school board, Peter Brown and James Power, were both Reform candidates for the district. The contest for Assembly seats, therefore, was but an extension into the public political arena of the school board dispute. As well, to the delight perhaps of Ridley and Prowse, Father Charles Dalton, Roman Catholic parish priest of Harbour Grace, played a prominent part in the Reform campaign; and the Tories were fond of charging that all Reform candidates were his nominees. Nevertheless, efforts at uniting Protestants fell far short of the expectations of Ridley and Prowse. First, the two Catholic Reform incumbents were joined in an aggressive campaign by the Protestant incumbent for Conception Bay district, Robert Pack, who, as the most influential local merchant in Carbonear, was able to acquire substantial support from his Protestant clerks and servants throughout the area. Rounding out the Reform ticket was a second Protestant, Anthony Godfrey, a small-time, local dealer. Together Pack and Godfrey could claim that, while the Protestants were unable to use the Bible in schools, the Reform program was the same for all – Catholics and Protestants; that it had the support of the heads of all the Protestant denominations in the colony; that Catholics and Protestants were to be found on both sides of the issue; that the governor had supported it; and that it had the backing of a majority in the last house. Nevertheless, Pack and Godfrey were not only attacked for not being real Protestants but were even accused of being closet sceptics. Rumours were circulated that Pack had "turned," that is, he had become Catholic; and that Father Dalton had baptized him as Patrick O'Pack. Pack had to take particular pains to point out in his addresses that he was not a Roman Catholic and that the charges were all lies, but that he was proud to defend Father Dalton and the Catholic priests from the libels uttered against them. Thus, the campaign revolved almost entirely around personal religious views, education, and use of the Bible. By the time it had begun, the crowds milling in the roadways were in feverish excitement about all the outlandish charges and counter-charges.

On 31 October, one day before the opening of polls in Harbour Grace, Robert Pack and James Power, the Carbonear men on the Reform ticket, led a huge parade of about five hundred men from Carbonear to Harbour Grace. They were met near the entrance to Harbour Grace by an equally large contingent of Brown and Godfrey supporters. Together they paraded through the town with drums beating and colours flying. Early the next morning they appeared on the hustings carrying sticks and bludgeons and creating as much noise as was humanly possible. When they spied Ridley's parade of about two hundred men, they hooted and jeered for they were itching for a fight. After Pack and Power had ascended the platform to commence their speechmaking, the first fighting began in the roads below. While Pack and Power called for peace, few of Ridley's men dared to enter the poll room for anyone who did was apparently brutally roughed up on exiting. When the results of the first several days of polling showed that Pack, Power, Brown, and Godfrey had averaged seventy-four votes each, while Ridley and Prowse had received a total of only seven between them, the first reports of violence and intimidation began to flow into the governor's office. One magistrate's report said that the Carbonear mob consisted of five hundred bloodthirsty wretches who were going round the Bay intimidating their opponents.[23] The magistrate stated that he had the Riot Act in his pocket all day on 1 November but would not read it because he was persuaded it would "mark out every Protestant for instant murder." Instead, he went around advising all Protestants to stay away from the polls. Another magistrate's report characterized the first day's campaign as "one of the most brutal and fierce outrages that ever disgraced a Christian land."[24] The Carbonear men were reported to have flattened everyone in Ridley's parade; victims "were left upon the ground weltering in their own blood." A continuation of similar occurrences prompted Ridley to retire from the contest on the second day; and Prowse, on the third. The returning officer forthwith declared the four Reformers elected by acclamation so that, before any results were known from the remote northern or western districts, the Reformers had captured a clear majority in the House of Assembly. They had won at least ten out of the fifteen seats: four of their wins were in Conception Bay, three in St John's, two in Placentia–St Mary's, and one in Ferryland. There was cause for celebration.

Yet the celebration in the Reform camp was short-lived. Less than a week after the results in Conception Bay, the governor announced that the entire election might be invalid.[25] The president of the council, Henry John Boulton, had discovered that the writs for the general election had not been sealed; as a result, the election should be declared null and void. Prescott, who appeared to have been startled by the revelation, appealed to the British government for assistance. He was told either to order new elections or to have the imperial Parliament validate the questionable writs by legislation. As it would be too late in the year to have the latter accomplished in time for an Assembly sitting before the next fishing season, the British authorities recommended the former. Consequently, Prescott ordered new elections for the spring of 1837.

The Reformers were shocked and indignant, and their strident cries of conspiratorial injustice knew no bounds. Parsons was convicted of libel, and Boulton ordered the presses of the *Patriot* seized and sold.[26] For almost two months in the fall and winter of 1836–37, when there was no house to sit and no *Patriot* to trumpet their charges and counter-charges, the Reformers were effectively muzzled. Nevertheless, the populace were secured in a high state of fervour by the trials arising out of the campaigns in St John's and Conception Bay, especially by those against the Catholic priests in the capital. The trials were exploited for all they were worth by the reformers, who claimed that it was all a conspiracy on the part of "another Political Term of the Supreme Court" to muzzle the Catholics and retain the ascendancy for the ruling oligarchy. When the *Patriot* recommenced business in February under new ownership, it trumpeted the court happenings daily as state trials and heralded those convicted as glorious martyrs.[27]

The daily reports from the various trials created a lasting sensation as serious bickering and quarrelling between Judge Boulton and the juries dominated the proceedings even to a greater extent than the charges made or evidence presented.[28] The cases in St John's and Conception Bay necessitated the use of petit juries, who met with a decided prejudice against them on the part of Boulton because they were composed of shopkeepers, coopers, and tradesmen. Boulton delivered highly partisan charges to the juries, remonstrated with them on several occasions over unwelcome verdicts, attempted a number of times to intimidate the foreman into changing decisions rendered, and in one celebrated case was believed to have registered a different verdict himself. Those events were later to form a fundamental part of the charges against Boulton in a case taken to the Privy Council. When the time arrived to try the main culprits – Morris, Troy, Kent, Carson, and Pack – the prosecution moved for special juries, a request immediately granted by the judge.

On 20 December 1836 a special all-Protestant jury returned a true bill against Father Troy, Father Ward, Patrick Morris, and others for a misdemeanour consisting of breach of the Sabbath. Before it came to trial in 1837, Morris and his co-defendants moved for a change of venue on the ground that they could not get a fair trial in St John's.[29] The request was denied and the case came up for trial on 4 January 1837. But Morris and his group need not have been so pessimistic. Frustrating Boulton's design to register as many convictions as possible was the difficulty in procuring witnesses to testify against their friends; and most of those subpoenaed played such a cat-and-mouse game that they frequently outwitted the prosecution. Despite all of the political troubles of 1836, few convictions were registered – a circumstance that Attorney General Simms blamed on the influence of the Catholic priests. In cases where the priests were interested, he told the governor, it would be best to use the grand and special jury system for almost all of them were merchants or their agents – and therefore Protestant. Simms told Prescott: "It is a very marked feature in the Irish character that few are found to be willing witnesses in any criminal proceedings and that is very difficult to extract the truth from them and very rarely the whole truth is to be got."[30] Nevertheless, convictions were registered in St John's against Patrick Brawders for assault and battery and against Patrick Power for pressing his face against a Tory supporter and shouting "bah!" – an offence described by Boulton as "a common insult of the Priests' Party."[31] Two others were convicted for riot and assault, but all the remainder, including the mob that thrashed the Tory committee room in St John's, the priests, the candidates, and all the others who violated the Sabbath, and the prisoners who were arrested for the election-day fighting, were acquitted.

In Conception Bay the Reform candidates, Pack and Power, and most of the others arrested were acquitted but convictions were registered against Edward Hayden, John Meaney, and Andrew Quirk for minor offences. Also, three of Pack's closest friends, William Harding, Roger Thomey, and William Saunders, were convicted on all charges and on these three Boulton took his revenge by announcing a severe sentence of twelve months' hard labour in the prison at St John's. The public, incensed and outraged, flooded the office of the governor and the Colonial Office in England with petitions protesting the severity of the sentence.[32] The protests were successful, and the governor was forced to release the prisoners with less than half the sentence served.

The last trial occurred in June and resulted in Michael Scanlan obtaining a guilty verdict against John O'Mara for assaulting him in church. But the Reformers hardly noticed that little setback, for, in the general elections that were held again in June, they had had no difficulty in repeating their victories of 1836. In fact, the Tories had resigned themselves to Reform control of the House of Assembly and had put little effort into their own campaign. Only one of their faction, W.B. Row, had let his name stand while the others apparently deserted the field on nomination day. In Trinity, Bonavista, Twillingate-Fogo, and Burin districts, Tory places were taken by middle- and lower-class unknowns, some of whom might even be expected to give a measure of support to the Reformers. In May 1837 the Reformers met a House of Assembly in which they almost totally prevailed.

In the 1837 session, as noted earlier, Peter Brown, Assembly and school board member from Conception Bay introduced an amendment to the Education Act to advance the Catholic policy regarding Bible teaching.[33] The bill ran into the opposition of Boulton in the upper house, and, in spite of a series of inter-house conferences, the session closed in late fall with no progress made on Brown's bill.[34] The Reformers, who suffered from no illusions about negotiating with Boulton, decided to place their major emphasis on efforts to remove him. Now, more than anyone else in the government or colony,

Boulton had come to embody all the anti-Catholic tendencies and characteristics of the ruling class. On 3 July, the first day of the new session, Patrick Morris called for a committee of inquiry into the administration of justice in Newfoundland. The move was aimed directly at Judge Boulton, who was unable immediately to counter it because the Assembly had chosen to fight on grounds where they held the greatest advantage free from interference by the upper house – that of enquiry at the instance of a simple house resolution. That strategy was strengthened by house resolutions that could command the appearance of witnesses on oath and order the production of records at will. With the huge majority the Reformers enjoyed in the lower house, they also set up committees to inquire into the fisheries, agriculture, John Stark's conduct at the Conception Bay election, and the state of the police. They next moved addresses to the governor for the following: production of the criminal calendars of the northern and southern circuit courts for the last twenty years; all the correspondence between the governor and the Colonial Office on the subject of the governor's privileges and powers and the privileges of the House of Assembly; returns of all writs and depositions in the cases involving the clergy and other political libel cases; and all records relating to the election-writ crisis of 1836.

Armed with their documents, the Reformers began to build up their case against Boulton for bias, bigotry, and gross partiality against Roman Catholics in general and against liberal Protestants in particular. For the most important inquiry, that on the justice system, they constituted the committee of the whole house as their inquiring body so as best to ensure the largest audience possible. After a summer of wild oratorical speeches condemning Boulton in every conceivable way, the committee ordered their first witnesses to appear.[35] On 29 August, to a packed gallery with the imposing six-foot, four-inch figure of Father Troy towering over all, the committee members began their interrogations of E.M. Archibald, chief clerk and registrar of the Supreme Court; Benjamin Garrett and Aaron Hogsett, sheriff and deputy sheriff respectively; and two members of the Newfoundland bar, George Lilly and G.H. Emerson.

For a month and a half the capital was transfixed by the quarrel between the Assembly and Boulton. While the Assembly made day-by-day gains in their plan of attack, Boulton was widely seen to be scurrying about town holding impromptu meetings with the witnesses in efforts to thwart the inquiry. In the first few days the committee made a strong case against Boulton charging that he had illegally changed the rules regarding the empanelling of juries. That case, based on the technicality that Carson had first revealed during the murder trial of Catherine Snow, now permitted them to charge justly that all those tried since Boulton's accession to the bench, half of whom had been executed, had been tried by illegally constituted juries.

But the Reformers were more interested in a particular charge with political overtones – namely, that Boulton's jury rules excluded Roman Catholics. The evidence given to the committee on that question was that in January 1834 Boulton had replaced twenty-three of the old rules regarding jury empanelling with but two of his own rules: 1) forty-eight jurors were to be summoned by the sheriff eight days prior to the court sitting for the trial of all issues therein; and 2) special juries were to be chosen in the following way: the sheriff would put names of all qualified candidates in a box and in the presence of the parties or their attorneys take out forty; plaintiff and defendant would alternatively strike off twelve each and the remaining twenty-four would form the panel to be summoned by the sheriff. Aaron Hogsett testified that, as deputy sheriff from 1825 to 1833, he had summoned jurors under the same old rules until Boulton made his changes. He was then asked what were those new rules by which he began to summon jurors. "By precept from the Judge," he answered, "and not under any particular rule."[36] The Reformers were jubilant since they now had evidence for a charge they had long been making – that the Supreme Court was being ruled by personal whim of Henry John Boulton. From the lawyer Emerson, they heard that, under Boulton's new rules, it was "possible to have Special Juries called without having a single Catholic on them but it couldn't have happened under the previous rules."[37] Aaron Hogsett testified to the same effect. It remained only for the Reformers to show that was what really happened; and records subpoenaed from the court would prove their case.

These records showed that, in the four years of Boulton's rule, only thirteen Catholic names had appeared on the grand jury rolls. Of these, James Kent, John Shea, and James Tobin had emigrated to other countries; another, John Dillon, had been excused by reason of age in 1834. That left nine Catholics currently on the grand jury list; according to Nugent, three of these – Hogan, Kough, and Tobin – had so distinguished themselves as supporters of the politics of the chief judge, particularly in his hostility to the Catholic bishop and clergy, that "Mr. Hogsett in his evidence did not count them amongst the Catholics." But, through some strange twist of logic or arithmetic, Nugent told the Colonial Office that there were but six Catholics on the grand jury list.[38] What Nugent did not say was that he himself was unwilling to consider Hogan, Kough, and Tobin as Roman Catholics and that, when their names did appear on jury panels in cases affecting the Reformers politically or religiously, they were consistently struck off by the Reformers.

However, the committee was able to show that, in the more important political cases of 1836–37 where grand and special jurors were used, all Catholics were stricken off before the cases went to trial. To cite an example, Patrick Morris and his seventeen co-defendants had petitioned for a change of venue for their trial on a misdemeanour arising out of their 23 October 1836, Sunday parade. The request had been denied and they went to trial before an all-Protestant, Chamber of Commerce jury. The same jury had tried the Conception Bay candidates and their committee members for riot and assault. Charges of partiality on political grounds were much stronger than those on religious grounds; the committee played down the fact that liberal Protestants had been stricken from the jury panels as well. Substantially bolstering the charges of political partiality was the fact that the jury members in the numerous libel cases against the *Patriot* and its supporters consisted of Tory candidates and their committee members. To make matters worse, the foreman of the jury that tried the leading political figures in the 1836–37 election riot-and-assault cases was none other than James Sinclair, member of the upper house and one of the leading disputants at Boulton's side in the political wars with the Assembly Reformers. In the trial of the Conception Bay rioters – Hayden, Meaney, and Quirk – the committee heard evidence which showed Boulton would not receive from the jury the verdict of "guilty of a tumultuous assembly" and desired instead the replacement of "tumultuous" with "unlawful." When the foreman denied the request, Boulton returned the jury to reconsider; but they insisted on standing by their original judgment. Then Boulton personally took the verdict and crossed out the word "tumultuous" in favour of the word "unlawful." More interference by Boulton was demonstrated against Father Duffy on 14 December 1835. Boulton delivered the charge as follows: "For riotously and tumultuously making a forcible entry upon the fishing flakes, stages and premises of certain merchants ... and pulling down and burning the flakes and taking possession of the land on which it stood."[39] Yet, when the copy of the true bill was presented to the inquiry, it was seen to make no mention of forcible entry, taking land, or burning flakes.

Again Nugent, as chair of the inquiry, charged that the proceedings of the court "exhibited a marked desire ... to crush what are denominated the Popular Party."[40] Petty election squabbles became grounds for the highest prosecutions in an effort to place every obstacle in the path of the Reformers. Nugent gave as an example the case of Patrick

Power, who was charged with shouting "bah!" in a Tory's face, and, more particularly, the case of a poor fisherman in St John's charged after the 1836 campaign with spitting in the face of a constable. When in the fisherman's case the jury returned with an acquittal, Boulton returned them to quarters for a decision on fact – whether or not the fisherman had spit. When the jury agreed that indeed Mackey had spit, the foreman felt obliged to tell Boulton that spitting was Mackey's habit; the jury, therefore, recommended mercy. But Boulton had heard enough; he banged down his gavel and immediately sentenced Mackey to a fine of £25, the equivalent of a full year's earnings for a fisherman of Mackey's status. Nugent concluded his testimony by saying that the public generally consider Boulton "as extremely partial and vindictive and ... in his decisions, a Partisan and a Bigot."[41]

The committee members claimed further interference with their inquiry itself. They charged that Boulton was actively involved in frustrating their efforts to procure witnesses and documents. This was particularly true in their efforts to build their case against him; they charged that he had substantially altered, in several judgments rendered, the relations between servants, fishermen, planters, and merchants to the great benefit of the merchants; and, in particular, that he had personally altered the writ of attachment (a legal document seizing property) to affect fishermen and their families adversely. On that score the committee went through a painful day listening to a protracted cross-examination of E.M. Archibald, who was less than forthcoming in his testimony and consistently refused to answer questions or deliver up documents. At length the House of Assembly cited him for protecting Boulton and charged him with a violation of its privileges. Then it unanimously moved an address to the governor demanding the documents and correspondence in question. Prescott agreed to hand over the court records but denied the request for the correspondence between Archibald and the colonial secretary on the subject before the committee.[42] Thus, the committee was forced to proceed without the records in question. More frustration came when the committee summoned assistant judges Edward Brabazon Brenton and Augustus W. DesBarres, who refused to appear on the ground that they were not aware of any instance "where a Judge in the Colonies has been summoned before any House."[43]

By early October the committee had tired of the wrangling with witnesses supporting Boulton and it closed the case on the tenth. Nugent reported to the whole house that "in consequence of their investigations having been obstructed in an early step by the improper interference ... of the Hon. Henry John Boulton ... their report cannot be as full ... as they had originally intended."[44] Nevertheless, they reported enough evidence to convict Boulton of 1) having illegally empanelled juries with the result that every grand jury since his arrival had been illegally constituted; 2) making his office ancillary to party vengeance; 3) conducting his court in a manner that was prejudicial to the Roman Catholic Church; 4) altering the writ of attachment and thereby essentially and radically altering the laws protecting the fisheries; 5) seriously damaging the fisheries by rendering judgments radically altering the customs and practices in the fishery. Members then moved an address to the queen embodying the recommendations and praying that Her Majesty would "be pleased to purify the Fountain of Justice" in Newfoundland by removing Boulton.[45] Carson, Nugent, and Morris were appointed as delegates to London to present the Assembly's case to the British government; and, anticipating additional obstructions from the upper house on any supply bill containing their expenses, the Assembly passed a resolution authorizing them to raise a loan on the credit of the colony to pay their way.

But Boulton had at least one more trick up his sleeve – he sued the three delegates for libel based on speeches made in the Assembly in debating the committee's report. That tactic delayed the delegates in St John's as they proceeded to defend themselves in open court while Boulton made a quick getaway to England in an attempt to head off his Newfoundland attackers. Yet, as Boulton hurriedly sailed the Atlantic, casting furtive glances in his wake, the assistant judges in late December threw out the case on the ground that the court was illegally constituted without the chief justice. The delegates in early 1838 followed on Boulton's tail. Against Morris's better judgment, they agreed to the Colonial Office's decision to refer the case for judgment to the Privy Council, whose verdict was rendered in July. The Reformers were not completely vindicated; the Privy Council reprimanded them for the language they had used against Boulton. Nevertheless, an era in Newfoundland politics ended when the highest court in the British Empire declared that, because Boulton "had allowed himself to participate in the strong feelings … of the … different parties in the Colony," it would be "inexpedient" for him to remain in office.[46] Reformers were exultant, Catholics were overjoyed, and Father Troy ordered the singing of a Te Deum in jubilation.[47]

For the Reformers, Boulton's removal was a fitting climax to the general elections of 1836–37. They had destroyed their archenemy and the almost complete rout of the Tories had given them control of the lower house. But the use of religion for political purposes had become so all embracing that the Reformers may have inadvertently delivered to the besieged Tories a most useful weapon with which to fashion their own recovery and to deliver a fatal blow to their opponents.

James Louis O'Donel, first Roman Catholic bishop of Newfoundland. (P.J. Kennedy, *Centenary Souvenir Book* [St John's: General Committee of the Cathedral Centenary Celebrations, 1955], 203)

Charles Inglis, first colonial bishop of the Church of England. (Owsley Robert Rowley, *The Anglican Episcopate of Canada and Newfoundland* [Milwaukee: Morehouse Publishing c. 1928], 10)

William Ellis, first chairman of the Methodist District of Newfoundland. (Gower Street United Church, St John's)

William Carson, Scottish doctor who originated the Newfoundland constitutional reform movement in 1808. (Joseph R. Smallwood, *The Book of Newfoundland* [St John's: Newfoundland Book Publishers 1979], 3:446)

Patrick Morris, co-founder with William Carson of the Newfoundland reform movement. (D.W. Prowse, *A History of Newfoundland from the English, Colonial and Foreign Records* [St John's: Dicks and Company 1971], 425)

Thomas Cochrane, first colonial governor of Newfoundland, 1825–34. (Smallwood, *The Book of Newfoundland*, 3:214)

Michael Anthony Fleming, Roman Catholic bishop of Newfoundland, 1830–50. (Kennedy, *Centenary Souvenir Book*, 216)

John Kent, leader of the Reformers in the first House of Assembly. (Smallwood, *The Book of Newfoundland*, 4:113)

John Valentine Nugent, Reform leader, 1836–41. (Paul O'Neill, *The Oldest City: The Story of St John's, Newfoundland* [Erin, Ont.: Press Porcepic, 1975], 1:161)

Robert John Parsons, famous printer, publisher, and editor of the *Patriot*. (Smallwood, *The Book of Newfoundland*, 1:268)

Henry Prescott, governor of Newfoundland, 1834–41. (Prowse, *A History of Newfoundland from the English, Colonial and Foreign Records*, 466)

Henry John Boulton, chief justice of the Newfoundland Supreme Court 1833–38. (Prowse, *A History of Newfoundland from the English, Colonial and Foreign Records*, 434)

John Harvey, Newfoundland governor who
inaugurated the amalgamated constitution
in 1842. (Prowse, *A History of Newfoundland
from the English, Colonial and Foreign Records*,
449)

Aubrey George Spencer, first bishop of the
Church of England in Newfoundland.
(Smallwood, *The Book of Newfoundland*, 4:96)

Hugh Hoyles, Conservative Party leader.
(Smallwood, *The Book of Newfoundland*,
4:113)

Philip Francis Little, first Newfoundland
premier under responsible government.
(Smallwood, *The Book of Newfoundland*,
6:113)

Edward Feild, second bishop of the Church of England in Newfoundland. (*Encyclopedia of Newfoundland and Labrador* [St John's: Newfoundland Book Publishers 1985], 2:31)

Ker Baillie Hamilton, Newfoundland governor, 1852–54, who split with the Church of England bishop over the latter's high church practices. (Prowse, *A History of Newfoundland from the English, Colonial and Foreign Records*, 466)

John T. Mullock, Roman Catholic bishop of Newfoundland, supported the Liberal Party and championed responsible government. (Kennedy, *Centenary Souvenir Book*, 223)

Laurence O'Brien, wealthy Roman Catholic merchant at the centre of the political crisis in 1840. (Prowse, *A History of Newfoundland from the English, Colonial and Foreign Records*, 492)

Colonial Building, St John's, seat of government. (Smallwood, *The Book of Newfoundland*, 1:32)

View of the Anglican cathedral and the narrows, St John's, 1855.
(Prowse, *A History of Newfoundland from the English, Colonial and Foreign Records*, 482)

St John's in 1770. (Prowse, *A History of Newfoundland from the English, Colonial and Foreign Records*, 350)

St John's from Signal Hill in 1831. (O'Neill, *The Oldest City: The Story of St John's, Newfoundland*, 1:16)

6 Checkmating Reform, 1837–41

Faced with the reverses of 1836–37, the Newfoundland Conservatives were forced to accept the fact that control of the House of Assembly was out of their reach for some time to come. Their future strategy would have to be based on a more realistic assessment of the local political scene as well as on lessons they had learned in their unsuccessful attempts to have Bishop Fleming removed. Perhaps, it was thought, a more comprehensive strategy on the constitutional front might be more rewarding than shortsighted efforts to blame all the discord on Fleming.

Nevertheless, Boulton's removal deeply rankled the Tories. He had been their hero, their unchallenged leader for a full five years. His loss deprived them of the greatest champion they had had to date. Not only had he been chief judge and president of the Legislative Council, but, next to the governor, he had also been chief executive officer of the government simply by virtue of his inclusion in the Executive Council. His removal left a void that they knew not how to fill, and so they anticipated the next session of the Assembly with fear and trepidation. Besides the loss of Boulton, one of their chief merchant friends and perennial supporters in the upper house, William Thomas, appeared to be deserting them and looking to compromise with the Assembly Reformers.[1] On top of that, Governor Prescott, smarting from a number of setbacks in several Colonial Office appeals against Assembly decisions, was retreating to safer political ground and attempting to placate the lower house. Tories now looked over their shoulders; while some, out of desperation, launched bitter personal attacks on the governor for inadequate defence of Boulton, others looked around for some new containment strategy.

Devising political strategy, however, never was a strong point for the ruling class and its Tory supporters in St John's. Over the years their political behaviour had been consistently marked by strictly defensive manoeuvres. Perhaps their fortress mentality pre-empted their feeling a need for anything other than defence; and their self-righteousness, so often and so comfortably exhibited by both governors and upper house politicians, prevented their even dreaming of the necessity of a constructive, carefully planned campaign. It is thus not surprising that, when opposition to them appeared in St John's in the first general election, the Tories were apt to consider it as more a nuisance than anything else. William Carson – regarded by the ruling class as symbolic of anti-officialdom, anti-establishment, anti-established church – was targeted for defeat. The Tories' weapon was not an offensive campaign strategy but the ruse of attempting to divide Carson's supporters, the Roman Catholics. To effect divisions they urged the Protestants, merchants, and Roman Catholics alike to champion the Catholic, Patrick Kough, in opposition to a bad bishop whom they castigated as unworthy to walk in the shoes of Bishop Scallan. When Kough won and Carson was defeated, they felt vindicated. Bishop Fleming had been rebuffed by his own kind, so they thought, and would never again venture into politics. Governor Cochrane told the British government that the election had been extremely peaceful and successful, especially in St John's. The ruling class and its Tory supporters returned to their ivory tower, only to be rocked severely by the 1833 by-election victory of William Carson.

When Fleming and his priests went to great lengths to ensure Carson's election in that year, Tories simply dusted off the old strategy of 1832 – that of attempting to divide the Roman Catholics. They found a willing Roman Catholic in the person of shopkeeper Timothy Hogan, a friend of Patrick Kough and a former friend and confidant of Bishop Scallan. Years before Fleming had become bishop, Hogan had fought with Fleming over control of the funds for the construction of the now famous cathedral. Hogan then placed himself at the front of the Catholic opposition to Fleming and allowed himself to be the spearhead for Protestant attacks on the Catholic Church, the bishop, priests, nuns, and everyone Irish and Catholic. Although the resulting crisis united the Protestants and split the Catholics, Bishop Fleming won the battle and the Tories launched a relentless effort to get rid of him.

The necessity of Fleming's removal became all the more clear in the session of 1834, when the Carson Reformers demonstrated both intensity and solidarity; the most elementary mathematician could calculate that a Roman Catholic campaign would produce a Reform majority at the next general election. Tories now raised their divide-and-rule strategy to a higher level with an organized plan, fully supported by the governor, to enlist the support of the British government and the Vatican in efforts to have Bishop Fleming transferred to Prince Edward Island.[2] Calculating that such a procedure might take more than a year, the Tories invested in a short-term strategy to enable them to hold their own ground until a new Roman Catholic bishop arrived.

First of all, the Tories attempted to restrict the number of voters by passing a registration bill through the session of 1834.[3] Reformers opposed the bill because registration would be a restriction on the present voting arrangements whereby any male claiming to be in possession of a dwelling could present himself at the polls and vote. Also, the bill required that registrars be the JPs, all of whom were appointed by the present government and, with the exception of one or two in St John's, belonged to the party being attacked by the Reformers. But Reformers could only delay the registration bill and were unable to prevent its becoming law.

Next, the Tories brought in a new representation bill expanding the present fifteen-member chamber to a twenty-five-member house.[4] Districts with Protestants majorities, under the bill, could elect fifteen members and Catholic districts were reduced to a maximum of ten representatives. Although Cochrane saw no merit in expanding a House of Assembly that he had opposed from the beginning, he signed the bill into law at the urging of his officials in the upper house. They convinced him, he told the Colonial Office, that the details of the bill were such as to diminish the Roman Catholic influence in the house by returning a majority of Protestants.[5] But he successfully persuaded the home government not to sanction the bill on the ground that the representative system in Newfoundland was still an immature creature. British officials agreed with Cochrane that an expanded Assembly would only add to a "disposition to contest and cabal" and lengthen the already protracted sessions of the Newfoundland legislature.[6] But this move did not deter the Tories, who straightaway brought in a bill to defer the general elections until 1840.[7] That tactic would enable them to buy more time in their campaign to remove Bishop Fleming. But they were rebuffed in that department too when the British government announced that it could not depart from the quadrennial principle now firmly established in the United Kingdom. Therefore, Newfoundlanders would have to face an election in the fall of 1836.[8]

In 1835 Cochrane's successor as governor, Prescott, earnest in his efforts to make the Assembly work, told the Colonial Office that he was prepared to argue on behalf of the Tory representation bill on the ground that "as the Protestant population predominate in some of the divisions" the increase would give confidence to those well disposed to sit in the house.[9] As soon as the Assembly opened in 1836, Tories brought back their representation bill; but, as severe winter weather and pressure of business had prevented some of the merchant members from travelling to St John's, the Carson Reformers were able to give the bill the six-months' hoist.[10] Tories now became resigned to face the next general election but kept their fingers crossed that the next mail would bring good news about Fleming's removal.

Their confidence in a strategy aimed at removing Bishop Fleming appears to have been based on the exaggerated notion that a new bishop would be able to work miracles among Roman Catholics by issuing the proper orders. Perhaps their view had been prejudiced by the Catholic tradition in Newfoundland whereby Fleming's predecessors had been loyal and obedient supporters of the government. Perhaps, too, they had in mind a bishop like O'Donnel, who was capable of enforcing perfunctory decisions in getting rid of "troublesome" priests and replacing them with those who refused to engage in "paper wars." Whatever their rationale, they fully believed all Newfoundland's political problems could be solved by banishment of Fleming.

The case against that bishop had been in detailed preparation since the Carson by-election victory of 1833.[11] The threat to the ruling elite posed by the solidarity and influence of the Carson Reformers early in the session of 1834 had alarmed the governor. Cochrane immediately led a concerted campaign to neutralize Fleming and deny the Reformers any further use of the "Catholic card." All the violence and discord were blamed on the bishop and his obedient priests while the Protestants were commended for their "conciliatory conduct and the deference with which they regarded Roman Catholics."[12] The present bishop, he lamented, was the reverse of his predecessor and did not hesitate to use all the power of his office to discipline his Catholic opponents. Timothy Hogan, the man defeated by Carson, withdrew from the contest, Cochrane claimed, because of threats from his bishop that "grass should grow before his door." That was no figure of speech, said the governor, for so fully was it carried out that hardly a customer would darken the door of his shop, and Hogan had to lower prices in an attempt to stay in business. When that did not work, Hogan resigned the contest; however, his capitulation notice was so displeasing to the bishop that he was forced to issue a public apology in the local papers.

Cochrane's communications to the British government now took on the characteristics of a regular vendetta, all aimed at blaming Bishop Fleming for every displeasing political event. The anonymous charges in the daily *Patriot*, the personal attacks on Cochrane himself, the libels uttered through the mouths of Reform members – all were blamed on Fleming, whom he labelled a deliberate liar with "a total absence of moral and upright feelings" and whose conduct was "unchristian and mischievous."[13] And why was Bishop Fleming so mischievous? "Because," answered Cochrane, "they [Catholics] hope to gain the ascendancy of which the present constitution affords the opportunity." It was perhaps typical of an evangelical governor immersed in advancing the interests of the Anglican establishment that he should interpret every Catholic-sponsored, political event as a threat to his church. But Cochrane conveniently, perhaps deliberately, ignored the role played by the individual priests and the local Reform leaders like Carson in rousing the lower classes for their own political advantage. Carson, Morris, and Kent had proven themselves experts in fomenting anti-government sentiments among the populace. They had become famous for their populist appeal on the hustings and had as much exploited the priests for their own political ends as the latter had used the politicians.[14] Bishop Fleming, for his part, told the Colonial Office that he had become involved in local politics only to defend his priests who had been so bitterly insulted. Cochrane disagreed, saying that Fleming had been stirring up trouble since he became bishop. But if that were true, the question arose as to why Cochrane had not reported it before 1834. Because he did not think Fleming's campaign would succeed – that was his answer. Now that the campaign had succeeded and an effective and disciplined Catholic party was waiting in the House of Assembly to take control after the 1836 election, Cochrane's strategy was to condemn Fleming, who, the governor argued, must accept the blame for all the troubles.

The British government had strong faith in the political strategy of supporting a bishop who, in its view, could silence any priest he wished and even force obedience from reluctant Catholic politicians by denunciations and intimidations. It yearned for a bishop like "the late lamented Dr. Scallan" and urged the Foreign Office to take up the matter with Rome.[15] As a result, Thomas Aubin, a British government representative, was sent directly to the cardinal in charge of the Office of Propaganda in Rome and laid at his feet the complaints against the Roman Catholic clergy made by the governor of Newfoundland and the Foreign Office of the British government. Aubin concluded a successful interview and informed the Foreign Office that the Office of Propaganda would be conveying to the Roman Catholic clergy its "disapprobation of their conduct."[16]

That message was transmitted to the governor in St John's, but, while he was exulting in triumph, Bishop Fleming was enjoying the last laugh. The bishop had received no such censure because Fleming's friends in Rome had outmanoeuvred the British representatives. It was November before the British Foreign Office, learning of the ruse, sent Aubin back to complain directly to the cardinal secretary of state, Monsignor Capaccini. The cardinal made a number of excuses to explain why Vatican officials had dragged their feet on censuring Fleming, one of which was that "it wasn't a good time to inform the Pope."[7] But Capaccini promised that, since he knew Fleming personally, he would write the bishop and provide a copy for the Foreign Office. Then at some future, more opportune moment he would inform the pope if the British government thought it desirable. The British representative believed that the letter would be just as effective as one from the Office of Propaganda and could see no reason to refuse the compromise. The Foreign Office respected the opinion of its representative and forwarded a copy of Monsignor Capaccini's letter to Cochrane's successor, Governor Prescott, in St John's. In the letter, received by both Fleming and Prescott in early 1835, Capaccini urged Bishop Fleming to "take an anxious part" in the affair mentioned in his letter and warned that word of such conflict reaching the pope would "excite his heavy displeasure." Then Capaccini referred to the complaints made by Cochrane and said, "You know how unbecoming it is to introduce the inflammatory topics of politics in a temple destined to the worship of the God of peace, of charity, and of mercy." Without directly charging that Newfoundland's Roman Catholic clergy had ever been guilty of any such misdeeds, Capaccini concluded by saying that he had no doubt that Fleming would in future "discountenance and stop the recurrence of similar unbecoming proceedings."[18] Pleased British officials were so convinced of the effective power of Roman Catholic clerical discipline that they believed there would be no further recurrence of Fleming's misdeeds.[19]

But Bishop Fleming had seen in Capaccini's letter more than had the British, who were unaccustomed to the workings of Catholic internal correspondence. For Fleming, the letter meant that his friend Capaccini had prevented the complaints from reaching the pope. Even though the monsignor had used condemnatory language, he had not actually censured the bishop but rather referred to certain reported proceedings. On closer scrutiny of the letter, Bishop Fleming saw himself as receiving no personal censure. Whatever his priests had done behind his back, Fleming knew that he himself had not been guilty of any such transgressions. The bishop therefore properly considered Capaccini's letter as a vindication and stated this opinion publicly.[20]

Within two days of reporting an end to clerical interference, Prescott, forced to contradict himself, asserted that Bishop Fleming had continued to exert undue influence so that "intercourse has been interrupted, friendship annihilated, and trade in some instances materially injured."[21] Prescott's evidence came from the press: several Roman Catholics had published capitulations to Bishop Fleming declaring that they would never again support an enemy of the Roman Catholic religion and were accordingly cancelling their subscriptions to the *Public Ledger*. Without producing any evidence, Prescott claimed that those public apologies had been elicited by Fleming's threats.

A few days later, there came to hand better evidence of those threats than published apologies. A number of Roman Catholics had forwarded sworn depositions to the governor's office to the effect that they and their relatives had been refused the sacraments on the grounds of their being Mad Dogs. Leading the charges against the Roman Catholic clergy was Michael McLean Little, who was a Roman Catholic, a St John's shopkeeper, a former confidant of Bishop Scallan, and now a political supporter of Kough and Hogan. Little submitted a diary of abuses meted out by the Roman Catholic clergy which had accumulated over a period of several months, abuses that he claimed cut him off from his friends and almost ruined his business. His quite detailed and extensive memorial to the governor was titled as follows: "Until MacLean Little is made a Beggar he cannot be a good Catholic – Observations made by the Reverend Edward Troy, a Priest of the town of St John's, Nfld."[22] Little claimed that he had been persecuted by the Roman Catholic clergy for his political views and that Fathers Waldron and Troy had specifically singled him out for denunciatory sermons during Sunday Masses. For proof he enclosed a placard that he claimed was posted in the Roman Catholic churchyard on 25 January 1835:

NO MISTAKE THE FIVE IS SEVEN

Yes Boys out of 75000 Catholics
in Newfoundland
Only Seven Support The LEDGER
There is one in every 10000 mind you
Who insults the Catholic religion
There they are
1. John Dillon takes the Ledger
2. Pat Keough

3. John Cusack
4. John Hogan
5. Scanlan
6. Malone
and Dirty McLean Little too
Will we deal with them!
No! the devil a bit!

That was the nature of the evidence on which Prescott based his charges. The evidence was quite obviously either a prank by lower-class mischief makers so common in Newfoundland at that time or else a fake put out by political opponents. It was the kind of ruse both sides had been wont to use since election campaigns had begun in 1832. Colonial Office officials were a little puzzled at hearing those charges so soon after Monsignor Capaccini's letter and especially so soon after having heard from the Newfoundland governor that clerical interference was at an end. Yet they had to take them seriously. Many of them came from Roman Catholic shopkeepers and servants and were supported strongly in public by both the *Ledger* and the *Times*, and in private by Governor Prescott, Attorney General Simms, the former governor, Thomas Cochrane, and the Church of England archdeacon, the Reverend Edward Wix.

Considering it unwise at this stage to involve the pope, the Colonial Office resolved instead to enlist the support of the well-known and respected Roman Catholic bishop of London, James York Bramston. At the instance of the British government, Bramston wrote Bishop Fleming about the abuses of which he had heard from the Colonial Office. Fleming was alarmed because it was the first official evidence he had had of charges being preferred against him by Governor Prescott. Once regarding Prescott as a friend, Fleming now accused him of double-dealing and of "whispering away" to destroy the bishop's reputation.[23] Worried about the nature of the charges, Fleming knew personally that in at least one instance Fathers Waldron and Troy had denied communion to a Roman Catholic woman – a serious transgression Fleming had to overcome by serving her himself at his office door. If episodes such as this had come to the attention of London and/or Rome, the result might be the removal of either or both of those priests. Then there was the possibility that charges, false or otherwise, could also have been made against the other politically active priests, namely, Bergin, Cummin, and Charles Dalton. If Fleming lost even some of those priests, he would find himself supported by only a minority of his priesthood. This loss, together with the substantial opposition arrayed against him from the middle-class, led by Hogan and Kough, would put him in an untenable position in the Newfoundland church.

Fleming immediately asked Prescott for copies of the charges so he could refute them.[24] Prescott denied ever having made any charges. But, when Fleming produced Bramston's letter, Prescott relented and, according to Fleming, agreed to provide the bishop with copies. When the papers were not forthcoming, Bishop Fleming went to Government House, where Prescott denied ever having made any such promise. Fleming professed to be astonished and wrote an official request, which Prescott also officially denied in writing. But Prescott must have been worried by memories of his predecessor's confrontation a year earlier – a clash that had directly led to Cochrane's unceremonious dismissal. At the same time, he must have realized that his secret efforts to tie the Catholic clergy to the mutilation of Henry Winton[25] would never stand up to critical cross-examination, and so, within a day of Bishop Fleming's most recent request, the governor wrote to extract himself entirely from the whole affair. As the so-called denunciations that had so often been reported, said Prescott, "had been discontinued," he and the British government had no desire to look to the past. As for complaints like those of McLean Little, Prescott said he had just simply transmitted them to the Colonial Office, as was his duty. Reassuring Bishop Fleming, Prescott spoke of feeling "as warm a regard for his fellow-countrymen of the R.C. as of any other persuasion whatsoever," and said that he looked forward in Newfoundland to a future of peace with His Majesty's Roman Catholic subjects.[26] That, however, was an outright lie because, at the urgent request of Governor Prescott, the Colonial and Foreign Offices of the British Government had referred all documents to Rome.

While Bishop Fleming was exulting over the kind partiality of the British government, delegates of that same government were then working feverishly at the Vatican to have the pope move against Fleming before the general election of 1836 got under way. Just two weeks before Bishop Fleming had thanked the British government for its kind partiality, the Foreign Office had warned the Vatican that unless something was done about Bishop Fleming and his clergy in Newfoundland, the British government would "be forced to resort to such extra-ordinary measures" as would be deemed necessary.[27] Under that threat, the cardinal secretary of state informed the Foreign Office that the Office of Propaganda in Rome would censure Fleming.

The news of a Vatican censure of Fleming was conveyed to Prescott in St John's and leaked to the press. The *Public Ledger* triumphantly teased the bishop to release the news. But the celebrations were premature. When the Foreign Office later received a copy of the Office of Propaganda letter, it proved only to be a worked-over version of the Capaccini letter of the previous year. The British Foreign Office representative in Rome said that Fleming had such a great reputation at the Vatican that he was "not likely to be called to very strict account."[28]

Busily at work that summer on his cathedral plans throughout the British Isles, Fleming heard rumours of the attempts made behind his back to discredit him at the Vatican. He wrote the Colonial Secretary, Lord Glenelg, requesting copies of the charges. Glenelg was more forthcoming than Prescott and the following charges were communicated to the bishop: that Fleming and his priests had played a prominent part in the 1833 by-election; that Father Troy had written to the *Patriot* several letters attacking the governor; that McLean Little and other Mad Dogs were denounced from the altar and threatened under pain of excommunication not to deal with the *Ledger*; that Henry Winton was frequently denounced from the Catholic altar and his mutilation came as the consequence of those attacks; and that Bishop Fleming had exhorted sealers to assault the people who signed the address supporting Boulton.[29]

Bishop Fleming gave a reasoned and quite detailed defence to each of the charges. As to the first, he acknowledged taking part in the election for that necessitated no defence on the part of a British subject. A priest, as he had pointed out at BIS functions in the past, was a citizen like anyone else; therefore, a priest had the same rights of participation in political life as a merchant or a shopkeeper. As for Father Troy's letters, Fleming had never seen a letter that reflected unfairly on the governor. Besides, Fleming wondered why he should be responsible for someone else's letters. Father Troy was never his secretary, and he flatly denied charges that he dictated any of the letters. With regard to the third charge, Fleming was not aware of any public denunciation of McLean Little and said that he refused to believe that any such denunciation had been made. As to the threat of excommunication, the bishop stated that he felt "humiliated that such an idea could be entertained."[30] Answering the fourth charge, Fleming saw Henry Winton's troubles as solely due to the *Ledger*'s outrageous attacks on the bishop, the Catholic priests, and the nuns. He further noted that, when he defended himself against calumnies, he found himself reported to the governor; yet, when Carson and two other Protestants were denounced from the Protestant pulpit in the governor's own presence, not a whimper was made. In reference to the last charge, Bishop Fleming declared that never in public or private, church or pulpit, did he counsel sealers to attack the signers of Boulton's address. On the contrary, when the sealers came to him complaining that St John's merchants had withheld their wages until they signed Boulton's address, he had borrowed money in order to tide them over and had advised others to sign in order to get their money. The bishop added to his defence an extensive review of Newfoundland society over the previous decade, detailing the Catholic community's struggle for equality, the impediments placed in its way by governors and their officials, and the hostility generated towards Catholics among the Protestants and merchants.

On the surface, Fleming's defence would have to be considered adequate. However, two serious strategic errors that he made would count heavily against him in the future. First, Fleming prepared his defence in England out of reach of detailed specific evidence on specific happenings in Newfoundland. There were confused dates and times, incorrectly identified names, and mistakes in the order of events. Further, Fleming was so confident of his own case that he neglected to engage the assistance of his friends and supporters in Newfoundland, and thus his communication alone was the only favourable evidence placed on file at the Colonial Office. Fleming himself recognized these shortcomings but possessed such faith in the British system of government that he recommended the calling of an inquiry to take evidence under oath as the proper course to get at the truth.

The Colonial Office did not take the bishop up on the offer. Fleming's flawed defence of his conduct became all the more significant when Governor Prescott had verbatim copies made of Fleming's statements, covertly supplied them to all the bishop's enemies, and requested detailed rebuttals. Extensive replies flooded the Colonial Office from former governor Sir Thomas Cochrane; former chief justice Henry John Boulton; Henry Winton, editor of the *Ledger*; and Patrick Kough, Ambrose Shea, Timothy Hogan, Michael McLean Little, Thomas Job, the Reverend Edward Wix, and Attorney General Simms. Also, affidavits were secured from James Tubrid, Stephen Malone, and Patrick Malone, who were election-committee members for Kough and Hogan. In addition, numerous Catholics made sworn depositions stating that there had been clerical interference with the sacraments.[31] Even worse for Fleming, the 1836 election had occurred while the bishop was in England preparing his defence and the troubles from the hustings in Conception Bay and St John's were all carefully reported, copied, and recopied to form part of the attack. Although Bishop Fleming had not put foot in the colony for any part of the 1836 or 1837 campaigns, the election trials were submitted as evidence against him without so much as a footnote to acknowledge his absence from Newfoundland while the events had occurred.[32]

In January 1838 Governor Prescott told the Colonial Office that Fleming's presence in Newfoundland was "incompatible with peace and harmony."[33] The Colonial Office felt humiliated to have to make another appeal to the pope against "that incendiary Priest." James Stephen[34] wrote: "I suspect that the Pope secretly enjoys the power of keeping a whole English Colony in a ferment which His Holiness alone can quell and which remains a standing monument to the fact that this Protestant country cannot entirely shake off its dependence, even in the nineteenth century, on the Papal Power."[35] All the documents were copied and forwarded to the British representatives in Florence, Italy, for presentation to the Vatican.

In early 1838 Fleming, still in England, caught wind of more rumours. He immediately approached the Colonial Office with a request for copies of any rebuttals made to his previous defence and declared himself ready to call as witnesses the Assembly delegates – Carson, Morris, and Kent – who were then in England fighting the Boulton case.[36] British government officials were baffled about what to do. They could not easily provide Fleming with a written copy of the numerous charges and personal attacks on the Catholic clergy made by so many prominent citizens in Newfoundland. If they did, one senior official warned, the "future tranquillization" of Newfoundland would be hopeless.[37] If Bishop Fleming were to learn, said another, what the Protestant clergy had said regarding the Newfoundland Catholic Church, then between them "no terms could be kept hereafter."[38] But an expert in the department concluded that such documents did not come under the category of confidential papers and they could not be concealed from Fleming since they had already been given to Henry John Boulton and others.[39] The officials pressed for a delay and wrote Fleming that their investigation was still incomplete because of the loss of some documents and the fullness of their schedules. But they promised Fleming that they would rule on both his request for documents and his political conduct as soon as possible.[40]

For weeks the Colonial Office pondered over what to do. Finally, the officials were forced to face the issue head on. James Stephen declared that the minister could not suppress the papers for the sake of peace in Newfoundland. If Fleming applied for the information to the House of Commons, the resulting furore in England would discredit the government.[41] But an escape route appeared for the British in the spring when news arrived from Rome that the pope had censured Fleming and had ordered the suspension of Father Troy.[42] The Colonial Office was immensely relieved and Lord Glenelg wrote Fleming that its investigation of his conduct had been discontinued. Further verbal or written communication on the subject would be inexpedient, Lord Glenelg said, because it was not possible to arrive at a definitive conclusion on events most of which had happened long ago. Moreover, since the British government had no power over the Catholic clergy in Newfoundland, it did not have the power to acquit or censure.[43] At last, the case was closed. It was an enormous victory for Fleming, who gave profuse thanks to Her Majesty's government. He set sail for Newfoundland in a triumphant mood.

News of the British government's decision regarding Bishop Fleming arrived in Newfoundland in the summer of 1838, hard on the heels of the news regarding Boulton's removal. Such setbacks unnerved Prescott, who began to retreat to safer political ground by taking a position midway between the political extremes then dominating the scene in Newfoundland. The Tories, on the other hand, were absolutely dismayed, for all their political strategies to contain the Reformers since 1836 had completely failed. Even their last line of defence, the upper house, might be breached because of Prescott's retreat and Thomas's apparent defection. The Tories lashed out in despair at Prescott and the British government. In their groping for a new strategy to contain the Reformers and checkmate the Catholics, the Tories were ably assisted by a bitter anti-Catholic newspaper campaign throughout the British Isles.

On 17 September 1838 the London *Standard* labelled Newfoundland "a half-Popish dependency" and compared it to French Canada and Ireland. For the most part, the *Standard* said, Newfoundland electors were "Irish Papists of the lowest order, not a few of them refugee ribbonmen."[44] Similarly, the Liverpool *Mail* regarded Newfoundland as "a Colony of horrid flavour arising from Maynooth priests, Irish felons, and entrails of codfish." In reference to Newfoundland legislation, the *Standard* said that they "must either be instantly transported to new South Wales, or, as we would propose, sent to the treadmill in England for six months, afterwards lashed at the Cat's tail from London to Portsmouth and finally shipped to a penal settlement, there to end their days in drudgery and chains."[45]

The Liverpool *Standard* called for an end to popish tyranny over the Protestants in Newfoundland, and the *Mail* of the same city said that the only way that could be effected was by "a regiment of good Protestant soldiers."[46] Calling Newfoundland a transatlantic Tipperary, the *Ulster Times* declared: "The convicts of Australia, the Negroes in Jamaica, or the Hottentots at the Cape would be scarcely less fit as depositories of power than the refugee ribbonmen who are elevated into an unnatural importance in Newfoundland."[47] Glenelg was condemned for his "Popish policy" in Newfoundland. The London *Conservative Journal* campaigned for his impeachment on the ground of his traitorous conduct in promoting the power of "a Romish sham Bishop from that nunnery of sedition and vice, Maynooth College."[48]

Throughout the fall of 1838 and the winter of 1839, the anti-Catholic, anti-Newfoundland campaign continued throughout England and Ireland, for the anti-government newspapers were bent on using it as a tool to fight the O'Connell movement for repeal of the union. They feared that the government's flirting with O'Connell might lead to a parliament in Dublin and Ireland would then become another Newfoundland. They called for the outright and immediate abolition of Newfoundland's legislature, which was "a rabble Assembly just such as one would meet in Ireland if the beggarman and his fetid monks had their will."[49]

Newfoundland Tories were encouraged by such talk. In December the Chamber of Commerce met to coordinate efforts to abolish Newfoundland's Assembly. To that end it initiated a petition to the queen. Throughout the winter of 1839, this petition was circulated around the island for the signatures of the merchants and traders. "The representation of the country," the petitioners claimed, "is entirely in the hands of the Roman Catholic Clergy who by their vast influence over their flocks can wield them at pleasure."[50]

But withdrawing representative government less than ten years after it had been granted was not a palatable alternative to a British government facing an increasingly liberal House of Commons. Besides, as one senior British official said, although little good had come from the Newfoundland Assembly, it was difficult to see what harm the institution had done.[51] Again, Governor Prescott was more circumspect in his admiration of the Tories and advised the British government that it would be premature to abolish an Assembly that had yet to be given an opportunity to prove itself. Additionally, Lord Durham had been appointed to investigate the troubles in the Canadas as a result of the rebellions there in 1837–38, and he had been advised to include Newfoundland in his recommendations. The Newfoundland Tories were, therefore, told in 1839 that no change would be contemplated in the colony's constitution until Durham had made his report.[52] Rebuffed once again, the Tories fell back on their old strategy of using the upper house to block Assembly desires, compiling charges against Fleming with the aim of achieving his eventual removal, and making demands for a revised constitution with substantially fewer Roman Catholics admitted to the franchise.

Meantime, the Reformers were riding the crest of a surge of public esteem as a result of their success against Boulton, who had been replaced in the Council with the neutral and highly regarded commandant, Colonel William Sall. The new appointee offered a promise of getting Reform legislation through the upper house. More significantly, Boulton's removal had considerably enhanced the stature of John Valentine Nugent as the pre-eminent Catholic political leader.[53] Just as Catholic grievances since 1833 had centred on Chief Justice Boulton, so Nugent had become the chief symbol of the Catholic struggle for equality. Perhaps it was destiny rather than coincidence that had landed both Nugent and Boulton on the shores of Newfoundland in the same year. As the leading judge in the colony, Boulton would become for the Protestants the chief legal expert; as the first Roman Catholic lawyer, Nugent would become for his co-religionists their premier legal advocate. It did not hurt that Nugent arrived with a reputation as an accomplished political advocate in Ireland's O'Connell movement, for he thus stepped immediately right into the front of the political spectrum as confidant and partner of William Carson and John Kent. In the Assembly between 1833 and 1836, Kent and Carson maintained their political assaults on Boulton and the ruling establishment and used Nugent's efforts to enrol at the bar as one of their main issues. Outside the house, Nugent established himself as the letter-writer for the Catholic clergy, especially for Father Troy; and, as court reporter for the *Patriot*, Nugent provided the detailed knowledge of the law and the ammunition that the Assembly reformers required in their struggle against Boulton. When it became evident to Nugent that the struggle to enrol at the bar would be a long-term one, he founded a private school, started a shop, and took over the proprietorship of the *Patriot* from R.J. Parsons.

By 1836 Nugent's reputation had soared. He easily took the Placentia–St Mary's seat in the House of Assembly; and William Carson was forced to strike a deal with Nugent in order to secure the speaker's chair.[54] The deal might have been a tactical error on Carson's part because Nugent became deputy speaker and, as chair of the committee of the whole house, took control of the case against Boulton. Moreover, Nugent's talents and debating skills were such that he was able to dominate debates on the floor of the house while William Carson, in the speaker's chair, was relegated to the position of an observer. Perhaps there is no greater testimony to Nugent's political stature than the fact that, when the veteran Reformer Patrick Morris wearied of the interminable struggle with the upper house over privileges and openly quarrelled with Nugent, Morris's own nephew, John Kent, sided with Nugent.[55] Kent, for his part, was brother-in-law to Bishop Fleming, a man whom Prescott and all the Tories regarded as the central figure in the troubles. Fleming himself, however, played no part in active politics after 1833 and instead immersed himself in church affairs. Consequently, among many Catholics, Kent lost political ground to Nugent, who had ingratiated himself with such politically active priests as Fathers Troy and Bergin. The fact that Nugent had headed the Assembly delegation to England to carry the case against Boulton to the Privy Council demonstrated that Nugent had taken effective leadership of the Reformers. By 1839 Prescott acknowledged Nugent as the indisputable leader of the lower house.[56]

With Boulton gone, Nugent approached the fall session of the legislature in 1838 optimistic that a favourable education bill would become law. The Assembly reintroduced Brown's bill of the previous year, and it came back from the Council with an amendment that Nugent accepted as an attempt at compromise.[57] The new Council, under the genial Colonel Sall, had made what appeared to be a basic change in its long-standing view and had amended the bill in the following manner: "No Board ... shall ... choose or select ... any Book or Books of a character or having a tendency to teach or inculcate the doctrines or peculiar Tenets of any particular or exclusive Church or Religious Society whatsoever."[58] For Nugent and the Catholics, that meant the Bible. The new Conception Bay board subsequently appointed by the governor accepted the same interpretation, with the result that the pro-Bible nominees on that board resigned in protest. They were immediately replaced by Roman Catholic and Protestant nominees who favoured exclusion of the Bible in mixed schools; and the new board continued to operate schools, establish new ones, and spend the government monies for the current and previous years.

However, the School Board in Trinity Bay put up a fight and insisted, once again unanimously, on including Bible teaching in all its schools. The Colonial Secretary informed the board that its rule on that score was contrary to the Education Act; whereupon, the Trinity board challenged the strict legal interpretation of that act as it applied to the Bible. The Holy Scriptures "being recognized by law as the rule of faith established in Her Majesty's Dominions," wrote the board chairman, the Reverend Bullock, "the Commissioners do not conceive that it can be classed with books of a sectarian character." The board insisted that it could not therefore "conscientiously become accessory to keeping back the unmutilated Word of God from Protestant children in Schools under their Superintendence."[59] The governor was forced to lay the matter before his attorney general who rendered a decision in June 1839, in favour of Bullock and the Trinity board.[60] Catholics in general and the Nugent Reformers in particular were painfully shocked; Nugent even charged dishonesty on the part of Attorney General Simms.[61] Nugent later claimed that he had put the question about the Bible to Attorney General Simms in the fall of

1838 and had received a favourable judgment, but that six months later Simms had reversed his position. Whether Nugent had been tricked or just plainly outwitted was irrelevant to the Reformers, who had suffered a significant setback that led to increased bitterness in the already vexed relations between the two houses.

For the remaining two sessions of the Assembly before the expected general election, Reformers tried to amend the Education Act but to no avail. The upper house consistently and stubbornly rejected the Assembly's amendments. For the Nugent Reformers, the Council without Boulton had proven to be a much more difficult obstacle than anticipated – a situation that surprised Prescott as much as it did Nugent. In an attempt to mollify the relations between the two houses and break the impasse on most of the legislation that had arisen since 1837, the governor tried to persuade the Council to be more conciliatory.[62] To his disappointment, Prescott discovered that he could effectively influence but two of its members, James Crowdy and Simms. The warmth of partisan political feelings dominated the remainder, still under the influence of Boulton. The governor could only stand by as a helpless observer as the Council killed ten out of the twenty bills sent up by the lower house in 1838, nineteen out of thirty in 1839, and thirty out of forty in 1840. The few bills that did get through the Council, such as the supply, contingency, road, and poor-relief bills, succeeded only after extensive delays, concessions on the part of the Assembly, and, in several instances, pointed admonitions to the Council from the British government.

The Reformers fully realized that Council obstinacy was a fundamental part of the Tory strategy to sabotage the constitution. Since 1836, merchants had boycotted the elections; in addition, the only one returned to the Assembly, William B. Row, consistently refused to attend its sessions. The mercantile members in the upper house attended regularly and continually used that body to frustrate and block Assembly wishes. The few bills that it allowed to pass – on roads, poor relief, and the like – were of such a necessity to the lower- and middle-class supporters of the Reformers that compromise was forced on both sides in order to prevent dire distress and/or outright rebellion in the colony. In efforts to advance Catholic equality, Reformers perennially sent up bills requiring such reforms as jury empanelling, lawyer incorporation, justice administration, and court procedure – bills that the Council amended and finally killed to preserve the status quo. But most of the bills advanced by the Reformers after 1836 can be placed in the category of class legislation.[63] They included bills on such subjects as merchant seaman's relief, insolvency, export of pickled fish, weights and measures, packing and inspection of fish, bread and butter inspection, pilots and pilotage, regulating sales of consumer goods, masters/servants relations, and attachment law. The council boycott was so comprehensive and effective that it gave not even first reading to a single one of these bills.

By late 1839 the governor, unable to report any Catholic troubles since 1837 and now finding occasions to praise Bishop Fleming, blamed the impasse on the upper-class merchants. "The existing dissensions proceed," he said, "very much from the natural mortification which the richer, more intellectual part of the community feel at being excluded from the influence which they should naturally possess."[64] The governor reported that William Thomas, a merchant in the upper house, tried to be independent but received such harsh treatment from his brother merchants that he relented. Rebuffed by the British government in early 1839 in efforts to have the Assembly abolished, the merchants in general and the council in particular were determined to have no truck or trade with what they referred to as the Catholic constitution of Newfoundland. They looked forward to a promised review of the constitution and centred their complaints on the present constitutional unfairness to Protestants. Those views were strongly reinforced by the singular political unanimity of the Protestants and by the strongly held anti-Catholic views of the Protestant clergy. In addition, Nugent pursued a political strategy on both the Bible question and Catholic patronage that tended to unite the Protestants and split his own ranks.

For half a century before the inauguration of a House of Assembly in Newfoundland, the Church of England had been complaining about losing ground to the Wesleyans and the Catholics. But what grieved them most after the granting of the Assembly was the banning of the bible in government schools throughout the colony. "Popery," declared the Reverend Henry Melvill in 1838, "is making great headway in Newfoundland" because of its "spurious system of education."[65] The Roman Catholic majority in the House of Assembly continually thwarted the Anglican clergy's efforts in Newfoundland to fight that system. A partial victory had been secured in 1839 when the Trinity Board launched what was later to prove a successful appeal against the interpretation of the act as applied by the Reform majority. But this victory came too late to be of any help in Conception Bay, where the pro-Bible advocates had already resigned in protest before Trinity had made its stand. The Anglicans justly regarded Conception Bay as their main battleground with the Wesleyans and Catholics because that bay was the most populous district outside St John's and the Anglicans were now in a minority in a district where they once had ruled the roost. The Reverend Charles Blackman walked all the way from

St John's to Harbour Grace in the winter of 1839 and "laboured hard to prevent some of the many evils which the Education Act" was "calculated to inflict on the Protestants."[66] But it was all to no avail, for the Reformers, Catholic and Protestant, had control of the board and pursued a policy of mixed, non-sectarian schooling. What rankled the Anglicans more than anything was the fact that they had met a number of Roman Catholic teachers and Roman Catholic parents who agreed with their position on the Bible but who felt they were forced "to adhere to certain rules."[67] A Roman Catholic faction in the House of Assembly, a faction that Anglicans believed was under the control and influence of Roman Catholic clergy, made these rules. In the Anglicans' view, the real evil of Newfoundland's constitution was that it provided an opportunity for a bishop like Fleming, together with some pliant clergy, to thwart the wishes of the majority of the people.

In February 1841 the Church of England called a public meeting of Protestant clergy in St John's, a meeting that a Methodist cleric, the Reverend Jabez Ingham, billed as a "Protestant Demonstration Meeting."[68] There, Anglican clergy condemned the present education system as not only unscriptural in its character but "opposed to the Established Church and all Protestant institutions."[69] One Conception Bay cleric stated that, "rather than allow their children to use mutilated versions of the Holy Scriptures, or submit them to the overseership of the Vicar General of the Romish Church," they had decided in his parish to boycott the schools.[70] Ingham called on all Protestant denominations to "come forward and unite in defending the cause of Protestantism." The Reverend Bullock echoed the same call and, amidst cries of "No Popery," called on all Protestants and Englishmen to refuse to be saddled with "the yoke of Rome."

Wesleyan clergy expressed the same strong feelings. They condemned the elections of 1836–37 and rejected the Assembly as a body under the control of a Romish faction whose main interest was popish ascendancy.[71] By 1838 the Reverend John Pickavant of Carbonear was hinting at cooperation between Anglicans and Wesleyans in "the necessity of doing something to save the island from the overflowing, domineering, and overbearing influence of the agents of the Church of Rome."[72] The opportunity to terminate that influence soon presented itself as the result of a series of divisions in the enemy camp.

In the face of a solid phalanx of opposition from the Council, the upper-class merchants, and the Protestant clergy, the challenge to Nugent to demonstrate a united Reform front proved more than he could handle. The controversial struggle on the education question, the failure of the supply bill in 1837, the poor-relief bill in 1839, the extensive delays of all money bills in the sessions of 1838, 1840, and

1841 – all brought their share of grumblings from within party ranks. First, James Douglas, a long-time party supporter, friend of Nugent, and former candidate in Bonavista Bay, was rumoured to be so discontented with the party that he was considering joining the Tories.[73] As commissioner of roads, Douglas had inherited most of the construction patronage once held under the first house by Patrick Kough. Perhaps the impasse on the money bills and the interminable delays in the road bills so adversely affected his financial interests that he could no longer take the pressure. When Nugent, in 1839, felt the necessity of publicly praising Douglas in efforts to keep him in the party, the danger passed momentarily.[74] Patrick Morris also had serious misgivings about the continual privileges battle that had led to such a legislative impasse with the upper house; also, on the subject of the road and poor-relief bills, he counselled compromise with the Council. "If we can't get 20 shillings to the pound," said Morris, in reference to the strict demands of Nugent, "then let's go for 19."[75] William Carson expressed a similar view, saying, "All Newfoundland needs is Roads, Bridges, and Schools to make her happy, glorious, and free."[76]

But greater anxiety came to Nugent because of an outright defection in his Catholic ranks. Just as Catholic rights' agitation was the chief Reform campaign tool, so was support in the Roman Catholic districts regarded as the sheet anchor of the Nugent party. The split in Catholic ranks occasioned by the Kough-Hogan faction had been a source of deep anxiety for the Roman Catholic bishop and the Reformers. The fact that parish priests like Father Timothy Browne of Ferryland aggressively supported this faction left Fleming and the Reformers in an extremely vulnerable position. They were continually outflanked because Browne had opened correspondence with Rome and the governor detailing all the alleged sins of Bishop Fleming and the political priests. The anxiety of the Reformers increased when, on the education question, they discovered that in the northern bays not only were Catholic parents and teachers willing to ignore the Bible ban but the Roman Catholic parish priest of King's Cove in Bonavista Bay, the Reverend Nicholas Devereux, paid no attention to it either. To add to the anxiety, one of Nugent's own colleagues in the House of Assembly, James Power, member for Conception Bay, refused to withdraw from the Harbour Grace school board in 1836 in favour of the boycott led by Father Charles Dalton. Power instead remained on the board and attempted a compromise over the Bible with the Protestants. When Governor Prescott, in 1838, was advised by the British government to make appointments without regard to religion, the governor chose Power to serve as stipendiary magistrate for Carbonear.

The Reformers, outraged, expelled Power from the house and demanded that the governor issue an election writ for Conception Bay. Prescott refused on the ground that the Assembly had no legal authority to expel Power. In spite of a year-long battle with the Assembly over the matter, the governor held his ground and eventually seized the backing of the British government. Nugent himself ultimately relented and allowed Power to resume his seat in January 1840.

A more serious problem for Nugent was the challenge to present a united position on a new constitution for the colony. Ever since the Rebellions of 1837–38 in the Canadas and the British government's appointment of Lord Durham to investigate and report on the constitutional problems of the British North American colonies, there had been speculation on all sides about Newfoundland's political future. Local Reformers were not immune to these tendencies, and William Carson soon returned to his old form in issuing epistolaries announcing his wide-ranging views. He greeted Durham's appointment as "A New Era" in British history and called for the union of Newfoundland with the other British North American colonies.[77] In another letter, Carson praised the present constitution, saying, "Newfoundlanders have no reason to complain of the want of responsibility,"[78] a statement that subjected him to a personal attack by Patrick Morris for having taken leave of his senses. Perhaps Carson, in failing health and in his declining years, expected a promotion to an official post in which to live out his final days or, as others suggested, he was finally in his dotage. Whatever had prompted the issuing of these surprising statements, they could not be left unrefuted. The debate drew R.J. Parsons of the *Patriot* into the fray.

Parsons, who prided himself on his advanced liberalism, personally castigated Carson and demanded full responsible government for Newfoundland.[79] That was a rather extreme position given that such a scenario existed in none of the British colonies at that time and that even in the United Kingdom it was only a relatively recent phenomenon. Carson returned to public print, rebutted Parsons, and attacked his views as a monstrous doctrine. The two men battled each other with such bitter displays of personal rancour that Carson soon personally boycotted the *Patriot*, the famous newspaper he had founded, and afterwards confined his epistles to the *Newfoundlander*.

Meanwhile, Nugent attempted to bring the two sides together and took a position midway between them. He articulated an interpretation of responsible government that emphasized making the government more responsive to public opinion through inclusion of some of the people's representatives (meaning themselves) in the Governor's Council and establishment of an executive separate from the

Legislative Council.[80] That proposal had the advantage of permitting the governor to share power with the elected majority in the House of Assembly without having to turn over completely all executive authority to a faction totally responsible to the electorate. As an alternative Nugent said that he would accept the amalgamation of the House of Assembly with the upper house as a way of breaking the legislative deadlock. It was an idea that had previously found favour with the highest-ranking officials in the Colonial Office. Placing his faith in the wisdom of Lord Durham, Nugent eagerly anticipated his report. The hope was that Durham would opt for the amalgamation, and Nugent succeeded in uniting all Reformers in carrying an address to Durham embodying this view.[81] But the issue was far from resolved when a crisis arose over the political future of Patrick Morris.

Perhaps the absence of Tories in the House of Assembly had led the Reformers to fall prey to attacking one another in house debates. As soon as the new, Reform-dominated Assembly met in 1837, the personal bickering and strident disagreements normally reserved for private party caucuses were heard on the floor of the legislature. An embryonic opposition to the Nugent majority developed over the first session of that Assembly and increasingly tended to coalesce around Patrick Morris. Always the dreamer, Morris was wont to think that political and economic difficulties could be removed by constructing a philosophical basis for change. He shunned the drudgery of debate in the house and had regard for neither the conventions of privilege nor the reality of constitution building. What he wanted done, he wanted done instantly with a pronouncement on the topic; he was impatient with the practical, everyday task of implementing a course of action. Although he had been accused of originating the cry of Mad Dog Catholics, during the election campaign of 1836 he counselled conciliation with the Kough-Hogan faction and was booed off the platform as a result.[82] In the Assembly, Morris grew tired of the struggle with the Council and gave only token support to the Assembly on a privilege question referred to the Privy Council in London. On the delegation that travelled in England in 1838 to have Boulton removed, Morris broke with Carson and Nugent in an open feud, claiming that those two delegates had ignored his advice. When, in 1839, Morris charged that Nugent and Carson had treated him "like a fifth-wheel,"[83] the latter two sought revenge by attempting to delete the supply vote compensating Morris for his expenses.[84] They failed, but a breach had been opened in Reform ranks that would widen irreparably in the early spring of 1840.

That March, Patrick Morris dropped a bombshell among the Reformers when he revealed that he had accepted the governor's invitation to sit in the council as colonial treasurer.[85] Nugent was embittered by the fact that, for two appointments in a row, Prescott had selected for office the two leading renegades in his party. Besides, Prescott had made the choices without any consultation with Nugent whatsoever, and in spite of the fact that Prescott had already recognized Nugent's de facto leadership of the Reformers in the lower house. Nugent became even more agitated when he learned that Prescott had been courting Morris for almost two years and that Morris had kept the matter secret.[86] Recognizing Prescott's tactic as an effort once again to divide them, the Reformers reacted with anger. They condemned Prescott and urged the expulsion of Morris from the Assembly. Nugent tried to heal the wounds by searching for some middle ground and offered Morris an opportunity to resign instead. They met at Douglas's house, where Nugent raised the resignation proposal in lieu of passing the condemnatory resolutions then being readied by the other Reformers. Such a debate, Nugent believed, could get ugly, with personal recriminations flying back and forth, and should therefore be avoided. Together, Morris and Nugent walked back to the House of Assembly on the afternoon of 24 March 1840, with Nugent under the impression that Morris would make the expected announcement.

But in the house Morris stood in his place and, instead of resigning, announced that on strict constitutional grounds he would be guided by the Power case as a precedent and would therefore keep his seat. He thereupon invited an open discussion of the question and declared that he would abide by any decision rendered on strict constitutional grounds and would not take disagreements as a personal attack. He thus cleverly sought to cut the ground from under Nugent's feet by attempting to relieve the members of party discipline and, by a free vote, divide the party and hold on to his seat both in the Assembly and in the Council. Nugent claimed that he was totally taken aback by Morris's manoeuvres and, steering clear of personal attacks against Morris, immediately focused the attention of the house on the governor. He therefore moved that "this House regard the extension of the influence of the Crown in the Representative Branch of the Legislature ... as subversive of the Constitutional rights and privileges of the popular branch of the Legislature, and pregnant with danger to the public interests." Nugent's motion further declared, "We regret that the Executive Government should ... embarrass the House" by placing another of its members in an office of emolument before the problem of James Power was finally resolved.[87] It was a clever move on the part of Nugent to link the Morris problem to the person of Prescott and James Power. It evoked all the Reformers' prejudices against Prescott and all the individual members' jealousies of both Power and Morris, who were seen as deserting the Reform cause for government jobs. Nugent's resolutions were carried on division, whereupon Morris, having expected to remain in the house, then interpreted Nugent's move as a personal insult, broke forever with Nugent and Carson, and withdrew permanently from the Assembly. The ensuing by-election created a serious crisis both for the Reform party and for the British government.

As soon as Patrick Morris dropped the news of his appointment to the Council, the race began for his St John's seat.[88] James Douglas, a Protestant Reformer, signified his intention of running with the blessing of Nugent. Reform supporters began to sign up a following for Douglas but met with less than an enthusiastic response. Some party members recalled that Douglas had returned home to Scotland after 1833 with the intention of permanently residing there and had only recently arrived back in the colony. Others remembered the rumours in 1837–38 that Douglas was tempted to join the Tories, while still others felt that Douglas's ill health would make him an ineffective candidate. Nugent's concerns heightened when William Walsh, a Roman Catholic, prominent member of the BIS, and friend of the Kough-Hogan faction, entered the field. Walsh, in a few days, received such an extensive display of public support from disaffected Catholics that visions of a repeat of the 1833 Carson-Hogan by-election struggle must have danced in Nugent's brain. Remembering the battle of seven years before to squeeze out a hotly contested, controversial victory for Carson, Nugent apparently concluded that with Douglas, a substantially less credible candidate, the Reformers would face inevitable defeat. He therefore approached Douglas with a proposal that he withdraw in favour of a compromise candidate, Laurence O'Brien.

As a Roman Catholic, O'Brien's candidacy against Walsh would be able to pre-empt the Catholic-Protestant campaign that had caused such trouble in 1832 and 1833. Besides, O'Brien was the wealthiest Roman Catholic merchant in the colony and had been previously favoured by the *Ledger* as a good choice for Prescott to place in his Legislative Council. O'Brien, according to Nugent, could appeal to all classes of the community and, as brother-in-law to one of the Mad Dog Catholics, had connections which extended also into the anti-clerical camp of the Catholics, by then perhaps the biggest part of the Catholic population. Douglas was prepared to listen to Nugent and concede, but his leading Reform supporters refused. They insisted on Douglas continuing the race, for, in the badly divided Reform party, they believed that he had as good a chance as any Nugent candidate.

The dispute over Morris's desertion was still festering, and the bitter personal feud between him and Nugent had left Morris's supporters in no mood to back Nugent. There was a great possibility that Douglas could siphon off the anti-Nugent Catholics and, as a Presbyterian, acquire enough Protestant support to defeat William Walsh. Nugent remained unconvinced, but his Reform opponents forced his hand by publishing Douglas's requisition with Nugent's name attached. Nugent was now faced with two possibilities: suffering public embarrassment by repudiating Douglas and supporting O'Brien; or seeing a repeat of the violent 1833 by-election with the strong possibility of a Walsh victory. Nugent chose to support O'Brien, reasoning that if Douglas could siphon off Protestant support from Walsh, then a pro-Catholic campaign would make for an easier victory than those experienced in either 1832 or 1833. Nugent made certain that he engaged the support of Bishop Fleming at the outset of O'Brien's campaign and ensured that Fathers Waldron,[89] Forrestall,[90] and Walsh[91] accompanied them to the hustings every day. But a severe shock shortly awaited Nugent and O'Brien: Walsh's anti-clerical supporters engineered his withdrawal and deserted en masse to Douglas in a blatant attempt to defeat their Catholic opponent. Leading observers later testified that Nugent recognized the danger of such a coalition and focused the campaign entirely around a defence of the Catholic Church.[92]

The Nugent faction held their own ground so that, after the first day of polling, Douglas was ahead by only nine votes. Then the *Patriot*'s R.J. Parsons, friend and supporter of Douglas, declared that Douglas's victory was in jeopardy. Parsons called on all Protestants to come forward and vote for Douglas. The *Ledger* then played right into Nugent's hands by launching a bitter personal attack on the Roman Catholic priests. Thousands of supporters from both sides milled into the streets, and by 5:00 P.M. on the second day the governor was forced to send in the troops to prevent violence. The contest was so evenly fought that the political battle depended upon which side could get more voters into the poll room and which tactic could be used to delay or discourage those from the opposite side. At the end of seven days of polling, Douglas was in the lead, but only by six votes.

Then a tactic Nugent had foreseen came into play and ultimately was to prove to be the decisive factor. Before the writ had been issued for the by-election, Nugent had persuaded Prescott to appoint Thomas Beck, a Reform friend of Nugent, as returning officer. Beck now introduced two strategic moves that allowed O'Brien to become the eventual winner. First, Beck began to slow down the voting process when Douglas brought his voters forward, so that in one day of six hours' voting only eighty votes were cast. This scheme allowed the O'Brien group to recruit desperately needed voters from the remoter sections of the district. Secondly, Beck looked for minor technicalities that would allow him to reject opponents. A combination of those tactics led to a ruckus in the poll room when Charles Fox Bennett – a wealthy, prominent, St John's merchant – came forward to vote for Douglas. Bennett, a close friend of the governor and brother of the former assembly speaker, Thomas Bennett, was carrying a concealed weapon and had publicly wagered £100 that O'Brien would be defeated. Beck considered that the wager acted as a bribe and searched for every possible means to reject Bennett's vote. He refused to receive Bennett's vote on the ground that Bennett, owner of several houses, would not be specific in naming the residence under which he wished to vote. When an argument and a shouting match ensued, the crowds outside pushed their way into the poll room. Beck then raised the matter of the concealed weapon, which Bennett was forced to produce: it turned out to be a piece of whalebone with lead at both ends. When, consequently, the returning officer ordered Bennett ejected, supporters and opponents engaged in a shoving match which ultimately led to several fist-fights. Bennett then used his influence with the governor to have the troops invade the poll room, an occurrence that the governor and all Tories later were to advance as proof that priestly influence in Newfoundland elections inevitably caused violence. The claim, of course, was nothing more than propaganda.

But, in spite of the violence, Beck's services paid off. After twenty days of polling during which almost everyone eligible had cast a ballot, O'Brien was neck and neck with Douglas at 1463 votes each. Beck then found a way to reclaim victory for his friend Nugent: he decided to receive unregistered voters and began to swear in those whose names had, for some reason or other, never been entered on the poll books. Douglas was able to round up 124 supporters who claimed ownership of some kind of dwelling. On 10 June, O'Brien, by eight votes, pulled ahead for the first time in the campaign. Beck then closed the poll, terminated the elections, and declared O'Brien the winner.

Nugent had won a pyrrhic victory. O'Brien would take his seat in the House of Assembly, but it was clear to all that not only was Nugent's leadership considerably weakened but that the Reformers were seriously divided. It was also clear that an Irish expatriate leading a Roman Catholic campaign in attempts to achieve electoral victory in St John's was henceforward no guarantee of success.

The governor compounded Nugent's difficulty by enlisting mercantile assistance in compiling a mass of evidence relating to the election in support of the Tory claim for a change in Newfoundland's constitution. The Tories based their case on the alleged interference of the Catholic priests. Every shouting match, fight, and crowded gathering was submitted to the British government as proof of the "propensity to violence" on the part of the Roman Catholic lower orders.[93] What William B. Grieve, a Protestant merchant himself, harmlessly referred to as a row was reported to the Colonial Office as another riot. Incidents where the soldiers were ordered into the streets and eventually into the poll room were submitted as proof of the intensity of the violence. Hordes of illiterate Roman Catholics who campaigned for Douglas and against priestly interference were handed depositions to which they were directed to swear that "they thought they were going to be killed!"[94] They were all dutifully marked with the careful X used by illiterates. Covering letters from Prescott pointedly told the British government what had caused all the troubles. Bishop Fleming, the governor said, "without the slightest pretence" had "again, from pure love of dissension, blown up the flame of religious strife."[95] As for the merchants, they had intended staying out of what appeared to be a purely liberal quarrel, but their indifference disappeared during the contest because "they wanted to help the oppressed." Fleming could do no right, and the so-called wealth and intelligence could do no wrong.

Nugent had hardly had time to assess the results of the St John's election when one of his sitting Assembly colleagues from Conception Bay, Anthony Godfrey, chose the worst possible moment to die, thereby necessitating another by-election. Within a few days the behind-the-scenes battles began with the search for candidates. The subsequent divisions among Reformers engendered by the Conception Bay by-election would further imperil Nugent's leadership and render the Reform party even more seriously divided.

Over the summer of 1840 a movement grew throughout Conception Bay in favour of two Reform candidates, James L. Prendergast of Harbour Grace and Edmund Hanrahan of Carbonear,[96] both Roman Catholics. The former was a semi-professional, jack-of-all-trades, sometime clerk, school board contractor, and political activist; the latter was a ship's captain and friend of Robert Pack, recent Assembly member for that district and friend of Carson and Kent. The St John's newspapers kept their silence on the campaign until October when it became clear that Prendergast was an anti-clerical and Hanrahan was the priests' candidate. Then the Protestant, Conservative newspapers began to emphasize the involvement of the Roman Catholic priests in the campaign. That fitted in rightly with their long-time strategy of boycotting the Assembly and condemning the present constitution as useless because of the undue influence of the Roman Catholic clergy. It also dovetailed with the strategy of the governor and his officials in the bay to depict the campaign as further proof of what they had said about the St John's campaign. Long before the campaign had begun, and even before the writ had been issued, the governor told the Colonial Office to expect violence. When magistrate Thomas Danson reported that he expected the contest to be hotly contested by the priests in favour of Hanrahan, Prescott reported that hunch to the Colonial Office with the comment that it would "manifest to the justness" of his previous apprehensions.[97] Nugent would later claim, with a great deal of credibility, that the governor's plan of action throughout the campaign, ably assisted by the Conception Bay magistrates and the Protestant merchants, had been part of a deliberate plot to sabotage the constitution.[98]

Meanwhile, the *Patriot*, in supporting Prendergast, betrayed no anxiety about the interference of the Catholic priests. That might be surprising in view of the bitter complaints the paper had made against them in the St John's campaign. But, since then, there had been considerable shifts in the political winds, for the results of the St John's election had been a moral victory for the *Patriot* and its supporters. Clerical support in St John's was no longer seen as the ticket to victory, and in Conception Bay, a day's journey from the capital and with fewer priests, it was even less so. Besides, Father James Walsh,[99] one of the three priests in Conception Bay, showed no desire to become involved in the campaign for Hanrahan and, to the delight of Prendergast's supporters, insisted on neutrality.[100] On the single occasion when Bishop Fleming did interfere in the campaign, it was not to support Hanrahan but to take a neutral stand by advising voters to keep the peace and vote as they thought fit[101] – a position that could easily be interpreted by Prendergast's supporters as support for their own candidate. But there was another factor, perhaps of even greater weight, that explained the *Patriot*'s new-found unconcern for clerical participation: Prendergast was widely seen to have an insurmountable lead, a fact borne out by the first two weeks of polling. The *Patriot*, so confident of victory, could only find praise for the clergy and even welcomed their involvement on all sides "as they know best how to instruct voters in their duties."[102] But near the end of the campaign, as Hanrahan's support surged and threatened Prendergast's victory, the *Patriot* whined about the "undue" influence of the priests. At the same time, the governor's official correspondence and the anti-Nugent newspapers became filled with news of "riots" at Carbonear.

One of the main reasons that Prendergast held a substantial lead for the first two weeks of polling was the fact that voting had first taken place in polls around Harbour Grace and southwards in the bay, areas where the Harbour Grace merchants, supporting Prendergast, had the greatest influence. The main stronghold of Hanrahan was his home town of Carbonear, while his chief campaign strategist was Robert Pack, the most influential merchant in that region. Pack was expected as well to command votes in the outlying villages north of Carbonear, principally Western Bay, considered to be located in his sphere of mercantile influence. Polling in Hanrahan's stronghold was due to begin on 1 December, at Western Bay, and continue at Carbonear where the election would be terminated.

In anticipation of the polling Prendergast and the Harbour Grace merchants led a parade northwards towards Carbonear on 30 November, intending to be in Western Bay for the next day's polling. On the outskirts of Carbonear they were met and attacked by upwards of fifty to sixty men with pickets. Magistrates Danson and John Stark immediately reported that a riot had broken out and made an urgent request to St John's for troops. When the returning officer, R.J. Pinsent, opened the poll at Western Bay the next morning, Prendergast had a lead of sixty votes, a lead that began to vanish throughout the day. According to Pinsent, some skirmishes broke out but he was able to restore peace and the polling resumed. The next day he was forced to abandon the poll because of "attacks on Lower Island Cove voters who came in to vote for Prendergast."[103] When polling concluded at Western Bay on 4 December, Hanrahan had cut Prendergast's lead to forty-eight votes. Carbonear, having upwards of eight hundred voters, was due to commence polling on Monday morning, 7 December.

Pinsent shot off an urgent message to St John's saying that feelings were running high and that he expected "2000 fighting men" would be on the hustings by Monday morning. "I am standing on a volcano," warned Pinsent, who feared the result.[104] The governor was later reprimanded[105] for not having sent troops at that juncture, but Pinsent had in fact become the victim of his own exaggeration. If one shouts fire at the slightest ember then one risks being ignored when the real conflagration takes place. Pinsent's volcanic assertions were typical of the crisis atmosphere created by the anti-Catholic Tories since 1833; hence, Prescott did not regard Pinsent's warnings as anything out of the ordinary. On Monday morning the poll opened at Carbonear as planned; and, in spite of the large crowds jostling in the roadways leading to the poll room, no breaches of the peace occurred. But later that same day Thomas Ridley, a wealthy and prominent Newfoundland merchant, campaigning for Prendergast, attempted to take a picket from the hands of a Carbonear man. A scuffle ensued, whereupon someone hit Ridley from behind, knocking him unconscious. That attack became the signal for a wild free-for-all as hundreds engaged in shouting, shoving, and fist-fighting. Pinsent immediately called off the election and declared it null and void on the ground of serious violence.

Prendergast's parade then decided to return to Harbour Grace. On the way back through Carbonear, they were continually harassed by picketers and stone-throwing youths. The fracas took a more serious turn when a Prendergast man, on the outskirts of Carbonear, pulling a pistol from his pocket, shot and wounded a Carbonear man. Supporters from Carbonear then turned on Prendergast's men still within the town and attacked the magistrates and constables as well. On the way home after darkness had fallen, several youths threw rocks at the house of Nicholas Ash, a Prendergast supporter. Ash panicked and, through the front windows of his home, unloaded the contents of several sealing guns in the general direction of the gang. Then he and his family ran for shelter into the woods behind his house. Unknown to Ash himself, he had seriously wounded six people – three who were innocent passers-by and three who had been standing in his line of fire some considerable distance down the road. Taking advantage of the diversions created by the screams of injured people, one young hoodlum set fire to Ash's house and the resulting night blaze brought the entire population to the scene. Throughout the violence, the magistrates were all busy scratching up hastily prepared messages to the governor in St John's with urgent requests for troops. Their messages were pointed and succinct – for example, "serious rioting had broken out, many lives were in danger, soldiers required immediately, if not sooner." To add to their theatrical sense of urgency, they dated their messages at hourly intervals as if reporting from the front in some kind of epic struggle of Napoleonic proportions: "December 8, 9:00 P.M.: Prendergast's men severely beaten; Ridley has fractured skull; pistols fired." By midnight on 8 December, the description ran: "two houses destroyed; one man's hip shot away; six men shot and wounded; military required right away!"[106] Prescott immediately submitted the messages verbatim to the Colonial Office with the terse comment, "I hold the Priests responsible,"[107] and forthwith sent troops marching out of St John's towards Carbonear.

The troops arrived not to a scene of war or battle but to deserted streets; there was no sign of destruction. They entered a peaceful town with a quiet people where the only sound or movement was that of a woman peering curiously out a window towards the embarrassed troops. For the soldiers, apparently, it all became a great joke. Six months after the termination of the trials arising from the election, the chief justice, Hohn Gervas Hutchinson Bourne, reported that everything had been exaggerated, especially the injuries, the rioting, and – above all – the numbers of people involved. If it had not been for the incident of setting fire to Ash's house, the chief justice said, there would have been only one crime committed through the entire election, "and that was a larceny committed by a deserter."[108] As for the thousands of people who were alleged to have been rioting, they, instead, were either innocent paraders or had come out to assist people who were hurt. The people actually involved in disorders "altogether formed but a small proportion of the thousands living in and around Carbonear at the time." As for the religious nature of the conflict, Chief Justice Bourne concluded, "the trials showed that it could be as much traced to local jealousy between Harbour Grace and Carbonear."

But the political and constitutional damage had already been done well before the election trials were completed.[109] Carbonear would no longer be a polling place; Bishop Fleming was forced to make an emergency trip to Rome in his own defence; and the British government warned the Vatican that, unless Fleming were removed from Newfoundland, no more government grants of money or land would be made to Roman Catholics in any of the British colonies. Even more devastating to the Reformers, Governor Prescott peremptorily dissolved the House of Assembly and purposely made no mention of a general election. The British government then proceeded with a House of Commons select committee of inquiry into Newfoundland's affairs.

On top of the political reverses arising out of the by-elections, the Reformers were stunned by the menacing twist of events. The sudden dissolution of the Assembly set them on their political haunches for it "came like a thunderclap upon the members of the House of Assembly who had been indulging in the reverie that they would be again called together."[110] The fact that such an inquiry would take place in London further seriously disadvantaged the Nugent supporters, who bitterly complained of the unfairness of settling Newfoundland's fate in the lap of its enemies in England, so far from the first-hand evidence available at home. But the Tories were exultant: "So there is some chance for us at last,"[111] the *Ledger* gleefully cried. The Tories, so confident that complete victory was at hand, bragged that the inquiry would produce such constitutional modifications "as will promote all that we desire."[112] After an almost decade-long struggle they appeared to be triumphant at last.

Carson, Morris, and Kent had begun the general election of 1836 with what they believed was a convenient tool to unite the Catholic populace. Although the pro-church platform did not prove as successful as they might have wished, it was sufficient to help them win control of the House of Assembly. Nevertheless, the pro-Catholic campaign tended to align the Protestants against the Catholic Church in general and against the Reformers in particular. That developmenmt was accentuated when the Reform party adopted an extremely hard-line, pro-Catholic position on the controversial Bible question. The result was to unite the Protestants and give the Tories a convenient tool to recover the political momentum. The advantage of using the sectarian tool now passed to the Tories. Having lost control of the lower house to a Reform party greatly feared by upper-class interests, the Tories were able to convince the governor and the British government that a Catholic mob ruled by political priests had control of Newfoundland. The subsequent suspension of the House of Assembly and the establishment of an inquiry into Newfoundland affairs were victories for which Tories had long yearned.

7 Constitutional Change, 1837-47

The dissolution of the House of Assembly on 27 April 1841 was the culmination of a series of bitter blows for the Nugent Reformers. It had struck with such abruptness that it pre-empted their stipends for the session then running. The break-up left Reformers without a forum from which to launch their political assaults upon the British Tory government's efforts to modify the Newfoundland constitution. Reformers were reduced to complaining once again about a conspiracy and to lashing out at former friends and allies such as Douglas and Edward Dwyer, whom they from time to time charged with abetting their own demise. A contemporary observer could not have been faulted had he expressed bemused perplexity about how, in less than three years, the Nugent Reformers had fallen so far from their recently occupied political heights.

In the fall of 1838, the Nugent Reformers had been in control. The Privy Council had removed Chief Justice Boulton; Fleming had been victorious at the Colonial Office; and Governor Prescott was in a conciliatory mood. The governor was now offering a cooperating hand to the lower house majority and endeavouring to induce his Council to adopt a less uncompromising attitude towards the Assembly. There were also encouraging signs that the mercantile politicians were breaking ranks in the upper house, an example being William Thomas's offer to placate the opposition. Yet, within two and a half years, the Nugent Reformers were seriously divided and totally humiliated, and the prospect of constitutional change threatened to relegate them to the political backwater.

Some Reformers undoubtedly had seen the victories of 1838 as an opportune moment to adopt a more flexible stance in order to bring about a thaw in the rigid relations which had developed between them and the Prescott government. But Nugent clung to his hard-line position while he waited for some concrete signs of executive favour towards Roman Catholics. Coincident with his preparation of the case against Chief Justice Boulton, Nugent had been busily preparing the Catholic case on the exclusive nature of the Newfoundland government. He claimed that the government service had become even more closed to Roman Catholics in the previous four years of Prescott's administration and that Protestants had solidified their monopoly on government patronage in the colony.[1] His strategy was aimed at heading off the Tory anti-Catholic campaign and proving that Newfoundland's Catholics had a just cause.

Shortly after Prescott had arrived in Newfoundland in September 1834, Bishop Fleming had begun his campaign for land on which to build his cathedral. To strengthen his case for an extensive grant of well-situated property, Fleming claimed that the Roman Catholics of Newfoundland were not convinced that the British government had their best interests at heart. That was, he said, because they had received no favours from the British government while the Protestants were in receipt of pensions, salaries, glebes, an episcopal residence, and even a vessel to transport the Anglican bishop around his diocese. The local government accentuated the injustice by excluding Catholics from the Legislative Council, the civil service, the bench, and the bar. The bishop declared: "This exclusion is not attributable to accident and when they see around them many Catholics competent to fill those offices, they see it is not to be attributed to a difficulty of finding them and therefore are they impressed with the idea that it is only for their religion they are thus disregarded."[2]

Prescott began his administration on good terms with the Catholic Church, and so he was delighted to support Fleming's request for land. The Colonial Office in London was soon happy to comply. It suggested that Fleming consult the local authorities in St John's,[3] including the governor and the British army garrison, in order to work out an arrangement respecting the actual site. But Prescott quickly came under the influence of Boulton, the Chamber of Commerce merchants, and the Tory party. Relations cooled between the governor and the Roman Catholic bishop, with the result that Prescott dragged his feet on the actual grant by placing a number of technical obstacles in the way of choosing the actual site. Even worse from Fleming's point of view, Prescott shortly became simply a conduit for transmission of complaints against the Roman Catholic bishop and clergy to which he did not hesitate to add his own personal stamp of approval.

With the Kent-Carson, Catholic, Reform party intensifying its sectarian campaign against the Prescott government, Bishop Fleming crossed the Atlantic to intercede directly with the Colonial Office on the subject of the land. He complained bitterly of Prescott's perfidy and double-dealing – of publicly telling Fleming of his support but privately acting in a contrary manner. Two years passed before the issue was finally resolved in Bishop Fleming's favour; by that time the Newfoundland political scene had become marked by a wide Catholic-Protestant cleavage. In the interim, Prescott's administration had become characterized by an increasing Protestant monopoly on appointments made locally; the Catholic Church and the Reform party were as much dedicated to ending the exclusive nature of the government as they were to effecting the removal of Chief Justice Boulton. Kent, Carson, and Nugent were now busily engaged in preparing the case against Prescott in order to prove to the home government the justness of their claims.

In July 1837 Kent published an open letter to Prescott containing a list of the civil servants; on that list the Protestant denominations claimed more than 96 per cent of the total. Kent wrote, he told the governor, to explain the cause of disaffection pervading the country. That cause was to be found in "the shameless exclusion of Roman Catholics from offices of emolument" under Prescott's government. Kent charged Prescott with running a party government; since the Reform party was almost exclusively Roman Catholic, the situation amounted to an almost complete exclusion of Roman Catholics from government favour. He was willing to acknowledge that the same exclusion was practised towards liberal Protestants but their insignificant numbers indicated that the exclusion was primarily religious in nature. Never "even in the most palmy days of Orangeism in Ireland," Kent declared, "was practised such unblushing exclusion." Kent was convinced, moreover, that such a system did not meet with the general support of the Newfoundland public, as Prescott's supporters assumed. Civil expenditures, he claimed, had been expanding at an alarming rate in order to prop up such a system in this colony. "The 'exclusive system would not last a moment,' he concluded, if situations were not multiplied for the purpose of binding an army of adherents to support its injustice."[4] That fall, when delegates were authorized to proceed to London to effect the removal of Chief Justice Boulton, they were also ordered by the Assembly "to awaken the attention of Her Majesty's Government to the exclusive character of the appointments to offices of trust and emolument in this Island, with a view to the procuring for the people of Newfoundland an impartial administration of Government."[5]

While in London awaiting the review of the case against Boulton, Nugent and Carson carried out extensive communications with the British Colonial Office on the sectarian nature of Newfoundland's administration. With the assistance of supporters in St John's, they submitted a carefully prepared and detailed report on the civil service of Newfoundland with special attention to Prescott's patronage from the time of his arrival in the colony down to the period of their own arrival in London that winter.[6] In this report, Nugent and Carson often used bitter words and rather intemperate language to describe the Prescott administration, but they never had anything less than complimentary to say about the colonial secretary, his staff, or the British government in general. And even though the Colonial Office was pestered almost daily throughout a period of seven months in 1838 by the delegates from Newfoundland, Nugent and Carson were never denied access to the minister, nor were they ever forced to endure the slightest impatience from even the highest-ranking civil servant in that department. Because of experiences such as this, the British government was highly regarded by the Catholic Reformers in Newfoundland. In fact, the Catholics gave such profuse sentiments of loyalty to the queen and the British government that both Governor Prescott and former Governor Cochrane had entertained anxieties lest Catholics earn more trust from the home government than its own gubernatorial appointments.

Throughout their exchanges with the Colonial Office, Nugent and Carson insisted that the political troubles in Newfoundland would entirely cease if Roman Catholics received their fair share of patronage from the local authorities. Since Prescott arrived, they pointed out, he had made not a solitary appointment of a Roman Catholic although forty appointments had been made during that four-year span. To prove their case, they submitted a table of statistics on the Newfoundland civil service that evidenced a rather damning case against the colonial government of that period.[7] (See Appendix, Table 1.)

The table contained a comprehensive list of all persons in receipt of salaries and fees from the government of Newfoundland. It named their official positions, gave their remuneration, and indicated their denominational affiliation as either Protestant or Catholic. It was a painstaking effort on behalf of both Nugent and Carson, who, first having had to gather the information from inhospitable sources, then had to transcribe it by hand in a shape and form to be read easily by the colonial secretary. In planning the table, sometimes in their zeal to make out their case as strongly as possible, they made a number of statistical and other errors, some deliberate to their own advantage, others perhaps through carelessness and fatigue. First, they wrongly numbered and therefore incorrectly counted the total number of positions in their table. They neglected to assign a number either to Thomas Read, subcollector in the colonial Customs Department, or to Thomas Bennett, speaker of the House of Assembly. In addition, they named Dr Edward Kielley as a "Reputed Catholic." Kielley, Carson's nemesis, had taken the latter's job as district surgeon. Despised by Nugent, Kielley had been denominated by Father Troy and his followers as a Mad Dog Catholic. Consequently he was anathema to the whole body of Roman Catholics. But calling Kielley a "reputed" Roman Catholic was not their greatest error, for, in reporting Kielley's second position as jail surgeon, they deliberately termed him a Protestant. That was no careless mistake but a deliberate falsehood intended to categorize the Newfoundland service in as exclusive terms as possible.

Towards the same end, Carson and Nugent practised another deception with regard to number 81, P. Gorman, jailer in Ferryland. On the pretext, it appears, of not knowing Gorman's religion with certainty, they marked him down as "not known to deputation." In fact, there was not much guesswork involved in ascertaining the religion of the Irish Gormans of Ferryland; however, Carson and Nugent had no scruples about seizing whatever opportunity lay at hand to strengthen their own case.

Nugent added one final note to the effect that, since his arrival in London, he had been informed from Newfoundland that Governor Prescott had appointed commissioners of charity for Conception Bay, all honorary positions. But, in spite of the fact that almost as many Catholics as Protestants lived in that bay and five Roman Catholic priests resided there as well, not one priest or Roman Catholic lay person had been appointed to that board while two of the Protestant ministers had received appointments in their stead. "Commentary," Nugent concluded, "is here unnecessary."

Notwithstanding their few mistakes, careless or otherwise, neither Carson nor Nugent had any need to doctor the statistical tables on the Newfoundland civil service to prove to the Colonial Office that there was something radically wrong. Even if all of their mistakes had been made in their own favour (which they were not), the clear picture still emerged of the true nature of the civil establishment of Newfoundland. Carson and Nugent were, therefore, able to reveal and document with names, numbers, and figures that an almost totally exclusive system operated in the colony. The Colonial Office could discover by a quick calculation that Protestants occupied 93 per cent of the public offices in Newfoundland. Indeed, as some Protestants possessed a number of sinecures (six to be exact), the real figures were even slightly more exclusive when the total number of civil servants were taken into account. The findings showed that as many as 94 per cent of the civil servants were Protestant and only 6 per cent Roman Catholic.

That might have been proof enough of the tendency to exclusivity, but the salary figures revealed an even more shocking discrepancy. Of the almost £20,000 expended on the civil and ecclesiastical departments in Newfoundland, Roman Catholics received only £400. And almost half that figure was composed of the £75 paid to Bishop Fleming by the imperial government and the £120 paid to Dr Kielley, the most implacable enemy of the Roman Catholic Church in the colony. Even including these two, Catholics still received only 2.3 per cent of the civil patronage in Newfoundland.

On having studied the table, the colonial secretary declared that the British government was decidedly opposed to exclusion of Roman Catholics from government patronage in Newfoundland. "However it may have originated," said Lord Glenelg, "it doesn't matter now"; and he therefore declared that the government was ready to instruct Prescott to appoint henceforward without regard to religious affiliation.[8] That was good news for Nugent; nevertheless, Prescott was summoned for a defence of the Protestant character of his government and also for a defence against the charge of bigotry preferred against him personally.

Prescott's subsequent defence was so weak – and in places so petty – that, had it not been for the fact that the British government was awaiting the report of Lord Durham into the affairs of all the British North American colonies, the Colonial Office might have removed him immediately and forthwith restructured the Newfoundland constitution. Whatever case Prescott might have possibly invented on his own behalf was nullified when he affirmed to Lord Glenelg the correctness of the Nugent/Carson table and confessed that indeed his appointments had all been Protestants. But, retorted Prescott, they "were not made on that account and ... I never instituted enquiry respecting Religion with a view to choice or rejection of any one."[9] Then he entered into what turned out to be an extremely feeble defence of the appointments made since his arrival in the colony. First, he attempted to take refuge in the argument that Nugent and Carson had made some mistakes in numbering and counting. Next, he denied that religion had influenced his choices and attempted to explain the real basis on which his appointments had been made. Naming the civil appointees individually, he contended that they were competent persons. Many of his appointments were made because they "benefit the public." One was appointed because he was "a native whose father was many years in the public service." Another got the job because he was "an exemplary person." Still others, especially the Sweetlands, magistrates in Bonavista and Trinity, were appointed because of their "general conduct" – and, more specifically, because they had not participated "in the violent Party spirit too prevalent here."[10]

The impression continually conveyed to the British government regarding the "violent Party spirit" rampant among Roman Catholics in Newfoundland was a deliberate ploy not just to defend the Protestant character of the government but to shore up the old Tory platform regarding the unsuitability of representative government in the colony. There had never been any sectarian campaign, let alone sectarian violence, among the substantial Roman Catholic populations in Trinity, Bonavista, and Notre Dame bays. The Nugent-Carson, proclerical, Catholic campaign had never extended beyond the majority Catholic populated areas on the Avalon peninsula; and Catholics in areas beyond the Avalon caused great anxiety even to Bishop Fleming by their lack of support for the Catholic, Reform education program. Even in St John's and Conception Bay, a substantial minority of Catholics had split with the Reformers and aligned themselves with Prescott's Tory supporters.

Given these conditions, Prescott could have had no difficulty in finding Catholics of "exemplary character" to fill positions at the lower levels of the civil service if he had had the courage to do so. It was impossible not to notice that in St John's sat a Roman Catholic member of the House of Assembly, E.J. Dwyer; if Prescott had been looking for a man of exemplary character, Dwyer was certainly one. Elected in 1836 and 1837 for the overwhelmingly Protestant district of Twillingate-Fogo, Dwyer had never taken any part in the sectarian squabbles in St John's and had been dismissed by Parsons, Nugent, and other Reformers as a C.F. Bennett nominee.[11] In fact, he was popular with neither Tories nor Reformers. The Tory newspapers in St John's continually referred to Dwyer as a perfect example of the violence and intimidation practised by the Roman Catholics; and, although he supported the Catholic campaign for equality, he never befriended the Nugent-Carson team to become a strict party man. In 1841 Nugent told the British House of Commons select committee on Newfoundland that the election of Dwyer had been part of the mercantile plot to sabotage the constitution, and that the charge that the violence of the Roman Catholic priesthood had ensured his election was nothing more than garbage.[12]

In time, the Colonial Office staff would weary of hearing how the minority Catholics in Newfoundland could intimidate the majority Protestants; but in 1838, Prescott could still maintain with some credibility at the Colonial Office that few Catholics of exemplary character were to be found in the colony. Speaking of the remainder of his civil-service appointments, Prescott tried to shift the blame in two ways. First, looking at total appointments since 1825, the governor informed the Colonial Office that his predecessor, Thomas Cochrane, had appointed more than half and that he, Prescott, ought not to be saddled with any blame regarding them. As for the constables on the list – all Protestants – they had been appointed by the magistrates; the Protestant jailers in Catholic St John's held their appointments from the sheriff, "appointments, with which," declared Prescott, " I do not interfere."

Here, however, Prescott ignored one of the Reformers' most bitter complaints: the lack of unbiased leadership both in Government House and at the local level led to Tories being consistently favoured over Reformers. Petty officials, such as sheriffs and magistrates, had been permitted to use their offices for the partisan exclusion of all but Tory supporters. Magistrate John Stark of Harbour Grace was a good example; a friend and sympathizer of the Tory candidates in Harbour Grace, Stark openly participated in their election committees in 1836 and 1837. The Reformers complained loudly against Stark and subsequently struck an Assembly committee to investigate him for improper conduct. They laboured as intensively for his removal as for that of Boulton but their efforts were in vain. Stark held his job because Prescott refused to intervene.

A worse situation existed in St John's, where Sheriff Benjamin Greer Garrett was as open a public enemy of the Reformers as were the members of the upper house. Garrett, who continually heaped indignities upon the Catholic priests visiting the jail, was widely known to be one of the notorious letter-writers in the *Times*, where the Roman Catholic bishop and his clergy were continually abused. Garrett, Parsons, and the *Patriot* engaged in a number of bitter libel suits over sentiments made by and in response to those letters.

John Kent argued that the practice of excluding Roman Catholics from public office was so deeply ingrained that it occurred as a matter of course. A case in point involving him happened in May 1838, when Sheriff Garrett, while calling out names for the grand jury list, skipped past Kent's name entirely. For years the Reformers had been making an issue of Roman Catholic exclusion from grand juries, and so Garrett's action did not surprise Kent. But Kent was more than puzzled a few days later when he received an official-looking letter addressed to John Kent instead of the usual John Kent Esq. He opened it to learn that John Kent Esq. had been dropped from the grand jury panel and that John Kent was henceforward a petty juror. It might seem petty, Kent pointed out, to complain about insults such as those; but when they occurred in succession over an extended period of time, they could be grating in their effects yet quite difficult to attack.[13]

Governor Prescott, on the other hand, having defended his appointments on individual grounds and shifted the blame to others, fell back on a defence that long had been the main campaign theme of the Newfoundland Tories: Roman Catholics were too ignorant to qualify for positions in the civil service. Although it was true that there were as many Catholics as Protestants in Newfoundland, declared Prescott, "the preponderance of that degree of Education which fits for public employment" is in favour of the Protestants.[14] As for the charge of personal bigotry against his character, Prescott repudiated it indignantly. The proof to the contrary, he said, was to be found in the manner in which he had handled the education dispute; he also offered the example that the person who cooked his meals was a Roman Catholic and the gardeners who worked on the grounds of Government House were of the same religion.

But the British government did not wait for Prescott's defence before applying pressure towards changing the sectarian character of the Newfoundland civil service. The colonial secretary told Prescott in May: "Her Majesty relies on your earnest endeavours to afford to all persons under your Government, irrespective of any political or religious distinction, the utmost protection in the enjoyment of their just rights and liberties."[15] Prescott was further informed of the British government's expectation that "no exertion would be wanting on your part to underrate the violence of party animosity and to induce all classes of the inhabitants to lay aside angry and excited feelings."[16]

In a second communication that same month, the British government again impressed on the Newfoundland governor that "a more favourable opportunity now exists than has hitherto presented itself for the successful exertion of your influence to promote concord and social kindness among all classes." It was referring to its decision to call off the case against Bishop Fleming; in fact, with Fleming having been rewarded with a generous gift of land for his proposed cathedral, British officials were firmly convinced of his sincere desire for cooperation. Again, in August of the same year, Prescott was urged to use all his personal and official influence "to allay the irritation which has formerly pervaded the society of Newfoundland, and to restore harmony and good feeling among all classes of the inhabitants."[17] Nugent returned to Newfoundland in the summer of 1838 in a triumphant mood. Boulton had been removed and the British government seemed to want an end to the exclusion of Roman Catholics from government patronage in Newfoundland.

Nugent approached the fall session of the legislature in 1838 with a great deal of optimism. Now that Boulton was gone from the council, there were indications that some of the remaining members were in a cooperative mood, and Prescott himself was taking a less rigid stance towards the Reformers. Nugent looked to Prescott for action on the patronage issue and appeared confident that a series of Catholic appointments would soon emanate from Government House.

But, for Prescott, that course of action was much more difficult than it appeared to Nugent. Even without Boulton, the Council soon shocked Prescott with further demonstrations of inflexibility. After an initial period of weakness following the reverses of 1838, the Tories regrouped and began to pursue an assertive, hard-line campaign against the House of Assembly in particular and against the Newfoundland constitution in general. That campaign apparently intimidated the governor and two others who were threatening to retreat from their previous inflexible positions – Attorney General Simms and William Thomas. Prescott thus discovered that the political atmosphere was extremely charged and hostile to Catholic, Reform appointments. It was possible that, if he were not overly cautious, he could lose the entire support of all his advisers and the Tory party while failing to win commensurate support from the majority Reformers in the lower house. Since Prescott had to tread carefully, he chose for his first Catholic appointment the maverick Reform Assembly member from Carbonear, James Power. While Prescott was likely pleased that the Tories did not condemn Power's appointment outright, he must have been more than shocked by Nugent's stand. Nugent stridently condemned the appointment and castigated Prescott for not having consulted the Reform leader on the issue. Although Power was a Roman Catholic, Nugent gave no thanks whatsoever to the governor for rewarding a member of that persuasion. Nugent sent the message instead that, in his eyes, only a certain, particular brand of Catholic would be suitable for government office.

Although Nugent had earlier rejected an outright demand for responsible government, his stance that the governor should consult the leader of the largest party in the Assembly meant that in effect he demanded little less than majority control. Nugent himself desired an appointment to the governor's Council, an idea that, from the governor's point of view, was totally impractical. Nugent had become the symbol of hysterical, partisan sentiments against every individual member of the upper house; doubtless few, if any, of them would be willing to serve with Nugent. Thus, Prescott found it impossible to contemplate appointing Nugent or even any of his detested Assembly followers to the upper chamber. As a result, Nugent soon lost faith in the governor's willingness to appoint Catholic Reformers to the Council; and, seeing that Power would be the lone Catholic appointment, he launched an ingenious initiative on the patronage issue that was destined to mark a new political and constitutional watershed in Newfoundland affairs.

Nugent appears to have felt confident that the Colonial Office would not suspend the constitution on religious grounds – the grounds put forward by the Conservatives. He believed that he had forced both the Conservatives and the governor into a political trap and that ultimately they would have no alternative but to accept his demands. He therefore elevated the struggle to a new level. In the House of Assembly the Reformers inserted into the supply, road, and poor-relief bills the names of all those who were to receive the salaries, expend the moneys, and administer the programs.[18] That tactic startled both the Legislative Council and the Assembly Tories, who were unsure at the outset how it could be checkmated. If the upper house blocked those money bills, the government of the colony would grind to a complete standstill. On the other hand, if the bills were passed, the entire patronage of the governor would be entrusted to the Assembly majority. This would be an intolerable situation for the Tories, the Upper House, the governor, the whole civil service, and their mercantile friends.

The upper house decided to thwart the efforts of the Assembly on the money bills and the succeeding impasse inaugurated a political and constitutional crisis in Newfoundland throughout 1839, 1840, and 1841. However, in the ranks of the Assembly Reformers, there were some who lacked the tenacity to back Nugent's hard-line position. William Carson and Patrick Morris expressed reservations on the adoption of such extreme tactics and served notice that they were willing to compromise. Prescott seized the opportunity to divide Reform ranks further and appointed Morris to his Executive Council. Carson would probably have been appointed, too, had he not possessed such a notorious personal reputation; Morris, on the contrary, was generally well liked even by his political enemies.

As recounted in the previous chapter, in the midst of this political and constitutional crisis, Nugent was forced to face a by-election for Morris's vacant seat in St John's. Nugent stood on fairly safe political ground in his pro-clerical campaign against the Kough-Hogan, Tory Catholic, William Walsh; but when Walsh withdrew and thereby left the field to James Douglas, Nugent's tactics became more of a liability than an asset. Instead of developing an alternative program to that of his former friend and colleague, Douglas, Nugent accentuated the pro-clerical, pro-priest campaign, to the embarrassment of a great many Catholics who had followed Morris and Douglas. Although Morris from his seat in the Council played no open part in the campaign, it was the threat represented by Morris's followers that posed the greatest danger to the Nugent Reformers.

Morris had been born in Ireland, yet he claimed he could be regarded as a native for he had taken up residence in the colony while only five years of age. Morris's followers in the BIS were mainly the native-born; and, as the Nugent campaign came increasingly under the control of Irish expatriates, there was a tendency for the natives to separate and vote for Douglas. Soon the native, Patrick Doyle, Assembly member for Placentia–St Mary's and colleague of Nugent, went over to Douglas, a detection that gave rise to predictions of an impending shift away from the Nugent camp. R.J. Parsons of the *Patriot* gave credence to a report that Nugent, in a street-corner speech, had declared he would "drive the copper-coloured natives into the sea."[19] Whether the charge was correct or not became irrelevant for it met with widespread acceptance, and Nugent spent the remainder of the campaign denying that he had ever uttered the remark. Shortly it appeared that the natives were deserting almost en masse to Douglas, and only the trickery of returning officer Thomas Beck allowed Nugent and O'Brien to rescue any semblance of victory.

But there was more to these events than the issue of national origins. In fact, the split in Reform ranks occurred more along economic than sectarian or national lines. Morris, Parsons, Douglas, and others who broke with Nugent in 1840 seem to have done so because their own political/economic interests did not coincide with those of Nugent.

Morris, for example, had been sufficiently long established in the colony and had become wealthy enough to break into the ranks of the respectable class. He grew impatient quite early with Nugent's hard line in the Assembly and wanted to withdraw from the privileges struggle shortly after it had commenced. To him, as had been the case with the middle class elsewhere,[20] Reform politics was simply an avenue to advance his own social and economic standing; and Nugent's appeal to fishermen and shoremen tended to make him rather nervous. As early as 1838, even before the victory over Boulton had been secured, Morris made it known that he would accept a seat in the governor's Council if Prescott tendered the offer.[21] It was perhaps only Nugent's facility to compromise that enabled Morris to remain in the party for another two years.

Carson, as well, was not long enamoured of Nugent's radical stance. Carson himself had clearly championed Reform politics and Catholic grievances as a tool to buck the establishment and forward his own causes. These causes were largely anti-Anglican and pro-farming; never even in his wildest days had he supported the fishermen-shoremen interest as opposed to that of the planter or merchant. In promoting one of his favourite schemes, the establishment of an academy in St John's for the children of the middle class, he opposed opening the doors of the school to the children of the lower orders.[22] On the subject of local improvements for the town of St John's, he advocated that such expenses be borne by the whole colony and not by rates levied in the capital, that is, by taxes on the middle class.[23] By 1839 Carson was expressing satisfaction with the system of government as long as expenditures were forthcoming on roads, hospitals, and schools;[24] such expenditures, of course, benefited the professional class most. Carson, if he could have secured the speaker's job in any other way, may perhaps have broken with Nugent earlier than 1840. When the break did come in that year, he threw his support behind Douglas.

James Douglas, a fellow Scot and Presbyterian, had early gravitated to Carson's side, backed him in founding the *Patriot*, and became co-owner of the paper with Parsons after Carson had abandoned journalism for a full-time political career. Douglas earned a name for himself among the populace as the secret author of the then-famous "Stick A Pin Here"[25] letter, for which Parsons served a prison term. He obtained influence with the "mob" after he secured the job as commissioner of roads, in which post he apparently made enough money to branch out to sealing with his own schooner and to the brewery business. He became sufficiently prosperous to acquire the business establishment of Patrick Morris when the latter retired from politics in 1840. Then, in partnership with a friend, William Wheatley, he established an extensive general dealership on Morris' waterside premises, catering to all classes in the colony. As an employer of many workers, Douglas could not have been particularly satisfied with Nugent's support of the fishermen-shoremen class. As soon as the 1840 by-election was declared, the Douglas-Nugent wings of the party eyed each other with much nervousness. William Carson was the first to propose Douglas and, as the requisition circulated through the capital for the usual accession of signatures, Douglas added the name of Nugent. He hoped thereby to acquire the support of the class of men behind Nugent and obviously to force the hand of the reluctant Nugent himself.

But Nugent held back. His hesitation was as much perhaps from the fear that Douglas might win as from the fear that he would be defeated.

Nugent had to be aware of his political mathematics and his calculations on that score gave him serious cause for concern. Since 1837 the House of Assembly, as a result of Row's boycott and the Buriner Henry Butler's poor attendance record, had been effectively a thirteen-member chamber. The opposition that had coalesced around Morris against Nugent consisted of the Conservative H.A. Emerson from Bonavista district, the liberal Dwyer of Fogo-Twillingate, a native-born relative of Morris, Patrick Doyle from Placentia–St Mary's, and – after 1839 – James Power from Conception Bay. Nugent's principal support came from Peter Winser of Ferryland and from the other three members from Conception Bay, Peter Brown, Anthony Godfrey, and John McCarthy. John Kent was also a supporter of Nugent, albeit a lukewarm one. Nugent, with the support of the clergy, felt perhaps that only this factor kept Kent in his own camp, a camp that had the tacit backing of Kent's brother-in-law, Bishop Fleming. The Trinity member, T.F. Moore, the only fisherman in the house, was also a Nugent supporter; but Nugent could hardly count on Moore, who had proven himself quite eccentric and totally unreliable. And even if he could indeed depend on Moore, Nugent realized that, since he occupied a tenuous position as leader of a slim majority, winning the St John's seat was a necessity. Thus, when the conservative, Catholic, and anti-clerical William Walsh threw his hat in the ring, Nugent spotted his chance and fielded a personal friend, Lawrence O'Brien, a devoted supporter of the Catholic Church, as a candidate.

R.J. Parsons and the *Patriot* quickly became the standard bearers for the Douglas wing of the party. Although Nugent's *Vindicator* did not appear until after the election, the *Patriot* campaign in the 1840 by-elections gives a good reflection of the widely divergent views of the liberal and conservative wings of the St John's middle class.

Parsons had always been hesitant to follow the Reform party line slavishly and had never demonstrated any reluctance about frequently chastizing Kent, Morris, and Carson. Parsons drew back, however, from attacking Nugent. Parsons hoped one day to sit in the House of Assembly, and so he could not afford to antagonize the powerful Reform leader. Instead, Parsons levelled his blasts at Peter Brown and Peter Winser, two of the most devoted supporters of Nugent. In defence of his two colleagues, Nugent was careful never to attack Parsons personally; indeed both Carson and Parsons had testified in an 1839 libel case that Nugent deprecated the use of personalities in politics, had always argued the merits of the case, and played the role of pacifier.[26] The breach that opened in 1840 between Nugent on the one hand and Parsons on the other, then, had little to do with personality and everything to do with issues of class.

Parsons had kept silent in the debate over Carson's project for a private academy, but he could not permanently conceal his true feelings regarding the legal regime governing the fishery. That question had become an open wound since 1824 and had started to fester as a result of the two perhaps most famous legal cases in the history of the Newfoundland fishery – Colbert versus Howley in 1835 and Nowlan versus McGrath in 1840. These landmark cases, which helped create a legal regime governing social relations in the fishery, became the litmus test for politicians in revealing their class sympathies.

In Colbert versus Howley, John Colbert, a fishing servant, was refused his full wages by his masters, planters Grant and Hamilton, because the latter claimed that the fish caught was insufficient to cover the full cost of the fishing supplies advanced at the commencement of the season. Colbert then sought his wages from the supplying merchant. When the latter denied any responsibility, Colbert sought redress through the court. The case came before Chief Justice Boulton in November 1835 and was decided in favour of the defendant. Nowlan versus McGrath was heard in November 1840 in the central circuit court in St John's before a special jury. A planter, Bartholomew McGrath, had hire John Nowlan to catch fish in the summer of 1840 but McGrath went bankrupt before the season ended and was unable to pay his servants' wages. When McGrath's supplying merchant refused to compensate Nowlan, the latter withheld his fish and oil and went to court for the recovery of his wages. In both Colbert versus Howley and Nowlan versus McGrath, the central question revolved around the lien system (whether the fishing servants had a lien for their wages on the fish caught) and the law of current supply (whether fishing servants could "follow" the fish and oil through a planter's hands right to the supplying merchant). Although the jury awarded the plaintiff his wages in the second case, the point of law, as in the first case, was decided in favour of the defendant.

Although Parsons launched a bitter frontal attack on Boulton's decision in the Colbert–Howley cse, he was careful to defend the interests of the planter and bewailed the harm that Boulton had done to that class. By early 1839 Parsons finally admitted that, in his view, the shield placed over the fishermen–shoremen class by the law of current supply was unjust.[27] In 1840 Parsons consistently defended the merchants who paid in truck, and during the Nowlan–McGrath trial he contended that the lien by custom for which Nowlan battled was a bad one. While it might have been right and just at one time, said the *Patriot*, it was now "unjust, unfair and injurious."[28] Later he defended the planters against an alleged attack by Nugent and condemned Nugent's legislative efforts to pass a bill through the House of Assembly giving the fishermen and shoremen a lien on their wages.[29] But most significant of all was the fact that, from the beginning of the election campaign in early 1840, the *Patriot*, in a attempt to defeat the Nugent candidate, advocated a union between the middle and upper classes. "The merchants in Newfoundland are, after all," declared the *Patriot*, "the truly Liberal party."[30] The "juncture of interests" of which the *Patriot* fondly spoke did take place, for the upper-class, Tory merchants came out to vote with the professional men, shopkeepers, and well-to-do planters to ensure a Nugent defeat.[31] But it proved insufficient to secure a Douglas victory because Nugent, with a popular fishery program, had constructed what was tantamount to a mass movement of fishermen in his party's interest.

Nugent had always stood with the fishermen and shoremen in the struggle against Boulton. In the House of Assembly after 1837, Nugent championed the poor and the fishermen/servant/sealer class. This position intrinsically conflicted with that later openly advocated by the Morris-Douglas-Parsons section of the party, and the differences between them were brought into sharper focus during the crisis of 1840–41. Nugent supported the cause of a lien on wages for the fishermen–shoremen class and in February 1841 attended a mass meeting of fishermen in St John's. This meeting was called expressly for the purpose of securing that lien. It was solely a fishermen-organized and fisherman-run demonstration; yet, of all the politicians in the colony, only Nugent and Kent played an official part in the proceedings. The *Patriot* almost completely ignored the event except to praise Patrick Morris for the few brief, unreported words he had to say there. But Nugent's *Vindicator* gave a detailed report of the fishermen's proceedings. It published verbatim all resolutions passed by the fishermen regarding their desired lien and gave them full and unqualified support.[32]

From such a position on fishermen's rights, Nugent approached the elections of 1840. When Conservatives expressed their fear of the propensity to violence on the part of the lower orders, they were simply testifying to the determination of the fishermen to ensure victory for their candidate. The fact that Douglas did so well was perhaps more because of the changing demographics in St John's than any weakness in popular support for the Nugent team. By the early 1840s, the fishermen and shoremen formed a minority of the voting population of the district. Although there are only inadequate statistics for that period, the 1836 and 1845 census records indicate that there was now an almost even split between the planter–fishermen–shoremen class, on the one hand, and the professional–tradesmen–farmer class, on the other. Throughout the district, those who were directly or indirectly involved in catching and curing fish barely outnumbered the others by 1845. But in the town of St John's, where the real political struggle took place, the class encompassing the professionals, tradesmen, and farmers, by that date, outnumbered those involved in the fishery by 1630 to 1617. It is tempting to think that, with just over three thousand votes cast, the almost even split signified a division along occupational lines. But one cannot ignore the fact that household ownership was a necessary qualification for the franchise and that there must have been a significant number of fishing servants who did not qualify on that account. While the 1845 census fails to throw light on the numbers in the servant category, the 1836 census had revealed that for every five servants only one was head of a family and thereby perhaps a householder. If as few as 20 per cent of the fishing servants, therefore, had no vote, the inescapable conclusion is that Nugent acquired support from the servants of the shopkeepers, of middle-class professionals, of printing establishments, and of upper-class merchants.

And so, in spite of the obvious cheating and delaying tactics of the returning officer, O'Brien did score a hard-earned victory in St John's and Nugent could look to Conception Bay with confidence. There, the demographic picture was much different from that in St John's. By 1845 the Conception Bay population was dominated ten to one by people in the planter–fishermen–shoremen category and was therefore susceptible to a movement catering to the fishermen. The fact that the Conservatives did almost as well as Nugent's candidate, Hanrahan, demands some explanation. First, the size of the middle class in Conception Bay was almost negligible compared to that in St John's, and so there were few middle class servants to cast ballots for Hanrahan. That meant that Hanrahan had to look almost exclusively to the fishermen and shoremen for support. Further, although the census does not give definitive figures on the question, we know from those available and from the nature of the fishery that significant numbers of the fishermen and shoremen were not householders and as a result did not possess the franchise. At the same time, Nugent's program held greatest appeal for the least secure of the fisherman class. They tended to be the less well established, the fishing servants who were the most recent arrivals. On that score, the pro-native, anti-foreign campaign of the Conservatives may have eaten into fishermen support for Nugent. But there is little evidence of such a campaign being conducted in Conception Bay to the extent that it had been in St John's.

The newspapers supporting the Conservative J.L. Prendergast, backed substantially by the government authorities both in St John's and Conception Bay, were strongly convinced that sectarianism on the part of Roman Catholics was the decisive factor in the campaign. That interpretation lacks credibility, however, primarily because the Tories had resolved in advance to blame any troubles on incendiary Roman Catholic priests. Their tactic dovetailed completely with the colonial government's strategy to label Newfoundland society as priest-ridden in order to aid and abet the campaign both in Britain and Newfoundland against the idea of a Catholic parliament in Dublin and to overthrow the colony's own existing constitutional structure. Besides, it would have been political suicide for Captain Hanrahan to have carried out a Roman Catholic campaign in Conception Bay, where approximately 60 per cent of the population was Protestant.

While a few Catholic priests campaigned for Hanrahan, support for both candidates crossed sectarian lines. It was generally conceded by both sides that Prendergast's substantial lead in the early part of the campaign came from the support of both Catholics and Protestants in Harbour Grace, where the two groups possessed approximately equal numbers.[33] That view is reinforced by the fact that Roman Catholic priests in Harbour Grace concentrated their campaign not in Harbour Grace itself but in the Carbonear section of the district where Catholics were outnumbered by the Protestants. At the same time, the returning Officer reported that, in the exclusively Catholic area of Harbour Main, right under the nose of the parish priest campaigning for Hanrahan, some Catholics had voted for Prendergast.[34] But the most significant evidence refuting a sectarian interpretation of the election is offered by the campaign in the area of Carbonear and northwards. There, Protestants constituted more than 60 per cent of the total population yet Hanrahan received such overwhelming support that he was coasting to inevitable victory when the election was suspended.

The fishermen's movement, sectarianism, and the tension between native- and foreign-born were undoubtedly all factors in the Conception Bay election campaign. But perhaps the decisive factor was the competition between the two chief towns in the bay, Carbonear and Harbour Grace. These two towns had been traditional rivals[35] and the competition between them accelerated in the 1830s when outport firms experienced increasing encroachment from St John's. Harbour Grace was in a much better position to cope with this pressure than Carbonear because it possessed a number of large mercantile firms such as the Ridleys, the Puntons, and the Munns, which operated in a manner quite similar to the big operations in St John's; that is, they had branches established in other centres of the colony.[36] Thomas Ridley and Sons of Harbour Grace was the largest mercantile business in Newfoundland outside St John's and created even further pressure on Carbonear by opening a branch firm there. Ridley was a government supporter and had run unsuccessfully as a Conservative candidate in the 1836 general election. Together with Punton and Munn of Harbour Grace, Ridley placed all his support behind Prendergast in an attempt to defeat the Carbonear man, Hanrahan.

In Carbonear the largest local mercantile operation was headed by Robert Pack, who had won the district for the Reformers in the general elections of 1832 and 1836. Pack now flung himself entirely into the campaign in an attempt to secure victory for Hanrahan. It was obviously in Pack's interest – and perhaps a necessity for him – to organize the fishermen in his area against the intrusion of firms backed by Harbour Grace and St John's. Pack's efforts account in large measure for the burgeoning support for Hanrahan from the Carbonear-Western Bay area. With Hanrahan's victory staring them in the face, the authorities, at the first pretext, called off the election and forwarded a mass of documentation to London claiming clerical interference with the franchise and demanding suspension of the constitution. In St John's Nugent and his supporters complained stridently and in the following months kept the momentum going with a mass meeting of fishermen. Nugent had successfully piloted the lien bill through the committee stages in the Assembly when news arrived of the abrogation of the constitution.

Following the by-elections, Nugent was surrounded by an air not of victory but of gloom and doom. This appears to have been due to Bishop Fleming's lack of enthusiasm for Nugent's cause. Following the St John's by-election, Fleming withdrew completely from active political campaigning, and he even announced, without even hinting at a personal preference, during the height of the Conception Bay election that voters should vote for whom they thought fit.[37] Fleming's lack of political commitment perhaps stemmed from his absorption in his church's worsening financial situation. In 1841, for the second year in a row, Fleming tried to found yet another Catholic society for the purpose of raising funds for the church.[38] With the church apparently suffering from the loss of middle-class support, the bishop became acutely aware of the utility of an alliance with people who not only had the cash to donate but played a fundamental role in collecting from their Roman Catholic servants and fishermen as well.

In the meantime, the British government announced the appointment of a select committee of the House of Commons to study the crisis in Newfoundland. The isolation of the Nugent Reformers meant that they enjoyed a minimum of political leverage with which to influence the final decisions of the British government, and thus the triumph of the Tory campaign to restructure the Newfoundland constitution seemed to be imminent. As it happened, the select committee had little time to complete its work because, in the midst of its deliberations, the British Parliament was dissolved for a general election. Subsequently, the new Tory government that took office, because of delays occasioned by communications with distant Newfoundland, dispensed with any further enquiries and presented its proposals to Parliament in 1842. Those proposals embodied a constitution aimed at overcoming three obstacles that, in the government's opinion, had caused the political difficulties in Newfoundland: the interference of the Roman Catholic priests at elections; the exaggerated notions of their privileges held by the two branches of the legislature in Newfoundland; and the conflicting interests of the resident and mercantile portions of the community.[39] To assist in overcoming the latter two obstacles, the new constitution provided for a single-chamber legislature where fifteen elected representatives would sit side-by-side with ten appointed members. The British government believed that the presence of representatives of all interests sitting side by side would help abate the ardour of political feelings. Formerly, each chamber held separate votes on all bills, an arrangement that often gave rise to deadlock on each one; now, representatives from each group would vote together and so pre-empt the possibility of deadlock. In the new unicameral legislature, there would be either a favourable vote or a negative one. There would also be no debate over privileges since both elected and appointed members operated under the same rules of parliamentary procedure. As for the interference of the Roman Catholic priests at elections, it was proposed to tackle that in the same manner as had been done in Ireland following Catholic emancipation in 1829 – by raising the qualifications for candidates and voters. Thus, the new proposals included a requirement that candidates for election to the Assembly must have an annual income of £100 or encumbrance-free property to the value of £500. Voters in outport ridings must possess at least a freehold worth forty shillings while those in the towns had to be in occupancy of a house with an annual rent of five pounds.

For the Newfoundland Tories, it was encouraging to know that a Tory government in Westminster had suggested such changes. And they were exceedingly pleased with several aspects of the new constitution. They were especially happy that the initiation of all money bills would be taken away from the lower house and reserved to the crown. Also, they were thrilled with the distribution of elected versus appointed members in the new Assembly. With ten positions reserved to the governor's patronage, the Tories had merely to win a minimum of three seats in a general election to preserve power in the governor's hands and maintain a thirteen-to-twelve majority in the legislature. Even if they continued to lose all seats on the Catholic Avalon, and win none in Conception Bay or Burin, they still held a monopoly of the four seats in Twillingate-Fogo district and the bays of Bonavista, Trinity, and Fortune. Even better, their old program of a franchise change to curtail the influence of Catholic priests seemed to be coming true at last. The Tories looked forward to the new house with eager anticipation.

R.J. Parsons, of the Reformers, initially condemned the new constitution because it failed to confer responsible government.[40] But, at that time, there was little support for that concept in Newfoundland either within or without the Reform party. Upon the inauguration of the amalgamated legislature, Parsons accepted it with great resignation. As for Nugent and his followers, they had previously demanded a separation of the councils and amalgamation of the two houses into one chamber. The changes of 1842, therefore, neither surprised nor disappointed them. Nugent, in fact, possessed a unique view of the amalgamated constitution. He personally considered it a signal victory for the elective branch. "They were no longer a Council," Nugent said, "they were discarded from their House by Act of Parliament." He considered that the status of his upper-house enemies had inflicted an embarrassing diminution as a result of the new constitution. "They had shown their unfitness to conduct the business of legislation by themselves," he boasted, "and they were sent to be instructed by those who knew how to conduct themselves properly – the Representatives of the people."[41]

Nugent's anxiety rested not on the specifics of the new constitution but on its effective implementation. His chief worry was that, in the newly constituted chamber, Reformers would need to win at least thirteen of the fifteen elected seats in order to establish a clear majority. While not an impossibility, for they had already performed that feat in 1837, it was an awesome burden which threatened to become all the more insurmountable because of the Tory, anti-Catholic attempts to restrict the franchise in the new constitution bill before the British Commons. In attempting to reduce substantially the numbers of Catholic voters, the British government was not only following the practice implemented in Ireland following the 1829 Emancipation Act but also bowing to the perennial complaints of the Newfoundland Tories. But liberals, reformers, and radicals in the British Commons succeeded in killing the proposed franchise change. Both sides were forced to accept a compromise on the issue and the final result – that of raising the voter-residency requirement to two years preceding polling day – was a major victory for the Nugent Reformers in Newfoundland.

For Nugent, debate over constitutional principles had never been much of a priority. To him, the form it assumed in practice determined the utility of a particular government. Government effectiveness, he thought, was built on a just distribution of patronage. For that reason Nugent's criticisms had primarily focused on the personalities of Boulton, Cochrane, or Prescott; he always maintained that, if fit and proper persons held high public office, Catholics would not have to suffer exclusion from government service. Nugent thus argued that the solution of Newfoundland's troubles rested in the hands of a governor who was prepared to be fair to Roman Catholics.[42] According to the general British practice of administering representative government in all its colonies, Nugent was stating an already accepted principle but one that had not yet been applied to Newfoundland.

The peace after the American revolution had revealed serious weaknesses in the old representative system as it existed in Newfoundland and the other British North American colonies.[43] The basic problem was that of attempting to control and direct from London colonies located thousands of miles away. This problem was complicated by the explosion in the range of responsibilities dumped into the laps of the governors as well as by the increasing aggressiveness of local, democratically elected assemblies. Efforts to manage in the face of such difficulties consisted of seeking collaborators in each colony by dispensation of patronage.[44] That system worked well where colonial elites were small and homogeneous, such as in Nova Scotia and New Brunswick, but failed in Upper and Lower Canada.[45] There, armed rebellions shocked the British government into initiating steps that led to union of the Canadas and eventually responsible government and confederation of all the British North American colonies.

In Newfoundland the collaborative system worked well for a time following the 1825 introduction of colonial administration. The small, but powerful, St John's mercantile elite expanded its influence during Cochrane's reign and further solidified it by taking almost complete control of the first House of Assembly. That had been facilitated partly by the weakness of the small middle class, which proved entirely unable to assume leadership over the population at large. But by 1833 the middle class had found an ally able to deliver the support of the populace. That ally was the Roman Catholic Church, which under Bishop Fleming was eager to build solidarity among the Catholic lower class for the purpose of establishing a church free of mercantile and government influence. By 1837 middle-class Reformers were able to

take complete control of the lower house and by 1840 they were able
to bring the system to a deadlock in pursuit of their objectives. Unresponsive governors, like Cochrane and Prescott, had been unable to
develop a system of conciliation that could incorporate the new
middle-class interests into the patronage system and the mercantile
elite and governing officials around them resisted even the slightest
attempt at compromise. At the same time, the British authorities
ignored the deepening crisis in Newfoundland because of their pre-
occupation with political crises at home and the attention demanded
by the rebellions in the Canadas. By the time the political and constitutional crisis in Newfoundland forced their hand in 1842, it was too
late to attempt placating any of the local interests other than by a
constitutional reorganization.

The year before the new amalgamated legislature came into being,
Prescott had been replaced as governor by Sir John Harvey. Harvey
had been born in England in 1778 to a family of modest means but
his father had been able to obtain an army commission for John by
the time he was sixteen. In the absence of money to purchase advance-
ment, Harvey displayed energy and raw talent in working his way slowly
through the ranks. In both the French Revolutionary Wars and the
War of 1812, Harvey demonstrated obvious courage, earned a medal
for bravery, drew the attention of his superiors and advanced to the
rank of lieutenant-colonel. With the coming of peace, Harvey continued to shine this time in civil administration. In 1828 he became
inspector general of police for the province of Leinster in Ireland.
The struggle for Catholic emancipation was then in full swing, and no
sooner was it concluded than tithe battles became a crisis. The eight
years Harvey spent there were the most turbulent years in Ireland in
the nineteenth century and some of the worst cruelties and retalia-
tions were perpetrated in the area under his jurisdiction. But Harvey
displayed such tact and common sense that he earned respect from
those on both sides of the issues. His suggestions for resolving the
problems were eventually adopted by the British government, and
when he left Ireland for Prince Edward Island in 1836, he went with
the blessings and congratulations not only of Dublin castle but of the
Roman Catholic and established churches as well as of the tenant
farmers and landlords. Following gubernatorial service in Prince
Edward Island, Harvey served in New Brunswick, where he earned the
support of Reformers. He pursued in that colony a policy that many
Reformers termed responsible government, a concept that had come
to mean the formation of an administration more responsive to public
opinion. While such a policy did not satisfy the more extreme, radical
Reformers like R.J. Parsons of the *Patriot*, it mirrored the views of all

moderate liberals and reformers in the British colonies at that time, including the Nugent group in Newfoundland.

The Roman Catholic and Irish expatriate elements of Newfoundland's population were extremely optimistic on Harvey's appointment, for they were fully aware of Harvey's past service in Ireland. Moreover, Bishop Fleming was now receptive to a new constitution that would afford an opportunity for a reunited middle class to regain its connection to the populace. Thus, both the bishop and his church were in a conciliatory mood. When Harvey landed at the St John's waterfront in September 1841, he was met with congratulations not just from Reform politicians but from a Roman Catholic procession led by none other than Bishop Fleming.[47] It was a confident beginning for the new governor, who began to build immediately on the good will.

Harvey consulted with leaders of all parties, classes, and religions, informing them of his desire to be just and fair to all in his decisions.[48] To accomplish fairness, he intended to confer patronage proportionately to each group. A happy coincidence, the birth of a prince, allowed him a symbolic occasion to demonstrate his skills at bringing opposing interests together. By a series of wise and carefully planned manoeuvres he succeeded in uniting, for the purpose of congratulating the queen, all the different religious and political representatives in the colony. That was an unprecedented occurrence for Newfoundland, and the British government was notably impressed. Next, Harvey played a leading role in the formation of an agricultural society for the promotion of local farming. Aimed at courting the resident, non-fishing interests, the society provided Harvey with annual forums for long-winded, grandiloquent speeches where he surpassed even Patrick Morris in exaggerating the farming potential of Newfoundland. Such speeches impressed the pro-native element in the population, who became endeared to him for his commitment to the colony. But Harvey's window-dressing in the form of social gatherings, wining, dining, and lofty speeches were all given a strong basis in credibility by the judicious nature of his appointments.

First, Harvey earned the gratification of the Roman Catholics and Reformers alike by appointing Patrick Doyle, Nugent's Assembly colleague from Placentia–St Mary's, as a stipendiary magistrate for St John's. He then appointed Henry Devereux as the first Roman Catholic notary public in the colony; and when, in 1843, he published his first list of JPs for the capital, the list included no less than six Roman Catholics. Then, to sit in the amalgamated legislature opposite the elected members, Harvey appointed three Roman Catholics: the veteran Reformer Patrick Morris; the long-standing Catholic leader John Kent; and James Tobin, an up-and-coming merchant. The fairest distribution on the basis of population would have been five Catholics out of the ten appointed members, but Harvey's appointments none-theless represented an enormous increase in patronage for Roman Catholics. Further, the governor had also been given expanded oppor-tunities for patronage appointments. Those included a first for Newfoundland, a separate Executive Council. To that body Harvey reappointed Patrick Morris as colonial treasurer; and, to the delight of Catholics and Reformers alike, he also included William Carson. While Harvey kept a preponderance of Protestants, Tories, and upper-class merchants in both councils, all classes, parties, and denomina-tional interests were willing to profess their support of his government.

Of all the leading Reformers, only John Valentine Nugent was without patronage. But an understanding grew between Nugent and the governor that, as soon as the education question was settled, Nugent would get an appointment in that field, an area where he personally possessed some experience and expertise. Harvey sounded out the different political and denominational interests on the wisdom of dividing the government education grants along Protestant-Catholic lines so as to remove the Bible controversy from the forum of public, political debate. For the Protestants, the issue of Bible education was the grievance that rankled deepest of all since the inception of repre-sentative government in 1832. If the colony were to have a respite from sectarian politics, Harvey knew that the Bible controversy must be settled. The Nugent Reformers had made that issue, along with Catholic exclusion, one of the main planks in their sectarian platform. When Harvey moved to settle an issue in such great favour with the Protestants, he must have cast an anxious glance in the direction of John Valentine Nugent.

But by 1843 Nugent's political position had considerably weakened beyond even what it had been even three years earlier. His two great clerical leaders, Fleming's so called "prime ministers," were no longer at hand to direct political affairs in St John's and Conception Bay. Under pressure from Rome, Bishop Fleming had removed Father Troy to a remote island parish in Placentia Bay, while Father J.M. Bergin of Tilting had suffered a premature death in September 1841. To make the situation even worse for Nugent, Father Patrick Ward, one of his devoted followers, was sent to replace the dead Bergin in distant Tilting, far out of reach of political campaigns on the Avalon.[49] Mean-while, the new priests recruited in the previous few years had shown little propensity to follow in the political footsteps of Bergin and Troy, and Sir Richard Bonnycastle, a British Royal Engineer stationed in St John's, reported that the anti-clericals in the Catholic community were now in command politically.[50] That advantage was borne out by

the elections for the new Assembly in 1842, when several indepen-
dents were elected in Catholic constituencies. They included James L.
Prendergast in Conception Bay, Patrick Morris's brother Simon in
Placentia, and a Presbyterian merchant, Thomas Glen, in Ferryland.
Nugent was therefore not well positioned to launch the Bible battle
once again. When Harvey sounded him out on the wisdom of setting
up separate school boards, he promised the governor that he would
give no "factious" opposition.[51]

Harvey continued to negotiate with the different denominations;
and as soon as he gained a consensus, he chose Richard Barnes, the
Protestant Assembly member for Trinity Bay, to take charge of the bill
in the new legislature. Barnes was a native Newfoundlander and, along
with the Protestant Reformer R.J. Parsons and the Catholic Tory
Edward Kielley, had played a prominent role in the formation of the
Natives Society of Newfoundland. It was an organization upon which
Nugent was wont to look with suspicion and jealousy – and, perhaps,
with good reason. An independent British observer noted at the time
that the natives then held the balance of power between the Reformers
on the one side and the Tories on the other.[52] Harvey's selection of
Barnes, then, to champion the most controversial and ground-breaking piece of legislation in Newfoundland's history was calculated to
give not only due recognition to Protestants but also a gentle reminder
to Nugent that he had been outmanoeuvred by native Catholics within
his own ranks.

Barnes introduced second reading of the now-famous Education Bill
on 13 March 1843 speaking extensively on the educational troubles
of the preceding ten years, he reviewed the controversy in the boards
of Conception, Trinity, and Bonavista bays and read into the record
the board minutes and correspondence of that period. The history of
the controversy, he said, had proven two things: that the Education Act
had failed, and that it had failed because the people had no confidence
in it. Nevertheless, Barnes did overlook the fact that, for the greater
part of the colony, especially the majority Roman Catholic districts,
there had been no educational dispute at all and the Education Act
of 1836 had been a resounding success. However, the subject was not
and had never been strictly an educational issue; in the mid-1830s it
had resolved itself quickly into a political and religious campaign. Now
Barnes was promoting the Protestant goal that the Anglicans had
sought as early as the mid-1820s. For the Roman Catholics, the anti-
Bible campaign had been strictly a defensive manoeuvre, and those
Catholics in the house listening to Barnes reluctantly agreed that "a
separation is unavoidable." That separation would protect Catholic
students from unauthorized versions of the Bible and leave the

Anglicans and Wesleyans to battle it out on grounds of their own choosing. "The two great religious bodies of the country," proclaimed Barnes, "are now like two armies, who, upon the subject of education, have got within each other's lines, and for whom there is no neutral ground to stand upon." He concluded, "We have no other course left to us."[53]

Sir John Harvey had done his preparatory work so well that not another member spoke in the debate, and second reading passed without a dissenting vote. But later in Committee stages, C.F. Bennett – who identified himself as remaining personally opposed to the principle of division – refused to press the issue to a vote. Nugent revealed that he entertained views similar to Bennett's on the subject of separate schools and was of the opinion that "a separate education was far better than no education" at all.[54] That same reluctance to revive the education wars of the previous decade was demonstrated by those outside the house as well. None of the partisan newspapers engaged in the least criticism of the bill. Within a few days separate education and Bible teaching were put to rest as issues dividing Protestants and Catholics.

Protestant feelings of injustice in education were greatly mollified by the 1843 act; but Roman Catholics, as well, had now good reasons to feel included in the system. In addition to the patronage conferred on Catholics since his arrival, Harvey, on passing of the Education Act, appointed Nugent as Newfoundland's first superintendent of schools. Thus, in 1844, the Reform leader embarked on a new career and in succeeding years he was to prove even ready to shower praise on Harvey's government. In the meantime, a final and successful effort was launched to terminate the last of the odious, infamous oaths which had embarrassed Catholics so much that Bishop Fleming, in 1832, had called it "sanguinary of the worshippers of juggernaut."[55] That was the oath that forced Catholics, upon accepting government office or seats in the Assembly, to swear against the doctrine that popes could order Catholics to murder excommunicated princes. When in 1843 R.J. Parsons opened his campaign for William Carson's vacated seat in St John's, he targeted that oath as his central campaign theme.[56] Parsons also cited removal of the Protestant oath as an essential component of the new Reform policy on oaths. That oath required Protestants to swear "that in the Sacrament of the Lord's Supper there is not any trans-substantiation." The oath also contained an article to swear defence of "the present Church establishment as settled by law within this realm." Parsons believed that these requirements were now anachronistic and an embarrassment to all denominations.

Such an argument, of course, could not fail to help Parsons's electoral chances in the Catholic constituency of St John's, where he had two opponents. His major adversary was a prominent Protestant businessman, Kenneth McLea, who had the backing of the *Newfoundlander* and its Catholic editor, Ambrose Shea. Neither of Parsons's opponents dared even to comment on the sensitive oath issue, and Parsons pressured the Reform caucus to bring in a bill on the subject in the house session then in progress. Nugent introduced a bill on 13 March to abolish the oaths in question. The Protestant oath, he said, was "irritating and vexatious" and insulting to Catholics, and perfectly unnecessary. As for the Catholic oath, he said, "it was framed in England on the pretence of protecting a Church establishment which does not exist here, and therefore was uncalled for."[57] Although Nugent's arguments were reasonable and logical with respect to the grounds on which the oaths were sworn in Newfoundland, his bill carved out a radical position that the British Commons was not then prepared to accept as far as the United Kingdom was concerned. At almost the same time that Nugent was arguing in favour of his oath bill in Newfoundland, an almost identical bill met a resounding defeat on second reading in the British Parliament.

The Church of England enjoyed a de facto establishment status in England, Ireland, and Wales; but the removal of that part of the oath protecting the Anglican establishment was not nearly as revolutionary a move in the Newfoundland, where the Church of England had never been officially established. For that reason, perhaps, Nugent's bill did not meet with general opposition from Protestants. Nevertheless, Patrick Morris led the opposition against the oaths bill in the house because he thought that it was useless to attempt what O'Connell, numerous Catholic lords and dukes, and the British Commons had failed to do. While all Protestants in the house remained silent in the debate, Morris – a Nugent-Parsons enemy since his elevation to the Council three years previously – attacked Nugent for his inflated ego in presuming to succeed where his betters had failed. Kent responded to what appeared to be Morris's effort to damage Parsons's chances in the by-election by defending Nugent and attacking his uncle's "pseudo-liberalism." But Nugent's strategy paid off. When the bill came to a vote on second reading, Morris would not dare vote against it; and the bill passed by a margin of twelve to eight, all opposed being Protestant.[58]

The general silence of Protestants in the house, specifically the eight opposed, could have been traceable to the fact that Kenneth McLea, one of their own, was running in the June by-election for St John's and the Protestants did not want to harm his chances in what appeared to be a close race. There was also some doubt as to the constitutionality of the act, and Nugent was forced to add a suspending clause to allay those fears. Governor Harvey, who felt the same way, reserved the act for the pleasure of the British government. The Colonial Office raised no objections to the contents of Nugent's bill but expressed doubts as to the proper mode of proceeding on such a topic. If the existing Newfoundland oaths had been imposed by a British parliamentary act, it said, then a Newfoundland bill would have to be placed before the British Commons instead. If, on the other hand, the queen under her royal prerogative had imposed the oaths, then the proper mode of procedure was for the Newfoundland legislature to address the queen. On reflection and study, the Colonial Office staff discovered that addressing the queen was the correct method and Newfoundland was so notified. But the information came too late to be of any advantage to Nugent in the session of 1844. In the interim Parsons had been the victor in the St John's by-election.

In January 1844 Parsons and the Protestant John Slade, a by-election winner in Twillingate-Fogo, presented themselves to take their seats in the house. When Governor Harvey stood in the committee room to tender the usual Protestant oaths to both members, Parsons created a scene by rejecting the Protestant oath.[59] He refused to take his seat unless tendered the same oath normally sworn by Roman Catholics. Governor Harvey, no doubt a little embarrassed, reached for the Catholic oath and, for the first time in Newfoundland history, tendered it to a Protestant member of the House of Assembly. From that day forward the Protestant oath was practically a dead letter. When, on 20 January 1845, Nugent moved for a select committee to prepare an address to the queen embodying the contents of his Oaths Act of 1843, there was hardly a whimper from the house. The committee reported in record time and the house quickly adopted the address. Governor Harvey was immediately pleased to accept it and on 1 February he transmitted the address to the queen. The following year the Newfoundland House of Assembly sent another petition to the queen calling for the tendering of the oaths of office and allegiance only, and the request was immediately granted. In December 1848, when the members of the newly elected House of Assembly presented themselves for business, history was made when the governor tendered to them all, Protestant and Catholic alike, the same oaths of office and allegiance. For Roman Catholics, the event was the culmination of their quarter-century-long struggle to be placed on the same footing as Protestants when taking oaths to serve the crown in Newfoundland.

The fact that a subject once as contentious and as sensitive as the oaths issue could be settled with so little fanfare was powerful testimony to the mollifying effects of Sir John Harvey's government.

Indeed, Harvey's conciliatory policy brought such immediate results that, within a year of his arrival, the 1842 general elections concluded with unprecedented peace and quiet. In the new legislature, with appointed and elected members sitting side by side, the deadlock that had paralysed the previous Assembly was non-existent. Partisan conflicts so rarely surfaced that some politicians yearned for the days of party politics. Only R.J. Parsons gave consistent opposition to Harvey's government and even his dissenting voice was muted by his own reservations that the constitution rather than Harvey himself should shoulder the blame.

By 1845 Parsons himself was contending that party lines had become so blurred that he could not tell one from the other.[60] Reformers themselves in fact were so enamoured with the success of the new constitution that, when the British government proved unprepared to concede true responsible government, they accepted an extension of the experiment for an additional year. When the original two-House constitution was revived in 1848, the elections came off with so little factious politicking that not only were the party standings identical to those of the amalgamated legislature but the campaign raised hardly a whimper throughout the colony. Politics, thanks to Sir John Harvey, were in a state of slumber that few cared to disturb.

Nugent's campaign for Catholic patronage had worked in an unexpected fashion: by the appointment of Catholics unacceptable to Nugent because of their conservative, upper-middle-class leanings. When a split occurred in Reform ranks, the resulting struggle revealed that there was a philosophical cleavage between the two factions. With the loss of Fleming's active support and desertion of a substantial part of the middle class, Nugent was politically isolated and left without a means of rallying the populace behind his party. Nugent's fall ushered in an era of conservative politics. For upper-class interests, the suspension of the constitution revealed that what they feared most was delivery of the Assembly into the hands of the fishermen. They thus swallowed their antipathies to Roman Catholics as the latter gained ground at all levels of government.

8 The Rise of Philip Little, 1848-52

Behind the quiet, non-sectarian politics of the 1840s powerful economic and political undercurrents were transforming Newfoundland society. Two immigrant, lawyer-politicians from Prince Edward Island were the first to acknowledge those new forces and the result was the birth of a new political movement. It eventually would transform the Newfoundland constitution yet again but this time into a progressive, instead of a regressive, instrument.

After the demise of the amalgamated constitution in 1847, a new governor, Gaspard LeMarchant, continued to enjoy the cooperation of the Nugent Reformers. Nugent still favoured the coalition on account of the patronage dispensed to him, to his fellow religionists, and to his middle-class supporters. Kent also had been considerably mollified as a result of government patronage and in the interim had developed a cosy relationship with many of the governor's officials, including Attorney General E.M. Archibald. Kent was not only close on personal terms with the governor but also personally indebted to him in financial terms as well. At the same time, the Roman Catholic Church was languishing. Its leader, Bishop Fleming, was in such a state of ill health that, in the few years preceding his death in 1850, he had been largely confined to his house. But disasters in the form of fire and storm and a severe recession were probably the chief factors contributing to the political quiescence that seemed to predominate after 1846.[1]

On 9 June 1846, a raging fire, the most destructive in the history of Newfoundland to date, tore through the capital destroying approximately 2000 houses and property to the value of four million dollars. The fire struck a devastating blow to the whole colony, and the government was forced to devote its entire attention and resources to the recovery. Then Newfoundland was hit by a storm unprecedented for its severity. The infamous gale of 19 September destroyed such an immense amount of property on both land and sea that it was considered a calamity greater than the fire itself.[2] To compound the adversities, poor fisheries and failure of the potato crops followed in 1847 and 1848. The failure of all the mercantile establishments resulting from the fire and the gale reduced the colony to a state approaching emergency. With provisions in short supply, prices doubled; the colony was faced with a huge budgetary deficit. Without an Assembly throughout 1847–48, the governor had to fall back on the issuing of treasury notes. For the first time in imperial history, the British treasury was forced to advance a loan to a colony in dire straits.

Perhaps hardest hit of all was the middle class of tradesmen, shopkeepers, and small merchants in St John's that had always formed the bedrock of the Reform movement. With their business establishments and homes destroyed in the great fire, those merchants were forced to turn to government for help. Politics was the least of their concerns. As a result, the 1848 election was such a quiet, dull affair that only half the voters went to the polls. "Politics are now a dead letter," noted the governor in the fall of 1849. With the return of good fisheries and abundant potato crops in that year, there followed a consequent improvement in the financial state of the colony and LeMarchant[3] felt in a buoyant mood. "Everything here is going on in the most perfectly satisfactory manner," he said, so that for the winter of 1850, "I hope to repose on a bed of roses."[4]

While Harvey and, his successor, LeMarchant could take steps to suspend party politics, they could not arrest all change. And while they blandished their way through their limited terms of office, significant changes were taking place in Newfoundland society – changes that were destined to have fatal consequences for their system of government.

In the British Isles, the view that colonial churches should stand on their own and not expect financial help from government intensified throughout the 1830s. By 1835 the British government had ended its long-standing grant to the SPG, an action that the Reverend Edward Wix considered to be a severe blow to the church in Newfoundland. But the move was not without its blessings for Newfoundland's Anglicans, because in 1839, after decades of complaining, the first steps towards the creation of a more effective and ambitious church organization were taken. As soon as the new bishop, Aubrey Spencer,[5] arrived in St John's, he commenced constructing a local church organization remarkably similar to that of the Roman Catholic Church under Bishop Fleming.[6] Spencer reorganized his diocese into three deaneries. He began a massive building program consisting of chapels, parsonages, and schools. In St John's he undertook the construction of a massive stone cathedral to rival that under construction by the Roman Catholic bishop. To solve the shortage of clergy, Spencer founded a theological seminary for the training of local men. In the interim, Spencer attempted to ordain the teachers of the Newfoundland School Society. To fund it all, it appears, he relied on traditional methods as well as on some innovative measures of his own. Friendly merchants were expected to continue to make deductions for Church of England clergy, but this method suffered from the vagaries of the infamous credit system as well from the hostility of certain merchants.[7] Some clergy tried to overcome those weaknesses by inaugurating their own fish-collection service[8] in the manner of Bishop Fleming. But this method was not a panacea either, and so Bishop Spencer also founded the Newfoundland Church Society, the objective of which was the assessment and collection of fees from every member of the church in the colony.

Perhaps this program was too ambitious. By 1845 Bishop Edward Feild,[9] Spencer's successor, was in despair at the sorry state of the Church of England in Newfoundland.[10] Feild held out dim hopes for the future of the theological college while the cathedral, he recorded, had died a natural death. Funds were not forthcoming and the shortage of clergy was worse than ever. "What creature far lower than tithe proctor," he moaned, "can be found to wring the dollars from the fishermen?"[11] He admitted that, by the strenuous efforts of himself and the governor, the church was making a dent in its financial problems, but the result was "only spasmodic charity." Feild's financial problems, although partly the result of the credit system and lower-class poverty in Newfoundland, were mainly a symptom of the difficulty of building on the voluntary system a church that for hundreds of years had eschewed that route in favour of government handouts. "The problem with our church," said the Reverend Benjamin Smith of King's Cove, "is that it started, supported by foreign aid, and gave gratuitous service and now it's difficult to break the habit."[12] Both Smith and Feild instituted a system whereby those who demanded baptisms, marriages, and the like were expected to pay a set fee or be denied the service. That policy aroused great opposition and eventually led to outright revolt on the part of some congregations.

Compounding the church's difficulties were the losses suffered to the Wesleyans. By 1840 the Wesleyans had 14 ministers compared to the Church of England's 10. On top of that, they had 10 local preachers,

107 Sabbath school teachers, and 9 day schools. Throughout the 1830s and 1840s they expanded faster than any other denomination – their membership grew by 33 per cent in the decade before 1845 and by 40 per cent in the decade following. Their gains alarmed the Anglicans, especially since Wesleyan gains were Anglican losses. The propensity of Anglicans and Wesleyans to attend each other's services indiscriminately tended to favour the Wesleyans, and the union of all evangelical Protestants in the mid-1830s for the purposes of education was generally believed to have greatly accelerated that trend. Then the evangelical movement scored a big victory with the successful conclusion of the Bible battle in 1843. However, the evangelical revival in the Church of England was checked in the United Kingdom by the late 1830s; and by the mid-1840s it was dead in its tracks in Newfoundland.

The arrival in St John's of the high churchman Bishop Feild, an enthusiastic proponent of the "tractarian" views of the Oxford movement, marked the institution of a church program that eventually alienated all low churchmen and dissenters. Feild's attempts to replace low church clerics with those of his own hue divided his clergy and congregations. At the same time, his questioning of the legitimacy of Wesleyan sacraments and his practice of remarrying and rebaptizing those who had received those services from Wesleyan clerics led to bitter disputes with Methodists all over Newfoundland. Feild's solution to Anglican financial difficulties and the clerical-recruitment problem – ordaining as clergy all the Newfoundland School Society teachers – led to the implacable opposition of the Wesleyans and an outright public rupture between the bishop and the Newfoundland School Society in 1848. Failing to gain control of the NSS, Feild announced that, when the 1843 Education Act expired in 1850, he would seek separate schools for Anglicans throughout Newfoundland. But by 1850 the Wesleyans held the balance of political power in the districts of Conception Bay and Burin, two formerly Anglican districts. Even with complete unity among Anglicans, they could now at best control only six out of the fifteen electoral districts. Political power had slipped to the Catholics and Wesleyans.

Supporting the coalition government led by Harvey and later LeMarchant, Bishop Fleming and his clergy immersed themselves throughout the 1840s in church affairs, particularly in the construction of the great cathedral in the capital. But Catholics were continually plagued with financial difficulties to such an extent that by 1847 Fleming begged even the king of France for a stipend. In 1848, by which date he was exhausted and in failing health, Fleming accepted a £300 annual salary from the British government. When he died in

1850, John T. Mullock, who in ecclesiastical circles was a giant figure with an international reputation, succeeded Fleming.[13] Mullock brought to the Roman Catholic Church in Newfoundland such imposing leadership that he was able to earn the unflinching loyalty of all his clergy.

Bishop Mullock had a signal list of achievements not only in clerical affairs but in the social and political sphere as well.[14] Perhaps his greatest accomplishment was the placing of his diocese and the whole church in Newfoundland on a secure financial foundation by the inauguration of a novel program of fund-raising.[15] Mullock inherited and perfected the fund-raising schemes of Bishop Fleming and added a new twist to the fish-collection program that overcame all its weaknesses. He instituted, in its stead, two days of special fishing for the church on the holy days of Sts Peter and Paul on 29 June and Lady Day on 15 August. It was such a novelty that Mullock had to check with the pope before its implementation. Setting aside special days obviated the difficulties of fish collecting by enabling the fishermen to compile a special catch on days when they would not have heretofore fished. The fish would be salted and cured separately and afterwards shipped to the church account. It worked so well that it soon passed into the folklore of the Irish Catholics of Newfoundland and was adopted by all Catholic parishes in the colony. Thus by 1850 the Roman Catholic Church was entering a new age in the history of Newfoundland, united under new and improved leadership.

Meanwhile, while Governor LeMarchant was reposing on his bed of roses, a rising political star was making plans that would soon greatly disturb the political landscape. An émigré lawyer named Philip Little, prospective by-election candidate, was extremely impatient with the Reform party then occupying the House of Assembly. Now popularly known as the Liberal party, the Reformers had entered the decade of the 1850s as a dispirited and leaderless political instrument. The political developments of the 1840s had done serious harm to their claim to be the party of reform and change. Their leading figures had been subdued with government jobs, and the conciliatory policy of Governor Harvey had robbed the party of its crusading spirit. The quest for Catholic equality had once been their driving force, but in the 1840s the Reformers could only sit quietly in the amalgamated assembly and observe first Harvey and then LeMarchant remove that problem from their list of grievances. Not only did Catholics advance in the civil service and, after the restoration of the old constitution, gain appointments to the upper levels of government, but the first Roman Catholic lawyer, Philip Little, obtained admittance to the bar. To top it all off, when Judge J.G. Bourne was suspended in 1844 by

Governor Harvey, an Irish Roman Catholic, Thomas Norton, took his place as the chief justice of Newfoundland. True liberals saw a desperate need for a new platform and cast anxious glances towards their fellow liberals in Newfoundland's sister colonies on the North American mainland. Then their wandering in the political wilderness of the 1840s came back to haunt them more painfully. While they had succumbed to the flattery and guile of a wily British governor in St John's, their sister liberal parties had acquired the full measure of responsible government on the mainland. Nova Scotia had been the first to acquire the coveted prize in January 1848; Nova Scotia was followed by New Brunswick in February; then followed the United Canadas in March.

Death had removed the two leading reformers of the last half-century. Carson had died in 1843 and Morris in 1849. Nugent, who had been the de facto leader since 1837, had taken one of the St John's Assembly seats in the 1842 election but shortly thereafter had accepted government patronage as school superintendent. He received fairly wide acclaim for his efforts in both Roman Catholic and Protestant schools, and, when a non-denominational academy was set up by legislative enactment in 1844, he was appointed the junior master. Following his electoral defeat in the election of 1848, Nugent left politics permanently to devote his life to college teaching and administration. The Liberals, therefore, entered the decade of the 1850s virtually leaderless.

Of the three leading Liberals remaining at the time, John Kent, Robert John Parsons, and Lawrence O'Brien, the first-named was the most experienced. A fiery orator and member for St John's, Kent had first been elected to the Assembly in 1832 and had continued to sit in the legislature for that riding. A Roman Catholic, brother-in-law of Bishop Fleming, and member of the middle class of general-merchandise importers, Kent was well qualified to lead an attack on the Church of England–wealthy mercantile class alliance. However, Kent's close identification with the Irish establishment and his past notorious allegiance to the pro-clerical cause severely weakened his potential to broaden the base of Liberal support. In addition, time apparently had mellowed his aggressiveness; having accepted governmental appointments under the amalgamated legislature, Kent continued the practice of compromising with the government by accepting the collectorship of customs in 1849. Much to the disgust of his colleague, Robert John Parsons, Kent believed that courting the governor's favour was a necessity in the colonies. Outright opposition, he thought, would tend to align the governor with the detestable Tories, thereby making that party too strong for the Liberals.[16] Kent, after the expiration of the amalgamated legislature, continued to court and be courted by the governor.

Parsons, on the other hand, desired no compromise with the existing political system and by 1850 was becoming extremely impatient with Kent.[17] Parsons had first gained public fame when he became printer of the *Patriot* after Carson had left the newspaper for a seat in the Assembly in 1833.[18] Later, after a series of damaging libel losses, Parsons relinquished ownership of the paper to Nugent in 1837. He then acted as the *Patriot*'s editor until 1840, when he reacquired full and sole ownership. As the *Patriot*'s editor, Parsons gained a reputation for his devastating attacks on the exclusiveness of the representative system and his vigorous support of the cause of Reform and Catholic equality. He made mortal enemies of the governor's officials, the upper-house councillors, and the judges. After his stinging rebuke of Chief Justice Boulton in the celebrated editorial of May 1835, "Stick a Pin Here: Beneficial Effects of Hanging Illustrated," Parsons became even more of a hero in Catholic eyes through his confrontation with Boulton in a legal suit. His imprisonment, at the hand of the same judge he had libelled, also spread his name throughout the British Isles and the British North American colonies. Subsequently, his early release, together with the British government's rebuke of Boulton, was the first Reform victory against the chief justice and made Parsons the toast of the colony.

To the Catholics, Parsons became as highly regarded as either Carson or Kent, but he fell from favour in 1840. In that year Parsons split with Nugent and the priests to support his friend Douglas in the by-election against the priests' candidate, O'Brien. Parsons severely castigated the Roman Catholic bishop and his priests for entering politics at all and flirted with the idea of the merchants becoming the basis for a new Liberal party. Within the year, however, he repudiated that alternative, made his peace with the priests, and embraced Bishop Fleming as once again the heart and soul of the Liberal party.[19] But the damage to Parson's credibility had been severe, and his re-conversion came too late to save his printing and newspaper business from serious losses. In the interim, Nugent had founded a rival paper, the *Vindicator*, and Assembly patronage had been diverted from the *Patriot*.[20] Parsons was forced to reduce his operations to a semi-weekly journal. In the 1840 by-elections, he opposed attempts by the Nugent Liberals to confine the party to non-natives. The pro-native elements gave their support to Nugent's opponents, and Parsons began to champion the native cause. Subsequently, he played a leading role in founding the Newfoundland Natives Society to promote native interests. He was soon able to re-establish himself as a political force to be reckoned with and, when William Carson died in 1843, Parsons won his seat in the Assembly for St John's. There he championed what had by then become his favourite cause, responsible government. Parsons had been the first to take up the cause of responsible government when, in the late 1830s, he publicly took issue with Carson on the subject. Parsons demanded full responsible government in the sense we know it today and personally condemned Carson for having the gall to oppose him on that topic. By 1850 Parsons was personally berating Kent for a lack of commitment to the same concept.

As a writer and orator, Parsons had an irrepressible tendency to indulge in gross exaggeration and extremism, a tendency that in the past had landed him in court to defend himself in numerous libel cases. He allowed that same proneness to reign so unchecked at times that, even in political disagreements with his own friends, he fell into the trap of personally defaming them for their audacity to disagree. In 1839–40 Parsons launched bitter personal attacks at various times on Carson, Morris, Kent, and Nugent.[21] By 1851 Parsons was so impatient with Kent that he charged the latter with embezzlement of charity funds.[22] Kent's subsequent libel suit proved that the Liberal party could not be expected to look to either Kent or Parsons for effective leadership.

Lawrence O'Brien entered the House of Assembly for the first time in 1840. Representing the district of St John's, the Roman Catholic O'Brien held a share, at least, in the Liberal leadership. It could be said, perhaps, that he held the titular leadership for in 1850 he introduced the Increased Representatives Bill in the House of Assembly. That measure involved an issue that was destined to dominate political debate in the 1850s. Party government, it was widely believed, could not work efficiently in a small elected house of only fifteen members; however, some believed that increased representation, once accomplished, would render responsible government inevitable.[23] Even the Colonial Office considered the existing legislature's limited size a major obstacle to the introduction of responsible government. A house of only fifteen members was, the colonial secretary told the governor, "quite inadequate to the efficient working of a system under which choice is to be made of the chief advisers of the Government, and of the principal officers of the administration, from the leading members of the Legislature."[24] On the other hand, the issue of responsible government could quite easily be reduced to the question of representation in the assembly, for the manner of enlarging that body would decide which Party would command the majority under the responsible system. And so, the Liberals, now in control of the lower house, wished simply to double existing representation, thereby doubling their numbers in the Assembly and enlarging their majority over the Tories. Liberals also sought to exploit Wesleyan-Anglican rivalries and resisted electoral subdivision, especially in Burin and Conception Bay, where Wesleyans held the balance of power between the two denominations. All of these objectives were at the heart of the Increased Representatives Bill of 1850

The purpose of the bill was, in keeping with the Liberal goals, to double the representation of each of the nine constituencies.[25] Nevertheless, in supporting the measure, O'Brien put forward the usual party line – that electoral subdivision would create a closed borough system under the control of the merchants. O'Brien failed to arouse any enthusiasm from his own side of the house, however, and no lively debate took place on the subject. Although the Representatives Bill passed the Assembly, it received little attention from the press other than a comment that it would provide a much more cumbrous mechanism for working out the colony's comparatively simple affairs.[26] Furthermore, because O'Brien had waited until near the end of the session to introduce the bill, and because it was not contemplated to come into effect until 1853, the Legislative Council passed it over until the next session.[27]

O'Brien's lack of enthusiasm and drive were not the only factors militating against his being the inspiration for the Liberals.[28] Engaged in extensive business operations, O'Brien, the wealthiest Roman Catholic merchant in the colony, was a member of St John's upper class. But, what was more significant, O'Brien as Irish expatriate, had, like Kent, been tarred with the pro-clerical brush in the 1830s. O'Brien's leadership would not, therefore, be totally acceptable to an anti-mercantile party attempting to enlist support from denominations other than Roman Catholic, and any presumption of his to that position was removed when, after the session of 1850, he accepted an appointment to the upper house.[29]

The void created by the inaction of Kent and his followers and by the elevation of O'Brien to the Council was quickly filled by John Little and his brother Philip, who for almost two years had been active voices crying in the political wilderness. The older brother John Little had been born in Ireland in 1817 but raised in Charlottetown, Prince Edward Island, where his family had moved when he was but a child. There he grew up in an atmosphere of struggle for tenant and Catholic rights.[30] In the 1840s he became an active reformer in the Irish movement for repeal of the union and also in the local struggle for responsible government. In the general election of 1846, he was returned to the House of Assembly in Charlottetown. Because of election violence in Little's district, however, the results were declared null and void and John Little and his running mate were expelled from the Assembly. In the ensuing by-election of March 1847 Little found himself in the midst of the most violent election disturbances in Prince Edward Island history. Then, Irish Catholics and Scottish Presbyterians fought each other in the famous Belfast riots which led to the deaths of at least four people. The election was suspended and held again three weeks later in the presence of about two hundred soldiers. Little refused to get involved a second time and shortly after left Prince Edward Island to join the law practice of his younger brother Philip in St John's. There, both apparently worked behind the scenes to create solidarity among Liberal party candidates for the general election of 1848. Although they achieved only small success in this respect, yet they came to understand the weaknesses in the Liberal party as well as the social and economic trends then transforming Newfoundland society. Those were trends that the Kent Liberals had been unable either to discern or to exploit by the adoption of a party platform that was at once futuristic yet practical.

The decades following the Napoleonic Wars in Newfoundland had witnessed an ever-expanding population against the background of a continuing decline in the quantity and quality of salt-fish production. Those developments imposed a severe economic strain on outport firms, especially those competing as branches of English companies. They began to lose ground considerably to firms located and controlled in the capital.[31] By the 1840s St John's had achieved a dominant position in the Newfoundland economy – a position it would never relinquish.

The consequent restructuring of the Newfoundland fishery was destined to have enormous social and political consequences. As the transatlantic firms gradually withdrew or went bankrupt, outport operations were transferred to small local firms that arose in attempts to fill the void. But the burden of providing credit and supplying fishermen through a hungry winter was more than these local merchants could bear and their reaction was to turn to St John's. This tended to increase the influence and the power of many St John's firms. But mercantile interests in St John's also found the financial obligations too great to shoulder and were eager to escape the responsibility of credit by passing it on to someone else. Governor LeMarchant noted that "the merchants as a body have determined to remove from their shoulders the burden of supplies." The result, he told the Colonial Office, was to "throw the people altogether on their own resources."[32] Together with the recession in the salt-cod industry and the population expansion, the increasingly tight-fisted attitude of St Johns's merchants occasioned more and more distress. Throughout the 1820s and

1830s these trends had been masked by the boom in seal-fishery production, especially in Conception Bay and the St John's area.[33] However, bad seal harvests in the late 1830s and early 1840s, along with the advent of steam in the mid-1840s, signalled the beginning of a permanent downward trend in the regional sealing industry. Henceforth, sealing would be dominated by St John's.

At the same time, Harvey's government had come to power, and his subsequent policy of attempting to placate all interests ultimately led to the charting of a new role for the state in the political economy of Newfoundland. Harvey expanded public spending, especially in the civil service and on public works such as roads and bridges. The object of civil-service spending was to placate the middle class, and work on roads and bridges was meant to gain the loyalty of the lower class. The ultimate result of Harvey's administrative efforts was to convince Newfoundlanders that the government belonged to them and was all-inclusive.[34] Just when economic and other forces were cutting the traditional ties between fishermen and merchants, Harvey's policies tended to replace such ties with fishermen-government ties instead. His successor, unwittingly it seems, accentuated the same phenomenon by involving the government directly in the economic development of the colony.[35] For the promotion of agriculture, Governor LeMarchant established a model farm at Bonavista in 1848. In the same year he founded a net-making factory in St John's, and in 1849 he drew up plans for an additional factory for the manufacture of homespun cloth.

Under the leadership of the Littles, the St John's middle class was quick to perceive its advantage. The colonial government could become the instrument by which the middle class might supplant the mercantile elite and also acquire leadership over the lower class. Of course, to achieve all of this, some program was required to mobilize the St John's middle class and extend its appeal throughout the colony. Tha program was supplied by John Little soon after he took over as editor of the *Courier* in January 1849.

In this position, Little soon staked out his incomparable claim as the champion of St John's middle-class interests. He adamantly opposed LeMarchant's idea of municipally incorporating the capital since it would mean an additional taxation burden for the middle class. Instead, Little proposed the alternative of administering St John's through the colonial civil service; general improvements such as water and sewerage would be financed by the colonial government, with additional taxation if necessary on luxuries, liquor, and absentee landlords. Almost daily, Little championed municipal improvements for the colonial capital ranging from garbage removal to rebuilding the burned town at government expense. But, most important of all, Little boldly advanced for the colonial government a developmental role that envisioned its main responsibility as creating a buoyant economy to ensure the prosperity of all. Government, he declared, should develop the interior of Newfoundland by sponsoring the immigration of thousands of experienced farmers from the British Isles. Only in this way could there be developed an agricultural industry independent of, and not subordinant to, the fishery. In addition, government should establish a series of factories for the manufacture of boots, nets, caps, and other supplies required by the fishing and farming population. While Little's opponents and pro-government forces ridiculed the *Courier* for its impractical and unrealizable goals, John Little had covered his tracks by announcing from the very beginning the program that would deliver the things he had in mind – responsible government.

As soon as Little took over the *Courier* editorship, he issued the clarion call for responsible government. Afterwards, while he continually elaborated on his developmental program, he never ceased to advance the cause of responsible government. The *Courier* seized the initiative on that issue, taking it away from Kent, Parsons, and the *Patriot*. Soon the *Courier* and responsible government were the talk of all the political pundits, and rival newspapers were drawn into the debate. The result was that the political agenda had been taken over by the *Courier*, which expanded in both size and circulation.[36] The *Courier* drew the attention of newspapers in other British North American colonies and the ire of the governor and his officials in St John's.

Responsible government, said the *Courier*, must be granted as the birthright of British descendants, and the newspaper scoffed at the idea that Newfoundlanders must earn such a government. Said the *Courier*: "It is a false cry kept up by official hyenas to deceive the unwary and gain for themselves and their patrons the lion's share of the public money."[37] In order to capture the attention of those unwary ones, Little put a human face on the grievances of all Newfoundlanders by focusing on the personal comforts of Governor LeMarchant, Attorney General James Simms, and Colonial Secretary James Crowdy – all Englishmen. Those three were personally maligned and abused as the Family Compact, a group of officials who were personally responsible for all the debt and pauperism in the colony. The *Courier* stated that the government of Newfoundland was generally given to such people as LeMarchant, Simms, or Crowdy. Thus, "some needy dependent, not having the slightest pretensions to statesmanship ... on his arrival in this country ... is always surrounded by the same family compact, who fattens upon the very vitals of the colony."[38]

The *Courier*'s focus on the persons of LeMarchant, Simms, and Crowdy struck a responsive chord with the populace of St John's. Many were accustomed to seeing Simms and Crowdy stiffly walking to Government House in their long coats and high hats – high hats that were often the sport of young boys with snowballs, a custom the *Ledger* was inclined to blame on the Roman Catholic priests. But the most telling blows struck by the *Courier* were those delivered over the distribution of the fire-relief funds.

The fire-relief funds were those collected from British and North American sources towards alleviation of the distress caused by the 1846 fire. By 1848 an enormous sum of more than £102,000, almost double the entire colonial budget, had been collected; however, there was a widespread perception that the money was squandered on needs other than those of the fire victims.[39] That perception arose principally from the fact that much of the money had been unbelievably spent on public buildings or at the personal whim of LeMarchant. The latter had constructed a controversial promenade around the mouth of the Waterford River. And upwards of one-third of the funds had been spent on the Church of England, much to the dismay of Roman Catholics and other Protestants. The *Courier* championed the rights of those religious groups in order to widen the breach between Anglican officials, on the one side, and Roman Catholics and Wesleyans, who were the majority of the population, on the other. LeMarchant was placed on the defensive with respect to the administration of the fire-relief funds but was particularly stung by *Courier* demands for a public inquiry. What rankled LeMarchant most of all was the charge that he himself had personally misappropriated the money.[40]

Early in his term of office it appears that LeMarchant had discerned the economic and political trends then remaking Newfoundland society and also understood the significance these trends carried especially for the St John's middle class.[41] The governor sought to place that group on the defensive by having his Assembly supporters advance the cause of a St John's municipal corporation. LeMarchant also attempted to throw the administration of poor relief on the capital by the introduction of a poor-rate system. But he was outmanoeuvred by the *Courier* and *Patriot*, which rallied public support for an elected corporation, an alternative damned by the Conservatives as a ruse to throw the city into the hands of the Roman Catholic rabble-rousers, the priests. LeMarchant's reaction was to place a severe restriction on further distribution of relief money and to centralize its administration in a small circle of officials around his office.[42] Thus, LeMarchant retreated to the security and comfort of his officials and the upper-class merchants. The St John's middle-class leaders, he believed, were a rapacious bunch of greedy, troublesome spirits who wanted a complete surrender of all relief money to them. On the other hand, LeMarchant believed that the mercantile elite had behaved admirably and deserved to be rewarded. In catering to that elite, LeMarchant played right into the hands of middle-class spirits such as the Littles and R.J. Parsons. The governor fired the relief committee once instituted by Governor Harvey. It was dominated, he charged, by Roman Catholics and Wesleyans who were too much involved in it for their own interests;[43] he replaced it with another committee, this one dominated by upper-class merchants. His move met with profuse praise from all shades of Conservatives[44] and with the universal condemnation of the middle-class leaders.[45]

However, LeMarchant felt secure in his own haven surrounded by his officials and upper-class merchants. Privately, he felt that a determined opposition to responsible government could maintain his position. He also decided to circumvent any Roman Catholic effort to exploit sectarian grievances by appointing Laurence O'Brien to the upper house. As soon as news of O'Brien's appointment leaked out, John Little made plans to capture the Assembly seat that would be vacated by O'Brien. But LeMarchant postponed O'Brien's appointment on the pretext of avoiding a winter election. It was more likely, however, that the reason for the delay was LeMarchant's desire to outmanoeuvre the troublesome Little.

The resulting lull in the political climate in late 1849 and early 1850 was destined to be only the calm before the political storm. But the governor could be forgiven for having thought otherwise. John Little, having resigned from the *Courier* apparently in anticipation of the by-election, quickly sank into obscurity.[46] When the by-election finally took place in November 1850, John Little's place was taken by his younger, much quieter, and less aggressive brother, Philip Francis. Supported by Kent, O'Brien, and Parsons, Philip Little won an easy election victory and in January 1851 took his seat in the Assembly for St John's.

To the surprise of many, Little quickly came to dominate the House of Assembly, and his behaviour throughout the session revealed a thoroughly planned, intelligent agenda. He immediately promoted the program that had been set out in the *Courier* over the previous two years – that of advancing the cause of responsible government through increasing representation in the House of Assembly. In order to keep the spotlight on that issue, Little would need to focus debate and to force divisions which, even if he lost, would give the perception that he was not losing momentum. As it turned out, Little was well aware of the potential for success as well as his limitations in the house, and he also knew the materials with which he had to work on the government and Opposition benches. Winser of Ferryland, and Hanrahan and Mulloy[47] of Conception Bay – elected as Liberals in the previous election – were expected to stand by Little. R.J. Parsons, his sitting colleague from St John's, had already been clamouring for new Liberal leadership, was unswervingly devoted to constitutional reform, and had nominated Little for the 1850 by-election. That gave Little five votes, three short of a majority in the fifteen-member house. But the controversial and imposing figure of Ambrose Shea, once a professed Liberal, now sat in the house as an elected Conservative for the district of Placentia–St Mary's. Shea had acquired a large personal following, so that in 1848 he had been able to select as his running mate John Delaney;[48] both Shea and Delaney scored easy election victories and sat opposite Little as government supporters. In response to *Courier* articles, however, Ambrose and Edward Shea of the *Newfoundlander* announced in 1849 that they favoured responsible government in principle;[49] the Liberals could have the Sheas' support if they avoided the excesses of former years. The challenge for Little was to prove that he was in command of the party, that it was a conservative middle-class movement, and that the Nugent-Troy style of priest campaigning belonged to the past. Then Little could reach out to Shea for the two Placentia votes needed to bring the Liberals even with the seven Conservative government supporters in the house. The two possibilities for the eighth vote were G.H. Emerson and John Kent. Emerson had confessed to having been converted to responsible government while studying law;[50] however, personal patronage and family ties had cemented Emerson to Governor LeMarchant, and he had been elected as a Conservative in Twillingate-Fogo in the 1848 general election. The most realistic possibility for that eighth vote was John Kent. As Little's sitting colleague for the district of St John's, Kent had once professed himself the champion of responsible government. While Kent never pretended to be other than a Liberal, he had accepted the governor's patronage and was widely believed to have led the Liberals to political obloquy. Yet by 1851 there was a widespread perception that, if someone could stir up the political waters in favour of constitutional reform, John Kent would have no choice but to fall in line. As soon as the 1851 throne speech was read, Philip Francis Little served notice that he was the person that the situation required.

Little was on his feet immediately in the debate on the address-in-reply and, supported by Parsons, launched a long, oratorical speech which made a vehement personal attack on LeMarchant and his officials.[51] Little and Parsons blamed them for every kind of wrong that they could see on the social and economic scene in the colony: for the debt and deficits, for bribery, intimidation, espionage, corruption, and misappropriation of government funds, and for neglect of the sick and the poor and those suffering from the fire. Their object, obviously, was to render LeMarchant's government so contemptible that it would become embarrassing for Kent and Shea to continue supporting it. Parsons said that the country had long enough been humbugged by such a paltry thing as the governor's speech, while Little declared that only responsible government would bring an end to the people's misery. The Conservative R.B. Job tried to adjourn the debate, but he was attacked by Little and Parsons for wanting to get to Government House where LeMarchant's favourites were all assembling "for the purpose of partaking of His Excellency's good cheer." Parsons charged that "the wine of Government House would furnish many a cordial to many of the sick poor," and, to torment LeMarchant and the Conservatives, he staged a mini-filibuster that lasted for several hours.[52] Members should not be lured from their sacred duty, warned Little, "by the siren song that had been so gracefully sung by the representative of Her Majesty."

Kent and Shea were aghast at the ferocity of the assault on LeMarchant, and, in reply, Kent chose to attack Parsons instead of Little. Defending Parsons, Little said that it was time "to ripple the placid waters of governmental corruption." The justification for such strong language as he and Parsons had used, he said, could be found "in the reprehensible conduct of the Executive towards the people of this country." The executive, which he termed "the official defenders of corruption and misrule," would no doubt cling to the pillars of the citadel of misgovernment, but it was the duty of the people's representatives "to burst open with sledge hammer force the portals of freedom."[53] Winser joined Parsons and Little in wielding the sledgehammer and Kent and Shea seemed to reel from the blows. Winser and Parsons wanted Little to focus attention away from LeMarchant personally, and Kent advised him to attack the system. Little, however was to have none of it. The system was made up of ideas and human agency, he pointed out, "and the individuals, through whose agency the nefarious system was carried out and maintained, must of necessity be the only tangible objects of attack and reprobation." Little, therefore, launched another assault on the person of LeMarchant. If the governor wanted to absolve himself of all blame, he thundered, "then why didn't he call as his advisers those who had the confidence of the people?"[54]

Between sittings of the debate on the throne speech, Little pulled off a political stunt more typical of modern-day politics. In order to draw public attention to the plight of the unhappy people suffering because of the fire, Little toured the so-called temporary wooden sheds still standing five years after the fire, with miserable inmates dying nearly every other day. Next day in the house, Little blamed all the misery on LeMarchant personally. "In one room were to be seen," he lamented, "an aged woman, about seventy years old – another woman who had two days before been delivered of an infant; and a little distance from her, in the same apartment, a sailor stretched on a bundle of shavings." This, he said, was all occurring while LeMarchant, "the head of the firm of misgovernment," was pocketing the people's money and enjoying the luxuries of Government House.[55] Shea now begged Little not to press his amendment, which was bitterly condemnatory of the governor personally, and said that if Little complied and fairly brought the responsible government question forward, then Shea himself would support it. Shea appeared to have become aware of the irrestible populist appeal of Little's strategy and program. Little was exultant, thanked Shea for his support, and allowed his amendment to die on the order paper.

During the days of the Throne Speech debate, Little had arranged for Liberal supporters throughout the Avalon to prepare petitions on responsible government. Upon the conclusion of that debate, Little, Parsons, and Winser began to present those petitions, using every such occasion to denounce the official oligarchy and expostulate on the merits of responsible government. One of the highlights of these debates came when Harbour Grace Liberals gave their petitions to the Conservative, James L. Prendergast, for presentation in the house. Prendergast, a close supporter and admirer of LeMarchant, was quite embarrassed when forced to stand in his place and read a long-winded petition denouncing the governor and demanding responsible government. Little and his cohorts laughed uproariously at Prendergast's predicament while Prendergast himself lost his patience and attacked Little as attempting to usurp the Liberal leadership from Kent.[56] When, after several weeks of debate, all the petitions were presented, Little introduced his Increased Representatives Bill and the momentum continued. (See Appendix, Table 2).

Like O'Brien's measure of the previous year, Little's Representatives Bill simply called for doubling the existing representation without any change in district boundaries. Little argued that, from his own point of view, it was a strictly non-partisan arrangement; and if opponents of the bill disagreed in any particular, then it was up to them to prove their case. In fact, doubling was a clever political trick. If the present Liberals could maintain their seats, then they would be guaranteed sixteen out of the thirty seats in a new house. Nevertheless, Little, who was aware that the Conservatives would seek to subdivide the ridings to their own advantage, tried a pre-emptive strike at their expected line of attack. Only traitors to their country, he declared, would even contemplate carving up or subdividing a district in any way. Subdivision, he said, everywhere allowed petty tyrants such as the landlords on Prince Edward Island to exert their sway. If districts were divided, he said, responsible government "would prove a curse to the country," adding, "Let there be a general system of representation established and the liberties of the country will be secured."[57] Kent followed with a speech giving full support to Little's bill, the principle of which he had supported in the amalgamated house. Subdividing districts, he said, would set up a system of close boroughs where class interests would prevail.

Hugh Hoyles, the Conservative leader, adamantly opposed the bill on the ground that it would place the House of Assembly entirely in the hands of the Roman Catholics. He wanted to subdivide districts, especially Conception Bay that had a majority of Protestants; he pointed out that in the last general election three Roman Catholics had been elected there. But, his opponents reminded him, one of those Catholics was a notorious anti-cleric who had even been returned as a government supporter. One anti-cleric did not matter, Hoyles retorted, because the district had a majority of Protestants who deserved to have the majority representation. The Catholics always made up for what they lacked in numbers, he charged, "by superior activity and unity of action." Thus, Hoyles rehashed the old anti-Catholic arguments of the 1830s, knowing that an anti-Catholic campaign could win a majority for the Conservatives only if he could unite the Protestants in Conception Bay. Little must have looked on with delight as Hoyles dragged sectarianism back onto centre stage, a move that prompted the Conservative Prendergast to stand up and denounce sectarianism. Prendergast thereafter took a stand diametrically opposed to Hoyles's position.

Hoyles and his supporters were placed on the defensive as Little denounced the idea of framing bills on the basis of denominational affiliation. If sectarian distinctions were adopted as the basis of representation, Little said, "there would follow confusion and turmoil without end, each denomination contending on some particular right or privilege which it might deem essential to the promotion of its own special interests." He would never permit the demon of denominational hostility and intolerance to run riot within the walls of the house. He lyrically declared: "He would rather lend his aid to chain the monster within its own dark corner or to some solitary rock, remote from the mansions of the poor and toil-worn thousands for whose well-being and harmony they were legislating; where the vultures of discord might prey upon its vitals, rather than permit, like another Prometheus, to snatch celestial fire from the altar of the Most High, for the purpose of inflaming the passions and prejudices of society, and eventually setting in flames the Temple of Freedom."[58]

Little revelled in the knowledge that he had made a great speech; the spectators in galleries created such a din that the speaker feared they would literally bring down the house. But, best of all, Shea was standing to oppose Hoyles's views; the very person who had deserted the Liberals because of the excesses of the 1830s now recognized in Hoyles's speech an attempt to resurrect them. Little anticipated victory for the Representatives Bill, and he also thought that, after the bill's passage, responsible government be achieved. But Hoyles had the house cleared several times, and the resulting chaos left the Assembly with reduced numbers. Hoyles, spotting an advantage, pounced on it immediately. Forcing a division in the report stage of the bill, Hoyles caused it to be defeated. Little was in a state of shock. For several days, confusion reigned about what had occurred. It eventually became clear that Shea and his colleague Delaney had, amidst the din, slipped out of the building altogether. Little bitterly attacked Shea for sabotaging the bill and Shea was forced to make his position unmistakably clear. He announced that he thought the bill had passed, that its defeat was a surprise to him, and that he would support Little's position unreservedly in the next session of the house. Little tested Shea's intentions by moving to rescind proceedings with regard to the bill. Shea gave him full support, but Kent ruled him out of order and berated Little on his mode of proceeding. Then Little for the first time lashed out at Kent personally, telling him, "Sir, I shall proceed in the way which appears best to myself."[59] When the galleries responded with a tremendous ovation for Little, Kent, now sitting as speaker, threatened to arrest everyone if they did not quiet down. But the crowd paid no attention to Kent, who, once with the tilt of his head, could dominate the galleries. Little waved his hand, and the overflowing galleries went instantly quiet. Kent had lost the galleries to a new populist agitator, Philip Little, and Prendergast taunted the latter with having surreptitiously dethroned Kent.

Little had no time to cherish the victory, for the Conservatives retaliated by bringing in supply, a tactic Little recognized immediately. The Conservatives' intention was to force supply through the house as quickly as possible and adjourn the Assembly with the address on responsible government still on the order paper. Little then raised the struggle to a new level by announcing that not one cent would be voted until the address was passed. This marked the start of one of the most celebrated filibusters in the political history of Newfoundland.

Little began the filibuster by speaking on the causes of the American revolution, continued with a description of the rebellions in the Canadas in 1837–38, and followed with a review of the struggle for responsible government in the other British North American colonies. It is time Newfoundlanders took a stand, he declared, and insisted on being placed on the same footing as the other British colonies in North America. Little dramatically asked: "The country is in a state of chrysalis – its political institutions are in their infancy. Were they satisfied to remain behind the spirit of the age?"[60]

It was of the utmost importance, Little said, that the government be fully cognizant that they depended upon "the people through that House for the means of carrying on the public business." If he had confidence in the executive, he admitted, he would vote supplies, but as he had none he would "oppose supplies to a government that employed its influence to oppose progress." Prendergast assumed the task of defending LeMarchant; Parsons and Winser took turns first speaking in the same vein as Little and then resting the voice in order to begin anew. Kent attacked the procedure and lyrically spoke of the virtues of moderation, saying: "It is by the operation of time that constitutional principles can be disseminated through the land and made to flash upon the mind and strike root in the heart of the country. As in the physical world the summits of the highest mountains are first illuminated by the rays of the rising sun and the gloom of the recumbent valley is gradually invaded by the spreading flood of light, so in politics, as also in morals, the diffusion of correct principles proceeds by gradation, till the public mind becomes irradicated [sic] with the advancing light of reason, and the darkness of doubt and unbelief is swept away before the spreading effulgence of truth."

In such a manner Kent had rationalized his compromising with the government while the party he presumed to lead had drifted off into the political wilderness. But Philip Little came to the rescue with a reply to Kent on the subject of moderation; even by partisans on the opposite side, the reply was seen to carry such force as to cause considerable political damage to Kent.

If Kent could not agree with Little's position, then the fault was not with Little but with Kent. "The government with which the country is cursed," said Little, "demands at their hands something more stern and truthful than soft words and bland phrases." Then, in dealing with the moderation argument, he intellectually demolished it to such an extent that even to mention moderation again risked personal embarrassment for Kent. He had no fear, Little confessed, that moderate men "would be seduced away from the cause of public justice and political honesty by the devices of pseudo-alarmists." He said that there was only one instrument that truly expressed the wishes of the people of Newfoundland, and that instrument was the House of Assembly through its Liberal representatives. Little had no intention of letting the British government believe that the existing corrupt oligarchy was supported by the mass of the people in the colony. Neither was he worried that moderate men would become enamoured of a government that was riding roughshod over the liberties of the country, and that was exploiting the cupidity, vanity, and weakness of the people's representatives in order to oppress the people.

Little continued by saying that he had confidence that the people would not suffer themselves to be blinkered and humbugged any longer. Nor should they remain attached to a system of government under which their labour was taxed in order to support a reckless and vicious executive intent on degrading and insulting them. People did not want a government that could not sustain itself for a day without employing public money to corrupt elected representatives. They did not want an executive that had misrepresented, vilified, cheated, and swindled them; on the contrary, corrupt government officials would be met with virtuous indignation. Elected representatives were sent to this house, said Little, to redress wrongs and stay the flood of executive aggressions; they were not sent to be corrupted, pinioned, and nailed to the mast of that same executive profligacy. He continued to the shouts of "Hear, hear!" from Winser and Parsons. Little warned those who recalled the suspension of the constitution in 1841 that the principal actors in that drama had transgressed the limits of the constitution; but, he pointed out "we kept within them." Stopping the supplies, he declared with telling effect, is a perfectly legitimate tool under the British constitution. Without its protective privilege the British government "would be nothing more or less than rank despotism."[61]

Little's speech left such an overwhelming impact that Kent felt constrained to reply. This rebuttal amounted, in effect, to an apology for Kent's lacklustre behaviour over the previous several years. The eventual result of the proceedings was a capitulation from the government benches. The colonial treasurer conceded that the administration would not oppose the introduction of the address on responsible government, and Little immediately dropped his filibuster on the supplies. However, he warned that, even though the Opposition would not withhold supplies altogether, it intended to scrutinize carefully every single line item on the grounds of economy.

Little's tactic of raising the economy question on every vote was aimed at attracting the support of Kent and Shea, who in the previous session had both spoken in favour of retrenchment. Little wished to remove from the clutches of government leaders that tactic which had never failed to outmanoeuvre the Opposition when carried to the public – the issue of economy in public expenditures. For two months, Little, Parsons, and Winser exhausted the government supporters with every delaying tactic imaginable. They moved reductions, pound by pound on every official vote, carried adjournments when possible, moved six-months' hoists, tired out the old men on the government benches with late-night sittings, and declared no quorum as soon as older Conservatives stepped out in the lobby for a break. They became further emboldened by reliable rumours that LeMarchant, in going home for the summer holidays, would be replaced with a new Governor. Parsons chanted in doggerel: "And joy be with him in a bag of moss, / If he never returns, he is no great loss."[62]

The economy issue became so effective throughout the remainder of the session that those who opposed Little had to defend their votes on the grounds of either consistency or courtesy to the governor. The Conservatives, therefore, not only refused to meet the governor on the grounds he chose but also suffered several significant defeats at Little's hands. One loss came on 2 April when the vote was taken for a new clerk in the colonial treasurer's department. Little, declaring that he would resist every attempt to carry that vote, appealed to Kent and Shea on the ground that out of a total expenditure of £60,000 as much as £25,000 was now being paid out to officers. Little argued that, if the colonial expenditure could not be lowered then the least the Assembly could do was to refuse to increase it. Kent and Shea both came on board to defeat the Conservatives. An extremely upset Emerson charged that the vote was a severe discourtesy to the governor; and Prendergast, who tried to adjourn the committee, lost.

One of the highlights of the filibuster came on Friday, 4 April, when Hoyles and Prendergast tried to increase by £50 the annual salary paid to the chief clerk and registrar of the Supreme Court. Little moved amendment after amendment until midnight so that the Conservatives were so tired they begged to go home. Hoyles wanted the question settled on its own merit – that of paying a just salary to a hard-working man. Parsons raised a much larger question related to the vote; he spoke "of a majority of the House composed of paid servants and hireling supporters attempting to sweep down the liberties of the people."

But the night belonged to Peter Winser, the seventy-year-old representative from Ferryland. As auditor of the public accounts, he revealed that he had found sums of money expended for which no satisfactory returns could be made; other sums intended for one object spent on a different one; some spent on doubtful objects; and even sums spent but not voted upon at all. Are "those violations of our constitutional rights to be tolerated?" he shouted. In answering his own question, he said that it were better they all went home and the house became extinct than for the house to exist as it was at that time. The house, Winser stated, "was only used as a screen to cover the monstrous acts of our government." He went on to condemn the profligacy of the government and its betrayal of the people. He did not have much strength left, he confessed, being seventy years of age; but whatever he had left, he would expend it all "in the cause of public justice and public liberty." Little and Parsons stood and cheered as Winser paused for breath. Then, quite deliberately, Winser began to move away from his seat towards the aisle of the house. All looked up in awe as Winser crossed the floor and headed for the government benches. While every neck in the gallery craned to see the sight, Winser stood behind the government members and announced in a strong voice, "I come to beard the lion in his den!" He knew what it was to fight for liberty, he declared to the hushed house, as he recalled how, as a captured prisoner during the French Revolutionary Wars, he had served time in a French prison. Winser stated: "He knew the value of good government, and the curse that followed in the train of despotism; it was, therefore, his duty to set the example of public virtue to his Honourable young friends."

When the cheering had subsided, Little rose again to continue the marathon sitting, commencing with the words, "Once more into the breach, dear friends," and as the Saturday dawn broke over the narrows of St John's, he spoke on the oppression and execution of King Charles I. "Till the Sabbath morning dawns upon us," he challenged, "we shall stand here and, unshrinking, fight the battle of the people's liberties." But a Sunday sitting was not necessary. By 6:00 A.M. the Liberal members were able to press their division to a 7–7 tie, which Speaker John Kent broke by casting in favour of Little. It was surely a victory to be savoured.

After supplies were finally voted, Little carried his responsible-government address on division with only four Conservatives remaining to continue the struggle. Shea and his Placentia colleague were on side as well as Winser, Kent, and the two Conception Bay members, Hanrahan and Mulloy. Following adjournment, Little could only conclude that the session, in spite of the defeated Representatives Bill, had been a signal success. He had reason to await with eager anticipation the government's reply. With a little patience on the

Representatives Bill next session, he anticipated that he could be premier of Newfoundland's first responsible government in time for the 1852 elections.

In the fall of 1851 strong rumours echoed that LeMarchant would be returning for one more year. Hearing this news, Parsons expressed the vain hope that LeMarchant would be bringing responsible government.[63] Liberals under Little, for their part, had focused so much of their attention on the person of LeMarchant that reports of his returning was unwelcome news to say the least. But not even his strongest critic among the Liberals of Little's following could have suspected the extent of LeMarchant's private vendetta against the supporters of responsible government. Even Emerson and Kent, who believed that the governor privately supported responsible government in principle, were destined to be deceived by LeMarchant's secret machinations behind the veil of imperial secrecy.

Since LeMarchant had spent his entire career in the army and had little experience in government and administration, it came as a surprise to many when in 1847 he was elevated to the gubernatorial office in Newfoundland.[64] Considering that he was at that time commanding a regiment in Limerick, even the Conservative *Public Ledger* was astonished at the appointment.[65] Throughout his administration, LeMarchant gained the reputation of a man too used to quarterdeck discipline. He brooked no interference whatever with his official duties and usually enforced orders peremptorily without seeking consultation. LeMarchant summarily dismissed several civil servants and he replaced them with relatives of government supporters. When questioned by opposition politicians, LeMarchant reacted with indignation at their audacity.[66] Said the *Courier*, he "introduces into his civil administration rather too much of the quick march without heeding any remonstrance from those he was sent to serve, not to command."[67] LeMarchant had the habit of interfering at the lowest levels of the civil service; he routinely ignored officials and served poor-relief favourites at his own door. When he overhauled the administration of fire relief and poor relief, those fired learned of their dismissal in public announcements. An Anglican clergyman said that "His Excellency is something of a tartar, I think, and so blunt and hasty, as to be almost uncivil."[68] When a Poor-Relief clerk, testifying on relief administration, made remarks placing the governor in a bad light, LeMarchant was reported to have cursed and shouted, "By God I'll skin him!"[69] But Bishop Fleming was perhaps the person who received the greatest fright from LeMarchant's lack of what the *Courier* called a cool head. Fleming, in a visit to Government House, cross-examined LeMarchant. He rebuked the governor for falsely claiming that he had consistently lied to the Colonial office and had constantly been stirring up sectarian political agitation. Fleming seemed to have had the better part of the argument when suddenly, as Fleming reported, LeMarchant jumped from his chair, assumed a boxer's stance in front of the bishop, and shouted loudly, "I am able to defend myself."[70]

LeMarchant seemed to have carried from the military to governmental administration the need to be in control at all times. Perhaps it was because of this compulsion to control that he took the unprecedented step of touring the St John's riding during the election campaign of 1848 with James Douglas, the Conservative candidate, by his side.[71] Obviously, it was that same compulsion that led him to avow, privately and secretly, that he would not accept responsible government in Newfoundland. From 1851 onwards, he threw every obstacle he could possibly devise before the responsible-government movement.

While Little in the fall of 1851 was waiting for his expected successful reply on the responsible-government address, the governor was busy conspiring against him. LeMarchant told the Colonial Office that the address emanated from only one member of the House of Assembly or, at most, represented the "sentiments of a very small section, or rather ... faction, of that body who have ever been most hostile to the Executive here." The only reason the address had passed, LeMarchant said, was that it came up so late in the session that the intelligent members had to go home to take care of business, leaving the Little faction in the majority.[72] He deliberately concealed several facts: that he had been referring to third reading only; that it had received majority support in a house of fifteen members; and that it had formed the subject of debate throughout the entire session. LeMarchant would not admit that the brilliant strategy of Philip Little had outmanoeuvred the Conservatives and that they and he had been defeated. Afterwards, LeMarchant journeyed to England and assured the Colonial Office that the responsible-government issue in Newfoundland was a Roman Catholic conspiracy. The priests in all districts, he told the British, announce the candidates from the altars and tell the people whom to vote for; indeed, elections are virtually decided at the bishop's palace. Nor does it stop there, for after the members are returned, he said: "they themselves are continued in the same thralldom and subjection as the electors and receive their orders how to vote on every subject of general interest – as the Bishop thinks proper; and should they venture to disobey or even remonstrate are treated as recusants and on the first opportunity are deprived of their seat by the same power that previously bestowed it."[73] If Newfoundland obtained responsible government, LeMarchant warned British authorities, the Roman Catholic bishop would in reality be the governor of the island "for he would possess the most unlimited and uncontrolled sway." Then LeMarchant sat down and drafted the Colonial Office reply which Philip Little was still naively expecting would favour responsible government.

LeMarchant returned to Newfoundland and on 29 January 1852, read the throne speech, all the while maintaining the pretence that he knew nothing of the British government's intentions. Kent was still defending LeMarchant's presumed views, and Emerson was saying that "he did not believe that His Excellency would interfere between that House and the Secretary of State for the Colonies."[74] But no sooner had LeMarchant withdrawn from the house than Little and the Liberals resumed the battle.[75] They launched an all-out assault on Le Marchant for neglecting to mention the responsible-government issue and carried an amendment regretting "the absence from" the governor's "speech of any indication as to the determination of Her Majesty's Government on this highly important subject." Then they brought in the Representatives Bill and were in the midst of its clause-by-clause debate when the British government's decision arrived.

In reply to the responsible-government address, Colonial Secretary Lord Grey defended the present system of government as well suited to the colony and doubted the expediency of granting responsible government because the House of Assembly was too small and because "no such preponderance of opinion in favour of the introduction of what is termed, responsible government, has as yet been discernible in Newfoundland."[76] Little immediately moved the house into committee on the address and launched a vigorous assault on the present executive. Upon the members of the executive he centred the complete responsibility for misleading the British government about the true state of Newfoundland. Point by point he savaged Grey's despatch, remarking that it had been written by persons "blinkered by interested motives." The opinions emanated, he charged, from "the local clique who had so long misgoverned this colony and made her boundless resources the means of personal and family aggrandisement." How did Grey know about Newfoundland's unfitness? Little answered, "only by the secret correspondence of the official clique." Still not knowing LeMarchant's part, Little claimed that the executive "had made use of the Governor to carry out their nefarious designs." As for Grey's contention that the present system worked satisfactorily, Little admitted sarcastically that it had indeed worked "for those who had ensconced themselves within the horns of the Executive and enriched themselves with the public plunder."

While Kent tried to calm the waters, Little was joined by a solid phalanx of six Liberals who, together with several absentees on Hoyles' side, gave him dominance of the house. Little's point-by-point refutation of Grey's despatch was so devastating and the arguments on the opposing side so weak that it became clear immediately that Newfoundland had been denied responsible government only because the governor did not want it. That was particularly frustrating to the Liberals, who had expected a positive reply since Newfoundland's sister colonies had already received responsible government and the British authorities themselves were in favour of such government in principle. The Liberals were particularly bitter towards LeMarchant, while Hoyles and the Bonavista representative, Robert Carter, the governor's chief defenders in the house, tried to escape the storm by attempting to adjourn the Assembly. When Hoyles and Carter could not carry the adjournment, they begged for a postponement on the ground that there was not a full house. Their position was demolished by Little, who pointed out the irony – the British government was requesting public debate on the question while the executive tried to stop it. Newfoundland owed nothing to an executive which "had conducted their movement underhand, and in deep secrecy; they had maligned the country in the dark; they had misrepresented the wishes of the people; they had betrayed the interests of the country."[77] Hoyles defended the denial of responsible government on the ground that the effect of granting it now "would be to place the government of the colony in the hands of the Roman Catholic clergy." When Shea, Winser, and Parsons attacked Hoyles for introducing the issue of sectarianism, Little moved the debate outdoors by instituting a round of public meetings to accelerate the movement for responsible government.

As disappointing as Grey's despatch was for the Liberals, they could easily see in it two causes for optimism. The British government had summed up what was needed. The House of Assembly had to be enlarged; and, if public opinion outside the House of Assembly in Newfoundland expressed itself in favour of that constitutional reform, then responsible government would immediately be conceded. For Little, the despatch defined the two necessary steps to be followed in order for him to assume the premiership; the Liberals would have to win a majority at the polls and immediately afterwards bring in a Representatives Bill. Once his side was in control of the house following a general election, Little was convinced that failure on that next step could be blamed only on the Council. And so, as soon as he finished his Assembly speech, Little and the Liberal party set out on the 1852 election campaign trail.

Just three days after the receipt of Grey's despatch, Little received from Bishop Mullock a letter of support that the Liberal leader published in the local newspapers.[78] The inflammatory remarks immediately raised the debate to a new level entirely and the whole colony was soon awash in a tide of sectarian charges and counter-charges. Mullock stated in his controversial and never-to-be-forgotten letter: "I was never more pained in my life, than when reading this evening the insulting document, forwarded by the Colonial Secretary, in answer to the address for responsible government ... I feel the ill-judged and irritating Despatch an insult to myself and to my people." Since Grey's despatch had complimented the existing government as being satisfactory for Newfoundland, Mullock took particular pains to repudiate the claim and did so in terms of such opprobrium that all observers were shocked. Mullock pronounced: "Acquainted as I am with many forms of Government, I solemnly declare that I never knew any settled government so bad, so weak, or so vile as that of our unfortunate country; irresponsible, drivelling despotism, wearing the mask of representative institutions, and depending for support alone on bigotry and bribery. I see the taxes wrung from the sweat of the people, squandered in the payment of useless officials; the country after three centuries of British possession in part an impassable wilderness, its people depressed, its trade fettered, its mighty resources undeveloped, and all for what? To fatten up in idleness, by the creation of useless offices, exorbitantly paid, the members of a clique." In fact, the present government was so corrupt that, Mullock pointed out, "my silence would betray the cause of justice and of the people."[79] There then followed a call for all honest men to unite and appeal to the British Parliament to reconsider its position.

To the Roman Catholics of the colony, the cause of constitutional reform now assumed quite a different nature entirely. While responsible government had hitherto been a subject of which Catholic priests had been accused of aiding behind the scenes, now the Roman Catholic Church had openly declared its official position. Mullock declared: "It is the duty of a Bishop to aid and advise his people in all their struggles for justice, and I have no other desire than to see justice done to the country, and equally administered to all classes."[80] With the battle cast in terms of good and evil, what had once been a subject for argument now became a duty for Roman Catholics.

Within a few days of the receipt of Mullock's letter, Little convened a mass public meeting in St John's.[81] Upwards of six thousand people, mostly Roman Catholics, attended. Resolutions in favour of responsible government were proposed by John Kent, Ambrose Shea, Philip Francis Little, R.J. Parsons, and an up-and-coming lawyer, George J. Hogsett.[82] Mullock's letter was read again to the cheering multitude. R.J.Parsons was the lone Protestant to take a prominent part in the proceedings.

Protestant reaction, especially to Mullock's letter, was swift and indignant. The *Public Ledger* condemned Mullock's language in reference to the Newfoundland government and declared that it was not befitting a bishop. Said the *Ledger*, "Its imprudence, its coarseness, and in some sort its fierceness ... all contribute to render it doubtful whether it was intended for the Press or not."[83] Winton expressed his astonishment at the arrogance exhibited in Mullock's letter and pronounced that "Dr. Fleming in the worst of times never committed himself half so egregiously." A writer signed "Anti-Maynooth" wrote the same paper to complain of the extreme injudiciousness of Mullock's letter. He declared: "Nothing since the days of Martin Luther and the Purgatorial tax of Friar Tetzel has been more ill-advised than the officious intermeddling of Bishop Mullock.[84]

The Presbyterian *Times* was just as astonished as the *Ledger* and asserted that Mullock had "come down from his high estate!" The *Times* stated, "That epistle was so ignominious and embarrassing that it would be the death thrust"[85] of the responsible-government advocates. A person writing under the name of "Ben Johnston" wrote to say that Mullock was encouraging religious warfare. "Are the scenes of the past to be repeated?" he asked rhetorically in reference to the 1830s. "Are we to be styled heretics and mad dogs again?" There followed a challenge to all Protestants to unite against Mullock and the Catholics. Ben Johnston wrote: "I hope that the Protestants of every denomination will lay aside their petty differences and unite, as one man, to put an end to this attempt to enslave them."[86] This call was re-echoed by the other Protestant newspapers and by a host of anonymous letter-writers fighting against responsible government. At the same time, Philip Little warned all liberal Protestants not to be seduced by the hypocritical alarms of a religious campaign aimed at preserving the present corrupt system. "I have received hearty assurances of support," he told them, "from influential gentlemen of Wesleyan and Episcopalian Churches."[87]

Governor LeMarchant, meanwhile, told the Colonial Office that the war of creeds was as bitter as it had ever been and rankled as deep as it had ever done in Newfoundland's political history. LeMarchant identified himself with the Hoyles party, echoed the latter's sentiments, and laid the blame for the uproar on the Roman Catholic Church and Catholic priesthood. Philip Little, he informed Secretary Grey, was the messenger of the Roman Catholic bishop and on those two LeMarchant fastened the responsibility for the failure of a Representatives Bill. The governor declared: "It would have been carried in 1850 as also in 1851, if the Roman Catholic Party in the House of Assembly had been contented with an equitable arrangement in the allotment of the number of members to the several districts; but that section having the preponderance of votes in their favour in the House as at present elected, was determined so to frame the measure, that the whole political power would be vested in their hands which was very naturally rejected with indignation by the whole Protestant Party."[88]

LeMarchant was representing the struggle as purely a religious battle prompted by the desire for power on behalf of the Roman Catholic Church. With exaggeration more extreme than that emanating from either of the political camps, the governor declared that no Protestant was in favour of any change in the existing constitution and that Grey's despatch had been received without a dissenting voice from the whole Protestant community. Although he could not have taken a poll of every Protestant in Newfoundland, he chose to ignore the obvious fact that R.J. Parsons, member of the Church of England and a sitting Assembly member from St John's, was a prominent advocate of responsible government. Also, LeMarchant completely overlooked the Presbyterian merchant Thomas Glen, a former Assembly representative from Ferryland district who also advocated constitutional reform. He made no mention either of Little's claims of Anglican and Wesleyan support or the fact that at least one Protestant member of the Law Society, Harcourt Mooney,[89] had taken a stand in favour of responsible government.[90] As for Mullock's letter to Little, LeMarchant said that it was "an inflammatory epistle" calculated to arouse "to the highest degree, all the worst passions of a populace of so easy and excited a temperament as that comprising the town of St John's where the Roman Catholics greatly outnumbered (three to one) the Protestant community." The time is coming, LeMarchant warned Grey, when it must be decided once and for all "whether the administration of this island is to remain in the hands of the Governor appointed by the Crown or whether it is to be surrendered into those of the Roman Catholic Party to be wielded by their Bishop at his own individual will and discretion."[91]

It was a damaging blow to Liberal expectations that LeMarchant should have taken such a definitive position with respect to responsible government. The communication of such one-sided views to the Colonial Office could serve only to delay the inauguration of constitutional reform. In fact, LeMarchant's adamant stand tended to aggravate the political struggles; for he expressed his determination to oppose and amend, in alliance with his Council, all representatives bills sent up by the present majority in the House of Assembly.

Unfortunately, because of the machinations of Catholic priests in the time of Bishop Fleming, it was natural for Protestants to look upon the Catholic Church with suspicion. But the almost complete unanimity with which the Roman Catholics greeted their bishop's recent pronouncements indicated that Protestant suspicions may have been unfounded. Instead of creating dissension among Catholics, as Bishop Fleming's campaigns had done, Mullock's public stand seemed to create unity instead. The presence both of the anti-clerical Ambrose Shea and of John Kent on the same platform, with each lauding the bishop's words, was perhaps a real indication that a new order had emerged. The catalyst seems to have been provided by Mullock's new style of episcopal leadership. In contrast to his predecessor, Bishop Fleming, Mullock demonstrated considerable respect for his adopted land by bringing his family to live in St John's and by advocating local improvements for the colony. In the same year of his consecration Bishop Mullock began to advocate Newfoundland telegraphic communication with Europe and the United States, and to this cause he later added steam communication with those parts of the world and road building in the outports. Furthermore, Mullock's Newfoundland orientation extended to his governing of the church. He proved that he held "wider and nobler views."[92] than Fleming. Instead of rejecting the idea of a native priesthood, as Fleming had, Mullock commenced almost immediately the construction of a diocesan seminary in St John's. His lack of prejudice against native sons was well demonstrated when, in 1850, he ordained the first native-born priest and received into the convent the first native-born nun. But perhaps the best signal that a new political era had begun was Mullock's refusal to back an Irish-expatriate for Liberal leader and his opting instead for Philip Little, the immigrant from Prince Edward Island. In addition, Mullock's advocacy of responsible government placed him in the class of liberal Reformers fighting for a cause that had widespread appeal around the British Empire – a luxury that Bishop Fleming had never enjoyed. There was a strong likelihood, therefore, that the Catholic feuds that had marked Fleming's time could be avoided and that the Liberal party might be accorded a real opportunity to develop along broader lines with a wider denominational appeal. Mullock's outright support of the Reform movement did not necessarily preclude wider Protestant support for the Liberals.

Meanwhile, the Commercial Society moved in a different direction, contributing to the degeneration of politics into religious warfare. That body declared its opposition to responsible government by passing a resolution sponsored by two wealthy merchants, C.F. Bennett and W.B. Row, both upper house councillors. In moving the resolution, Bennett stated that responsible government would be inexpedient and unjust at that time: inexpedient because there were only fifteen members in the House of Assembly; unjust because "under the present division of the electoral districts the majority are returned by the influence of the Roman Catholic clergy, although the majority of the population are Protestants."[93] To concede responsible government now, charged Bennett, would be to transfer the government of the colony over to the government of the Roman Catholic bishop. In support of Bennett, Row declared himself against government from the bishop's palace and expressed a desire for a division of districts so that "all denominations of Christians in the colony should be so cut up and divided that sectarian views could not be carried by one party to the injury of another."[94]

Lawrence O'Brien opposed Bennett's motion by reminding Bennett that the only Roman Catholic in the Legislative Council was O'Brien himself and that the Wesleyan Methodists were totally excluded. O'Brien, therefore, charged that the real ascendancy was to be found in the present system – an ascendancy enjoyed by the very sect of which Bennett was a prominent supporter, the Church of England. O'Brien condemned Bennett for seeking to maintain Anglican ascendancy. Bennett retorted that O'Brien ought to look at past elections for evidence of Roman Catholic attempts at ascendancy. Protestants were, he charged, "waylaid in the open day, mutilated, handcuffed, gagged, blindfolded, taken to places unknown, and submitted to the interrogation of a secret inquisition."[95]

Catholics were outraged at the severity of the charges made by Bennett and Bishop Mullock felt obliged to reply. For the second time in two weeks, he rushed into public print an extensive epistle that had the effect of further immersing the Roman Catholic Church into Newfoundland's political struggles.[96] Denying that Roman Catholic priests had participated in the previous general election, Mullock went on to define the role of the clergy in election contests in what became a manifesto for Catholic priests in politics. He pronounced: "Let me not however be understood to condemn the interference of the clergy at elections. I cannot see why a priest is to be deprived of his right of citizenship more than anyone else; he pays his portion of the public burthens; he is subject to the same laws; his interests are affected by the return of a member as well as those of another ... A priest by his ordinance does not forfeit the privileges of a British Subject; every elector under a Representative Government has not alone a right to vote for himself, but to canvass others to vote with him. Deprive any citizen of that right, and he is a free man no longer." Mullock stood on solid ground in advocating political rights for his priests on the basis of their common citizenship with other British subjects. However, in oratorical tones, he unfortunately proceeded to accord to each priest a role far superior to that of any other person. Bishop Mullock postulated:

Every man's position gives him a certain amount of influence. The landlord has it in England; the merchant in Newfoundland; the priest everywhere ... But while the influence of the former two was exercised by worldly pressure, the influence of the priest is moral influence – vote for such a candidate for he will make the best representative; he is no jobber, no place seeker, no bigot; he will represent your sentiments better than the other. The one appeals to the pocket, the other to the people's feelings, or prejudices as some would say. The people know that individually to the priest the return is of little importance; that he only influences them to do what he considers best; that his interests and theirs are identified; they believe him to be a disinterested guide; they venerate his sacred character; they respect him as a man superior in education and acquirements to themselves; all this gives him a powerful influence which they believe has never been exercised except for their benefit.

Mullock's epistle, charged with superlatives and emotionalism, proved that his sense of reason had been overcome by vanity. In one paragraph he declared election returns to be of little importance to the priests individually, yet in another he pronounced their interests to be as affected by the returns as everyone else's. On the one hand, Mullock had claimed a political role for his priests on the basis of their equality with other citizens – a claim that none could with justice deny. On the other hand, he maintained that his clerical servants exercised their priestly influence so effectively by reason of their priestly character alone. But the influence of the priest, with the sanction of the "One, Holy, Catholic, and Apostolic Church" behind him, carried such legendary weight in the Roman Catholic community that it tended to become an undue influence. While the average Roman Catholic could easily overlook the union of priest and common citizen, it was precisely the priest-as-politician image to which the Protestants made greatest objection. Admitting the right of priests to vote and use lawful influence in electioneering, a correspondent of the *Public Ledger* nonetheless put it very well for all Protestants when he declared that "it would have been more candid for Dr. Mullock to have informed us that the Confessional was the great source of priestly influence as few like to run counter to the wishes of their soul-breakers and keepers of their conscience."[97] He then called on all Newfoundlanders to awake from their apathy and save the colony from priestly domination.

Another correspondent, declaring that "liberty and the Romish faith are incompatible," appealed to all Protestants to unite and save Newfoundland from the tyranny of the Roman Catholic priesthood.[98] The

Newfoundland Express, another government supporter, pointed out that the main point was not the legitimacy of the priest's influence; the problem was, according to the writer, "such power exists, that the intention of exercizing it is avowed, and that the present division of districts will with ease enable the clergy to command a majority in the Assembly who, of course, would be subservient to their wishes." The same writer concluded that an Assembly so constituted would serve as the exponent "of the very worst description of despotism."[99]

What the *Express* and *Ledger* most clearly realized was that Mullock's latest pronouncements bordered on the compulsion once attempted in the notorious days of Father Troy. Surely the conservatism of the Catholic Church and its tendency to direct matters as it saw fit were plainly visible in the bishop's grandiose conception of the character and roles of his priests. Behind this exposition of their good purposes lurked the temptation to control and direct political fortunes. To Philip Little, whose political salvation lay in preventing the Liberal party from coming too closely under the control of the church, the latest warning of the *Express* must have served to arouse great personal anxiety.

Meanwhile, before the house was dissolved for the 1852 election, church rivalries had emerged as the dominant feature of debate on the Representatives Bill. Little advanced the same bill as he had done in the previous session and urged its adoption with a repetition of his traditional arguments. When he produced a table showing the relative party returns under the bill, the table disclosed for the first time a new interest openly influencing his conduct on the question.[100] A brief glance at the table proves that Little had divided the districts into Roman Catholic and Protestant. In one column were placed the predominantly Roman Catholic districts while in the other were found the Protestant districts. But 11,500 Roman Catholics in Conception Bay were placed in the Liberal column, while the 16,500 Protestants were placed on what the compiler called the other side. Nobody could, or did, argue with Little's returns for seven of the nine districts, but Conception Bay and Burin were different. In this regard, Little's official admission of political divisions based on religious lines was perhaps a tactical error. His placing of Roman Catholics in the Liberal column and of Protestants on the Conservative side was an indication of the difficulty of preventing religious denominationalism from influencing political deliberations. Little, however, may have been attempting to drive a wedge between the Wesleyans and Anglicans in Conception Bay and Burin by forcing Hoyles's Tories to focus on what they had hitherto had referred to as "a special case" in those two districts. His Catholic district divisions were undoubtedly revelatory of his inability to ignore the fact that, within his Liberal ranks in the persons of Kent, Hanrahan, and Winsor, there lay a core of pro-clerical advocates who tended to bristle at any diminution of Catholic influence.

Hoyles, charging that Little's bill would return a preponderance of members in favour of the Liberal party while the Conservatives had a majority in the country, moved for a division of Conception Bay into three districts returning six representatives.[101] Though he did not want to admit that his divisions were based on religion, Hoyles moved for a subdivision of St John's so as to ensure a mercantile return while subtracting one from Placentia–St Mary's in order to add it to Trinity Bay. The Catholics attacked immediately. Kent charged that Hoyles altered the representation in favour of the Protestants by taking a member from Placentia–St Mary's and by trying to get a Protestant return in St John's. "The great difficulty in bringing this subject to a satisfactory conclusion," Kent argued, "lay in the religious distinctions which pervaded the minds of honourable members." Hoyles's inten-tion, Kent charged, was to diminish Catholic influence and "create ascendancy of his own sect."[102] Quite correctly, Kent then pointed out that merchants were well represented in the Legislative Council. Upon that group, Winser then centred his attack. Blaming the merchants for all Newfoundland's troubles, Winser declared: "If it were not for the well-directed influence of the Catholic priests, the country would be in a most pitiable condition, for there would not be a vestige of liberty in it and the people would be reduced to the most degraded condition of serfdom."[103]

With those remarks Winser had isolated an important factor, for to the merchants' influence he opposed that of the priest. The strength of the merchants owed its origin to their economic power, a force to be reckoned with in Newfoundland politics. Bishop Mullock, Winser, and the Catholic Liberals obviously felt that such power could best be constrained by the force of religion, which they intended to apply to their advantage. Little's bill passed the committee stage by a large majority. While that bill was in the process of passing to the upper house, Bishop Mullock published his second letter. Consequently, the political atmosphere became denominationally charged in a much more partisan fashion; and, as expected, the Council attacked the bill with a vengeance. Immediately following second reading, Council reduced the representation from thirty-one members to twenty-nine by subtracting two from Placentia–St.Mary's and one each from Con-ception Bay and Bonne Bay. It then increased by one member each the two districts of Trinity Bay and Bonavista Bay.[104] Bennett argued that in Little's bill Placentia–St Mary's had too many representatives compared to Trinity Bay, Bonavista Bay, and Fogo. But Bennett ignored the fact that Fortune Bay had too many compared to Ferryland or that Fortune Bay and Bonne Bay had too many compared to St John's. Disregarding the bill as a totality, Bennett and his followers emphasized sections that appeared to disadvantage their side. Second reading passed, however, with only Lawrence O'Brien dissenting.

While both sides admitted that, according to the census, Protestants deserved a majority of one, the problem was centred on the districts of Conception Bay and Burin. Those were the two districts that had such a peculiarly mixed population that the particular brand of Protestantism favourable to Hoyles and Bennett had no guarantee of capturing either district while Wesleyans held the balance of power. Nevertheless, the Council came to grips with the problem in committee when Row moved for a subdivision of Conception Bay.[105] His amendment guaranteed the return of four Protestants while definitely securing the return of at least one Roman Catholic.[106] However, in his third division, where Protestants outnumbered Catholics, Row granted two representatives to the Roman Catholics; his reasoning was that Protestants were equally divided between Anglicans and Wesleyans and thereby unsure of returning a member. (See Appendix, Table 3.) The Liberals had shown themselves eager to exploit the Wesleyan-Anglican rivalry to gain a member from the Protestants, but O'Brien proved reluctant to depend on it for what he considered a just return for the Catholics. In objecting to Row's divisions, O'Brien pointed out that they would render certain the return of only one Roman Catholic. Roman Catholics, he charged, would regard Row's amendment as "a gross insult to them." The amendment carried against O'Brien's objections. Then, before the committee rose, it divided St John's into three districts to ensure a mercantile return and transferred a member from Fortune Bay to the area west of Bonne Bay. The plan came back to the Assembly on 31 March in an entirely new shape.

When debate resumed on the Representatives Bill in the Assembly, Little urged that the house dispense immediately with the Council's amendments because they were of such a nature as to warrant prompt rejection.[107] Pro-mercantile and anti-Catholic sentiments were behind the Council's amendments, Little charged. As for Ferryland and Placentia–St Mary's, in Little's opinion they had received no increase from the Council because they were Roman Catholic. The Liberal leader laid most of the blame on the desire of the merchants to combine their influence and stifle liberal sentiments. Notre Dame Bay, he pointed out, was not divided because the House of Slade already ruled it. As for Fortune Bay and Burgeo–La Poile, they should be divided as follows: "the one district included within the first and last pages of the ledger of Newman and Company, and the other included within the first and last pages of the ledger of Nichol and Company."[108] When Prendergast suggested making an effort to amend the bill further, Little declared it preposterous to expect the Council to give justice to the country. He continued with his oratory, claiming that the bill encouraged sectarian opposition: "It was the latest dark intrigue, the latest design of corruption – the last gigantic imposture which emanated from this government of intrigue, of political depravity, and unchecked, unscrupulous plotters against the rights, privileges, and liberties of the people ... It would set the country in one blaze of religious and sectarian animosity."

While some members of the Liberal party thought the bill could be amended and sent up again, Little insisted that the bill be discarded entirely. His opponents expounded on the lack of freedom in Catholic countries, but Little attempted refutation by remarking on the good graces of the Catholic kings Alfred and John. Amidst the uproar Shea continually shouted that the subject be referred to the country in the next general election. Little, however, led his followers in complete unison in carrying his motion on a strict party vote. The Council's amendments were rejected as too insulting to demand consideration while the Liberals looked to the coming election for a wider and stronger base of power.

Little himself was brimming with confidence. He had wrested the spotlight and the Liberal leadership from Kent in less than a year. His populist program and populist rhetoric seemed to have secured for him a fairly broad base of public support. He had attracted to his side conservative middle-class men from around the Avalon peninsula who had deserted the party in the days of Nugent. His prospects for victory received no better testimonial than the course that circumstances forced on the Conservatives – that of using the Protestant, anti-Catholic, sectarian tool in attempts to stop him.

9 Religion and Electoral Representation, 1852–54

The anti-Catholic campaign launched by the Conservative press at the beginning of the 1852 general election was reminiscent of the conflicts of 1840–41. But the seeds of disunion among Protestants had been deeply sown in the last three sessions of the legislature prior to dissolution. And, in contrast to the Conservative successes of 1841, the 1852 election campaign was destined to be a great disappointment to the Conservatives.

In the dying moments of the 1852 session of the House of Assembly, Philip Little had decided not to pursue the representation dispute with the Council. His decision came not from reluctance to press the issue; on the contrary, realizing the importance of that subject for the responsible-government campaign, Little wished to appeal to the public because a broader base of power would strengthen his chances for victory in the coming struggle between the two houses. It had become rather evident since the receipt of Grey's despatch in February 1852 that the acquisition of self-government depended to a large degree on the results of the campaign.

Apathy on the subject of responsible government had completely disappeared. Indeed, throughout the colony, responsible government had become the all-absorbing, all-embracing topic of the day. The Roman Catholic Church, representing half the population, had officially declared its support of the cause. Signifying to all Roman Catholics that they ought to support the Liberal party, Bishop Mullock's controversial letter to Little had been also an official proclamation that Little was his chosen representative and leader of the party. To

Little, who represented a Catholic constituency while leading a party consisting of either Roman Catholics or representatives of Roman Catholic districts, it must have come with some gratification to receive the public backing of the Roman Catholic bishop. The Liberal Leader was still faced, however, with the problem of acquiring substantial support from other sections of society.

Particularly as a result of Grey's despatch, the Liberals would need to garner almost immediate support from other denominations. They, therefore, began to give paramount attention to the Wesleyans. Politically speaking, the Wesleyans as a group occupied much the same position as the Roman Catholics. Both were almost totally excluded from the civil service; no Wesleyan held a government position. In enunciating their grievances against the establishment, Roman Catholics usually made the Wesleyan grievances part of their cause too. So consistently did the Liberals follow that line that, from 1850 onwards, Roman Catholics in the Assembly had interjected themselves into a specifically Anglican-Wesleyan dispute to champion the cause of the Wesleyans.

By 1850 the educational system, which had been set up in 1843 on a seven-year trial basis, was no longer acceptable to the Church of England. Roman Catholics had been given control of their own separate schools while Protestant denominations could have unfettered use of the Bible and prayer book in schools under their own direction. The Protestant alliance in the field of education, however, did not prove to be as peaceful as had been expected. Within the Church of England, the 1840s witnessed a series of conflicts that were seriously to impair relations between Anglicans and Wesleyan Methodists.

Tractarianism,[1] having become a powerful force in the Church of England in the early 1840s, gathered momentum after 1850 and prompted many public complaints against Bishop Feild from members of his own church. In 1853 Feild faced a revolt from his congregation in St John's because of the appointment of a tractarian clergyman to St Thomas's Church,[2] and that same year residents of Harbour Buffet, Placentia Bay, published a pamphlet accusing Feild of encouraging anti-Protestant practices in the Church of England.[3] Those who knew of Bishop's Feild's past, however, would not have been surprised by his theological leanings, for, before coming to Newfoundland in 1844, he had been a follower of Henry Manning and John Henry Newman, leading figures in the Oxford movement.[4] He initiated high anglican practices in the Newfoundland church and began to install tractarian clergymen and remove those opposed to him.[5] The result was that the church became so moulded to Feild's image that low churchman Governor Ker Baillie Hamilton[6] felt constrained to withdraw as patron of the Newfoundland Church Society. He told the archdeacon Thomas Bridge that he could no longer "sanction proceedings which were not in harmony with the character of the Church of England" and of which he entirely disapproved.[7]

But the growth of tractarianism in the Church of England was not only a bitter disappointment to all low churchmen but also a great threat to the Wesleyans. The Wesleyans became highly incensed at tractarian clergymen who condemned Wesleyan sacraments and rechristened, rebaptized, or remarried those who had already received those rites from Wesleyan ministers.[8] Tractarian tendencies in the Church of England destroyed any chance of cooperation with the Wesleyans in the field of education and contributed to the forging of a political alliance between Wesleyan Methodists and Roman Catholics.

The 1843 Education Act, which had instituted a separate Roman Catholic and Protestant education system, was due to expire in 1850. By that time, tractarianism had transformed the Church of England to such an extent that its alliance with all other Protestants was a burden that Anglicans wished to unload.[9] Hugh Hoyles, the leading Assembly spokesman for the Church of England, moved for subdivision of the Protestant education grant early in the session of 1850.[10] By that measure the Church of England sought complete control of its own schools; this meant that the existing Protestant education grant would have to be divided on a per-capita basis while existing Protestant school board property would have to be shared in the same manner. That, of course, would be beneficial for Hoyles's church, which constituted approximately 70 per cent of all Protestants. But the same division would seriously adversely affect the education of other Protestants. Scattered thinly throughout a large geographical area of the colony, these denominations would not be capable of maintaining their own schools on a grant given on a per-capita basis. In addition, Wesleyans, especially because of the inaccuracies in the 1845 census, were not confident of retaining school property in areas even where they enjoyed a majority.[11] Adequate education for their children, therefore, meant a continuation of the alliance with the larger Church of England. In the Assembly, the low churchman J.G. Falle and the Congregationalist T.B. Job, members for Burin and Trinity respectively, engaged in protracted debate with Hugh Hoyles on the issue; but their efforts would have come to nought had it not been for the intercession of the Roman Catholic Liberals. Sensing the importance of an issue that potentially could split the Wesleyans from the Anglicans, the Roman Catholics banished subdivision from the house and re-enacted for another year the Act of 1843.[12]

At the beginning of the session of 1851, Wesleyan congregations throughout Newfoundland presented numerous petitions against subdivision.[13] Ignoring those protests, the Anglican Hugh Hoyles repeated his performance of 1850 by producing the same education bill which had been defeated in the previous session. His efforts, however, met with identical results because the Catholic Liberals once again defeated subdivision.[14] Moreover, in the course of the debate, a significant defection from the Anglican camp took place. The Anglican and Conservative member for Twillingate-Fogo, George Emerson,[15] who had been a consistent supporter of the government, now cast his vote against subdivision.[16] The opposition of the low churchman Emerson to Feild's education policy was an encouraging sign to the Liberals that the Anglicans, especially the Conservatives, were divided.

The controversy over educational subdivision became much more intense in the election year of 1852. It subsequently developed into an issue rivalling responsible government itself. While Anglican petitions in favour of subdivision poured into the Assembly from every area of the colony, they were met with counter-petitions from the Wesleyans. The question came up for debate almost immediately when the session commenced.[17] Hoyles once again led the advocates of subdivision; but this time Philip Little, Liberal leader and Catholic member for St John's, emerged as the undisputed leader of the opposition to the idea. Taking statistics as his guide, Little demonstrated that subdivision would adversely affect Wesleyan educational interests in St John's, Brigus, Harbour Grace, Carbonear, all of Trinity Bay, all of Bonavista Bay, Fogo, Twillingate, Burin, and Bonne Bay. Little pointed out that it was a difficult question for Roman Catholics because it was a question of bitter rivalry between Wesleyans and Anglicans.[18]

Roman Catholic members had played a prominent part in the controversy since 1850, but they had not completely acted as a unit in opposing subdivision. In 1851 Ambrose Shea, member for Placentia–St Mary's, claimed to have voted for subdivision because his conscience had dictated that Anglicans should be given the same justice that had been accorded to the Roman Catholics in 1843.[19] For the same reason, he supported subdivision in the session of 1852 while two Catholics, Winser and Prendergast, wavered between opposition to subdivision and support of a compromise measure.[20] But in response to urgent appeals from the Liberal leader, who was keenly aware of the political significance of the measure, all Catholic members except Ambrose Shea joined Little in defeating subdivision once again.[21] In the last session before a general election, that move brought on a struggle between the Assembly and the Council which threatened legislative deadlock.

Charles Fox Bennett, a wealthy Anglican and St John's merchant, led the campaign for subdivision in the Council by declaring that "the Episcopalians are unwilling to be controlled in the management of their schools by their Dissenting brethren."[22] Three other Anglican councillors, Archibald, Crowdy, and Row, supported Bennett while the Catholic O'Brien, the Congregationalist Joseph Noad, and the low churchman William Thomas constituted the opposition. While third reading was adopted under the official protest of these three opposing members, the Education Bill was returned to the lower house amended beyond recognition.[23]

The lower house immediately rejected the Council's amendments, and a subsequent conference with the Council brought no results. In Council, Bennett moved that the members stand by their own amendments and condemned the part played by Roman Catholics in the controversy. He could understand why the Wesleyans wanted to keep the unnatural union of 1843 – because of the advantages given to them to the prejudice of Anglicans. Lashing out in other directions, he condemned the Anglicans who opposed him and charged that the Roman Catholics exhibited a poor spirit "which he could not regard in any other light than that of gross persecution and unfair play towards their Episcopalian neighbours." An alliance had taken place, he charged, between Catholics and dissenters for the purposes of stripping the Church of England of its rights and privileges; this union he deprecated as unnatural "because there was no other common bond of union between them."[24] As expected, Bennett's motion was adopted; and a committee was appointed to prepare instructions for a conference with the Assembly.

Once again the lower house rejected the amendments while Philip Little showed no hesitation in urging the alliance of which Bennett had spoken. They would not assent to the upper house amendments, explained Little, for too great an injustice would be done to the dissenters. Catholics and dissenters must be firm, he warned: "The government of the colony was in the hands of one religious party, the Episcopalians, and they made use of their position to strengthen their own power to weaken the efforts of all other denominations; and to better secure their ends in this respect, they used every means to raise a cry at an attempt at religious ascendancy on the part of the Catholics."[25]

Little had delivered his most extreme speech ever but it was characteristic of the intense feelings that had been generated. After a week of fruitless debate, the Trinity representative and Congregationalist,

T.B. Job, reported that the conference between the two houses had broken down and that they had arrived at a complete deadlock on the subject of education. The next day Job brought in a new education bill which simply re-enacted the bill of 1851 for another year. Hugh Hoyles once again launched a vigorous assault on non-division, moving that the house go into committee on the Council's amendments to the former Education Bill. The motion was seconded by Ambrose Shea but defeated by a large majority. Consequently, Hoyles withdrew from the Assembly in protest. He soothed his wounded feelings by scornfully expressing the hope that a different spirit – a spirit of justice to the Church of England – would activate the next house. Job's bill then easily passed with an amendment subjoined at Emerson's demand requiring Protestant boards to furnish by the end of the year full and detailed reports of the probable effects of subdivision. Emerson foresaw a long struggle and realized that the subject would not be put to rest for a number of years.

Nevertheless, the Legislative Council pressed the same amendments as they had previously presented.[26] On 9 June, because of the lateness of the session, O'Brien was worried lest Catholics be deprived of their education funds as a result of the feud between Anglicans and other Protestants. Bennett and Row took this opportunity to castigate O'Brien and his co-religionists in the lower house for continuing the dispute. While Bennett laid the blame on a Roman Catholic-Wesleyan alliance, Row charged that the Catholic majority in the Assembly had been the sole cause of the deadlock.

In the House of Assembly, Emerson, charging that the Council had interfered with the privileges of the lower house by amending a bill appropriating expenditures, moved that the amendments not be received on those grounds.[27] For the first time since the subdivision controversy began, Ambrose Shea voted with his Catholic colleagues and a large majority carried the motion. James Prendergast now came forward with a compromise bill conceding subdivision in St John's and Conception Bay. Still not satisfied, Hoyles put forward numerous amendments and resorted to protracted delaying tactics. His patience exhausted, Philip Little engaged in immoderate exchanges with Hugh Hoyles; each attacked and insulted the other's religion. Then the Congregationalist Job announced that, because of the lateness of the year and the absolute necessity of coming to some arrangement, he would accept Prendergast's measure. Hanrahan, Winser, and Parsons admitted that they would have to vote for it out of expediency as the dissenters had accepted it. The dissenters' choice had been largely dictated by the fact that no moneys for education would be voted at all that year if the struggle were to continue. Little bemoaned the lack of constitutional power to overcome the Council and regretted the compromise, noting that, if the government had been properly constituted under responsible government with the Liberals in power, the compromise would not have been necessary. The Council subsequently adopted Prendergast's measure so that, after five months of contentious debate, an Education Bill became law.[28]

The intrusion of Roman Catholics into a dispute between Anglicans and Wesleyans had severely strained relations between Catholics and Anglicans. Also, the behaviour of Roman Catholics on subdivision of the Protestant education grant had drawn Catholics and Wesleyans closer together, a tendency encouraged by the behaviour of the Church of England. At the same time, Liberals in the Assembly had shown little reluctance to represent Wesleyan grievances against the establishment as a common cause with that denomination and all Roman Catholics. There remained only the task of channelling those grievances in the direction of reform under the guidance of strong leadership and a thoroughly disciplined Liberal party.

As the general election neared, Wesleyans were reminded that defeat of subdivision depended on Roman Catholic votes. The Catholic *Pilot* informed all dissenters that their support would be expected at the ensuing elections, declaring that "the Dissenters, having received the efficient support of the Liberal members of the Assembly, in thus defeating the common enemy of our civil and political rights … will prove themselves at the next general election worthy of a continuation of that support."[29] In other words, if the Liberals did not receive Wesleyan support, the latter should not expect Catholics in the Assembly to continue to vote against subdivision. Throughout the campaign, the *Pilot* continued to champion the dissenters' cause while declaring that there had never been exhibited "such a spirit of religious rancour and sectarian hatred as that which Sir Gaspard LeMerchant and his Councillors … manifested on the Education question."[30] Similarly, the Catholic *Newfoundlander* considered the question of subdividing the education grant as "an election issue next in importance to responsible government,"[31] and R.J. Parsons, one of the Liberal candidates for St John's, also made subdivision one of the most important planks in his election platform.[32] In addition, Liberal intentions to cooperate with Wesleyans were openly demonstrated when the attempt of James L. Prendergast to run as a Liberal was rebuffed.[33] Prendergast, a political maverick who had discounted both the mercantile and the denominational basis of representation, was pushed aside by the Harbour Grace merchants in favour of more pliable candidates. Prendergast had been the initiator of the bill that had brought educational subdivision to St John's and Conception Bay.

With a Catholic from Brigus declaring that the betrayer of the Wesleyans on subdivision would never get a Catholic vote,[34] Prendergast was left to run as an independent.

The Liberal design to capture Wesleyan support remained in continuous operation until election day, and considerable gains were made in that direction throughout the year. Early in 1852 the Liberals received a big boost when the Wesleyan publisher of the *Morning Courier*, Joseph Woods, assumed the editorship as well.[35] Billing itself as the only Wesleyan newspaper in the colony, the *Courier* became the advocate and champion of Wesleyan rights while at the same time calling for responsible government.[36] A strong critic of the sectarian aspect of the governing establishment, the *Courier* in the first three months under Woods devoted itself almost exclusively to the battle over educational subdivision. Lambasting the establishment for its sectarian ascendancy, continually attacking Hoyles and his followers, the *Courier* concerned itself almost wholly with the Wesleyan cause. Such a campaign could not have been entirely satisfactory to the Liberals. They wanted nothing less than all-out support for their party and they were also chagrined that Woods believed in subdivision of electoral districts.[37] On the other hand, Liberals took satisfaction from the *Courier*'s advocacy of responsible government.

While Woods, in the early months of his editorship, continually praised Roman Catholic Liberals for their behaviour on educational subdivision and discounted the idea of Roman Catholic ascendancy, not a word was spoken on the subject of the Representatives Bill. As the struggle between the two houses over both education and representation reached a climax near the session's end, however, the *Courier* realized that nothing could be expected from the establishment. Having received Liberal support on its important cause of education, the *Courier* announced early in the spring that it had reconsidered its position on increased representation. Chopping up a district, it now confessed, would only afford certain interests a greater opportunity to exert control whereas "an undivided district gives each man a fair chance of bringing him away from such local coercion."[38] The *Courier* was then completely in the Liberal camp.

Throughout the remainder of the campaign, the *Courier* concentrated on proving how valuable had been Roman Catholic support in the education controversy and on ridiculing suggestions that a Roman Catholic government would result in the loss of civil liberties.[39] Specifically, Wesleyan Methodists in Conception Bay and, particularly, Burin, would either have to remain neutral or switch their votes to the Liberal candidates in order for the campaign to bring practical results. As for the education question, the Roman Catholic *Pilot* felt constrained to assist the *Courier* with the headline, "A WORD TO THE DISSENTERS." The *Pilot* reasoned that Dissenters should thank Roman Catholics for defence of the dissenters' rights against Anglican sectarianism. But, warned the *Pilot*, dissenters must take broader ground than the education question or they would find that they had "reckoned without their host."[40]

That they did take broader ground was particularly demonstrated by the election in Burin district. There the leading Wesleyans announced their support for a former member of the Assembly, the Catholic Clement Benning.[41] A Roman Catholic, one Furlong, who had been canvassing the district, withdrew in Benning's favour while the *Courier* scorned the Conservative, Wesleyan candidate. Contesting the district on the Liberal party ticket, Benning won an easy election victory.

In Conception Bay the Liberals opposed James L. Prendergast with a Carbonear teacher, William Talbot.[42] The former had been the object of attacks by the *Courier* for his betrayal of the Wesleyan cause on the education question; and, on his subsequent defeat, Liberals argued that Wesleyans should feel grateful to the Catholics of Conception Bay. In addition to Talbot, the Liberals sponsored two other Catholics in that district while the candidacy of the Anglican John Hayward[43] as an independent favouring responsible government demonstrated the Conservatives' difficulty in preserving Protestant unity.[44] Protestants, of course, had always been less susceptible to church-sponsored politics than had Roman Catholics; yet the Conservatives also faced the problem of attempting to activate Protestants against a popular cause – that of democracy and responsible government. Instead of backing an Anglican, the Hoyles party concentrated on splitting the Wesleyan-Liberal alliance by supporting Wesleyan merchant John Bemister of Carbonear. While Bemister succeeded in defeating the third Catholic, his victory perhaps demonstrated more than anything else a reluctance to disturb the existing sectarian pattern of returning equal numbers of Protestants and Catholics for Conception Bay. Even the Liberal *Courier* disliked the idea of disturbing the present arrangements; and, while the denominations split the district, Liberals could be happy that three responsible-government men had been returned.

However, although the support of the Roman Catholic Church and its priesthood was of considerable advantage to the Liberal party, that very support contributed certainly to impairing relations between Liberals and Protestants. Protestants had, generally speaking, an innate fear of the supposed monolithic power of the Church of Rome and its legendary authority to command obedience from its subjects. Such fears undoubtedly had some basis in fact for the open participation of the Roman Catholic Church in Newfoundland politics had in large measure contributed to the Liberal sweep of Catholic districts since 1836. Because of the fervour generated by church-driven politics, however, anxiety about Roman Catholic power and conspiracy had become grossly exaggerated. Perhaps Governor LeMarchant typified the most extreme of those views when he reported to the Colonial Office on the absolute power of the Roman Catholic bishop and his priests. Blaming Little and Mullock for sparking all the religious discord, LeMarchant declared that any doubter would be convinced of Newfoundland's unfitness for responsible government if he had witnessed "the violent proceedings of the Roman Catholic party in the House of Assembly in the session just closed." With respect to the coming elections, LeMarchant said that the Catholic Church was setting on foot an agitation to return Catholic candidates "and with such irresistible power and such crushing weight does the Roman Catholic Church control the minds and direct the conduct of the whole of that creed in this Colony that the end results of this agitation may be most clearly foreseen."[45] LeMarchant's bias had completely eclipsed his reason. If he had bothered to read the despatches of his previous fellow governors, a practice always followed by incoming governors, he could not have failed to notice the deep divisions generated in the Catholic camp in the 1830s and early 1840s. And even if he had not read his predecessors' despatches, he surely must have known that the Catholic candidates had prominent anti-clericals in their midst in the persons of Ambrose Shea, John Delaney, and, above all, R.J. Parsons and James L. Prendergast. But, sadly, LeMarchant had simply abandoned his responsibility to play the role normally associated with that of a British governor, that of impartial arbiter. Instead, LeMarchant simply pandered to the political whims of Hoyles and the Conservative party.

The Conservative campaign against responsible government was now based on the same exaggerated assessment of Roman Catholic power as that found in the governor's reports. The Conservative *Public Ledger* imputed to Mullock the most disgraceful of motives and remarked upon "the mysterious control which he sways over as deluded a population as may be found under any other canopy of heaven."[46] Charging the *Pilot* with treason, the *Ledger* proclaimed that there was "no such thing as civil liberty tolerated in the Romish church," and therefore its ecclesiastical domination was "for all purposes omnipotent."[47] Responsible government, then, must be resisted for it would make the executive responsible to the Roman Catholic bishop, "whose allegiance to the Queen ... we hold to be at least questionable ... and not VERY questionable either."[48] The *Newfoundland Express* trumpeted much the same charges.[49]

In the face of such a campaign, the Wesleyans must have hesitated to forge an alliance with the Catholics. Indeed, some aspects of the Catholic campaign were of such a nature as to contribute to the justification of the opposition charges. "Religion is supreme over politics," declared a *Pilot* article addressed to Catholic electors. "Politics," it argued, "are a part of ethics and Ethical Sciences are only a part of Moral Theology which, therefore, includes politics."[50] Reasoning from the premise that the state had its origin from God, the *Pilot* concluded that its laws must be in accordance with the laws of God. As to who would decide whether any law was or was not in accordance with the laws of God, the implication was clear that Roman Catholic theology would decide that. Another article on the definition of the province of religion in politics compared it to the soul in the body, with "death beginning as soon as its vivifying action was stopped." The *Pilot* concluded, "There is no religious principle except in Catholicism; Protestantism is nothing more than absolute negation."[51] To some extent the basic intolerance of the Catholic Church was emerging into public view; and, to an objective observer, the problems inherent in an alliance between such a conservative organization and a liberal political party must have foreshadowed even greater difficulties for Liberals in the future.

Nevertheless, the Liberal party did win three of the five seats in the districts of Conception Bay and Burin. Having won St John's without a contest, Ferryland with only token opposition, and the two Placentia–St Mary's seats, the Liberals had a total of nine representatives in the new House of Assembly. But what gave the Liberals greatest satisfaction was the support of the Anglican Hayward for responsible government; that, together with Emerson's later defection from the Conservatives,[52] considerably enhanced the Liberal claim to represent all denominations. Certainly the Protestants of Conception Bay had refused to some extent to be blinded by fears of Catholic ascendancy. Such backing was very welcome to the Liberals, who had now extended their base of support into once Conservative strongholds. With this in mind, the Liberals considered the political advantages to be reaped from the support of the Anglicans, Emerson and Hayward, and they also took stock of the fact they were relieved of the necessity of depending on Roman Catholic votes, at least in Conception Bay. In the end, they therefore compromised on the Representatives Bill by conceding several points to the Conservatives and Protestants.[53] When they sent it to the Council in 1853, the Conservatives there were placed on the defensive.

The Liberals had deducted one member from Placentia–St Mary's while Conception Bay had been subdivided into five electoral districts.

Now it was more imperative than ever for the minority Conservatives to make their cause a Protestant one. When an uproar developed in the Assembly on the question of responsibility for dragging sectarianism into the debates, the Conservative leader, Hugh Hoyles, rose to declare proudly that there was nothing wrong with bringing up what was on everybody's mind. To neglect the religious character of representation, he stated, "would be downright hypocrisy and criminal indifference."[54] From that premise Hoyles could easily prove that, where Anglicans and Wesleyans were divided, as in the second division of Conception Bay, Roman Catholics could be returned for Protestant ridings. Little had, of course, cleverly devised the bill in that fashion in order to force Hoyles to admit that the Protestants of whom Hoyles spoke were Anglicans. If the Conservative leader were forced to declare that pro-Anglican divisions were his object, the breach between his party and the Wesleyans would become much wider. However, with the backing of such a small minority in the Assembly, Hoyles dispensed with the task of proposing formal amendments and passed that duty over to the Legislative Council.

The Council showed more reluctance than ever to meet the Assembly's demands on the subject of increased representation. In spite of the fact that the Assembly had demonstrated a desire to compromise, the Council produced the most drastic amendments to date.[55] It reduced the representation to twenty-six members by taking one member each from Placentia–St Mary's, Ferryland, and Burin, while adding an extra one to Trinity Bay. Dividing St John's into two districts so as to give a mercantile return, the Council maintained that its division would return an even number of Protestants and Catholics. While no one could disagree that the arrangement would guarantee the return of thirteen Protestants, it could easily be seen to guarantee the return of only twelve Catholics. Naturally, Catholics did not want to depend on Burin to furnish their complement of members any more than the Anglicans did for theirs. In addition to this objection, the Assembly maintained that the third division of Conception Bay would give a divided return. Even though the Roman Catholic majority there was small, the Assembly's argument was curious.

In fact, with the exception of the quandary of Burin, one must admit that, in the four years of debate, the Council had produced the most reasonable divisions to that point. Yet objection to the division of St John's was to take a new turn in the Assembly. Formerly, Liberals in the lower house had objected to the divisions of St John's because such divisions would create a measure of mercantile control as well as fashioning a close borough in the business section of the capital. Maintaining that by the Council's amendments two Protestants would be returned for St John's, the majority Liberals in the Assembly based their opposition to the divisions on the ground of religion.[56] Refusing to entertain the Council's amendments, the Assembly rejected them on second reading and requested conferences with the Council. The Assembly-Council conferences dragged on for three weeks and proved fruitless as each side refused to budge from their original positions. Before the conference broke up in despair, the Council reminded the Assembly that the appellations, Liberals for Catholics and Conserva-tives for Protestants, were "mere titles of assumption or opprobrium" and "such terms and all others of the like tendency had better be avoided."[57] The Council considered the terms Protestant and Catholic to be more appropriate so that, henceforward, in the political debates of the two houses, the terms Liberal and Conservative were rarely heard.

Perhaps because he had anticipated an agreeable Council that might even be open to the prospect of responsible government and perhaps because he was unwilling to add insult to injury after a bitter election, Little had, at the beginning of the debate, admitted a division of Conception Bay. His move amounted to formal recognition that the crux of the problem rested with the apportioning of members according to religious affiliation. The validity of this view was proven when the struggle between the two houses was reduced to a quarrel over the key districts of Conception Bay and Burin. The Council's stubbornness in the course of the struggle likely stemmed from con-tinuing fears of Catholic ascendancy. Indeed, if one can judge from the governor's views, those fears had now become of paramount importance.

In reporting on the results of the election and on the responsible-government question, Governor Hamilton revealed his deeply held suspicions of the Roman Catholic Church.[58] First, Hamilton consid-ered the power of that church so immense that it could move the whole Catholic population at will. In political as well as in religious matters, he considered the entire Roman Catholic population to be completely subservient to their clergy and bishop. Yet, if his charges were really true, it is curious that "intimidation and actual coercion by the priests"[59] – to use his words – were necessary during the elections in Ferryland and Placentia. The Roman Catholic Church, no doubt, did wield immense power over its flock; but to insist that it was as complete as Hamilton alleged was to fly in the face of reality. Hamilton charged as well that the Catholic Church's power was being exercised for the purpose of gaining a permanent ascendancy. But that was not a credible argument given that Catholics constituted less than half the total population. It was difficult to imagine even a short, temporary ascendancy. Hamilton was convinced, however, of the church's real motives and was even more certain of the evil results. Newfoundland, he believed, was unique among North American colonies in that the concession of responsible government would result in control by the Roman Catholic bishop. That state of affairs, he warned, would "involve consequences so momentous in their results to the moral, social and political condition of the people that Her Majesty's Government" should "hesitate as to its adoption." With the Roman Catholic bishop and clergy in control of the executive and legislature, "the proceedings of the legislature would be characterized by injurious excesses and those of the Executive by tyranny and caprice." Hamilton concluded, "An oligarchy would be established, subversive of that freedom the enjoyment of which is the vaunted advantage of the desired change."[60]

No wonder the Council fought such a stubborn battle when the governor supported its position without reservation. No wonder the two houses failed to arrive at a compromise when the person who was to act as an impartial arbitrator possessed such strong opinions in favour of one of the parties. In any event, since the Council and Assembly had arrived at a deadlock on the question, the Liberals did not force the issue but decided to appeal to the British government, appointing two representatives to present their case. Then, while Little and Parsons were on their way to London as delegates from the House of Assembly, the Colonial Office finally made up its mind to grant responsible government to Newfoundland.[61] The Liberal campaign of 1852 had been successful for, in spite of Conservative warnings about Catholic ascendancy, the support garnered from Wesleyans and Anglicans had convinced the Colonial Office that the responsible-government campaign was not wholly a Roman Catholic movement.

The Liberals could look forward to the session of 1854 with unrestrained glee. Their aspirations had been fulfilled, and responsible government would soon be a reality. Only an increase of members with a geographical division of districts was required before they would form the government.[62] But the Council could argue that the home government in a sense had given it some degree of support by calling for a division of districts. To the Liberals, it was somewhat frustrating to realize that only the stubborn Council was preventing their party from taking power. Early in the session, therefore, the Assembly adopted an address to the Colonial Office objecting to the granting of responsible government being made contingent on a geographical division of the present districts. Division based on territorial extent, it argued, "would throw the elective power into the hands of the most scattered and isolated portions of our population and thereby unjustly act upon the more populous and wealthy settlements."[63] The Liberals then reiterated old arguments against subdivision. Content with that case, they re-introduced their bill of 1853 and, with three more compromises to please the Council, passed it by a strict party vote.[64] Subdivision had now been acknowledged in two more districts, St John's and Fortune Bay–La Poile; and an extra member had been given to the Protestant district of Trinity. Little pointed out that those were concessions to the Conservative party and provided for fair denominational returns. A thorough study, he said, would disclose that there were "fifteen Protestants for 49,523 inhabitants and fourteen Catholics for 46,983 inhabitants according to their absolute majorities in the several districts; one Protestant member for 3,300 Protestant inhabitants, and one Catholic for 3,355 Catholics; while the average representation for the whole island is one for 3,327; thus giving the Protestants an advantage of twenty-seven on the general average for every one of their fifteen members and the Catholics a disadvantage of fifty-five on each of their fourteen members compared with the Protestants, or an actual loss of twenty-eight inhabitants for every one of fourteen members, on their general average right."[65]

The problem of allocating members according to religious denomination had become a question of meticulous mathematics. Before concluding his lengthy speech, Little warned that this was the last time that the Assembly would attempt legislating with the Council. It was doing so now, he declared, only to meet the suggestions of the Colonial Office. There were few objections, however, that could with justice be offered against the bill. Only Burin, which had proven an insoluble puzzle, really remained in doubt. Yet no opposition was offered on that score; the sticking point proved to be Conception Bay. Two Wesleyan merchants, John Bemister[66] and Stephen March,[67] objected to the divisions of the district.[68] They contended that two Wesleyans should be secured for the area, but John Hayward, an Anglican who helped frame the measure, would not agree to any change. While Hugh Hoyles remained conspicuously silent, Philip Little suggested that, if they could work out an arrangement among themselves to guarantee the return of two Wesleyans for Conception Bay, he would accept it. Apparently Hoyles did not want the Conception Bay divisions disturbed either; and the result was that March moved, instead, for a division of Trinity Bay into three districts. One of those districts, the south shore of Trinity Bay, contained a large majority of Wesleyans that March used as a pretext for dividing the Bay into three ridings. But the same south shore of that bay was the centre of March's mercantile operations, and Little objected to March's desire to create what Little referred to as nomination boroughs and suggested instead that the Wesleyan section of Conception Bay, Freshwater to Bay de Verde, be extended round the peninsula to Trinity Bay to return two members. That was an equitable arrangement for the Wesleyans, but March refused to accept it. He apparently wished to capitalize on Wesleyan discontent to serve his business interests in Trinity Bay. He and Bemister were both condemned by the *Courier* for betraying the Wesleyan cause.[69] Little's bill passed the Assembly with three Anglicans – Parsons, Emerson, and Hayward – having given strong support for it all through the session. Liberals could justly be confident that the legislation no longer could be considered merely a Roman Catholic measure.

However, over the protests of Lawrence O'Brien, the Council reduced the representation of Placentia–St Mary's and gave an additional member to Bonavista Bay.[70] It also altered slightly the divisional boundaries in Conception Bay and introduced a unique principle into the division of Burin. Attaching a proviso that Burin electors were to have only one vote each, the Council ingeniously thereby secured an equal return of Protestants and Catholics for that district. It was a clever arrangement, no doubt, the first one that guaranteed the return of fifteen Protestants and fourteen Catholics. In their frustration to pass a Representation Bill and acquire responsible government as quickly as possible, the Liberals met in party caucus and – over the objections of John Kent – decided to accept the Placentia–St Mary's amendment. Their action would prove to the British government that "there was no endeavour," as had been represented, "on the part of the denomination of Christians to which he [Little] belonged to grasp the government for themselves."[71] They based their opposition to the remaining amendments, however, on the novelty of the Burin proviso; and, deleting that section, sent the bill back to the Council, where the same Burin proviso was added. Rejecting the bill once again, the Assembly endeavoured to seek some arrangement with the Council, failing which the lower house adamantly refused to vote supplies and sent delegates to London to seek concession of responsible government on the Assembly's own terms.[72]

Meanwhile, Hugh Hoyles had carried his resistance to responsible government to broader fields. Shortly after the concession of responsible government had been made public, the Hoyles Conservatives began to organize subcommittees among Protestants in the outports under the direction of a central committee in St John's.[73] The objective was to oppose the granting of responsible government on the basis that it was a Roman Catholic plot dangerous to the interests of all Protestants. Fearing that the struggle in the Assembly had been lost, the St John's Conservative merchants had seized upon the creation of a grass-roots, anti-Catholic campaign as their last forlorn hope to prevent power from slipping from their hands. Requesting the queen to withhold responsible government, the Central Protestant Committee circulated petitions to be signed by every male Protestant of the age of discretion. Having collected the petitions by 20 June 1854, the committee resolved to send its chairman, Hugh Hoyles, to London as a delegate to urge its claims.

Hoyles prepared a statement of the case marked by understatement and gross exaggeration. In evaluating the struggle for responsible government, he represented it purely and simply as a religious question with all the Protestants on one side and all the Catholics on the other. Hoyles conveniently forgot that three of his prominent co-religionists had fought for the Representation Bill, which, he charged, tended to "perpetuate Roman Catholic ascendancy." Pleading that the Protestants "should not be deprived of liberty," he begged that "the majority should not be placed at the mercy of the ecclesiastical ruler of the minority."[74] Notwithstanding the fact that the Protestants had a majority, particularly in Conception Bay and Burin, the Catholics were "always ready to resort to violence and intimidation" and were thereby able to win a Protestant seat. Ultimately, the petitions Hoyles presented were found to contain such irregularities that the Colonial Office initially refused to present them to the queen unless further explanation were given. Receiving a partial but not completely satisfactory reply, the colonial secretary presented the petitions to the queen with some reluctance.[75]

In the meantime, Governor Hamilton had become more closely identified with the anti-Catholic campaign, for, when submitting Protestant petitions to the Colonial Office, he unreservedly championed their cause.[76] Condemning the Representatives Bill which had passed the Assembly, he reiterated all his old arguments against Catholic ascendancy and doubted whether a government could be carried on with a majority of one, considering "the intolerance of control which characterized those by whom the Roman Catholic members are returned."[77] By this time the Colonial Office had become belatedly convinced of the governor's inability to mediate the conflict and was seriously considering his removal.[78] But it contented itself at the time with remaining aloof from the struggle and warned Hamilton that the constant endeavour of the local government should be "to mitigate those hostile feelings and to prevent merely political questions from being mixed up with religious disputes."[79] Meanwhile, Hoyles on the one hand, and Little and Emerson on the other were plaguing the Colonial Office. However, neither delegation received a particularly warm reception, and both were forced to travel back home to receive from the governor the results of their entreaties.

Those results were of little comfort to the Central Protestant Committee and its supporters, for the home government declared support for the Assembly's stand on Burin. In addition, Hamilton was ordered to use his good graces to bring the conflict to a resolution and not to expect any interference from Britain. The governor's only option, the colonial secretary informed Hamilton, was to advise "Her Majesty to remodel the Council in such a manner as to make it act harmoniously with the Assembly."[80] The Council, Hamilton, and the Central Protestant Committee had to face the possibility of complete defeat. Their wishes had been ignored, and the governor now faced either the prospect of striking the best possible bargain with the Assembly or the alternative of a remodelled council and a Representatives Bill framed solely on the terms favoured by the Liberal party.

On 10 October a special session of the house was convened. Faced with the urgency of forming the government, the Liberals rushed their Representatives Bill through three readings on 16 October. The Council, however, gave no indication that its back was to the wall for it fought the bill for two weeks, finally reducing by one the representation of each of the districts of Bonavista Bay, Placentia–St Mary's, and Burin.[81] The change in the Burin clause was made on the reasoning that, with one representative, there would be greater certainty that Burin would return a Protestant. Reducing the representation of Bonavista Bay and Placentia–St Mary's would guarantee an even return of thirteen Protestants and Catholics with Burin holding the key. With those arguments, the Council moved for a conference with the Assembly, a conference that was promptly rejected.

Through all of this, Governor Hamilton demonstrated no desire to act as the impartial mediator he had been instructed to become. Early in October the official members of the Council intimated their desire to follow Hamilton's instructions in the event that the subdivision dispute between the two houses arose again.[82] In spite of the fact that after 16 October it was clear that no agreement could be reached between the two bodies, Hamilton remained aloof until 9 November. On that date, under threat of a remodelled Council, the councillors were forced to accept the Assembly bill[83] and a new Representatives Act became law immediately.[84]

In retrospect, the 1852 election had been a key event in the struggle for responsible government. For Little had steered his party through the sectarian winds blowing from all sides and had been able to extend its support into Protestant and hitherto Conservative districts. From such a position of strength, the Liberals were able to compromise on the representation bills such that the anti-Catholic tactics of both the governor and the Council were somewhat circumscribed. The end result was that electoral boundaries had been drawn along denominational lines. It then became inevitable, especially with respect to the political climate in Britain, that the Newfoundland Liberals would be rewarded with responsible government.

10 The Election of 1855

In late 1854 the Conservatives were licking their wounds, embarrassed by the threat of a remodelled Council and the awarding of responsible government. As for the Liberals, they were inclined to believe that, with the Representation Bill now law, only an election campaign lay between them and their taking office. But there were unexpected obstacles ahead.

When the Council had passed the Representation Bill, the Liberals rushed a supply bill through the Assembly and made provision for the registration of voters in the new district of Burgeo–La Poile in eager anticipation of a general election. The Conservatives, however, had other plans. They amended the supply bill in the Legislative Council and sent it back to the Assembly minus the clause relative to the registration of voters.[1] The lower house rejected the amendments altogether and endeavoured to suspend the Registration Act entirely. Soon, however, they became aware of a plot to postpone the elections until the spring. The Liberals were confident of winning a majority and wanted an election as quickly as possible. But, because of the difficulty of winter transportation and communication, a December election was hardly a realistic possibility. That was especially true in the northern and western districts, where no election could possibly be carried out before spring. As the north and west possessed Protestant majorities[2] and were likely in the Conservative camp, a December election would without doubt short-change the Conservatives. The election would thus be determined by the results in the southern, or Catholic, districts, a matter of crucial significance to the Liberals. Thus,

while the Liberals urged an early election, their Conservative opponents hoped to defer the elections until spring in order to postpone
the almost inevitable accession of a Liberal government and to secure
an advantage for themselves. The coming of spring heralded the
beginning of the fishing season. The merchants would then hold in
their hands significant powers of manipulation that could be of crucial
assistance in winning that extra seat in Conception Bay or Burin.

But the Conservative campaign, however, would have come to
nought had it not been for the staunch support given it by Governor
Hamilton. Since his arrival in St John's, Hamilton had shown little
impartiality in dealing with political disputes and now had, even more
than Bishop Mullock, descended fully to the level of a political party
leader. Before the opening of the special session of the house, Hamilton had contemplated holding the elections following the passage of
the Representation Bill.[3] Yet, by 14 November, however, he had
changed his mind. The change had been occasioned by the passage
of a Representation Bill which he considered "not such a one as, in
the estimation of the Protestants generally," secured to them "that
share in the representation" to which they conceived themselves entitled. He believed that the returns would be different "from what they
would be if the electors were left to exercise their free choice." The
truth is that Hamilton seems to have secretly decided to postpone the
elections until May 1855.[4] Meanwhile, the Liberals had detected the
plot and demanded that Hamilton close the session and hold the
elections that fall.[5] Upon his response that the elections could be held
no sooner than May,[6] the Assembly refused the granting of supplies
and instituted proceedings for the removal of the governor.[7]

While Hamilton's opponents prepared their case for his dismissal
and appointed Philip Little as a delegate to England to effect the
change, the governor concentrated on fashioning arguments in
defence of his stand on the election issue, arguments that appear
somewhat muddled. First, Hamilton protested that transportation difficulties rendered a fall election impossible.[8] That was a credible
argument. Next, he argued that a registration of voters should precede
an election. Then he retreated to his first-stated position and adopted
the strict, Tory party line.[9] Finally, Hamilton voiced an additional
defence, which, perhaps, best represented his views. If, he argued, in
addition to the unjust Representation Bill, elections were held when
the Protestants did not want them, "exasperation would have been
occasioned which would increase, embitter, and perpetuate existing
local differences."[10] Hamilton was determined to salvage some measure of victory for his Conservative friends, and to this end he sent
off Hugh Hoyles as his personal representative to counteract the

accusations of Philip Little at the Colonial Office.[11] There followed the cleverest political move of the whole period. Hamilton dissolved the House of Assembly. Philip Little was suspended in London as the delegate from an Assembly which did not exist. Yet that must have been cold comfort for Hamilton, who, although upheld on the election timing, later received word of his own dismissal.[12] The Liberal leader's mission had been successful, and Little returned to Newfoundland to find several of his colleagues already on the campaign trail in the most important election to date in the colony's history.

Newfoundland voters must have faced the polls in the spring of 1855 with an almost certain foreknowledge of the results. The Liberals had been riding the crest of a wave of popularity that had continued to build momentum for more than three years past. And both the Conservatives and the government that they defended had receded deeper and deeper under a cloud of defeat. While everything seemed to be going right for the Liberals as the election grew ever closer, much had been going wrong for the government and its Conservative supporters.

In the first place, the Conservatives had been cast in the role of defenders of the officials Archibald, Crowdy, and Noad. Perhaps Little's populist attacks on those "greedy" officials with their "top hats" and "high salaries" might have been sufficient to alienate the general public from the Conservatives. But in the Assembly Little had also led successful attempts to reduce these officials' salaries forcing the Conservatives to defend a very unpopular cause.[13] Worse, the officials were non-native and, as the colony prepared for the advent of responsible government, they departed for retirement in England, clutching their Newfoundland pensions.

Then there was the fact that in the few years previous to the election, the Newfoundland economy had not performed well. In 1852 the potato blight had descended on the colony causing widespread potato failure,[14] and a dreaded failure of the cod fishery in the same season exacerbated the distress to almost unbearable proportions. These calamities were followed in 1853 by the failures again both of the potato crop and of the fishery.[15] In 1854 there was only a partial recovery of the fishery and destitution was reported to be rampant, especially in Conception Bay.[16] The consequent rise in prices of all supplies added to the great misery. The price of flour was said to have risen so high in 1854 that bakers in St John's reduced the size of their loaves without any subsequent reduction in price.[17] The result was a litany of bitter complaints and severe disaffection with the government.

Considerable labour unrest coincided with the potato failures and the fishery setbacks. In the spring of 1853, widespread discontent among the sealers led to a strike involving demonstrations, which some observers labelled as riots.[18] When in the fall of 1853 adverse verdicts were recorded against the sealers, there were fresh demonstrations and protests.[19] Throughout 1854 there was considerable unrest among the mechanics and labourers because of low wages. In May 1854 the coopers and shipwrights in St John's went on strike for higher pay.[20] A wave of alarm swept through the capital as hordes of men marched the streets with placards threatening those who settled for less than the group's demands. A general strike hit the city on the 22 May as everyone downed tools and took to the streets. The new Electric Telegraph Company, planning to lay a telegraph line across the island, was forced to settle at higher rates with 400 men. New labour organizations emerged from the unrest. The coopers founded an association for the protection of their interests and in October 1854 announced their first action, a boycott of imported casks. They resolved not to "line or head those casks ... because they consider it an injury to their trade ... ."[21]

In the face of the growing unpopularity of the government and its supporters, the economic setbacks, and the labour unrest, the Conservative party found itself in an embarrassing situation while preparing for the 1855 election. They experienced great difficulty in finding a slate of candidates. Having opted for a union of Protestants, they decided to forego fielding candidates in districts that had a Catholic majority, a tactic that reflected their view of the elections as strictly a Protestant-Catholic struggle. Thus, they aimed at Fortune Bay, Burgeo–La Poile, Notre Dame Bay, Bonavista Bay, Trinity Bay, Conception Bay and Burin, districts accounting for nineteen representatives in the new thirty-member house. These had been the traditional Protestant areas which, Conservatives had continually argued, justly belonged in the Conservative camp. Burin and Conception Bay, they had always maintained, should be electing all Conservatives but Catholic mob violence had stolen some of the seats there in the past. For the 1855 election, Conception Bay had been subdivided into five sections, three of which had Protestant majorities; in total, that district would send seven members to the Assembly. One of the three Protestant districts, Harbour Grace, was entitled to two members and those, plus the two, single-member Protestant districts of Port de Grave and Bay de Verde, could give the Conservatives four representatives out of the seven-member bay. In Harbour Grace, however, the largest mercantile firm, which had traditionally supported the Conservatives, had now swung away from Hoyles and placed its support behind the Liberals. It backed two populist candidates who appeared to have the support of all groups in the district. Thus, Hoyles' Conservatives were shut out of

Harbour Grace and managed merely to nominate but two candidates for the whole bay, one in each of the districts of Port de Grave and Bay de Verde. In Burin they fared but little better. There, they sent James Seaton of St John's, editor of the *Newfoundland Express* and secretary of the Central Protestant Committee. Following a tour of the riding, Seaton withdrew in consequence of finding little support. Then Seaton, a Presbyterian, recommended fielding a Wesleyan in an attempt to break the apparent Catholic–Wesleyan alliance there. Eventually, the Conservatives nominated William T. Freeman, a seventy-one-year-old Wesleyan from St John's. Yet, even if by some miracle they won that seat in Burin, it was destined to be of no avail. In fact, the Conservatives had been beaten on nomination day, when they managed to field but thirteen candidates for the thirty-member House of Assembly.

As Liberal leader in 1855, Philip Little could face the electorate in a rather triumphant mood. Throughout the colony his party attracted fairly widespread support and this support seemed to be distributed among all classes. His populist program of public works and government intervention in the economy had engaged the attention and support of the fishermen and labouring classes in most of Newfoundland. In the House of Assembly he and his followers had not failed to champion the interests of the fishermen and sealers at every opportunity in the four sessions he had sat as a St John's member. His advocacy of the fisherman's lien had been a prominent plank in his platform since taking office. As well, sealer rights were advocated in the same vein when Liberals defeated Conservative efforts to define relations between sealers and their employers to the detriment of the former.[22] At the same time, Little kept his feet firmly planted in the midst of the consevative middle-class in St John's.

The middle class had been fertile ground for Little's responsible-government program since he and his brother John had first championed that cause in the *Courier* more than five years before. His platform of doubling the number of representatives, expanding the Legislative Council, and acquiring a self-governing expanded executive with new powers and responsibilities for hiring civil servants opened up tantalizing opportunities for aspiring middle-class business dealers and professionals. The Liberals' pet scheme of reciprocal trading privileges with the United States increased those possibilities. Since 1853, Liberals in the house had advanced that proposal with renewed vigour. They pursued an agreement whereby the United States would open up its doors to Newfoundland fish on the same basis as American fish. In return, Americans would get free and equal access to the Newfoundland fishery. This prospect generated a great deal of enthusiasm throughout Newfoundland, for it was widely believed that a substantial percentage of the labouring population would find new work processing fish from American schooners expected to use Newfoundland harbours for drying their cod. The treaty was also expected to open the colony to cheaper supplies, lower prices for provisions, and new fields of endeavour for the shopkeepers and middle class dealers. For these and other reasons, middle-class leaders flocked to the Liberal banner in 1855.

In adition to the two lawyers who had run for the Liberals in the previous election, there were two new ones this time, George Emerson in Twillingate-Fogo and John Hayward in Harbour Grace. Two newspaper proprietors and journalists, R.J. Parsons and Ambrose Shea, were joined by two more for the campaign: E.D. Shea in Ferryland and Joseph Woods in Burin. Two fellow teachers joined teacher William Talbot, who was running in Harbour Main: M.J. Kelly in Placentia–St Mary's and John Haddon in Bonavista Bay. Local contractor Clement Benning in Burin was joined by fellow contractors: Patrick Morris, also in Burin; James L. Prendergast in Harbour Grace; Thomas Byrne in Harbour Main; and John Delaney in Placentia–St Mary's. Joining John Kent on the campaign trail from the class of shopkeepers and middle-class merchants were Edward Morris in St John's, Thomas Glen in Ferryland, David Walsh in Bay de Verde, and James Stewart in Bonavista Bay.

The Liberals had even broken into the ranks of upper-class merchants. First, the old west country firm of Slade and Sons was now backing the Liberals in the northern bays.[23] For several years, companies like the Slades had been in a tailspin as a result of restructuring in the fishery and the resulting competition from St John's firms. The Slades were soon to wind up their business in Newfoundland entirely. Their weakened position by 1855 was demonstrated by the fact that their St John's-based competitors, Thomas Knight and C.F. Bennett, were able to carry the day in Twillingate-Fogo. Their nominees, William Ellis and Thomas Knight, took the two seats against the Slade supporter George Emerson, now the Liberal candidate.

In Conception Bay the most substantial mercantile firm in the region, Punton and Munn of Harbour Grace, in addition to its closest rival there, T.H. Ridley and Sons, was now in the Liberal camp. In St John's, upper-class, Chamber of Commerce merchants such as J.J. Rogerson, James Tobin, John Fox, and William Warren had also lined up behind the Liberals. The division in the upper class seems to have been caused by the proposed reciprocity treaty with the United States.[24] The leading mercantile firms feared the new competition from American suppliers. Since the St John's firms were now concentrating on supplying the outport fishery, the prospect of American traders freely plying the coast laden with American consumer goods caused them great anxiety. This prospect did not generate the same kind of concern on the part of many outport firms for two reasons. First, firms like Ridley and Sons in Harbour Grace were focusing their attention on the cod and seal fisheries and did not have the same stake in the suplying trade as did the well-known Chamber of Commerce men in St John's. Also, for many of the outport firms, American competition with St John's-based operations would serve to lower prices and so would be a boon to their trade. Similarly, many of the St John's merchants like John Fox and William Warren, Jr, had exclusive interests in the wholesale trade. They thus welcomed the news of free access to American suppliers and were delighted on that account to champion the Liberal cause. As a result, Philip Little could stand in the House of Assembly and announce that he represented the St John's Chamber of Commerce as much as any Conservative on the Hoyles side of the House.[25]

The Liberals in fact faced the general election with a problem directly opposite of that troubling the Conservatives: instead of a shortage of candidates, the Liberals had too many. Making final decisions on the Liberal ticket was a taxing responsibility for Little and the Liberal party. In St John's seven leading Liberals had publicly announced their intentions for the six seats; three had announced for the two-member constituency of Burin, three for the double-riding of Harbour Grace, and four for the three-seat constituency of Placentia–St Mary's. And there were strong rumours that more were waiting in the wings as they gauged the proper timing for their political leap. The principal weakness of the Liberal party relative to its choosing of candidates lay in the nature of party organization at that time. There really was not any formal strucure as in modern party organizations, and it was generally accepted that the various parties existed through the form of their elected caucus. Normally, this structure served well enough to perpetuate incumbents in a re-election bid but the 1855 election was a special case. The house had been doubled to thirty members and, while the previous Liberal caucus contained but nine members, Liberals now required more than triple that number for a full slate. Accentuating the difficulty was the fact that several caucus members possessed extensive personal followings on their own account, were relatively independent, and were but loosely attached to the party. Such was the case with John Kent especially. With an extensive personal following dating back more than twenty years, Kent had only belatedly been detached from the reigning "irresponsible" government to support Little's party line. R.J. Parsons also had a large personal following and was no doubt untouchable as regard to a position on the Liberal ticket.

Philip Little, on the other hand, although an able politician in many respects, had limitations as a leader. His youth and inexperience among a group of seasoned veterans militated against his commanding that loyalty reserved for the likes of Kent, Parsons, Ambrose Shea, or O'Brien. Moreover, Little lacked the oratorical powers necessary to hypnotize a crowd of supporters, let alone his opponents in the House of Assembly. Much of his appeal had been largely based on a populist program of reform rather than on his personal characteristics. His eligibility for leadership stemmed mainly from the fact that he was a compromise candidate, whose selection avoided the nasty local jealousies that Kent, Parsons, Shea, or O'Brien would have to confront. The lack of personal inspirational leadership from Philip Little was demonstrated when his efforts on the Representatives Bill and responsible government had failed to arouse the populace until Bishop Mullock had made public his support for those causes. Further confirmation came barely three months before the election, when Little was almost defeated as vice-president of the Benevolent Irish Society. He won by only one vote, and he would have been beaten had Edward Morris, the other nominee, voted for himself.[26]

That kind of lacklustre performance was much less than was required to distribute the six St John's seats among the Roman Catholics, many of whom had political aspirations. Indeed, there were strong tensions sweeping through the political climate in St John's through the winter of 1855, apparently generated by edginess over the upcoming party nominations. John Kent became so anxious regarding his own position that, even when Bishop Mullock invited him to form a Liberal club to promote party unity, Kent declined on the ground that it might serve to threaten his own nomination.[27] The campaign thus began slowly for, mainly out of courtesy to the absent Little,[28] few Liberals wished to impose themselves on the constituency before he returned.

Nevertheless, John Kent could not restrain his impatience indefinitely and finally issued an address to the electors of St John's East.[29] The address of R.J. Parsons quickly followed.[30] The campaign then gathered momentum as Edward Morris, who had been waiting in the wings for some time and who had saved Little's reputation as vice-president of the BIS, issued his address to the electors of St John's West.[31] Cashier of the Newfoundland Savings Bank, personal friend of the bishop, and first cousin of John Kent, Morris was seen by many to possess the qualifications necessary to represent St John's for the Catholic party. The Morris family had a history in politics and Morris could stake his claim to a share in the representation. The late Patrick Morris, the famous Reformer, had been his uncle; his father, Simon Morris, one of the closest friends of Bishop Fleming, had previously sat in the Assembly for Placentia–St Mary's.

But the announcement of Morris's candidacy caused consternation in some circles. While Kent and Parsons had been long-time representatives for the party, Edward Morris was a newcomer. His address to the electors could set off a chain reaction and bring a flood of aspirants into the field. Some of his friends, therefore, urged him to wait and see if the bishop had any objection to Morris's candidacy.[32] Reluctantly, he agreed to consult Mullock. On the night of 22 February 1855, he was ushered into the inner sanctum of the bishop's study. Having cordially greeted Morris, Mullock declared that he entertained no personal objections whatsoever to his visitor. Nevertheless, the bishop stated that he intended to give no preference to one candidate over another. Remarking that there was a great necessity for unity in the party, Mullock suggested a committee as the best means to achieve it. Morris reminded him that the suggestion had already been made to John Kent and Lawrence O'Brien, who had done nothing about it. Morris then openly confessed to Mullock his doubts that a committee could "secure his object from the materials at hand – of a batch of politicians every one of whom was at war, or in contention with, the other." In confessing the inability of the Liberal politicians to reach an agreement on the subject, Morris had, by inference, suggested that the bishop himself make the decision. But Mullock refused. Presumably, while still in the good graces of the bishop, Morris departed to let things take their course.

Three days later, Morris and Robert Kent, brother of John Kent, learned indirectly of a meeting of Liberals called by John Little, brother of the Liberal leader. Forthwith they repaired to the expected meeting place, the Legislative Library in the Colonial Building, only to find that the location had been changed. Following a search of the building, they discovered the meeting in an adjoining room that they entered uninvited. There, in addition to John Little, they found John Kent, George Emerson,[33] Peter Winser,[34] Thomas Glen,[35] brothers Edward D. and Ambrose Shea, George Hogsett,[36] William Talbot,[37] and James Tobin.[38] Subsequent to the passage of a resolution affirming the desirability of unity in the party, Hogsett moved a resolution that the meeting decide on the St John's candidates as follows: Little, Kent, Parsons, Shea, Winser, and Parsons.[39] Immediately Morris protested that such "a one-sided meeting composed alone of the persons interested in the nomination" should assume the right to dictate to the district. Supported by the Kent brothers, Irish ex-patriates like himself, he received the reply that the bishop and the priests had decided the course.

Failing in his efforts to modify the plans, Morris called a public meeting for the following night and addressed "seventy or eighty notes to shopkeepers requesting their attendance." Meanwhile, Father Edward Condon of St John's had changed his mind about the propriety of Morris's candidacy and notified Morris to that effect, saying that the nominations came from the bishop and ought to be respected. At the same time, Father Walsh cautioned the Kent brothers to avoid blaming Hogsett or Little for what had happened at the meeting for they, too, had been ordered to take the course they did. Had they refused, others would be found to replace them. Just before his planned public meeting, Morris consulted with the Kent brothers and decided to retire "rather than act in opposition to the wishes of the Priests." Ultimately heard by only a very small audience, Morris explained his reasons for withdrawing; then the original resolution respecting the nominations was carried unanimously. Subsequently, the chosen candidates carried the two St John's districts by acclamation. Morris summed it up sarcastically, saying, "So triumphed the popular cause and the voice of the constituency." But Morris accepted his defeat in a resigned manner and went to a friend's house where, as he described in his diary, he remained for some time, all "laughing over my misfortunes and disappointments for half an hour and washing off their recollection in a glass of brandy and water."[40]

Although the dispute had been settled peaceably, the candidacy of Morris had represented for the Liberals the greatest danger to party unity. Having considered the opposition of the bishop and the priests as sufficient cause for his withdrawing, Morris typified the Irish Catholic conservative elements that had found such favour in the time of Bishop Fleming. Bishop Fleming had tolerated priests and politicians who believed that support of the clergy constituted eligibility for political favour; Bishop Mullock, on the other hand, had enough political sagacity to realize the suicidal political results of Catholic divisiveness. When therefore, the conflict at the election committee meeting demonstrated that the Morris camp was aligned against a basically non-Irish, native group, Bishop Mullock did not lack the capacity to accept the latter. He also understood that the former, in their devotion to the church, could accept clerical decisions with greater resignation. It was this shrewdness, along with an ability to compromise, that accounted for a great deal of Mullock's influence. For the Liberal party, the necessity of retaining his support was urgent; for, if Mullock tended to dispense his favours towards pro-clericals of the Morris variety, the liberal elements in the party could not so easily be consoled. If, on the other hand, he withdrew the use of his name entirely, then perhaps the party would fall into disarray.

In Placentia–St Mary's the Liberals decided on the incumbent George Hogsett, merchant James Tobin, and teacher M.J. Kelly. But a general contractor and former Assembly member, John Delaney, made a successful canvas of the riding in his own favour for the Liberals. It must have caused a great annoyance to Little, who engineered Tobin's withdrawal by apparently promising him a seat in the upper house following the election. The agreement was soon effected and Delaney was accepted on the Liberal ticket, thus carrying the district for the Liberals on nomination day with Hogsett and Kelly.

In Harbour Grace the parish priest had been sponsoring a candidate, John McLean, against Prendergast and Hayward. But apparently a liberal use of Mullock's name succeeded in convincing McLean to withdraw. The same strategy seems to have been successful in Harbour Main and Ferryland, where the Liberal candidates carried the district on nomination day. But the same strategy wasn't as successful in Burin. There, a third Liberal, Patrick Morris, a local contractor, contested the district against the chosen two, Benning and Woods. The latter had remained in St John's to fight the Liberal campaign through his *Courier*. That perhaps shortchanged him on election day, for, while Benning topped the poll, Morris squeezed by Woods to take the second seat by eight votes.

In spite of the socio-cultural, economic, class, and other factors bearing on the 1855 election, the campaign itself resolved almost entirely around issues of religion. That was principally due to the fact that the Conservatives had been placed in such a defensive position that "Protestant Union" was adopted as their main campaign slogan. Since their 1852 election defeat, the Conservatives had hastened to champion the Protestant cause in the fight over the representation bills. Having succeeded in making it an issue of religious affiliation, they had forced the framing of the Representation Bill along denominational lines, incorporating the Conservative claim that Protestants justly deserved a majority of one. Now, finally realizing that the only majority they could win was a Protestant one, they did not hesitate to cast the campaign as purely a religious struggle against Roman Catholic ascendancy.

That campaign was directed from St John's by the Central Protestant Committee. Hugh Hoyles was initially the committee's chairman, but, once the campaign got under way, he resigned in favour of a fellow committee member, Henry King Dickenson, a partner in the St John's firm of W. and H. Thomas. Hoyles was designated for his old riding of Fortune Bay, while committee members James Seaton, John H. Warren, and Stephen March ran for Burin, Bonavista, and Trinity Bay in that order. All committee members except Dickenson, who remained in the capital to direct affairs and resolve any conflict that might arise over conservative nominations were eventually appointed candidates.

Eventually, Seaton pulled out of Burin because of a lack of support, whereupon the last remaining committee member, William Freeman, was appointed in his stead. A mere serious issue arose when long-standing Conservative and former Assembly member for Fortune Bay, lawyer Bryan Robinson, decided to contest the La Poile appointment of Robert Prowse. The problem was overcome with the assistance of Governor Hamilton, who promised that, if Robinson left La Poile to Prowse, then Hamilton would ensure Robinson's appointment to the upper house.[41] Robinson accepted and the issue was settled. In the remaining districts where the Conservatives had a reasonable chance of success candidates were appointed with little difficulty except in Bonavista Bay. There, William Warren, Jr, merchant of St John's, was upset with the Central Protestant Committee because he did not receive the appointment as their candidate.[42] He protested, publicly attacked the committee, and, when it proved unresponsive, defected to the Liberals, running in Bonavista Bay against his brother, John H., a Conservative and member of the Protestant Committee. Both the Warrens appear to have been acting quite consistently with their own economic interests. They had once been allied as Warren Bros Ltd in the trade and fisheries on the same basis as their fellow Chamber of Commerce merchants in St John's. But they had gone bankrupt in 1851, following which John H. set himself up in Bonavista Bay as an agent of St John's suppliers while William entered the wholesale trade. Thus, William found that, with little difficulty, he could go off to Bonavista Bay to champion free trade with the United States and responsible government in an unsuccesful bid to deliver that riding for the Liberals.

James Seaton, editor of the *Newfoundland Express*, spearheaded the anti-Catholic campaign from his position in the capital. For three full months prior to polling day, the *Express* was fixated on attempting to break what it regarded as a Roman Catholic-Wesleyan alliance. The attack was a two-pronged affair. First, the *Express* continually pointed out to the Wesleyans and all Protestants the danger posed by the Roman Catholics in the colony. The latter were not free in the exercise of their political franchise and, if the Liberals won, the Roman Catholic clergy would be in control. Bishop Mullock would be the new head of the government and the Wesleyans were warned to shrink from that horror. Only in Burin, claimed the *Express*, would a Catholic-

Wesleyan alliance benefit the latter. It produced population figures purporting to prove that, as in Twillingate-Fogo, Bonavista Bay, Trinity Bay, and Port de Grave, a Catholic-Wesleyan alliance would leave the Wesleyans politically isolated.

The second part of the *Express* campaign was a defence of the Anglican establishment. The main body of Anglicans throughout the colony had nothing to do with any appointmenmts under the government, claimed Seaton. Those appointments were all blamed on the various governors. Besides, the *Express* pointed out, under responsible government Anglicans and Wesleyans would arrange for themselves their respective shares of government patronage.

The Conservative *Times* and *Public Ledger* carried out similar anti-Catholic campaigns. According to the *Times*, Roman Catholic electors were automatons performing the bidding of their dictator, Bishop Mullock. The case was so hopeless, they believed, that not even the secret ballot would be of any help. The *Ledger* campaign, as befitting Henry Winton, was extremely bitter especially against Woods. While Winton promoted Protestant Union throughout the colony, he specifically feared the Catholic-Wesleyan alliance in Burin. Woods was attacked continually as a servile tool of Catholic interests, as a "nominal" Protestant and a political Catholic. The *Ledger*'s constant theme was that there was no liberty in the Roman Catholic Church and the Liberal party was manipulated from above. "To show how completely liberty of action is ignored by the Catholic Party here," claimed the *Ledger* in a reference to the St John's nominations, "we may mention that Mr Edward Morris had addressed the electors of St. John's last week, but it appears that he had not obtained episcopal sanction to enter the political arena, and he is completely extinguished."[43]

On the Liberal side, the *Newfoundlander* boycotted the religious issue entirely and almost completely ignored the anti-Catholic attacks from their contemporaries. Instead, the *Newfoundlander* focused on attacking the supplying system, defending free trade, and promoting middle-class interests. But the *Patriot* and *Courier* were much less charitable with the religious issue. The *Patriot*'s religious campaign centred around defence of the Catholic church, countering the attacks from the *Ledger, Times,* and *Express* and promoting the Wesleyan cause. Parsons condemned the anti-Catholicism of Winton as he had in the past and praised Roman Catholics for their support of Wesleyan interests. He did not attack the Church of England, however, or the clergy of any denomination in the same vein as did Winton and Seaton. He continually referred to the Central Protestant Committee as "the Orange Society" and directed his barbs against the *Ledger, Times,* and *Express.* "Which of those imposter prints," he rhetorically asked, "ever defended Wesleyan Methodism against the 'iron-heel' of 'prelatical' despotism?"[44]

The *Courier* replied in kind to its opponents' attacks. For Woods, the political campaign was a struggle against a Church of England conspiracy to wipe out Wesleyan Methodism in Newfoundland. He published the statistics on civil-service appointments and referred to them continually to prove that Anglicans had never done justice to the Wesleyans. In every district of the island where there was an Anglican majority, claimed the *Courier,* Wesleyan claims were completely ignored. Woods resurrected the debates over patronage to show that it was the Roman Catholics who had stood by the Wesleyans, not the Anglicans. The objective of the Anglicans in house education debates since 1852 had been "the extermination of Wesleyan Methodism from the outports of the Colony."[45] The Catholics had proven to be the true friends of all dissenters and the coming election results would prove it. The *Courier* was contemptuous of the Protestant Union cry, labelling it "the forlorn hope of a party, the leaders of which are the representatives and supporters of what is termed the Tractarian or Puseyite aschool."[46] To add insult to injury, the *Courier* reprinted newspaper articles dating back four years that detailed disputes between Wesleyan clergy and high church Anglican clerics over baptism and marriage in the outports. At the same time, the *Courier* published a series of pamphlets by Thomas E. Collett of the Church of England wherein he attacked his own church for abuses connected with clerical fund-raising.

It seems to be the nature of religious prejudice that those who suffer from it are inclined to overstate the influence of the religion they oppose. Following the conclusion of the 1855 campaign, the *Newfoundlander* bitterly noted that "No Popery" charges in Twillingate and Bonavista had rung "with orange frenzy and droves of poor ignorant dupes were found to dance to the tune."[47] And, on learning of the defeat of Woods and Emerson, the *Express* jubilantly declared that their rejection "clearly shows that the misnomer of liberal Protestantism finds no favour with the Protestant electors of this country."[48] But the issue was not so clear-cut, especially in the Protestant districts. For, as we have already learned, there were decisive influences affecting the returns in each district that had nothing at all to do with religion. Undoubtedly there were some electors, as at all times, who fell victim to the anti-Catholic dodge. But it is impossible to determine the size of this group. In the one district where the numerical returns are extant, Burin, there is no evidence of any voting pattern along the lines of religion. For William Freeman, the Protestant party candidate, finished such a distant third[49] that Anglicans, Roman Catholics, and Wesleyans must have split their votes evenly between the three Liberals, the Catholics Benning and Morris and the Wesleyan Woods. The fact that Woods lost by a mere eight votes can be explained more easily by the fact that he had been unable to tour the district in person and that his conqueror was a popular local man who, as commissioner of roads, had substantial patronage power in his own hands.

In the Catholic districts, there was no contest. Voters in these districts had been ecumenical enough to elect two Protestants, R.J. Parsons in St John's and Thomas Glen in Ferryland. Nevertheless, no Catholic district had elected a Conservative. But that was hardly surprising given the pro-Protestant, anti-Catholic nature of the Conservative campaign. In fact, religion was a factor – even a critical one – in the Catholic districts, but not in the manner suggested by Henry Winton. Bishop Mullock seems to have played a key role in the 1855 election in the Catholic districts. Yet he exercised his influence in a quite conciliatory fashion in helping to settle the nominations. Apparently, no Liberal politician could dominate the political scene sufficiently to bring a decisive influence to bear in a contentious nomination squabble. Mullock did not interfere directly in this sphere, but his parish priests invoked his name to quiet disaffected aspirants, as in the case of Edward Morris. In Ferryland, Father Cummin worked feverishly for the Liberal cause but was careful, he told Little, not to do it from the altar.[50] There is no reason to believe that the same caution was not shown in Placentia–St Mary's, Harbour Main, and Carbonear.

The candidacy of several Protestant candidates for the Liberals in the 1855 election took the steam out of the Conservative anti-catholic campaign. The Conservatives' main mistake, however, was to think that an anti-Catholic campaign would be just as successful as it had been in 1841. The Bible controversy, which had earlier tended to unite Protestants against Catholics, had been put to rest in 1843. Little's Liberals benefited not only from that arrangement but also from not having to campaign on a platform of Catholic grievances. Little, too, was fortunate to have as an ally the cautious and moderate Bishop Mullock. The end result of all of this was that the Liberals had the advantage of a divided Protestant community. Thus, it was easy for them to extend their support beyond the Catholic St John's middle class to encompass other denominations and classes in all regions of the colony.

While observers had different views on the determining factors in the campaign, none could dispute the final results. Liberals had beaten the Conservatives eighteen to twelve and an era in Newfoundland politics had come to an end. On 14 June 1855 the curtain rose on a new epoch when Governor Charles Darling tendered the oaths of office to Philip Francis Little as premier of the first responsible government in the history of Newfoundland.

Conclusion

Although Newfoundland was claimed for England by right of discovery in 1497, permanent settlement did not really commence on the island until the seventeenth century. Then, for two hundred years, it developed only haphazardly and slowly. As a result, its constitutional development lagged far behind that of British colonies on the mainland of North America. No governor remained permanently on the island until 1818, and full colonial status was witheld by the British government until 1825. Thus, an indigenous Newfoundland state did not receive an oppportunity to develop until the nineteenth century. One of the victims of this state of affairs was the Church of England, which was denied the type of assistance in Newfoundland that it received by right and by law in England. The result was that, instead of being able to lean on an indigenous local state, it was forced to depend for staff and financing on a London-based voluntary society, the SPG. It was not therefore surprising that, when serious competition appeared in the eighteenth century, from the Methodists and the Catholics, the Church of England was not capable of responding effectively.

In the decades following 1765, Methodists made slow progress. They were hampered by the fact that many Newfoundlanders equated them with the Anglican establishment. However, after 1790 the Methodists began to distance themselves from the Church of England, and they then began to spread rapidly, especially in the Protestant bays outside St John's. The support of local merchants in major fishing centres such as Harbour Grace, Carbonear, and Trinity was critical to their rapid development in the decades preceding and following 1800.

Anglicans, alarmed about the defection of a constituency it regarded as their own, began debating how best to cope with Methodist gains.

While the Methodists were flourishing in Newfoundland in the post-1790 period, so too were the Roman Catholics. The grant of religious liberty to Catholics in Newfoundland in 1779 might have been aimed at fulfilling a political agenda for the British, but for the Roman Catholics it became the basis of their church's development. Indeed, the Roman Catholic Church became so firmly established so quickly that both Methodists and Anglicans would have welcomed restrictions. When it became clear they were not forthcoming, the Protestant churches began to search for alternative strategies.

The 1820s was a watershed decade for both church and state in Newfoundland. The local state was officially established with the grant of colonial status in 1825, while the Methodists, Anglicans, and Roman Catholics launched their churches on new paths. An evangelical revival embracing both the Methodist and Anglican churches and backed by the new colonial government made great headway in the colony. And the new evangelicals launched an initiative in education that was destined to have repercussions down to the end of the twentieth century. In order to combat Roman Catholicicism and to promote Protestant Christianity, the evangelicals combined forces to establish religious schooling based on Bible teaching. Hitherto there had been mixed secular education on a cooperative basis, but in the early 1820s hard-line evangelicals aroused Roman Catholic jealousies. These were accentuated upon the founding of a local House of Assembly, for evangelical Protestants then began the battle for the Bible in the public schools of the colony. The Bible battle tended to unite Protestants and alienate Roman Catholics, who, in response, began to display a new aggressiveness of their own.

In the years following Catholic emancipation in 1829, Bishop Fleming instituted a radical departure in the Roman Catholic Church in Newfoundland. Having been schooled in the anti-British, anti-Protestant, Catholic tradition in Ireland, Fleming brought that point of view to bear on his episcopal career in Newfoundland. Under his leadership, Newfoundland's Irish Catholics asserted their identity both as Irish Catholics and as British citizens. Fleming himself attacked the Anglican, mercantile, political, and economic oilgarchy while simultaneously attempting to construct a church dependent on fishermen only. This sharpening of identity, in religious, ethnic, and class terms, was combined with an aggressive program of encouraging the Newfoundland Irish to rebel against the local British Protestant government in favour of their own civil rights. Fleming's revolutionary church movement reached its climax in the late 1830s while the evangelical movement reached its apex at the same time. Both movements had played right into the hands of Conservatives and Reformers who were battling for control of the government.

Following the grant of a local House of Assembly, Conservatives took control of the elected chamber by electing almost all mercantile men from St John's. A Reform movement, however, took root among the St John's middle class when two Irish expatriates, Patrick Morris and John Kent, and a Scottish dissenter, William Carson, combined to wrestle the political monopoly away from the capital's upper class. Faced at first with limited success, they enlisted the support of all anti-Anglican forces in the colony. Portraying the government as an established church monopoly, they sought to arouse the jealousies of all dissenters and Roman Catholics. The Catholic community especially became a fertile field as several political priests enthusiastically joined the ranks of the Reformers to lambast the Anglican monopoly on government patronage and promote the political aspirations of the Irish Catholics. Matters tended to get out of control, however, when behind Fleming's back several of his over-zealous priests identified the Reform movement with Fleming's church policy and attempted to compel Catholics to vote for Reform candidates only. As divisions appeared in the Catholic community, Reformers William Carson and Patrick Morris began to have serious reservations about that political strategy. But their positons were ursurped by an agitator who viewed Fleming's assertions about the fishermen's church in a very serious fashion. John V. Nugent took control of the Reform Party, began to foment a fishermen's movement, and so controlled the House of Assembly by 1840 that complete deadlock with the upper house occurred. The resulting party developments under Nugent split the middle class as its more conservative representatives deserted.

In the meantime, the Reform party had had little success in spreading its roots among the dissenters of the colony. Roman Catholic activism had scared them off but, more significantly, the evangelical movement and the Bible controversy tended to unite all Protestants and draw a solid line, of demarcation bewteen them and the Roman Catholics. Conservatives, terrified of the threat posed by Nugent, were able to take advantage of the resulting Protestant unity and successfully represent the struggle as a dastardly Irish Catholic plot to establish a Popish ascendancy in a British colony. Thus, they were able to convince the British government to suspend the House of Assembly and repeal the constitution in 1841. The Reformers were so beaten that they did not fully recover for more than a decade.

The inauguration of a new constitution with the experiment of an amalgamated assembly in 1842 ushered in a decade of conservative politics. And, in the midst of tranquility, Newfoundland underwent significant social and economic changes. A fishery restructuring that had been under way for some decades quickened to the extent that, by the early 1850s, the bulk of cod harvesting rested in the hands of individual fishermen. Together with poor markets for fish and high prices for supplies, changes in the fishery led the traditional firms to withdraw entirely from the industry, especially in the bays to the north, south, and west of St John's. New firms centred in the capital arose to take their places, this time placing their major emphasis on providing supplies for the fishing trade. That development tended to create a dependency on large firms based in the capital to the detriment of those located elsewhere.

In the vacuum that emerged between the disappearance of the old structures and the emergence of new ones, the Newfoundland state discovered for itelf a new role. In place of the winter credit once offered by the failing firms, the government filled the breach by offering seed potatoes, relief works, and government-sponsored industries. Coinciding with those governmental developments, a political philosophy and movement arose to further the same ends. Earlier, there had been murmurings among some Reformers that the route towards ending Newfoundland dependence lay in transforming the constitution so that responsible government would be the new form of administration. If the choice of government could be placed in the hands of electors, ran the new thinking, then the people would have under their own control the mechanism for economic survival that had once been in the grasp of mercantile firms. But, at first, the voices making this argument were crying in the political wilderness.

Complementing the economic developments of the 1840s were enormous changes in church and society. Bishop Fleming's attempt to build a church on the backs of the fishermen failed. He lost his enthusiasm for Nugent and, under the new amalgamated constitution, he threw the church fully behind the new middle class–upper class administration. The rift in the Catholic community was healed as Fleming steered the church towards internal growth, with a massive construction program being its outward manifestation. In the meantime, the Protestant community rejoiced over the widespread acceptance of their solution to the Bible question. Protestant schools were separated from Roman Catholics when a bi-denominational system received legislative sanction in 1843. Since evangelical Christianity had been sweeping the Protestant community since the early 1820s, separate Protestant education proved to be a great boon to Wesleyan Methodists in particular. High church Anglicans grew worried and, with the arrival of a tractarian bishop, again began to debate means of halting the losses to the Wesleyans. By 1850 they had resolved on a split with other Protestants and begun a campaign for separate Anglican, sectarian schools. That crusade, plus the installation of both tractarian clergy and High church practices within the church, alienated all dissenters and split the Protestant community in Newfoundland. The issue of Anglican sectarian education forced itself into the political arena and tended to align the Wesleyans in the colony against the Anglican establishment and alongside the liberal Reformers. Those developments took place against a background of radical changes in the British Empire.

The British government had adopted free trade in 1846 and it now became possible for each colonial executive to chart its own economic policy. The result was that the British government began to transfer responsibilities to each of the colonial capitals in the form of responsible government. The mainland North American colonies of Nova Scotia, New Brunswick, the United Canadas, and Prince Edward Island were the first to receive responsible government. A Conservative government then in power in Newfoundland, backed by supporters in both houses of the legislature in St John's, allowed the great boon to pass them by. But two immigrant lawyers and veteran politicians from Prince Edward Island, John and Philip Little, realized that Conservative domination of Newfoundland had been constructed on a platform of Protestant unity and anti-Catholic bias. Circumstances had changed and the way was open for a Liberal revival. The Littles began to advance a realistic program for building a new Liberal party and acquiring responsible government.

In order to combat the responsible-government movement, the Conservative party enlisted the aid of religious bigotry. It cast the struggle in terms of an attempted religious ascendancy on the part of Roman Catholics and opted for "Protestant Union" to save the day. That had been a successful rallying cry in the 1830s and early 1840s. But the Bible question that had once alienated the Catholics from the Protestants had been put to rest while an evangelical debate had now split the hitherto united Protestant community. Perhaps no greater testimony to the fact that the Liberals were on a successful path in the 1850s was that Conservatives were forced to use an old campaign ploy that, ultimately, was widely believed to have been a failure.

In the end, Liberals were able to assemble a coalition of middle class–upper class interests crossing religious boundaries and win responsible government in 1855. Nevertheless, the intensity of the pro-Protestant, anti-Catholic campaign of the Conservative party was to have long-lasting repercussions. In the first place, establishment of Anglican schools in St John's and Conception Bay further fragmented the education system. But, most important, Conservatives had forced the construction of electoral boundaries along the lines of religious separation. That would serve to ensure the survival of sectarian politics for another century.

Appendix

Table 1
Exhibiting the extent of the "exclusive system" in Newfoundland Civil Department
Exclusively Protestant

#	Office	Name	Persuasion	Remarks	Salary	Totals
1	Governor	Henry Prescott	Protestant		£3000-0-0	
2	Secretary	James Crowdy	Protestant		£500-0-0	
3	Clrk of Council	Do	do		200-0-0	
4	Secretary's Clerk	Jos Templeman	Protestant		200-0-0	
5	2nd do	Chr Ayre	Protestant		200-0-0	
6	Clerk of Council	Do	Do		100-0-0	
7	Office helper	Val Born	Protestant		60-0-0	
8	Messenger	John Howston	Protestant		60-0-0	
9	Treasurer	N W Hoyles	Protestant		400-0-0	
10	Surveyor Gen	Jos Noad	Protestant		300-0-0	
11	Chainman to do	John Maddox	Protestant		20-0-0	
12	Dist Surgeon	Edwd Kielly	Reputed Catholic		80-0-0	
13	Gaol do	Do	Protestant		40-0-0	
14	Collector	Jas Spearman	Protestant		800-0-0	
15	Comptroller	Geo Bayley	Protestant		500-0-0	
16	Waiter & Searcher	G J Hayward	Protestant		350-0-0	
17	2nd do	G M Blyth	Protestant		200-0-0	
18	Clk & Ware House Keeper	Ed J Stewart	Protestant		150-0-0	
19	2nd clerk	James Winter	Protestant		100-0-0	
20	3rd do	Saml Prowse	Protestant		100-0-0	
21	4th do	Wm Lilly	Protestant		100-0-0	
22	Sub Collector	Jas Bayley	Protestant		250-0-0	
23	Clerk & locker	Ed E Brown	Protestant		100-0-0	
24	Sub Collector	Andw Pearce	Protestant		100-0-0	

No.	Office	Name	Religion	Salary
25	Do	Robt Carter	Protestant	100-0-0
26	Do	Robt Bayley	Protestant	150-0-0
27	Do	Josh Greene	Protestant	100-0-0
28	Do	Thos E Gaden	Protestant	100-0-0
29	Do	G King	Protestant	100-0-0
30	Do	W G Bradshaw	Protestant	100-0-0
31	Actng do	Lorenzo Moore	Protestant	100-0-0
	COLONIAL CUSTOMS			
32	Tide Surveyor	J R H Cooke	Protestant	
33	Land waiter	E L Moore	Protestant	
34	Clk to Collector	John Canning	Protestant	
35	Sub-Collector	Jas M Winter	Protestant	
Sic	Ditto	Thos Read	Protestant	
36	Preventive	John L McKie	Protestant	
	JUDICIAL DEPARTMENT			
37	Chief Judge	H J Boulton	Protestant	1200-0-0
38	Asst Judge	A W DesBarres	Protestant	700-0-0
39	Do	E B Brenton	Protestant	700-0-0
40	Attn General	James Simms	Protestant	450-0-0
41	Chief Clerk of Supreme Court	E M Archibald	Protestant	300-0-0
42	Crier of Supreme Court	Jas Lambord	Catholic	60-0-0
43	Solicitor Gen	H A Emerson	Protestant	no salary but has fees
44	Clk N Circuit	John Stark	Protestant	200-0-0
45	do S Circuit	Geo Simms	Protestant	200-0-0
46	Sheriff	B G Garrett	Protestant	655-0-0

no salary but the fees of this office after meeting all the expenses of SubSheriffs, Bailiffs, Houses,Light, Stationery, etc. returned in the Blue Book =655

#	Office	Name	Persuasion	Remarks	Salary	Totals
47	Judge of Vice Admiralty	Wm Carter	Protestant		500-0-0	
48	Registrar do	G W Carter	Protestant			To Protestants
49	Marshall	Chr Ayre	Protestant			£4905:
						to Catholics £60
STIPENDIARY MAGISTRATES						
50	St John's	James Blackie	Protestant		350-0-0	
51	Do	P W Carter	Protestant		350-0-0	
52	Hr Grace	Thos Danson	Protestant		350-0-0	
53	Carbonear	Jno Buckingham	Protestant		120-0-0	
54	Brigus	Rt J Pinsent	Protestant		120-0-0	
55	Trinity	Benj Sweetland	Protestant		120-0-0	
56	Bonavista	Wm Sweetland	Protestant		100-0-0	
57	Twillingate	John Peyton	Protestant		100-0-0	
58	Bay Bulls	John Mckie	Protestant		100-0-0	
59	Ferryland	Robt Carter	Protestant		100-0-0	
60	St Mary's	Josh Blackburn	Protestant		100-0-0	
61	Placentia	F L Bradshaw	Protestant		100-0-0	
62	Burin	Wm Hooper	Protestant		100-0-0	
63	Grand Bank	Wm Gaden	Protestant		100-0-0	
64	Fortune Bay	Thos Gaden	Protestant		100-0-0	To Protestants 2110; to Catholics 0-0-0
CORONERS						
65	St John's	Aaron Hogsett	Protestant	paid in fees voted by the Assembly		
66	Concep Bay	Josh Greene	Protestant	paid in fees voted by the Assembly		
67	Greenspond	Jas Winter	Protestant	paid in fees voted by the Assembly		

#	Place	Name	Religion	Notes	Amount
					Brought up 16385-0-0
68	Concep Bay	John Stark	Protestant	paid in fees voted by the Assembly	
69	Trinity	Robt Bayley	Protestant	paid in fees voted by the Assembly	
70	Hr Britain	Thos E Gaden	Protestant	paid in fees voted by the Assembly	

CONSTABULARY DEPARTMENT

#		Name	Religion	Notes	Amount
71	High Constable	John Findlay	Protestant		80-0-0
72	Constable	Ml Glinn	Protestant		45-0-0
73	Constable	Polk	Protestant		45-0-0
74	Constable	Toor	Protestant		45-0-0
75	Constable	Heney[2]	Catholic		45-0-0
76	Constable	Boyd	Protestant		45-0-0
77	Constable	Geary[3]	Catholic		45-0-0
					To Catholics, £90; to Protestant, £260

GAOLERS.

#		Name	Religion	Notes	Amount
78	Saint John's	R Perchard	Protestant		50-0-0
79	Hr Grace	John Currie	Protestant		50-0-0
80	Trinity	C Granger	Protestant	Also a Constable and Servant to the Protestant Clergyman Mr Bullock. This salary was reduced by the Assembly nearly to its former standard.	25-0-0
81	Ferryland	P Gorman	Not known to Deputation		25-0-0
82	Placentia	Luke Collins	Protestant		25-0-0
83	Burin	Ed Glynn	Protestant		25-0-0
					To Protestants, 175-0-0; to? not known, 25-0-0

#	Office	Name	Persuasion	Remarks	Salary	Totals
	CLERK OF THE PEACE					
84	Saint John's	A Hogsett	Protestant	The fees of this office are considerably underrated in Blue Book at	274-0-0	
85	Hr Grace	Alfred Mayne	Protestant	Fees and salary	156-0-0	
86	Ferryland	Thos Wright	Protestant	No return of fees	No salary	
87	Trinity	Robt Bayley	Protestant	No return	No salary	To Protestants, 430-0-0; to Catholics, 0-0-0
	LEGISLATIVE DEPARTMENT					
88	Usher of the Black Rod	Jos Templeman	Protestant		50-0-0	
89	Door-keeper	Val Born	Protestant		30-0-0	
90	Clerk	C Ayre	Protestant	These two are not	100-0-0	
91	Master in Chancery	B Robinson	Protestant	Returned in the Blue Book	100-0-0	To Protestants, 280-0-0; to Catholics, 0-0-0
	HOUSE OF ASSEMBLY IN 1836					
92	Speaker	Thos Bennett	Protestant		No salary	
93	Clerk	E M Archibald	Protestant		100-0-0	
	Sergeant-at-Arms	Hy Rendal	Protestant		50-0-0	
94	Door-keeper	John Stephenson	Protestant		35-0-0	
95	Messenger	Wm Kelly	Catholic		30-0-0	
96	Under Door-keeper	John Cox	Protestant	These two are not	25-0-0	
97	Solicitor	Charles Simms	Protestant	Returned in Blue Book	100-0-0	To Protestants 210-0-0; to Catholics, 30-0-0

ECCLESIASTICAL DEPARTMENT

PROTESTANT CHURCH			
98 Arch deacon	Ed Wix	Beside a most commodious Church in the centre of the Town, Glebe, House and Gardens & grounds for the Rector and a piece of ground also beautifully situated granted to the Archdeacon lately for a new Church	300-0-0
CATHOLIC CHURCH			
99 Bishop	Dr Fleming	Dr Fleming has been these five years seeking a patch of ground for the purpose of erecting Schools, a Church, a Cemetery etc for his Congregation who form full three fourths of the population of the District, but in vain but the Executive have always found means to defeat him. At [sic] this hour the Catholics owe nothing to the government but the recollection of wrongs which they hope now to have amply redressed [text missing]	75-0-0

---

[1] As there is no return of the names of the Constables there is no opportunity afforded of showing how the Exclusive System works in this department; however, the following seven positions from Saint John serve as an example.

[2] Heney is very many years in office.

[3] Geary was one of the prosecutors of the priests representatives in Autumn of 1836 and immediately after that trial was rewarded with a constableship, a Catholic constable having been displaced for not having been more active on the state prosecutions at that term to make room for him. In Conception Bay 13 constables are paid 270-0-0. In other parts of the island constables are paid 490-0-0.

[Source: CO 194/103, 7, Carson and Nugent to Glenelg, 31 Jan. 1838, encl.]

Table 2

Distribution of members, by districts, according to the Representation Bill produced by Philip Little in the House of Assembly, St John's, February 20, 1852

Liberal Party:

St John's	would return	6 members for 25,196 population
Conception Bay	would return	3 members for 11,500 population
Ferryland	would return	2 members for 4,370 population
Placentia–St Mary's	would return	4 members for 6,472 population
		15 liberals in all, or 1 for every 3,175 population

Other side:

Conception Bay	would return	5 members for 16,500 population
Trinity Bay	would return	2 members for 8,800 population
Bonavista Bay	would return	2 members for 7,227 population
Twillingate-Fogo	would return	2 members for 6,744 population
Burin	would return	2 members for 4,385 population
Fortune Bay	would return	2 members for 2,920 population
Bonne Bay	would return	1 members for 2,180 population
		16 members in all, or 1 for every 3,040 population

Source: Assembly Debates, 20 Feb. 1852

Table 3

The electoral division of Conception Bay, according to W.B. Row, Legislative Council, March 19, 1852

	Population		Representatives	
Districts	*Roman Catholics*	*Protestants*	*Roman Catholics*	*Protestants*
Western Section (St John's to Brigus)	3,230	767	1	0
Port de Grave (Brigus to Bryant's Cove)	2,627	7,262	0	2
Harbour Grace (Bryant's Cove to Crocker's Cove Brook)	4,772	Episcopalians and Dissenters even	2	0
Eastern Division	1,441	3,998	0	2

[*Source:* Council *Journal,* 19 March 1852.]

Table 4
Probable returns under the bill passed by the House of Assembly and sent to the Council for their concurrence on the 28th March 1853, according to the census of 1845

	Population	Protestant	Catholic	Members Protestant	Catholic
St John's district	25,196	6,210	18,986		6
Conception Bay is divided into 5 districts, to return 7 members, viz: Horse Cove to Cupids, incl.	6,719	2,611	4,108		2
Port de Grave to Bay Roberts	4,612	3,806	806	1	
Spaniards Bay to Harbour Grace	6,182	3,698	2,484	2	
Carbonear and Musquito	5,070	2,339	2,731		1
Freshwater to Bay de Verds	5,370	3,929	1,441	1	
Trinity district	8,801	7,518	1,283	2	
Bonavista district	7,227	5,418	1,809	2	
Fogo and Twilingate district	6,744	5,616	1,128	2	
Ferryland district	4,581	109	4,412		2
Burin district	4,358	2,407	1,951	2	
St Mary's and Placentia district	6,473	1,018	5,455		3
Fortune Bay and LaPoile district	5,100	4,708	392	2	
				14	14

[*Source:* Assembly *Journal,* 1853, 239.]

Table 5
Legislative Council amendments to the Representation Bill passed by the House of
Assembly, March 28, 1853

				Members	
	Population	Protestant	Catholic	Protestant	Catholic
St John's district to be divided in 2 districts	25,196	6,210	18,986		6
Conception Bay to be divided into 4 districts, viz:					
Horse Cove to Colliers, inclusive	3,183	672	3,141		1
Colliers to Bryant's Cove	9,574	7,358	2,216	3	
Bryant's Cove to Crocker's Cove	9,200	4,428	4,772		2
Cocker's Cove to Bay-de-Verd	5,439	3,998	1,441	1	
Trinity Bay district	8,801	7,518	1,283	3	
Bonavista Bay district	7,227	5,418	1,809	2	
Fogo district	6,774	5,616	1,128	2	
Ferryland district	4,370	169	4,201		1
Burin district	4,358	2,407	1,951		1
Placentia & St Mary's district	6,473	1,018	5,455		2
Fortune Bay and LaPoile district	5,100	4,708	392	2	
	96,296	49,521	46,775	13	13

[Source: Assembly Journal, 1853, 279.]

Table 6
Representation Bill passed by the Assembly, April 11, 1854

Distribution of members according to the census of 1845	Population	Protestant	Catholic	Members		Proportion for each member
				Protestant	Catholic	
St John's district is divided in 2 districts, by a line running North from Beck's Cove to Broad Cove	25,196	6,210	18,986		6	4,199
District of Trinity	8,801	7,518	1,286	3		2,933
District of Bonavista	7,227	5,418	1,809	2		3,613
District of Fortune Bay	2,920	2,557	363	1		2,920
District of LaPoile	2,180	2,151	29	1		2,180
District of Ferryland	4,581	182	4,399		2	2,290
District of Burin	4,358	2,407	1,951	2		2,179
District of Placentia–St Mary's	6,473	1,018	5,455		3	2,157
Conception Bay is divided into 5 districts, to return 7 members, for a population of 28,026, averaging 1 for every 4,000, viz:						
Horse Cove to Cupids, inclusive	6,722	2,614	4,108		2	3,361
Port de Grave to Bay Roberts	4,612	3,806	806	1		4,612
Spaniards Bay to Harbour Grace	6,182	3,698	2,484	2		3,091
Carbonear to Musquito	5,071	2,340	2,731		1	5,071
Fresh Water to Bay de Verde	5,439	3,988	1,451	1		5,439
Twilingate & Fogo, inclusive	6,744	5,616	1,128	2		3,372
	96,506	49,523	46,983	15	14	

Note: The Council stated last session, in their conference, that 13 Protestant members and 13 Catholic members would result from their amendments on the Representation Bill of that session. The bill of this session gives the power of returning 15 and 14. While the Assembly do not recognize the necessity or justice of obliging the districts to effect that result, it is more than probable the number of Protestant returns would be much larger under this bill than 15, as Catholic districts would, doubtless, continue to return independent Protestants, as they have done previously.

[*Source: Assembly Journal*, 1854: 193.]

Table 7
Legislative Council amendments to the Representation Bill passed by the Assembly,
April 1854

Districts	Population	Protestant	Catholic	Members Protestant	Catholic
St John's	25,196	6,210	18,986		6
Trinity	8,801	7,518	1,286	3	
Bonavista	7,227	5,418	1,809	3	
Twilingate & Fogo	6,744	5,616	1,128	2	
Ferryland	4,581	182	4,399		2
Placentia–St Mary's	6,473	1,018	5,455		2
Burin	4,358	2,407	1,951	1	
Fortune Bay	2,920	2,557	363	1	
LaPoile	2,180	2,151	29	1	
Conception Bay					
1st subdivision Horse Cove to Turk's Gut, inclusive	3,997	769	3,230		2
2nd subdivision Brigus to Port de Grave, both inclusive	5,538	4,150	1,388	1	
3rd subdivision Bay Roberts to Harbour Grace, both inclusive	7,981	5,198	2,783	2	
4th subdivision Carbonear and Musquito	5,071	2,340	2,731		1
5th subdivision Fresh Water to Bay de Verde, inclusive	5,439	3,988	1,451	1	
				15	14

[*Source:* Assembly *Journal,* 1854, 188.]

Table 8
The Representation Bill passed by the Assembly and finally accepted by the Legislative Council, November 9, 1854

Distribution of members according to the census of 1845	Population	Protestant	Catholic	Members		Proportion for each member
				Protestant	Catholic	
St John's district is divided into 2 districts, by a line running North from Beck's Cove to Broad Cove	25,196	6,210	18,986		6	4,199
District of Trinity	8,801	7,518	1,286	3		2,933
District of Bonavista	7,227	5,418	1,809	3		
District of Fortune Bay	2,920	2,557	363	1		2,920
District of LaPoile	2,180	2,151	29	1		2,180
District of Ferryland	4,581	182	4,399		2	2,290
District of Burin	4,358	2,407	1,951	2		2,179
District of Placentia–St Mary's	6,473	1,018	5,455		3	2,157
Conception Bay is divided into 5 districts, to return 7 members, for a population of 28,026, averaging 1 for every 4,000						
Horse Cove to Turk's Gut, inclusive	3,996	769	3,230		2	1,998
Turk's Gut, exclusive to Port de Grave, inclusive	5,538	4,150	1,388	1		5,538*
Port de Grave, exclusive to Harbour Grace, inclusive	7,981	5,198	2,783	2		3,990
Carbonear to Musquito, inclusive	5,071	2,340	2,731		1	5,071
Fresh Water to Bay de Verde	5,439	3,988	1,451	1		5,439
Twilingate & Fogo, inclusive	6,744	5,616	1,128	2		3,372
	96,506	49,523	46,983	16	14	

* *Note:* The relative numbers of these districts, as altered by the Council, stand as here stated. The population was more equally divided in the Bill as sent up by the Assembly.
[*Source: Assembly Journal*, 1854, 192.]

A Note on Sources

This study makes intensive use of primary sources in the various archival institutions recorded in the notes that follow. For historical developments within each church, however, I have had to rely on a number of secondary studies. Although general in scope and neglectful of the total environment within which the churches operated, these works contain much useful information. In the case of the Church of England, the best studies are Thomas Beamish Akins, *A Sketch of the Rise and Progress of the Church of England in the British North American Provinces* (1849); Philip Carrington, *The Anglican Church in Canada* (Toronto: Collins 1963); Thomas R. Millman and A.R. Kelley, *Atlantic Canada to 1900: A History of the Anglican Church* (Toronto: Anglican Book Centre 1983); C.F. Pascoe, *Two Hundred Years of the SPG: An Historical Account of the Society for the Propagation of the Gospel in Foreign Parts, 1701–1900* (London: SPG 1901). Recent years have witnessed the publication of numerous Anglican parish histories, the most valuable of which are Thomas G. Ford, *Short History of St. Pauls Harbour Grace, Parish and Church 1764–1935* (Harbour Grace, Nfld.: 100th Anniversary Committee 1935); P.B. Rendell and E.E. Knight, eds., *History of St. Thomas' Church 1836–1961* (St John's: St Thomas' Chruch 1962); C. Francis Rowe, *In Fields Afar: A Review of the Establishment of the Anglican Parish of St. John's and Its Cathedral* (St John's: A SeaWise Enterprise Book 1989); Naboth Winsor, *Through Peril, Toil and Pain: The Story of the First One Hundred Years (1825–1925) of the Church of England in the Northern Settlements of Greenspond Mission, Bonavista Bay, Newfoundland* (Gander, Nfld.: BSC Printers 1981).

On Methodist history, the following are useful: William Wilson, *Newfoundland and Its Missionaries* (1866); Naboth Winsor, *Hearts Strangely Warmed: A History of Methodism in Newfoundland 1765–1825* (Gander, Nfld.: BSC Printers

1982); and also by Winsor, *Building on a Firm Foundation: A History of Methodism in Newfoundland, 1825-1855* (Gander, Nfld: n.d.). The only history of the Roman Catholic Church available is M.F. Howley, *Ecclesiastical History of Newfoundland* (Boston: 1888). Though this work is much more than a compilation of clerical appointments and parish foundings, Howley's tendency to see all developments through a coloured, Roman Catholic lens seriously hampers his view. Then, too, he does not proceed beyond 1850. Cyril Byrne's *Gentlemen-Bishops and Faction Fighters: The Letters of Bishops O'Donel, Lambert, Scallan and Other Irish Missionaries* (St John's: Jesperson Press 1984) is an essential supplement, not just for the presentation of precious archival evidence but for the editor's incisive comments and his translations and explanations of Latin and idiomatic phrases long since buried in the folklore of the period. Raymond J. Lahey's *James Louis O'Donel in Newfoundland 1784-1807* (St John's: Newfoundland Historical Society 1984) is a useful pamphlet on O'Donel's role in founding the Catholic church in the colony. The reader should also consult Michael Brosnan's *Pioneer History of St. George's Diocese, Newfoundland* (Toronto: Mission Press 1948).

The published political history of Newfoundland is marked by the same shortcomings as characterize published church history. Until 1966 the only published monograph on Newfoundland's nineteenth-century politics was Gertrude Gunn's *Political History of Newfoundland, 1832-1864* (Toronto: University of Toronto Press 1966). Though church history does not fall within the range of her study, Gunn's work is especially valuable for the exposition of Conservative Party politics and for the treatment of the convoluted constitutional developments of that period. I have complemented Gunn's work with a comprehensive study of the various churches from 1745 onwards and with details of the various post-1832 campaigns collected from primary sources not accessible to Gunn in the 1960s. The best study of constitutional developments in the half-century preceding 1832 is A.H. McLintock's *The Establishment of Constitutional Government in Newfoundland, 1783-1831: A Study of Retarded Colonisation* (London: Longmans, Green 1941). The remaining published sources are general histories. Those published prior to 1900 are valuable reading especially for the personal comments from the various authors on developments to which they themselves were first-hand witnesses. The best of these, in order of importance, are D.W. Prowse, *History of Newfoundland* (London: Macmillan 1895); Charles Pedley, *The History of Newfoundland from the Earliest Times to the Year 1860* (1863); John Reeves, *History of the Government of the Island of Newfoundland* (1793); Lewis Amadeus Anspach, *History of the Island of Newfoundland* (1819); Joseph Hatton and Moses Harvey, *Newfoundland, the Oldest British Colony: Its History, Its Present Condition and Its Prospects in the Future* (London: 1883).

My research has been ably assisted by several excellent articles on selected topics of Newfoundland's nineteenth-century political history. Chief among them are several articles by Philip McCann: "Bishop Fleming and the Politicization of the Irish Roman Catholics in Newfoundland, 1830–1850," in Terrence Murphy and Cyril J. Byrne, eds., *Religion and Identity: The Experience of Irish and Scottish Catholics in Atlantic Canada* (St John's: Jesperson Press 1987), 81–97; "Culture, State Formation and the Invention of Tradition: Newfoundland 1832–1855," in *Journal of Canadian Studies*, vol. 23 (1988), 86–103; "Class, Gender and Religion in Newfoundland Education, 1836–1901," *Historical Studies in Education*, 1 (1989), 179–200; and "The 'No Popery' Crusade and the Newfoundland School System, 1836–1843," *Société canadienne d'histoire de l'Église catholique: Étude d'histoire religeuse*, 58 (1991), 79–97. These articles represent the first successful published attempt to identify factors other than religion influencing political and educational developments in nineteenth-century Newfoundland. Hans Rollmann's "Religious Enfranchisement and Roman Catholics in Eighteenth-Century Newfoundland," in Murphy and Byrne, *Religion and Identity*, 34–52, should be studied for an assessment of how the Roman Catholic Church achieved religious liberty. Terrence Murphy's "Trusteeism in Atlantic Canada: The Struggle for Leadership among the Irish Catholics of Halifax, St John's, and Saint John 1780–1850," in Terrence Murphy and Gerald Stortz, *Creed and Culture: The Place of English Speaking Catholics in Canadian Society 1750–1930* (Montreal: McGill-Queen's University Press, 1993), 126–51, is extremely valuable for its consideration of relationships between lay Catholics and their clergy over that period. In the same volume, 49–78, Raymond J. Lahey's "Catholicism and Colonial Policy in Newfoundland, 1779–1845" is a comprehensive survey of British behaviour towards Newfoundland.

Notes

INTRODUCTION

1 Peter F. Neary and Sidney J.R. Noel, "Continuity and Change In Newfoundland Politics," in Ian McDonald, ed., "Selected Readings, History
3120: Newfoundland since 1815" (St John's: Memorial University
1976), 278.
2 J. Murray Beck, *Politics of Nova Scotia, Volume One, 1710–1896* (Tan-
tallon, N.S.: Four East Publications 1985), 23; W.S. MacNutt, *The Atlantic Provinces: The Emergence of Colonial Society, 1712–1857* (Toronto:
McClelland and Stewart 1965), 145–8.
3 MacNutt, *The Atlantic Provinces*, 125–8.
4 See ch. 5.
5 Hans Rollmann, "Religious Enfranchisement and Roman Catholics in
Eighteenth-Century Newfoundland," in Terrence Murphy and Cyril J.
Byrne, eds., *Religion and Identity: The Experience of Irish and Scottish
Catholics in Atlantic Canada* (St John's: Jesperson Press 1987), 36, 40–3.
A note on terminology is in order at this point. Strictly speaking, the
term "dissenter" should not be applied either to Wesleyan Methodists
or to Presbyterians. In Newfoundland, however, adherents of the
Church of England commonly used the word "dissenter" in referring to
all Protestants outside the Anglican fold. This study follows the same
practice.
6 Ibid., 38–9.
7 See, for example, M.F. Howley, *Ecclesiastical History of Newfoundland*
(Boston: Doyle and Whittle 1888), esp. ch. 13.

8 MacNutt, *The Atlantic Provinces*, 104–7; John S. Moir, ed., *Church and State in Canada 1627–1867: Basic Documents* (Toronto: McClelland and Stewart 1967), 31–2, 38, 58–60, 77–86, 111–120.

9 S.D. Clark, *Church and Sect in Canada* (Toronto: University of Toronto Press 1948), esp. chs. 1–2.

10 *Census of Canada, 4, 1665–1871: Nova Scotia*, 232–9.

11 Clark, *Church and Sect*, 93–100.

12 *Census of Canada, 4: Upper Canada*, 178–99.

13 S.J.R. Noel, *Politics in Newfoundland* (Toronto: University of Toronto Press 1973), 21.

CHAPTER ONE

1 SPG, *Sermons Preached and an Abstract of Proceedings* (London: SPG, 1732), 5: *Proceedings*, 42–3; Thomas R. Millman and A.R. Kelley, *Atlantic Canada to 1900: A History of the Anglican Church* (Toronto: Anglican Book Centre 1983), 19.

2 William Peaseley was born in Dublin in 1714 and, following ordination as an SPG missionary in 1742, came to Newfoundland. See *DCB*, 3: 504.

3 D.W. Prowse, *History of Newfoundland, 3rd ed.* (St John's: Dicks 1971), 7.

4 John S. Moir, *The Church in the British Era from the British Conquest to Confederation* (Toronto: McGraw-Hill Ryerson 1972), 4–5.

5 Erasmus Stourton (1603–58) was born in England; for a brief biography see Melvin Baker and Robert D.W. Pitt, eds., *Dictionary of Newfoundland and Labrador* (St John's: Harry Cuff Publications 1990), 330.

6 Prowse, *History*, 101; Moir, *The Church in the British Era*, 10; also Philip Carrington, *The Anglican Church in Canada* (Toronto: Collins 1963), 23; and F.M. Buffett, *The Story of the Church in Newfoundland* (Toronto: General Board of Religious Education 1939), 9.

7 R.J. Lahey, "The Role of Religion in Lord Baltimore's Colonial Enterprise," *Maryland Historical Magazine*, 72/4(1977), 506–8.

8 Hans Rollmann, "Anglicans, Puritans, and Quakers in Seventeenth-Century Newfoundland" (http://www.ucs.mun.ca/~hrollman/index.html: home page of Dr Hans Rollmann, Department of Religious Studies, Memorial University of Newfoundland), 2–3.

9 Carrington, *The Anglican Church*, 29–30; Prowse, *History*, 229.

10 Ruth M. Christensen, "The Establishment of S.P.G. Missions in Newfoundland, 1703–1783," in *Historical Magazine of the Protestant Episcopal Church*, June 1951, 214.

11 PANL, CO Records, Series 194(Newfoundland Incoming Correspondence, hereafter cited as CO 194), vol. 7: 275. This series of extensive correspondence is the most important primary source for the student

of Newfoundland history. Encompassing the period from 1696 to 1922, it is a veritable gold mine on the social, economic and political conditions of Newfoundland. The governor's reports are not only regular and detailed for the period of his stay but they contain enclosures from the principal players in church, state, and the economy. These enclosures are replete with statistics, comments, and personal observations on the social, political and economic culture of Newfoundland. They were preserved at the Colonial Office headquarters in London and microfilm copies have been made available to the PANL. Their value to the Newfoundland historian is reinforced by the fact that Newfoundland governors failed to preserve locally any originals or copies of their Colonial Office correspondence until 1824. And, although their local records after that date have been preserved intact, the historian must be wary of relying on them alone for the valuable and frequent enclosures were rarely copied before being forwarded to London.

12 Millman and Kelley, *Atlantic Canada*, 20; Carrington, *The Anglican Church*, 32.

13 Millman and Kelly, *Atlantic Canada*, 21.

14 Christensen, "The Establishment of SPG Missions," 213–14, 218.

15 R.J. Lahey, "Newfoundland Material Contained in the Annual Reports of the United Society for the Propagation of the Gospel in Foreign Parts, 1704–1800" (St John's: typescript, Centre for Newfoundland Studies, Memorial University of Newfoundland, n.d.). These extracts are not paginated but are organized in chronological order.

16 Charles Inglis (1734–1816) was born in Ireland, served as an Anglican cleric in the American colonies before the American revolution, and afterwards he was appointed the first colonial bishop in 1787. See DCB 5: 444–8.

17 Moir, *Church and State*, 54.

18 The most authoritative and detailed study of the Newfoundland fisheries is Keith Matthews, "A History of the West of England–Newfoundland Fishery" (D. Phil. thesis, Oxford University 1968). See also Harold A Innis, *The Cod Fisheries: The History of an International Economy*, rev. ed. (Toronto: University of Toronto Press 1954), and C. Grant Head, *Eighteenth Century Newfoundland* (Toronto: McClelland and Stewart 1976). The best study of the nineteenth-century cod fishery is Shannon Ryan, *Fish out of Water: The Newfoundland Saltfish Trade, 1814–1914* (St John's: Breakwater Books 1986).

19 S.D. Clark, *The Social Development of Canada* (Toronto: University of Toronto Press 1942), 3.

20 Prowse, *History*, 331.

21 Ibid., 254–5.

22 Lahey, *Newfoundland Material*, 2–3.

23 Millman and Kelley, *Atlantic Canada*, 21.

24 C.F. Pascoe, *Three Hundred Years of the SPG: An Historical Account of the Society for the Propagation of the Gospel in Foreign Parts, 1701- 1900* (London: SPG 1901), 92.

25 *Calendar of Letters from Canada, Newfoundland, Pennsylvania, Barbados and the Bahamas 1721–1793, preserved at the Society for the Propagation of the Gospel* (London: Swift(P&D) 1972), 57–8.

26 CO 194/6, 276–7, Commodore Scott to William Popple, 16 Nov. 1718; 8, 173–8, Lord Vere Beauclerk to Mr Burchett, 18 Oct. 1728; 60, 185–6, Merchants of Bristol to Bathurst, 11 March 1817.

27 Paul O'Neill, *The Oldest City: The Story of St John's, Newfoundland* (Erin: Press Porcepic 1975), 227.

28 CO 194/6, 321, William Keen to the Commissioners of Trade and Plantations, 30 Oct. 1719.

29 Ibid., 8, 173–8, Beauclerk to Mr Burchett, 19 Aug. 1728.

30 Griffith Williams, *An Account of the Island of Newfoundland* (London: 1765), as quoted in Peter Neary and Patrick O'Flaherty, eds., *By Great Waters: A Newfoundland and Labrador Anthology* (Toronto: University of Toronto Press 1974), 43.

31 Clark, *The Social Development of Canada*, 2–3.

32 Pascoe, *Three Hundred Years*, 91.

33 Clark, *Church and Sect*, ch. 1.

34 Pascoe, *Three Hundred Years*, 92.

35 Lahey, *Newfoundland Material*, 1778.

36 Ibid. The soldier was the Congregationalist minister John Jones, who founded a tiny, but successful, congregation among a few elite families in St John's. See James S. Armour, *John Jones and the Early Dissenter Movement in Newfoundland* (St John's: Newfoundland Historical Society 1975).

37 Prowse, *History*, 171, 183, 209, 215–22, 235, 239–45, 248–9, 305–9.

38 Millman and Kelley, *Atlantic Canada*, 14; Moir, *The Church in the British Era*, 31; William Wilson, *Newfoundland and Its Missionaries* (Cambridge, U.K., 1866), 34–5. Thomas Beamish Akins says in *A Sketch of the Rise and Progress of the Church of England in the British North American Provinces* (Halifax, 1849) that, when the SPG officially appointed Coughlan in 1768, he had already been residing there three years.

39 Wilson, *Newfoundland*, 140–2.

40 Ibid.,158.

41 McGeary was an Irishman and previously had been on a mission in the United States; Baker and Pitt, *Dictionary*, 208.

42 Wilson, *Newfoundland*, 176–7.

43 O'Donel had been born in Ireland *c.* 1737 and ordained a priest in 1770. For a brief biography, see *DCB* 5: 631–3.

44 Howley, *Ecclesiastical History*, 177–80.

45 PANL, MG 598, Correspondence of the Society for the Propagation of the Gospel in Foreign Parts(hereafter cited as SPG correspondence), Rev. John Harries, Placentia, to Dr Morice, London, 1788. The incoming correspondence of the SPG has been preserved at the organization's headquarters in London and has been made available to various archival institutions by means of microfilm copies. The corespondence, which embraces the period between 1702 and 1928, includes letters, journals, and calendars for all North American stations as well as the West Indies and Australia. In addition to reporting on church developments, the correspondents frequently forwarded extensive comments on the habits, customs, and economic conditions of the people. These letters are a highly valuable source, second only to the governor's correspondence, on the history of Newfoundland.

46 PANL, GN2/39/A, Census Materials, 1675–1884: Census, 1675.

47 Keith Matthews, *Lectures on the History of Newfoundland 1500–1830* (St John's: Breakwater Books 1988), 18.

48 Idem, "A History of the West of England–Newfoundland Fishery," esp. ch. 1; Innis, *The Cod Fisheries*, ch. 4.

49 Matthews, *Lectures*, 23.

50 Prowse, *History*, 76–7.

51 Matthews, *Lectures*, 23.

52 Gerald S. Graham, "Fisheries and Sea Power," in G.A. Rawlyk, ed., *Historical Essays on the Atlantic Provinces* (Toronto: McClelland and Stewart 1967), 7–16.

53 Ibid., 7.

54 Ibid., 8–9; Matthews, *Lectures*, 26–7.

55 Prowse, *History*, 55.

56 Graham, "Fisheries," 10.

57 Matthews, *Lectures*, 26–7.

58 Graham, "Fisheries," 8.

59 Prowse, *History*, 87.

60 Ibid., 192.

61 Ibid., 192–6.

62 Matthews, "A History of the West of England–Newfoundland Fishery," ch. 1.

63 John P. Greene, *Trial and Triumph: The History of Newfoundland and Labrador* (Toronto: Doubleday 1982), 132–5.

64 The best studies of Newfoundland settlement history are: W. Gordon Handcock, *Soe longe as there comes noe women: Origins of English Settlement*

in Newfoundland (St John's: Breakwater Books 1989), and John J. Mannion, ed., *The Peopling of Newfoundland: Essays in Historical Geography* (St John's: Memorial University of Newfoundland 1977). See also Matthews, *Lectures,* chs. 10, 14, and Head, *Eighteenth Century.*

65 Matthews, *Lectures,* ch. 21.

66 Handcock, *Soe longe,* 75–6.

67 CO 194/16, 108 (1764); 57, 11–12 (1815); 72, 390 (1826).

68 CO 194/7, 246, Commodore Bowker to the Board of Trade, 29 March 1725, enclosure: "Proceedings of the Harbour of St. John's on the 26th day of November in the 10th year of the Reign of King George and in the year of our Lord 1723."

69 Prowse, *History,* 287; A.H. McLintock, *The Establishment of Constitutional Government in Newfoundland, 1783–1832: A Study of Retarded Colonization* (London: Longmans, Green 1941), 56.

70 Henry Osborn was a captain in the Royal Navy; for a brief biography see Baker and Pitt, *Dictionary,* 255.

71 Millman and Kelley, *Atlantic Canada,* 23; Moir, *Church and State,* 54.

72 William Pilot, "Historical Sketches of the Church of England in Newfoundland," in Thomas G. Ford, *Short History of St. Paul's Harbor Grace, Parish and Church, 1764–1935* (Harbor Grace: 100th Anniversary Committee 1935), 11, says that Bishop Stanser visited Newfoundland in 1807 but Pilot was mistaken at least about Stanser's status for he did not become bishop until 1816. See Judith Fingard, "Robert Stanser," in *DCB* 6: 731–2.

73 Clark, *Social Development,* 3.

74 Anspach had come to Newfoundland as a schoolteacher in 1799; Baker and Pitt, *Dictionary,* 5.

75 SPG correspondence: Anspach to headquarters, 18 Dec. 1805.

76 H. H. Walsh, *The Christian Church in Canada* (Toronto: Ryerson Press 1956), 106.

77 Wilson, *Newfoundland,* 193.

78 Ellis was born in Ireland in 1780 and ordained a Methodist clergyman in 1808; Baker and Pitt, *Dictionary,* 98.

79 SPG correspondence: Carrington to headquarters, 23 July 1817. Frederick Hamilton Carrington (b. 1780) was an SPG missionary from England who served in Newfoundland for twenty-six years before his death at St John's in 1839; *ENL,* 1, 357.

80 John Leigh had been born in England *c.* 1789 and came to Newfoundland as an SPG missionary in 1816; Baker and Pitt, *Dictionary,* 197.

CHAPTER TWO

1 Cochrane had been born in London in 1789; Baker and Pitt, *Dictionary,* 62.

2 Statistics on population distribution and its denominational make-up have been collected from a variety of sources, principally the annual "Returns of The Fishery And Inhabitants ..." in CO, Series 194. See, for example, CO 194/72, 1826, 390–1: "Returns of the Fishery and Inhabitants of the Island of Newfoundland for the year ending 30 June, 1826." See also the *Census of Newfoundland, 1827*.

3 CO 194/72, Cochrane to Bathurst, 30 Jan. 1826; 74, Cochrane to Coster, 10 May 1826, and Cochrane to Bathurst, 29 Jan. 1827; 76, 60–4, Tucker to Huskisson, 25 Jan. 1828; 70, 218, E.B. Brenton, governor's secretary to the inhabitants of Tilton Harbour, 7 Nov. 1825; 74, Cochrane to Bathurst, 6 Feb. 1827; 79, W.A. Clarke to R.W. Hay, 9 March 1829.

4 Prowse, *History*, 405.

5 For clerical attitudes towards the fishery and inhabitants of Newfoundland, I am indebted to the Newfoundland correspondence of both the SPG and the WMMS, whose eighteenth- and nineteenth-century correspondence is to be found on microfilm at the PANL. The records of the WMMS consist of twenty-one microfilm reels of incoming correspondence and mission-committee minutes for various locations in North and South America.

6 CO 194/77, Cochrane to Huskisson, 11 April 1828.

7 CO 194, annual "Returns of the Fishery and Inhabitants..." for the period 1800–25.

8 Ibid.

9 *Newfoundlander*, 5, 19, 26 Sept., 3 Oct. 1827; 7 Aug. 1828; 1, 22 Jan. 1829.

10 Patrick Morris (1789–1849) was born in Ireland and came to Newfoundland as a boy; *DCB*, 7: 626–34.

11 CO 194/76, Cochrane to Huskisson, 11 April 1828; 78, Cochrane to Murray, 22 Dec. 1829; 83, Tucker to Goderich, 24 Jan. 1832.

12 My assessment of the relations between Protestants and Catholics in Newfoundland for the period encompassed by this study is based on extensive readings of the correspondence in CO 194, files of the SPG and the WMMS.

13 PANL, Newfoundland Blue Book, 1825.

14 *Newfoundland Patriot*, 17 Jan. 1844.

15 W.E.H. Lecky, *A History of Ireland in the 18th Century* (London: Longmans, Green 1892), vol. 1, ch. 2, 138–42.

16 Ibid., especially vol. 2, 180–217, and vol. 4, 1–3.

17 Ibid., vol. 5, ch. 13, esp. 441–6 and 458–60.

18 *Newfoundlander*, Fleming to the editor, 30 Aug. 1832.

19 *Patriot*, 17 Jan. 1844.

20 CO 194/70, Cochrane to Bathurst, 29 Dec. 1825; 73, 142, Stephen to Horton, 6 Jan. 1826; also, PANL, Sir Thomas Cochrane Papers

(hereafter cited as Cochrane Papers), mss 2371, 114, Bathurst to Cochrane, 10 April 1826.

21 Scallan had been born in Ireland in 1765, ordained a priest in 1791, and succeeded to the bishopric at St John's in 1817 on the death of Bishop Lambert; Baker and Pitt, *Dictionary*, 305.

22 Newfoundland Blue Books, 1824, 1825.

23 CO 194/74, Cochrane to Bathurst, 6 Feb. 1827; 75, Hamilton to Horton, 12 March 1827; 79, W.A. Clarke to R.W. Hay, 9 March 1829; 85, Cochrane to Stanley, 26 Dec. 1833; 87, Cochrane to Stanley, 8 April 1834.

24 CO 194/72, Cochrane to Bathurst, 10 Nov. 1826. Cochrane proposed, among other things, that the government engage clergy to serve in the various bays and that all Church of England clergy be paid out of government coffers.

25 My statistical assessments of the relative strength of the various denominations are based on studies of the annual "Returns of the Fishery and Inhabitants," found in CO 194; also *Census of Newfoundland, 1827, 1836*.

26 My account, in succeeding pages, of Wesleyan Methodists and Anglicans in Newfoundland – their rise, progress, and interrelationships – is based primarily on two sources: the correspondence of the WMMS from 1800 to 1867; and the correspondence of the SPG from 1772 to 1855. In order to keep references to a minimum, sources are given for only direct quotations.

27 SPG, "C" Series, Balfour to secretary, 8 Dec. 1784.

28 During the same period the Anglicans were conducting an identical strategy in the Maritimes. See Moir, *Church and State*, 58–62.

29 William Waldegrave (1753–1825) was governor of Newfoundland from 1797 to 1800; Baker and Pitt, *Dictionary*, 348–9.

30 CO 194/39, 191, Proclamation of Governor Waldegrave, 4 Oct. 1797.

31 Pickmore was a lieutenant in the Royal Navy and governor of Newfoundland from 1816 to 1818; Baker and Pitt, *Dictionary*, 269.

32 CO 194/59, 1–3, Pickmore to Bathurst, 7 Jan. 1817.

33 WMMS, George Cubit, St John's, to Mission Committee, London, 16 Sept. 1817.

34 Ibid.

35 Ibid.

36 SPG, "C" Series, Rev. Carrington, Harbour Grace, to secretary, 23 July 1817; also Rev. Leigh, Harbour Grace, to secretary, 1822; and Rev. John Burt, Harbour Grace, to secretary, 27 Dec. 1833.

37 D. George Boyce, *Nineteenth Century Ireland: The Search for Stability* (Savage, Md.: Barnes and Noble 1991), 34–6.

38 The varied Anglican views are reflected in the SPG correspondence of the period.

39 Howley, *Ecclesiastical History*, 194, 204–5, 212–17; Cyril J. Byrne, ed., *Gentlemen-Bishops and Faction Fighters: The Letters of Bishops O Donel, Lambert, Scallan and Other Irish Missionaries* (St John's: Jesperson Press 1984), 120–2, 124, 139, 160–2, 171–2, 187–8, 191, 201–6, 207–13, 221–2, 224–6, 240–2. See also CO 194/44, Gower to Camden, 25 Oct. 1804, enclosure: Memorial of Merchants, Magistrates etc. of St John's, 9 Aug. 1804.

40 General John Skerret (*c.* 1743–1813) was military commander at St John's, 1799–1807; Baker and Pitt, *Dictionary*, 314–15.

41 Howley, *Ecclesiastical History*, 206, 242–3, 254.

42 CO 194/77, Cochrane to Huskisson, 11 April 1828.

43 SPG, "C" Series, Rev. Harries, Placentia, to secretary, London, 1788.

44 G.I.T. Machin, *The Catholic Question in English Politics 1820 to 1830* (Oxford, U.K.: Clarendon Press 1964), 7, 55, 145–6.

45 SPG, "C" Series, Dr Skelton, Trinity, to secretary, London, 5 Jan. 1819.

46 WMMS, reel 1, letter 191, Rev. Cubit, St John's, to mission committee, London, 1817.

47 Ibid., reel 2, partially readable letter between 134 and 139, dated 1819.

48 Ibid., reel 2, letter 26, James Hickson, Harbour Grace, to mission committee, London, 9 Jan. 1819.

49 CO 194/76, Cochrane to Huskisson, 11 April 1828; 72, Cochrane to Bathurst, 10 Nov. 1826.

50 Ibid., vol. 72, Cochrane to Bathurst, 10 Nov. 1826.

51 SPG, "C" Series, Rev. John Leigh, Twillingate, to secretary, London, 8 Dec. 1818.

52 Ibid., Rev. George Coster, Bonavista, to Bishop Inglis, 2 Nov. 1826.

53 CO 194/74, Cochrane to Bathurst, 26 Sept. 1827, encl: Bishop Inglis to Cochrane, 10 Sept. 1827.

54 Moir, *Church and State*, 54–7; MacNutt, *The Atlantic Provinces*, 188–90.

55 Ibid., 54.

56 Moir, *The Church in the British Era*, 129–30.

57 SPG, "C" Series, John Leigh, Twillingate, to secretary, London, 17 April 1817.

58 Ibid., correspondence of Rev. Spencer, Trinity, 1821.

59 Ibid., calendars of Rev. Bullock's correspondence from Trinity, 1822.

60 Greene, *Trial and Triumph*, 211–12.

61 SPG, "C" Series, Dr Skelton, Trinity, to secretary, 5 Jan. 1819.

62 Elie Halevy, *The Liberal Awakening 1815–1830: A History of the English People in the Nineteenth Century*, vol. 2 (New York: Peter Smith 1949), especially 138–45.

63 E. Jane Whateley, *Life and Correspondence of Richard Whateley, D D* (London: Longmans, Green 1875), 66.

64 Desmond Bowen, *The Protestant Crusade 1800–1870* (Montreal: McGill-Queen's University Press 1978).

65 SPG, "C" Series, Archdeacon Wix to Bishop Inglis, 23 Dec. 1830.

66 George Henry Bolt, *The Codner Centenary: or the Performance of a Vow: A Short Review of the Rise and Progress of the Colonial and Continental Church Society, 1823–1923* (St John's, 1923), 1. See also the Colonial and Continental Church Society (commonly known as the Newfoundland School Society), Annual Reports and Minutes, vol. 1; these reports and minutes are located at PANL on nine reels of microfilm and encompass the period between 1823 and 1872 inclusive.

67 Bolt, *Codner Centenary*, 1.

68 CO, Series 195, Newfoundland outgoing correspondence(hereafter cited as CO 195), Bathurst to Cochrane 8 June 1826; this corespondence, on microfilm at PANL, encompasses the period from 1623 to 1867.

69 SPG, "C" Series, calendars of Nova Scotia correspondence, Bishop's letters: Inglis to Cochrane, 10 Sept. 1827.

70 PANL, St John's, BIS, minutes, 22 May 1825.

71 *DCB*, 7: 626–34.

72 Machin, *The Catholic Question*, 136.

73 SPG, "C" Series, Rev. George Coster, Bonavista, to secretary, 9 Nov. 1836.

74 Ibid., Inglis to Cochrane, 10 Sept. 1827.

75 Ibid., Coster, Bonavista, to secretary, 21 July 1827.

76 Frank Smith, *A History of English Elementary Education* (New York: Augusta M. Kelley 1970), 76–84.

77 Edward Wix (1802–66) had been born in England, ordained church of England priest in 1825, and came to Newfoundland in 1830; Baker and Pitt, *Dictionary*, 368.

78 SPG, "C" Series, Wix to Bishop Inglis, 8 Sept. 1830.

79 Ibid., Wix to secretary, 12 Sept. 1832.

80 Ibid., Rev. Bullock, Trinity, to Archdeacon Wix, 25 Oct. 1833; also, Wix to Campbell, 28 Oct. 1833, and encl., Bullock to Garland, 23 Sept. 1833; Bullock to Garland, 7 Oct. 1833; Bullock to secretary, 8 Oct. 1833, and Willoughby to Governor Cochrane, 22 Oct. 1833 enclosed in James Crowdy to Edward Wix, 20 Oct. 1833.

81 Ibid., Bullock to Wix, 24 Sept. 1833.

82 Charles Blackman (c. 1798–1853) had come to Newfoundland in 1819 as tutor to the governor's son, was ordained as Church of England priest in 1822, and served until his death; Baker and Pitt, *Dictionary*, 22–3.

83 *Patriot*, 2 Sept. 1834: Fleming to the editor, 28 Aug. 1834.

84 CO 194/80, Tucker to Hay, 24 May 1830.

CHAPTER THREE

1 *Ledger,* 8 May 1829.
2 *Newfoundlander,* 7 May 1829.
3 CO 194/78–83, Governor Cochrane's correspondence, Dec. 1829–Dec. 1832.
4 Ibid., 70, Cochrane to Bathurst, 11 Oct., 29 Dec. 1825.
5 Ibid., Cochrane to Murray, 22 Dec. 1829, encls: Simms, Tucker, Des-Barres, and Brenton to the governor.
6 Ibid., 80, Tucker to Hay, 24 May 1830, encl.: *Newfoundlander,* 21 Dec. 1829, with copy of correspondence between Joseph Shea and the governor.
7 *Newfoundlander,* 21 Jan., 28 Jan. 1830.
8 CO 194/81, Cochrane to Goderich, 4 May, 14 Sept. 1831.
9 David Alexander, "Newfoundland's Traditional Economy and Development to 1934," in James Hiller and Peter Neary, eds., *Newfoundland in the Nineteenth and Twentieth Centuries: Essays in Interpretation* (Toronto: University of Toronto Press 1980), 20–1.
10 Shannon Ryan, *The Ice Hunters: A History of Newfoundland Sealing to 1914* (St John's: Breakwater Books 1994), 406; also idem, *Fish out of Water,* 60–1.
11 CO 194/82, 24–78, Tucker, DesBarres, and Brenton to Governor Cochrane, 23 Aug. 1831. There is considerable diversity of opinion in modern historical studies over the actual nature of those fishery laws. See, for example, Sean T. Cadigan, *Hope and Deception in Conception Bay: Merchant-Settler Relations in Newfoundland, 1785–1855* (Toronto: University of Toronto Press 1995), esp. ch. 5; Robert M. Lewis, "The Survival of the Planters' Fishery in Nineteenth and Twentieth Century Newfoundland," in Rosemary E. Ommer, ed., *Merchant Credit and Labour Strategies in Historical Perspective* (Fredericton: Acadiensis Press,1990), 102–13, and, in the same volume, James K. Hiller, "The Newfoundland Credit System: An Interpretation," 86–102, and Patricia Thornton, "The Transition from the Migratory to the Resident Fishery in the Strait of Belle Isle," 138–66. See also Steven David Antler, "Colonial Exploitation and Economic Stagnation in Nineteenth Century Newfoundland" (D. PhD thesis, University of Connecticut 1975); Ryan, *Fish out of Water,* 60–1.
12 CO 194/72, Cochrane to Bathurst, 10 Nov. 1826.
13 J.C. Beckett, *The Making of Modern Ireland, 1603–1923* (London: Faber and Faber 1981), 303–4.
14 Howley, *Ecclesiastical History,* 245–6; Byrne, *Gentlemen Bishops,* 297- 9.
15 *Newfoundlander,* 30 April 1829.

16 CO 194/87, Cochrane to Stanley, 8 April 1834.

17 Howley, *Ecclesiastical History*, 245.

18 CO 194/79, W.A. Clarke to R.W. Hay, 9 March 1829.

19 Ibid., 80, 405, Tucker to Hay, 24 May 1830, encl., *Newfoundlander*, 31 Dec. 1829, Bruce to Joseph Shea, 22 Dec. 1829. Bruce was the governor's secretary at that time and Shea was the secretary of the public meeting.

20 Ibid. R.A. Tucker (1784–1868) served as chief justice of Newfoundland from 1822 to 1833; Baker and Pitt, *Dictionary*, 342.

21 Lecky, *A History*, vol. 2: 63–5.

22 *Ledger*, 1, 11 June 1830; *Newfoundlander*, 3, 10 June 1830.

23 Ibid., 11 June 1830.

24 CO 194/44, Gower to Lord Camden, 25 Oct. 1804; 77, Cochrane to Huskisson, 11 April 1828; 87, Cochrane to Stanley, 8 April 1834.

25 Michael MacDonagh, *Daniel O'Connell* (Dublin: Talbot Press 1929), chs. 8–10.

26 Since Fleming's death in 1850 it has been unanimously reported that he had been born in Tipperary. But recent microfilm copies of what were believed to be hitherto extinct 1834 Newfoundland *Patriots* have thrown serious doubt on those assertions. See *Patriot*, 2 Sept. 1834, "Brutus" to H.J. Boulton, 31 Aug. 1834, where "Brutus" says that Fleming was born "… in Kilkenny, about 10 miles from Waterford and 3 from the town of Carrick-on-Suir."

27 Archives of the Sisters of Presentation, St John's, folder 6, no. 10, M.X. Lynch, St John's to "My Dearest Ann," 6 Jan. 1834.

28 Tom Inglis, *Moral Monopoly: The Catholic Church in Modern Irish Society* (Dublin: Gill and Macmillan 1987), esp. 110–21; S.J. Connolly, *Priests and People in Pre-Famine Ireland, 1780–1845* (New York: Gill and Macmillan 1982), 6–15; Oliver MacDonagh, "The Politicizaton of the Irish Catholic Bishops, 1800–1850," *Historical Journal*, 18 (1975): 37–40.

29 Lecky, *A History*, vol. 5: 467–8; G. Locker Lampson, *A Consideration of the State of Ireland in the Nineteenth Century* (New York: E.P. Dutton 1907), 95–100.

30 "Papers of Richard Joachim Hayes, Part I," *Collectanea Hibernica*, nos. 21–2, 82–6.

31 Howley, *Ecclesiastical History*, 261.

32 Ibid., 262–3: Fleming to Protestant rector, April 1829.

33 *Newfoundlander*, 28 May 1829.

34 Howley, *Ecclesiastical History*, 269.

35 *Newfoundlander*, 5 July 1832, Fleming to the people of Carrick-on-Suir, 3 June 1832.

36 Ibid., 30 Aug. 1832, Fleming to the editor, 29 Aug. 1832.

37 *Dublin Freeman's Journal*, 3 Dec. 1834, Fleming to Spratt, 24 Sept. 1834; 13 Jan. 1835.

38 Ibid.

39 *Newfoundlander*, 17 Jan. 1833; *Ledger*, 15 Jan. 1833.

40 AASJs, Papers of Bishop Fleming(hereafter cited as Fleming Papers), folder 103/10, Fleming to Lord John Russell, Dec. 1840 [sic].

41 AASJb, Dollard Papers, Fleming to Dollard, bishop of Moncton, 9 May 1848.

42 Fleming Papers, Folder 103/10, Fleming to Walsh, bishop of Halifax, 8 Sept. 1843.

43 AAH, Bishop Walsh Papers, Fleming to Walsh, 22 Nov. 1842.

44 Ibid.

45 Michael Anthony Fleming, *Relatio of Bishop Michael Anthony Fleming Vicar Apostolic of Newfoundland to Propaganda 26 November, 1846* (1846), 16.

46 Ibid.

47 Patrick Kough (1786–1863) was born in Ireland and came to Newfoundland *c.* 1804; Baker and Pitt, *Dictionary*, 192.

48 Timothy Hogan (1789–1869) was born in Ireland and came to Newfoundland *c.* 1820; *ENL*, 2: 994.

49 See chs. 4 and 5.

50 BIS, minutes, reel 1, 1834–36, 98–145.

51 See ch. 5.

52 Howley, *Ecclesiastical History*, 263.

53 Bishop Walsh Papers, Fleming to Walsh, 2 May 1843.

54 Father Browne (*c.* 1786–1855) came to Newfoundland from Ireland in 1811 and spent most of his twenty-eight years in the colony at Ferryland; *DCB*, 8: 106–8; Howley, *Ecclesiastical History*, 242.

55 Byrne, *Gentlemen Bishops*, 109, 147, 246.

56 Innis, *Cod Fisheries*, 152, 154–6, 305–7; Ryan, *Fish out of Water*, xxii; Cadigan, *Hope and Deception*, ch. 2.

57 WMMS, reel 8, letter 178, Ellidge to the London Methodist Conference [c. 1832]. See also in ibid., James Hennigar, Burin to the London Methodist Conference, 1 Dec. 1835, and J. Peach, Hermitage, to the London Methodist Conference, 22 Nov. 1842.

58 Byrne, *Gentlemen Bishops*, 218, O'Donel to Pope Pius VII, 15 July 1804.

59 Ibid., 117, O'Donel to Troy, 8 Dec. 1791.

60 *Newfoundlander*, 11 Oct. 1832.

61 Joseph Michael Bergin born 1809 in Dublin, was recruited to Newfoundland by Bishop Fleming, appointed parish priest of Tilting in 1835, and died at St John's in 1841; *Vindicator*, 2 Oct. 1841; *Star and Newfoundland Advocate*, 2 Oct. 1841.

62 PANL, MG 46, records of Slade, Cox and Slade, Fogo, box 21–2, Ledgers, 1834–38; MG 458, records of Cox and Co, Fogo, box 1, Ledger. 1838–39.

63 See map 1.

64 See ch. 4.

65 *Patriot*, 13 Jan. 1835, Fleming to Spratt 24 Sept. 1834; *Newfoundlander*, 3 Dec. 1840, Fleming to the editor; Walsh Papers, Fleming to Walsh, 2 Feb. 1843; National Library of Ireland, P.J. Little Papers, doc. 3854/125, Fleming to the Central Society of Lyons, 2 Jan. 1845; Fleming, *Relatio*, 1846, 5–6.

66 *Ledger*, 4 Sept., 30 Oct., 1835; 5 Feb., 5, 19 July 1836.

67 CO 194/90, Prescott to secretary of state, 16 Feb. 1835.

68 PANL, MG 366, notebook of Rev. Benjamin Smith, King's Cove, 1844–50, Smith to Rev. B. Jones, 7 Feb. 1848.

69 *Newfoundlander*, 21 Oct. 1841.

70 Ryan, *Ice Hunters*.

71 See ch. 4.

72 CO 194/93, 260–3, Fleming to Grey, 5 June 1835.

73 AASJs, Mullock Papers, 104/1/29, Pastoral Letter, 22 July 1850; Ibid., 104/2/17, "Seal Fishery 1858."

74 J.T. Mullock, *The Cathedral of St John's Newfoundland with an Account of Its Construction* (Dublin, 1856), 44.

75 *Annals of the Propagation of the Faith: A Periodical Collection of Letters from the Bishops and Missionaries Employed in the Missions of the Old and New World, vol III, Jan. 1840 no XIII* (Dublin, 1840), 384–89, "Missions of Newfoundland," extract of a letter, Bishop Fleming to members of the Council of the Association, January 1842 [sic].

76 Fleming, *Relatio*, 7–8.

77 Ibid., 4.

78 E.R. Norman, *The Catholic Church and Ireland in the Age of Rebellion, 1859–1873* (Ithaca, N.Y.: Cornell University Press 1965), ch. 1, 5–25.

79 BIS minutes, 107, 29 Aug. 1847.

80 *Dublin Freeman's Journal*, 3 Dec. 1834.

81 CO 194/92, 74–114: Foreign Office correspondence, Extracts: Fleming to Capaccini 13 June 1835.

82 BIS minutes, 22 May 1825.

CHAPTER FOUR

1 *Newfoundlander*, Sept.–Dec. 1832; also, *Ledger*, Sept.–Dec. 1832; *Times*, Sept.–Dec. 1832; CO 194/84, correspondence of Thomas Cochrane, Jan.–March 1833; vol. 92, 1835, 74–112; vol. 99, 1837; for electoral districts see map 2.

2 William Bickford Row (1786–1865) was born in England and established business in St John's *c.* 1816; Baker and Pitt, *Dictionary*, 296.

3 William Thomas (*c.* 1785–1863) came to Newfoundland in 1801 and by 1815 had founded the family firm which shortly grew to be one of the larger merchant houses in St John's; Baker and Pitt, *Dictionary*, 337.

4 *Ledger*, 14 Sept. 1832.

5 *Newfoundlander*, 13 Sept. 1832, Kent to the editor, 12 Sept. 1832.

6 *Ledger*, 18 Sept. 1832.

7 Ibid.

8 *Newfoundlander*, 20 Sept. 1832, Fleming to the editor, 19 Sept. 1832.

9 *Ledger*, 21 Sept. 1832.

10 Ibid., 5, 12 Oct., 2 Nov. 1832, 15 Jan., 9 April, 1833 etc.

11 Ibid., 5 Oct. 1832.

12 CO 194/99, 1837. This entire volume, entitled "Dr. Fleming," contains a complete documentation of all the charges and counter- charges made against the bishop over the previous eight years. Included, also, are: the detailed testimony of a large number of his accusers, Fleming's own defences, and a variety of reports on the 1832 election. For special reference to the effect of Kough's backers on Bishop Fleming, see especially CO 194/113, 1841, T. Browning, Brigus, to the secretary of state, 29 March 1841.

13 *Ledger*, 9 Oct. 1832, "A Bookkeeper," St John's, to Fleming, 6 Oct. 1832.

14 CO 194/85, Cochrane to Goderich, 3 Jan. 1833; vol. 87, Cochrane to Stanley, 1 May 1834.

15 *Ledger*, 6 Nov. 1832.

16 Peter Brown (1797–1845) was born in Ireland and emigrated to Newfoundland where he became a dealer and shopkeeper in Harbour Grace; he also supplied vessels for the seal fishery and was president of St Patrick's Free School, Harbour Grace. See *Star and Conception Bay Journal*, 28 Nov. 1838, 29 March 1839; Baker and Pitt, *Dictionary*, 34; ENL, 1, 276.

17 James Power (*c.* 1796–1847) was apparently born in Carbonear where he became a fish merchant; he withdrew from that business upon appointment to the magistracy in 1838. See *Star and Conception Bay Journal*, 14 Nov. 1838; *Patriot*, 21 June 1847; *Courier*, 19 June 1847.

18 CO 194/72, Cochrane to Bathurst, 10 Nov. 1826; vol. 74, Cochrane to Bathurst, 26 Sept. 1827; vol. 80, Cochrane to Sir George Murray, 11 March 1830.

19 *Newfoundlander*, 14 Oct. 1830.

20 CO 194/81, Cochrane to Goderich, 14 Sept., 4 May 1831.

21 Ibid., vol. 85, Cochrane to Goderich, 3 Jan. 1833.

22 CO 194/87, Cochrane to Stanley, 8 April 1834.

23 Joseph R. Smallwood, *Dr. William Carson, The Great Newfoundland Reformer: His Life, Letters and Speeches* (St John's: Newfoundland Book Publishers 1978), 20–1.

24 *Times*, 26 Sept., 7 Nov. 1832.

25 *Ledger*, 28 Aug., 11 Sept. 1832.

26 CO 194/99, 1837, testimony of Patrick Kough.

27 *Times*, 7 Nov. 1832.

28 Ibid.

29 *Ledger* and *Times* for the months following Oct. 1832.

30 CO 194/99, 1837, testimony of Bishop Fleming and Henry Winton.

31 Ryan, *Fish out of Water*, 60–1.

32 CO 194/87, Cochrane to Stanley, 8 April 1834.

33 *Patriot*, 10 Dec. 1833.

34 *Times*, 21, 28 Aug., 4, 11, 18 Sept. 1833; *Ledger*, 9, 30 Aug., 6, 15 Sept., 29 Nov., 10 Dec. 1833.

35 Edward Troy (d. 1872) was recruited from Ireland in 1831 by Bishop Fleming and served in St John's before becoming parish priest of several parishes; Howley, *Ecclesiastical History*, 264–6.

36 *Times*, 4 Dec. 1833, address of Timothy Hogan "To the Independent Electors of St. John's," 3 Dec. 1833.

37 Patrick Ward was recruited from Ireland in 1833 by Bishop Fleming and served first in St John's before being sent to Ferryland and Tilting; Howley, *Ecclesiastical History*, 281.

38 My account of the dispute over the military intervention following the 1833 by-election is taken from a number of sources including, principally, CO 194/85, Cochrane to Stanley, 26 Dec. 1833; vol. 87, Cochrane to Stanley, 8 April 1834; vol. 88, Cochrane to Stanley, 28 July 1834.

39 CO 194/87, Cochrane to Stanley, 1 May 1834.

40 Ibid., vol. 85, Cochrane to Stanley, 26 Dec. 1833.

41 Ibid., vol. 88, Cochrane to Stanley, 28 July 1834, encls. 1 and 2, correspondence with Fleming.

42 Robert Pack (1786–1860) came to Newfoundland from England in 1801 and soon established a business at Bay Roberts which grew to become one of the largest firms in Conception Bay; Baker and Pitt, *Dictionary*, 257.

43 *Journal of the House of Assembly* (hereafter cited as *Journal, Assembly*), 30 Jan. 1833; *Newfoundlander*, 31 Jan. 1833; SPG, "C" Series, box A 168, correspondence of Rev. Edward Wix, 1833; Howley, *Ecclesiastical History*, 271–4.

44 Howley, *Ecclesiastical History*, 274.

45 DCB, 8: 673–5.

46 WMMS, reel 10, letter 61, James Hennigar, Burin, to Mission Committee, 1 Dec. 1835

47 Ibid., reel 11, Rev. John Pickavant, Carbonear, to mission committee, 8 Jan. 1840.

48 Roger F Sweetman (?–1862) was born in Ireland and came to Newfoundland *c.* 1814 where he ran the Placentia-based operations of the transatlantic firm of Saunders and Sweetman; DCB, 7: 840–2; *Journal, Assembly*, 1854 (2nd session), app. 207; *Express*, 9 Dec. 1862.

49 *Ledger*, 7 Feb. 1834.

50 *Journal, Assembly*, 29 Jan. 1834.

51 *Patriot*, 4 Feb. 1834.

52 CO 194/87, Cochrane to Stanley, 8 April 1834.

53 *Proceedings of the House of Assembly* (hereafter cited as *Debates, Assembly*), 29 Jan. 1834. Extracts of proceedings in both houses of the Newfoundland legislature were printed from time to time in the various newspapers but no complete file exists anywhere before 1908.

54 *Patriot*, 14 Feb. 1834.

55 CO 194/87, Cochrane to Stanley, 8 April 1834.

56 Edward Kielley (*c.* 1790–1855) was born in St John's and trained as a surgeon in the Royal Navy; ENL, 3: 171–2.

57 CO 194/87, Cochrane to Stanley, 8 April 1834, and Cochrane to Stanley, 14 Aug. 1834 and encl. 1, petition of William Carson.

58 The issues of the *Patriot* of 11 Feb. and 4 March 1834, in which first appeared the letters of "Junius," are not extant.

59 *Patriot*, 1 July 1834.

60 CO 194/88, Cochrane to Stanley, 28 July 1834.

61 CO 195/18, 211–12, Rice to Cochrane, 4 Aug. 1834.

62 *Ledger*, 4 Nov. 1834.

63 Henry Prescott (1783–1874) was born in England, followed a career in the navy and was appointed governor of Newfoundland in 1834; DCB, 10: 600–1.

64 Boulton (1790–1870) had emigrated from England to Toronto where he practised law; Baker and Pitt, *Dictionary*, 27.

65 Prowse, *History*, 433–4; Howley, *Eclesiastical History*, 380–1.

66 Prowse, *History*, 434.

67 Cochrane Papers, mss. 2350, Simms to Cochrane, 6 June 1835.

68 CO 194/92, 1835, 74–112: copies of Foreign Office correspondence with Vatican officials and Bishop Fleming, July 1835–Feb. 1836.

69 Ibid., 91: Fleming to Mons. Capaccini, 13 June 1835.

70 *Journal, Assembly*, 1837, app., 459–537, Committee of Enquiry into the Administration of Justice in Newfoundland (hereafter cited as the Justice Enquiry); *Vindicator*, 5, 12, 19, 26 Feb., 5, 12 March 1842. See esp. CO 194/103, 1838, 66–70.

71 *Journal, Assembly*, 1836, 60, petition of John Kent on behalf of John V. Nugent, 19 Feb. 1836; *Vindicator*, 1 Jan. 1842.

72 *Patriot*, 15, 22 July, 2 Sept. 1834. See CO 194/88, Cochrane to Stanley, 2 Aug. 1834, with encls. of correspondence between Troy, Boulton, and the *Patriot*.

73 CO 194/88, Cochrane to Stanley, 2 Aug. 1834, encls: correspondence between Troy, Boulton and the *Patriot*.

74 *Ledger*, 29 Aug. 1834.

75 Ibid., 26, 29 Aug. 1834.

76 T.B. Job (1806–78) was born in England and came to St John's where he established the firm of Job Brothers; Baker and Pitt, *Dictionary*, 177.

77 C.F. Bennett (1793–1893) came from England to Newfoundland as a boy and eventually established in St John's a succession of businesses in manufacturing and merchandising; Baker and Pitt, *Dictionary*, 19–20.

78 Newman Hoyles (1777–1840) emigrated from England to St John's where he established a fishery supply business in 1807; Baker and Pitt, *Dictionary*, 168.

79 John Dunscombe (1777–1847) emigrated from Bermuda to Newfoundland where he served as an agent for, and partner with, several trading firms; Baker and Pitt, *Dictionary*, 93–4.

80 James Crowdy (1794–1867) came from England to Newfoundland in 1831 to serve as colonial secretary; Baker and Pitt, *Dictionary*, 73.

81 William Haly (*c.* 1771–1835) came to St John's as a soldier with the British forces; ENL, 2: 783.

82 *Ledger*, 26, 29 Aug. 1834.

83 *Ledger*, 26 Aug. 1834.

84 *Patriot*, 2 Sept. 1834, Fleming to the editor, 28 Aug. 1834; 13 Jan. 1835, Fleming to Rev. John Spratt, 24 Sept. 1834; *Ledger*, 9 Sept. 1834, "Omicron" to the editor.

85 Cochrane Papers, mss. 2370, 59, Cochrane to Bathurst, 12 Jan. 1826.

86 *Patriot*, 23 Dec. 1834.

87 Ibid., 30 June 1835.

88 SPG, "C" Series, esp. Rev. Leigh's correspondence from Twillingate, 1817, and Rev. Bullock's correspondence from Trinity, 1822 and 1824; also WMMS, Newfoundland Letters, 1819.

89 Ibid., esp. correspondence of Archdeacon Wix for 1831.

90 CO 194/91, Prescott to Glenelg, 1 Dec. 1835, encl.: Wix to Glenelg, 30 Nov. 1835.

91 *Journal of the Legislative Council* (hereafter cited as *Journal, Council*), 1837, app.: Edward Wix to J. Templeman, 21 July 1836, "Bye-Laws, Rules and Regulations for … St. John's adopted on the 15th day of July, 1836."

92 D.H. Akenson, *The Irish Education Experiment: The National System of Education in the Nineteenth Century* (London: Routledge and Kegan Paul 1970), ch. 5.

93 *Journal, Council,* 1837, app., reports and proceedings of the Board of Education for the electoral district of Conception Bay, 1836.

94 John Stark (*c.* 1791–1863) came from Scotland to Newfoundland as a clerk to the governor's secretary in 1821, later becoming chief clerk and registrar of the northern circuit court at Harbour Grace; see PANL, Newfoundland Blue Book, 1822; Cathedral of St John the Baptist marriages, box 3, no. 534.

95 Robert Prowse (1798–1873) came from England to Newfoundland as an apprentice at the age of ten years and by the 1830s was in charge of the Conception Bay branch of the St John's firm Brown, Hoyles; *ENL*, 4: 467; *DCB*, 14: 850–3.

96 *Journal, Council,* 1837, app., reports and proceedings of the Board of Education for the Electoral District of Conception Bay, 1836: J. Templeman, Acting Secretary to Reverend John Burt, Chairman of the Board of Education, Harbour Grace, 14 [sic] Aug. 1836. A printing error gave the wrong date for this letter; a critical textual examination has proven the correct date to be 5 Aug. 1836.

97 Charles Dalton (1786–1859) was recruited from Ireland to Newfoundland in 1831 by Bishop Fleming; Baker and Pitt, *Dictionary,* 77.

98 *Journal, Council,* 1837, app., reports and proceedings of the Board of Education for the electoral district of Conception Bay, 1836, Dalton, Brown, and Power, Harbour Grace, to governor's secretary, 31 Aug. 1836.

99 Ibid., J. Templeman, acting secretary to Rev. John Burt, 1 Sept. 1836.

100 Ibid., minutes of Conception Bay Board of Education, 1 Nov. 1836.

101 Nancy Ball, *Educating the People: A Documentary History of Elementary Schooling in England, 1840–1870* (London: Maurice Temple Smith 1983), 17; Neil J. Smelser, *Social Paralysis and Social Change: British Working-Class Education in the Nineteenth Century* (Berkeley: University of California Press 1991), 202–7; Machin, *The Catholic Question,* 7; Akenson, *Irish Education,* ch. 5.

102 *Patriot,* 9 July 1836; CO 194/95, 1836, Prescott to Glenelg, 4 July, encl.: Troy to Carrington, 29 June 1836.

103 CO 194/95, 6, Prescott to Glenelg, 4 July 1836; see note attached by James Stephen of the Colonial Office.

104 *Patriot,* 10 Sept. 1836.

105 *Ledger,* 19, 23 Aug. 1836.

106 Ibid., 16 Sept. 1834, "Z," Conception Bay, to the editor.

107 *Patriot,* 18 Jan. 1840, 29 June 1842, 22 Feb., 15 March, 18 Oct., 1843, and *Debates, Assembly,* 3 April 1844, speech of John Kent.

108 *Journal, Council,* 1837, app., proceedings of the Board of Education for Conception Bay, J. Burt to Joseph Templeman, 30 Aug. 1836.

109 Ibid., reports and proceedings of the Board of Education for Trinity, 1836.

110 Ibid., J. Templeman to George Skelton, 22 Aug. 1836.

111 Ibid., George Skelton to J. Templeman, 12 Sept. 1836.

112 *Ledger*, 11 March 1836, letter from "Censor" and editor's note as well.

113 *Journal, Council*, 1837, app., reports and proceedings of the Board of Education, Bonavista, 1836–37.

114 Nicholas Devereux (1787–1845) was recruited from Ireland to Newfoundland in 1816 by Bishop Scallan; Baker and Pitt, *Dictionary*, 82.

115 *Journal, Assembly*, 1837, 231–2.

116 Ibid., 251–7; also *Journal, Council*, 1837, 52–4, 57–9.

CHAPTER FIVE

1 *Patriot*, 2 Sept. 1834, "Brutus" to H.J. Boulton, 31 Aug. 1834.

2 Ibid., 16 Sept. 1834.

3 Ibid., 26 May 1835.

4 CO 194/93, Stephen to Hay, 5 Aug. 1835; CO 195/118, 372–4, Glenelg to Prescott, 13 Aug. 1835

5 Ibid., vol. 90, Prescott to Aberdeen, 21 May 1835, encls. 1–5; also, ibid., Prescott to Grant, 29 May 1835, and Prescott to Aberdeen, 30 May 1835; *Ledger*, 2 June 1835.

6 Ibid.

7 *Patriot*, 12 Jan., 14 May 1836; *Times*, 23, 30 Dec. 1835; *Ledger*, 15 Dec. 1835, 1 Jan. 1836; CO 194/94, Prescott to Glenelg, 4, 11 Jan. 1836, encls.

8 *Patriot*, 12 Jan. 1836; CO 194/94, Prescott to Glenelg, 11 Jan. 1836, encls.

9 *Ledger*, 1 Jan. 1836

10 *Patriot*, 9 July 1836.

11 Fleming Papers, 103/4, Fleming to Troy, 10 Sept. 1836.

12 *Patriot*, 9 July 1836, Troy to Rev. Carrington, 27 June 1836; *Ledger*, 19 July 1836.

13 CO 194/95, 6, Prescott to Glenelg, 4 July 1836.

14 *Ledger*, 19 July 1836.

15 The information on the campaigns of 1836–37 has been drawn from a variety of sources, principally CO 194, 94–6, 1836; 97–9, 1837; 100–3, 1838; 106, 1839; 113, 1841; also, *Patriot*, 1836–37; *Ledger*, 1836–37; *Times*, 1836–37; *Newfoundlander*, 1837; Fleming Papers and Cochrane Papers, mss. 2353.

16 *Patriot*, 10 Sept. 1836.

17 CO 194/95, Prescott to Glenelg, 10 Dec. 1836, encls: depositions of constables, St John's.

18 *Patriot*, 12 April 1836; *Times*, 23 March, 13 April 1836.

19 Ibid.; CO 194/94, 1836, Prescott to Glenelg, 16 March 1836, encl.: petition of Michael McLean Little; also, Prescott to Glenelg, 15 July 1836.

20 CO 194/95, Prescott to Glenelg, 10 Dec. 1836, encl.: deposition of Michael Scanlan; vol. 97, Prescott to Glenelg, 2 March 1837, encl.: Boulton to Prescott, 25 Jan. 1837.

21 Thomas Ridley (1799–1879) emigrated from Ireland to Conception Bay where in 1826 he established a large fishing and supply firm; Baker and Pitt, *Dictionary*, 290–1.

22 *Journal, Assembly*, 10 July 1837.

23 CO 194/95, Prescott to Glenelg, 9 Dec. 1836, encl. 2, Stark to Crowdy, 2 Nov. 1836.

24 Ibid., encl. 5: Magistrates Danson and Stark to Crowdy, 17 Nov. 1836.

25 *Ledger*, 17 Jan. 1837; *Times*, 18, 25 Jan. 1837; CO 194/97, Prescott to Glenelg, 11 Jan. 1837; 103, 7–228, complaints against Judge Boulton by Nugent, Carson, and Morris, Jan.–July 1838. See esp. vol. 95, Prescott to Glenelg, 11 Nov. 1836.

26 *Ledger*, 3 Jan. 1837; *Patriot*, 20 May 1837.

27 *Patriot*, 4, 18, 25 Feb., 11 March 1837.

28 Ibid; *Ledger*, 6, 10 Jan., 16 June 1837; CO 194/97, Prescott to Glenelg, 21 Feb. 1837, encls: reports on the trials at St John's and Harbour Grace; also, Prescott to Glenelg, 11 April 1837, encl.: Nugent to Crowdy, 28 March 1837, with petition on behalf of Harding, Thomey, and Saunders.

29 CO 194/103, 1838, 73, petition of Patrick Morris et al.

30 Ibid., vol 97, Prescott to Glenelg, 2 March 1837, encl. 4: Simms to Prescott, Feb. 1837, "Reports on the State of Society." [The exact date cannot be discerned because of imperfect microfilming.]

31 Ibid., Prescott to Glenleg, 2 March 1837, encl. 3: Boulton to Prescott, 25 Jan. 1837.

32 Ibid., Prescott to Glenelg, 11 April 1837; *Patriot*, 25 Feb., 4, 11 March 1837.

33 *Journal, Assembly*, 30, 31 Aug., 2–6 Sept. 1837.

34 Ibid., 4, 10 Oct. 1837; *Journal, Council*, 4, 9 Oct. 1837.

35 Ibid., 1837, app., 459–537, Justice Enquiry, Aug.–Sept. 1837.

36 Ibid., testimony of Aaron Hogsett, 29 Aug. 1837.

37 Ibid., testimony of G.H. Emerson, 2 Sept. 1837.

38 CO 194/103, 66, 1838, House of Assembly report to Colonial Office.

39 Justice Enquiry, 1837, testimony of John V. Nugent, 10 Oct. 1837.

40 Ibid.

41 Ibid.

42 *Journal, Assembly*, 8 Sept., 1837, Prescott to Nugent and Morris, 8 Sept. 1837.

43 Justice Enquiry, Brenton and Desbarres to Nugent, 5 Sept. 1837.

44 *Journal, Assembly,* 10 Oct. 1837.

45 Ibid., 14 Oct. 1837.

46 CO 194/103, 450, Report to cabinet of the Privy Council committee on the Boulton case, 5 July 1838.

47 *Ledger,* 21 Aug. 1838; *Times,* 21 Nov. 1838.

CHAPTER SIX

1 CO 194/106, Prescott to Normanby, 4 July 1839.

2 CO 194/92, Public Offices and Individuals, Foreign Office Correspondence, Strangsways to Hay, 28 Oct. 1835 (see notes in margins by Colonial Office staff, also draft of a despatch to the foreign secretary dated 18 Feb. 1836 and notes in the margins as well).

3 *Journal, Assembly,* 3 April 1834.

4 *Statutes of Newfoundland,* 1834.

5 CO 194/88, Cochrane to Spring Rice, 22 Oct. 1834.

6 Ibid.

7 *Journal, Assembly,* 26 Jan. 1836.

8 CO 194/90, Prescott to Aberdeen, 16 Feb. 1835 (see notes by Aberdeen for draft of a despatch to Prescott). See also CO 195/18, 304–10, Aberdeen to Prescott, 15 April 1835.

9 CO 194/90, Prescott to Spring Rice, 17 Jan. 1835.

10 *Journal, Assembly,* 26 Jan. 1836.

11 My detailed information on the subject of the political involvement of Bishop Fleming and his supporting clergy has been recovered from the extensive files of the British Colonial Office correspondence with Newfoundland governors between the years 1833 and 1841 inclusive. These files include, as well, a special volume, no. 99, compiled in 1838 exclusively on the subject of Fleming and labelled as such.

12 CO 194/87, Cochrane to Stanley, 8 April 1834.

13 Ibid., 88, Cochrane to Stanley, 28 July 1834.

14 See also Phillip McCann, "Bishop Fleming and the Politicization of the Irish Roman Catholics in Newfoundland, 1830–1850," in Terrence Murphy and Cyril J Byrne, eds., *Religion and Identity: The Experience of Irish and Scottish Catholics in Atlantic Canada* (St John's: Jesperson Press 1987). McCann shows the extent to which the populace and Reform politicians pursued their own objectives independent of clerical leadership.

15 CO 194/89, Lord Palmerston, Foreign Office, to Spring Rice, 12 Sept. 1834.

16 Ibid., encl.: H. Hamilton Seymour, Florence, Italy, to Palmerston, 22 Aug. 1834.

17 Ibid., extract from a private letter dated Rome, Italy 12 Nov. 1834; encl.: Aubin to Seymour, 19 Aug. 1834. Enclosed in Bidwell to Hay, Foreign Office, 3 Dec. 1834.

18 Ibid., encl.: Capaccini, Rome, Italy, to Fleming, 9 Nov. 1834.

19 Ibid., vol. 89, correspondence with Foreign Office, 3 Dec. 1834, encls.

20 Ibid., 92, 74–85, notes in margins and blank spaces of correspondence between the Colonial Office, Foreign Office, and the Vatican.

21 CO 194/90, Prescott to Aberdeen, 14 May 1835.

22 Ibid., encl.: memorial of Michael McLean Little.

23 Ibid., 96, Public Offices and Individuals, Foreign Office Correspondence, Lord Grey to Palmerston, 4 Feb. 1836, encl.: Fleming to Bramston, 25 Jan. 1836.

24 Ibid.

25 Ibid., 90, Prescott to Aberdeen, 21 May 1835.

26 Ibid., 91, Prescott to Grey, 30 Nov. 1836, encl.: Templeman to Fleming, 30 Nov. 1836.

27 Ibid., 92, 74–85, correspondence between the Colonial Office, the Foreign Office, and the Vatican, June 1835–Feb. 1836; 96, 44–50, Foreign Office correspondence, Ralph Abercrombie, Florence, Italy, to Palmerston 1 April 1836, encl.: Abercrombie to Aubin, 15 March 1836.

28 Ibid., 96, 70, Aubin, Rome, to Abercrombie, 11 April 1836.

29 Ibid., 102, 289, Glenelg to Fleming, 19 Sept. 1836.

30 Ibid., 99, Prescott to Glenelg, 14 Oct. 1837, encl. 1: statement of Fleming.

31 Ibid., encls. 2, 3, etc.

32 Bishop Fleming left Newfoundland for Europe early in July 1836 and was absent not only for the 1836 general election but for the 1837 one as well. While in Ireland he wrote Fr Troy and ordered him, in case any election occurred, not to "interfere in any public manner with it"; see Fleming Papers, box 1, folder 103.

33 CO 194/100, Prescott to Glenelg, 5 Jan. 1838 (confidential).

34 James Stephen (1789–1859) was an English lawyer who became undersecretary in the Colonial Office; DCB, 18: 1050–1.

35 CO 194/100, Prescott to Glenelg, 5 Jan. 1838 (confidential). See James Stephen's marginal notes.

36 Ibid., 102, 258–60, Fleming to Grey, Feb. 1838.

37 Ibid. See inter-office memo on above by Thomas W.C. Murdoch.

38 Ibid.

39 Ibid., Stephen to Murdoch.

40 Ibid., Grey to Fleming, 9 Feb. 1838.

41 Ibid., notes made by James Stephen on above correspondence.

42 The news was unreliable, however for Bishop Fleming had received no personal censure whatsoever and, although the bishop had been ordered to "remove immediately the said Father Troy from all ecclesiastical ministries there" (Fleming Papers 103/16/6: Pope Gregory XVI to Bishop Fleming, 5 Jan. 1838), Fleming subsequently so successfully appealed the ruling directly to the pope that Cardinal Franzoni told Fleming on the authority of the Holy Father that "concerning Father Edward Troy you may do whatever prudence and conscience dictate you should do in the Lord"; Fleming Papers, 103/16/7, Franzoni to Fleming, 23 March 1839.

43 CO 194/100, f.289, Grey to Fleming, 2 Aug. 1838.

44 *Ledger,* 16 Oct. 1838.

45 Ibid.

46 *Times,* 17 Oct. 1838.

47 Ibid.

48 *Ledger,* 20 Nov. 1838.

49 Ibid., 16 Oct. 1838.

50 CO 194/105, Prescott to Glenelg, 2 March 1839, encls.: petitions from merchants, traders, etc.

51 Ibid., 106, 22–3, Henry Labouchere to Marquis of Normanby, 18 Aug. 1839.

52 Ibid., 101, Prescott to Glenelg, 3 Oct. 1838, notes made in margin at Colonial Office by "T.W.C.M." See also CO 195/18, Russell to Prescott, 6 Oct. 1839 and 195/19, Glenelg to Prescott, 4 Jan. 1839.

53 Biographical information on John V. Nugent has been gleaned from a variety of sources principally the *Patriot, Ledger, Times,* and *Newfoundlander* for the post–1833 period, the despatches of the governors from 1833–55 and House of Assembly petitions relating to Nugent's attempts to enrol at the bar from 1834 to 1841 inclusive.

54 *Ledger,* 3 Nov. 1837.

55 Ibid., 11 July 1837, 9 Oct. 1838.

56 CO 194/106, Prescott to Normanby, 4 July 1839.

57 *Journal, Assembly,* 1841, address to the queen presented to the House of Assembly by John V. Nugent, 23 April 1841.

58 Ibid.

59 *Journal, Council,* 1839, app., education returns, Trinity, Bullock to Crowdy, 12 June 1839.

60 Ibid., Simms to governor, 17 June 1839.

61 CO 194/113, 410–490, Nugent *et al.,* London, to secretary of state, 1841.

62 Ibid., 106, Prescott to Normanby, 4 July 1839.

63 *Journals, Assembly,* 1834–41.

64 CO 194/106, Prescott to Normanby, 4 July 1839.

65 NSS, *15*th *Annual Report,* 1838, anniversary sermon by Rev. Henry Melvill.

66 SPG, box A193, Rev. Charles Blackman to secretary, 14 Jan. 1839.

67 Ibid., box A194, Rev. Boone to the bishop, 13 Oct. 1839.

68 *Times,* 17 Feb. 1841.

69 Ibid.

70 Ibid., speech of Bryan Robinson at monthly meeting of the Church Society, 15 Feb. 1841.

71 WMMS, Rev. John Pickavant, Carbonear, to mission committee, 12 Sept. 1838; ibid., Rev. Faulkner, St John's, to mission committee, 25 Aug. 1838.

72 Ibid.

73 *Times,* 2 Aug. 1837.

74 Ibid., 7 Aug. 1839.

75 *Debates, Assembly,* 20, 21 Jan. 1840.

76 *Newfoundlander,* 7 Nov. 1839, Carson to *Newfoundlander,* 5 Nov. 1839.

77 Ibid., 24 May 1838, "Essay on the Contemplated New Era in the Destinies of the British North American Colonies," by William Carson.

78 Ibid., 31 Oct., 7 Nov. 1839.

79 Ibid., 7 Nov. 1839.

80 *Debates, Assembly,* 18 Nov. 1837; *Journal, Assembly,* 1837, 365.

81 Ibid., 13 Aug. 1838.

82 *Ledger,* 11 Oct. 1836, letter from "A Freeman."

83 Ibid., 9 Oct. 1836, speech of Patrick Morris in House of Assembly.

84 *Debates, Assembly,* 23, 24 Oct. 1838.

85 Ibid., 22 March 1840.

86 Ibid.

87 *Journal, Assembly,* 24 March 1840.

88 My information on the St. John's and Conception Bay by-elections comes from a variety of sources, principally co 194/109, June–Dec. 1840; vol. 3, Jan.–July 1841; vol. 114, ff.126–36, 1842. Also: *Patriot,* March 1840–Oct. 1841, *Newfoundlander,* May to Dec. 1840, *Ledger,* May 1840– June 1841, *Times,* May–Dec. 1840, and *Vindicator,* Jan.– Oct. 1841.

89 Thomas Waldron had been recruited from Ireland in 1833 by Bishop Fleming; Howley, *Ecclesiastical History,* 281.

90 John Forrestall (*c.* 1813–1850) was born in County Kilkenny, Ireland, and ordained for the Newfoundland mission by Bishop Fleming in St John's in 1838; *Patriot,* 1 Dec. 1838, 19 Nov. 1850; *Gazette,* 19 Nov. 1850; *Ledger,* 19 Nov. 1850.

91 Kyran Walsh (1808–68) was recruited from Ireland *c.* 1839 by Bishop Fleming and served in several parishes before becoming vicar general in 1857; DCB, 9: 819–20.

92 CO 194/109. This volume has a considerable quantity of reports on the controversial by-elections of 1840 in St John's and Conception Bay, but one must remember in studying that evidence that all such reports were made by opponents of the Nugent Reformers.

93 Ibid., Prescott to Russell, 10 Dec. 1840.

94 Ibid., Prescott to Russell, 10 June 1840, encls.: depositions of Prendergast's supporters.

95 CO 194/109, Prescott to Russell 10 Dec. 1840.

96 Edmund Hanrahan (1802–75) was born in Carbonear and became a famous ship captain; Baker and Pitt, *Dictionary*, 142.

97 CO 194/109 Prescott to Russell, 7 Nov. 1840.

98 Ibid., 113, 410–90, Nugent et al. to secretary of state, 1841.

99 James Walsh (*c.* 1803–1873) was born in County Kilkenny, Ireland, and ordained *c.* 1836 by Bishop Fleming for the Newfoundland mission.

100 *Patriot*, 12 Dec. 1840, 2 Jan. 1841. Father Walsh, however, paid the penalty for his reluctance to interfere on Nugent's side. Nugent successfully induced Bishop Fleming to remove Walsh forthwith; the bishop appointed Walsh parish priest of Placentia, effective immediately. As a dedicated parish priest, Walsh was determined to reach his parish as quickly as possible, especially in view of the fact that Advent was under way and Christmas was near. He set out on foot from Carbonear in what was a near superhuman endeavour of crossing the uncharted, trackless Avalon peninsula. It was then an almost impassable wilderness of thick forest undergrowth, intermixed, as it is today, with bog, swamp, and thick clusters of brooks, ponds, and lakes. A heavy fall of snow had occurred the night before he left Carbonear and the walking was thus made so difficult that, when he reached Spaniard's Bay that evening, he was exhausted. A well-to-do Roman Catholic merchant put him up for the night and influenced him to take companions on the next leg of his perilous journey. The next morning Walsh, accompanied by two friends, set out for New Harbour. But the walking was again so difficult that they were trapped on the barrens throughout the night. Heavy snow, bitter cold, searing wind, and the lack of any means of making a fire resulted in Walsh's companions being severely frostbitten. One of them, Robert Timm, was so overcome that Walsh knew he would never reach New Harbour and encouraged him to return to Spaniard's Bay. Timm set out on the return journey and, although he successfully reached that village, he expired soon afterwards. Walsh and his remaining friend continued their journey to New Harbour, arriving the next day. After resting at that harbour, they struck out south for Chapel Arm on the narrow isthmus of the peninsula separating the bays of Trinity and Placentia. Having

gained that destination they apparently attempted to cross the isthmus without further delay. But they were overcome on the barrens that night and, were it not for the accidental discovery of a winter hut they might not have survived. They straggled in to Long Harbour, Placentia Bay, the next evening and, instead of resting for a few days, Walsh ordered a crew to launch a punt to row him down the Bay to Placentia.

101 *Ledger*, 1 Dec. 1840, extract of a letter received by a Roman Catholic of St John's and dated "Harbour Grace 24 Nov. 1840." See also ibid., "Argus," Harbour Main, to the editor of *Ledger*, 27 Nov. 1840.

102 *Patriot*, 14 Nov. 1840.

103 CO 194/109, Prescott to Russell, 10 Dec. 1840, encl.: report from returning officer R.J. Pinsent, Dec. 1840.

104 Ibid.

105 CO 195/19, Russell to Prescott, 14 Jan. 1841; CO 194/111, Prescott to Russell, 3 March 1841.

106 CO 194/109, Prescott to Russell, 10 Dec. 1840, encls.: reports of magistrates, Conception Bay. The shooting had actually been done by Prendergast's supporters.

107 Ibid., Prescott to Russell, Dec. 1840.

108 Ibid., 112, Colonel Sall to secretary of state, 10 June 1841, encl.: chief justice to Colonel Sall, 5 June 1841.

109 Ibid., 109, Colonial Office Secretary to Foreign Secretary, 16 July 1840.

110 *Ledger*, 30 April 1841.

111 Ibid., 27 April 1841.

112 Ibid., 30 April 1841.

CHAPTER SEVEN

1 CO 194/103, 7, Nugent and Carson to Glenelg, 31 Jan. 1838.

2 Ibid., 92, 112, Petition of Fleming to Lord Duncannon, 4 July 1835.

3 Ibid., 100, Prescott to Glenelg, 1 Jan. 1838, encl.: report on meeting, Roman Catholic church, Christmas Day, 1837, with speech of Fleming; ibid., 102, Fleming to Glenelg, 7 March 1838, with enclosures of correspondence on the subject of the land grant.

4 *Patriot*, 29 July 1837.

5 *Debates, Assembly*, 14 Oct. 1837.

6 CO 194/103, Jan.–July 1838. This period is replete with correspondence between Carson and Nugent, on the one side, and the Colonial Office, on the other, over the question of Newfoundland's grievances.

7 See appendix, table 1.

8 CO 194/103, Glenelg to Nugent, 2 March 1838.

9 Ibid., 100, Prescott to Glenelg, 29 Aug. 1838.

10 Ibid.

11 *Patriot*, 24 June 1837.

12 CO 194/113, 410, Nugent et al. to secretary of state, 1841.

13 PANL, Newfoundland government records, Group 2/2, Incoming Correspondence of the colonial secretary, June–Sept. 1838, Kent to colonial secretary, 22 May 1838.

14 CO 194/100, Prescott to Glenelg, 29 Aug. 1838.

15 CO 195/19, Glenelg to Prescott, 18 May 1838.

16 Ibid.

17 Ibid., Glenelg to Prescott, 12 Aug. 1838.

18 *Journals, Assembly*, 1839–41.

19 *Patriot*, 8 Aug. 1840. See *Newfoundlander*, 18 June 1840, where Nugent responds to the *Patriot* of 13 June 1840 (an issue that has unfortunately not survived). See also *Vindicator*, 30 Jan. 1841, where Nugent attacks Parsons over the "Copper Coloured Natives" issue.

20 E.J. Hobsbawm, *The Age of Revolution, 1789–1848* (New York: New American Library 1962), 80–100, 103–10, 148–50, 153–4, 166–70, 222–33.

21 *Debates, Assembly*, 15 July 1839.

22 Ibid., 10 Aug. 1837, 15, 18 July 1839.

23 Ibid., 25 July 1839.

24 *Newfoundlander*, 31 Oct., 7 Nov. 1839.

25 *Vindicator*, 3 Feb. 1841.

26 *Patriot*, 5, 17 Jan. 1839.

27 Ibid., 30 March 1839.

28 Ibid., 19 Dec. 1840.

29 Ibid., 9 Jan., 13 Feb. 1841.

30 Ibid., 1 Oct. 1840.

31 In 1838 John V. Nugent was at the apex of his political power, and there is no greater testimony to that fact than the *Patriot*'s publication on 3 Feb. of a "Nugent Tribute" to which a veritable "Who's Who" of middle-class figures from the principal towns in the colony appended their names and gave a monetary donation. A perusal of the newspapers and other available records during the 1840 by-election reveals that, in addition to those of the upper-class merchants, the names of Douglas's supporters came from the "Nugent Tribute" list.

32 *Vindicator*, 27 Feb., 6 March 1841.

33 *Patriot*, 13 Nov. 1840; *Ledger*, 17, 24 Nov. 1840.

34 CO 194/109, R.J. Pinsent to colonial secretary, 21 Nov. , 9 Dec. 1840.

35 Ryan, *Ice Hunters*, 132–3.

36 Ibid., *Fish out of Water*, 62–3.

37 *Ledger*, 1 Dec. 1840.

38 *Newfoundlander*, 21 Oct. 1841; *Vindicator*, 16 Oct. 1841.

39 CO 194/112, Harvey to secretary of state, 6 July 1842, encl.: copy of reply of secretary of state. See also CO 195/20, Stanley to Harvey, 3 Sept. 1842.

40 *Patriot*, 5 Jan. 1842.

41 *Debates, Assembly*, 22 May 1843.

42 CO 194/103, Nugent to Glenelg, 26 March 1838.

43 Phillip A. Buckner, *The Transition to Responsible Government: British Policy in British North America, 1815–1850* (Westport, Conn.: Greenwood Press 1985), 6–9.

44 Ibid., 9–10.

45 Ibid., 70–3.

46 A biographical sketch of Governor Harvey is included in DCB, 8: 374–84.

47 *Patriot*, 22 Sept. 1841.

48 The author has consulted a variety of sources to determine the character and details of Harvey's administration, especially CO 194 for the period 1841–47 along with the extensive newspaper files and Assembly *Journals* for the same period.

49 Bergin had been able to spend unusually lengthy periods of time in St John's because he suffered from a serious illness and was detained there "under the care of the Doctor." The doctor was, undoubtedly, William Carson.

50 CO 194/113, Bonnycastle to James Stephen, 14 Jan. 1841.

51 *Debates, Assembly*, 23 March 1843.

52 Richard Bonnycastle, *Considerations upon the Political Position and Natural Advantages of Newfoundland*, enclosed in CO 194/113, 262–93, Bonnycastle to Stephen, 14 Jan. 1841.

53 *Debates, Assembly*, 13 March 1843.

54 Ibid., 23 March 1843.

55 *Newfoundlander*, 30 Aug. 1832, Fleming to editor, 29 Aug.

56 *Patriot*, 8 March 1843.

57 *Debates, Assembly*, 9 March 1843.

58 *Journal, Assembly*, 17 May 1843.

59 *Debates, Assembly*, 10 Jan. 1844.

60 *Patriot*, 29 Jan., 10 Sept., 13 Sept. 1845.

CHAPTER EIGHT

1 CO 194/127, 183–203, LeMarchant to secretary of state, 10 May 1847; also, despatch 7, 10 May 1847, and LeMarchant to secretary of state, 24 June 1847; 129, LeMarchant to Grey, 24 Jan., 1 May 1848; and 131, LeMarchant to Grey, 2 June 1849.

2 *Patriot*, 7 Oct. 1846.

3 John Gaspard LeMarchant (1803–74) was an English military officer who had replaced Harvey as governor of Newfoundland in 1847; Baker and Pitt, *Dictionary*, 197.

4 CO 194/132, 69, inter-office memo: "A.B." to Herman Merrivale enclosing an extract from a private letter from LeMarchant.

5 Aubrey George Spencer (1785–1872) was born in London, ordained a Church of England priest in 1819, and became Anglican bishop of Newfoundland in 1839; Baker and Pitt, *Dictionary*, 322.

6 Millman and Kelley, *Atlantic Canada*, 94–5.

7 SPG, box A194, Thomas Boone to the bishop, 8 Dec. 1841.

8 Rev Benjamin Smith, "Notebook," Smith to "Dear Sir," 20 Oct. 1846.

9 Edward Field (1801–76) was born in England, ordained a priest of the Church of England in 1827, and succeeded Spencer as bishop of Newfoundland in 1844; Baker and Pitt, *Dictionary*, 105–6.

10 SPG, box A195, Correspondence of Bishop Feild, Feild to Hawkins, 19 June 1845.

11 Ibid., 15 Oct. 1845.

12 Rev. Benjamin Smith, "Notebook," Smith to Rev. B. Jones, 7 Feb. 1848.

13 John T. Mullock (1807–69) was born in Limerick, Ireland, and was ordained a Catholic priest in 1830. He came out to Newfoundland as coadjutor to Bishop Fleming in 1847. See AASJS, Howley Papers, unfinished "Draft of an Ecclesiastical History of Newfoundland," ch. 2; J.B. Ashley, "Literary Works of Bishop Mullock," in P.J. Kennedy, ed., *Centenary Souvenir Book* (St John's: General Committee of the Cathedral Centenary Celebrations 1955), 246; John J. Delaney and James Edward Tobin, "John T. Mullock," *Dictionary of Catholic Biography* (New York: Doubleday 1961), 833.

14 Ibid; Rev. E.P. Roche, "The Right Reverend John Thomas Mullock, D.D., 1807–1869," in Kennedy, *Centenary*, 222–32; also, Edward B. Foran, "Right Reverend Doctor Mullock, Bishop Militant," in Kennedy, *Centenary*, 233–46.

15 AASJS, Mullock Papers, 104/1/31, "Pastoral of 2 June 1853"; ibid., 104/1/29, "Pastoral of Bishop Mullock 14 July 1856 giving, on completion of Cathedral, account of receipts and expenditures for 1853, 1854 and 1855..."; ibid., 104/1/6, Bishop Hughes to Mullock, 3 May 1855; PANL, MG 920, B7/2, Diary of Robert Carter, Ferryland, 1832–52, entry for 29 June 1852. Robert Carter (1790–1852) was a JP and subcollector of customs at Ferryland.

16 National Archives of Canada, Howe Papers, Kent to Joseph Howe, 22 July 1846 as quoted in Elizabeth A. Wells, "The Struggle for Responsible Government in Newfoundland, 1846–1855" (M.A. thesis, Memorial University of Newfoundland 1967), 12, 15–18.

17 *Patriot*, 3, 17 Aug., 8, 15 June 1850.

18 Biographical information on R.J. Parsons has been drawn from a variety of sources, principally CO 194 and the extensive newspaper files covering the period 1832–83.

19 *Patriot*, 18 Aug. 1841.

20 *Debates, Assembly*, 29 Jan. 1841; *Patriot*, 23, 27, 30 Jan. 1841.

21 *Ledger*, 28 Sept. 1839; *Newfoundlander*, 7 Nov. 1839, 20 Feb. 1840; *Patriot*, 22 Feb., 14 March, 16 May, 8 Aug., 8 Sept. 1840.

22 *Newfoundland Express*, 13 Nov. 1851.

23 *Newfoundlander*, 17 Oct. 1850.

24 *Journal, Assembly*, 1852, app., 83–5: Grey to LeMarchant, 16 Dec. 1851.

25 *Debates, Assembly*, 27 March 1850.

26 *Ledger*, 19 April 1850.

27 *Debates, Council*, 14 April 1850.

28 The biographical information on Laurence O'Brien is drawn from the extensive newspaper files of the period 1832–50.

29 CO 194/133, LeMarchant to Grey, 3 May 1850.

30 H.T. Holman, "The Belfast Riot," in *The Island Magazine*, 14 (1983), 3–7; Duncan Campbell, *History of Prince Edward Island* (1875), 99. See also *Journal*, Prince Edward Island Assembly, 1847, 31–2 and app. 1, report on 1 March 1847 election violence. For Philip Little's biography, I am indebted, principally, to the CO correspondence for the period between 1844 and 1865 inclusive, to the extensive newspaper files of the same period, and to debates in the two houses of the Newfoundland legislature, 1850–61.

31 Ryan, *Fish out of Water*, esp. 59–60.

32 CO 194/129, LeMarchant to Grey, 1 May 1848.

33 Ryan, *Ice Hunters*, 55–9, 121–3, 215–16.

34 Phillip McCann, "Culture, State Formation and the Invention of Tradition: Newfoundland, 1832–1855," *Journal of Canadian Studies*, 23, nos. 1–2 (spring/summer 1988), 86–103. This is a ground-breaking essay on the general relations between government and people in the colony at that period. McCann advances the appealing theory that Harvey sowed the seeds of a political culture that for the first time gave the Newfoundland state genuine local roots.

35 CO 194/132, 69, "A.B." to Merrivale enclosing extract of a private letter from LeMarchant, dated St John's, 18 Oct. 1849; *Ledger*, 15 Oct. 1847; *Courier*, 8 April 1848, 27 Oct. 1849.

36 *Courier*, 17 April 1849.

37 Ibid., 6 March 1849.

38 Ibid., 20 Feb. 1849.

39 *Courier*, 7 April 1847, report of meeting of fire victims; ibid., 26 June 1847, 18 Jan. 1849; also, *Ledger*, 29 June, 30 July, 12 Nov. 1847.

40 Ibid., 24 Feb., 13, 20 March 1849.

41 CO 194/127, LeMarchant to Grey, 10 May , 27 Aug. 1847; vol 129, LeMarchant to Grey, 1 May 1848.

42 Ibid., 131, LeMarchant to Grey, 12 July 1849; *Courier,* 4 July 1849.

43 Ibid., 127, LeMarchant to Grey, 19 Aug. 1847.

44 *Times,* 23 June 1849; *Ledger,* 2 Jan., 2 Feb. 1849

45 *Courier,* 4, 7 July 1849.

46 John Little's low profile in the following years may have been induced by a premature, but severe, heart attack. When he died in 1864 at the early age of forty-seven, it was said that he had suffered from a "long and painful illness" (*Patriot,* 25 Oct. 1864) and that he had died from "disease of the heart" (*Day Book,* 24 Oct. 1864). It appears that his brother Philip had a share in the editorship of the *Courier* as well and they may have been joint editors. No private papers have survived to settle this issue for us.

47 Nicholas Mulloy was born in New Ross, Ireland, *c.* 1796 and served in Brigus, Newfoundland, as a medical doctor until his death in 1857; *Journal, Assembly,* 1851, 207; *Patriot,* 23 Nov. 1857.

48 John Delaney was born in Ireland and emigrated to Newfoundland, where he initially was appointed doorkeeper to the House of Assembly; Baker and Pitt, *Dictionary,* 81.

49 *Newfoundlander,* 1 March 1849.

50 Ibid., 26 April 1849.

51 The discussion that follows on the 1851–52 Assembly struggle is based on the house debates as they were published in the *Morning Post* from Jan.–July 1851 and in the *Newfoundland Express* from Jan.–July 1852; the debate of 28 Jan. 1851, which was not reported in the *Post,* can be found in the *Newfoundlander* and the *Times.* All debates are clearly identified in the respective newspapers under the heading "House of Assembly," and the dates appearing in the notes that follow are the actual dates of the debates in the house and not the dates of the newspapers.

52 *Post,* Assembly debate, 23 Jan. 1851.

53 *Newfoundlander, Times,* Assembly debate, 28 Jan. 1851.

54 Ibid.

55 Ibid.

56 *Post,* Assembly debate, 21 March 1851.

57 Ibid., 20 Feb. 1851.

58 Ibid., 21 Feb. 1851.

59 Ibid., 12 March 1851.

60 Ibid., 21 March 1851.

61 Ibid., 22 March 1851.

62 Ibid., 28 March 1851.

63 *Patriot,* 3 Nov. 1851.

64 P.B. Waite, "Sir John Gaspard LeMarchant," in *DCB*, 10: 438–9.

65 *Ledger,* 29 Jan. 1847.

66 *Post,* Assembly debates, 19, 24 March 1851, speech of P.F. Little.

67 *Courier,* 1 Feb. 1849.

68 Rev. Benjamin Smith, "Notebook," Smith to T. Wells, *c.* 1847.

69 *Newfoundlander,* 1 July 1852.

70 CO 194/129, 274, Fleming to Grey, 6 Nov. 1848.

71 *Patriot,* 17 Oct. 1848.

72 CO 194/134, LeMarchant to Grey, 4 June 1851.

73 Ibid., f105: see inter-office memos and notes.

74 *Express,* Assembly debate, 10 Feb. 1852, speech of Emerson.

75 The most complete reports of the Assembly debates for 1852 are to be found in the *Newfoundland Express* and the discussion that follows is based on those reports.

76 *Express,* Assembly debate, 4 Feb. 1852.

77 Ibid., 6 Feb. 1852.

78 *Patriot,* 16 Feb. 1852: Mullock to Little, 7 Feb. 1852; *Newfoundlander,* 12 Feb. 1852.

79 *Patriot,* 16 Feb. 1852: Mullock to Little, 7 Feb. 1852.

80 Ibid.

81 Ibid.

82 George James Hogsett (1820–69) was born in St John's and admitted to the bar in 1846; Baker and Pitt, *Dictionary,* 159.

83 *Ledger,* 17 Feb. 1852.

84 Ibid., "Anti-Maynooth" to the editor.

85 *Times,* 14 Feb. 1852.

86 Ibid., 25 Feb. 1852.

87 *Newfoundlander,* 12 Feb. 1852: Little to the editor, 11 Feb. 1852; *Ledger,* 17 Feb. 1852.

88 CO 194/136, LeMarchant to Grey, 13 Feb. 1852.

89 Harcourt Mooney (*c.* 1811–1853) was a barrister of the Middle Temple, London, and in 1844 was sworn in as a barrister of the Supreme Court in St John's where he practised law until he died; *Ledger,* 27 Dec. 1844, 3 June 1853.

90 *Ledger,* 24 Feb. 1852, report of the meeting of the Law Society; *Times,* 28 Feb. 1852.

91 CO 194/136, LeMarchant to Grey, 13 Feb. 1852.

92 Howley, *Ecclesiastical History,* 390.

93 *Pilot,* 28 Feb. 1852, report of a meeting of the Commercial Society.

94 Ibid.

95 Ibid.

96 *Patriot,* 1 March 1852, Mullock to the editor, 25 Feb. 1852.

97 *Ledger,* 5 March 1852, "Janus" to the editor.

98 Ibid., 12 March 1852: "Juvenis" to the editor.

99 *Newfoundland Express* 6 March 1852.

100 Appendix, table 2.

101 *Express*, Assembly debate, 20 Feb. 1852.

102 Ibid.

103 Ibid.

104 The debates of the Legislative Council were published sporadically in various newspapers and no complete file exists anywhere. Those that were reported are clearly identified under the heading "Legislative Council," and, as with Assembly debates, the dates cited here refer to the debates themselves rather than to the newspapers. *Council*, debate, 16 March 1852.

105 Ibid., 19 March 1852.

106 Appendix, table 3.

107 *Express*, Assembly debate, 31 March 1852.

108 Ibid.

CHAPTER NINE

1 At Oxford University in the 1840s several prominent Anglicans began the "Oxford Movement," which endeavoured to revive the high church tradition. They and their followers, called Tractarians because of the "Tracts for the Times" that the movement published, urged adoption of forms, ceremonies, and practices in Anglican services that many viewed as Roman Catholic.

2 CO 194/140, f.12, Hamilton to Newcastle, 31 Oct. 1853, encl.: petition from the pewholders of St Thomas' parish to Governor Hamilton.

3 Thomas E. Collett, *The Church of England in Newfoundland* (1853).

4 AASJs, Edward Morris, Diaries and Journals, 12 June 1876. Morris, 1813–87, was a commission agent, auctioneer, cashier of the Newfoundland Savings Bank, one-time editor of the *Courier*, and, after 1858, member of the Legislative Council.

5 Collett, *Church of England*.

6 Ker Baillie Hamilton (1804–89) was born in England, educated at the Royal Military Academy, and, following service in several British colonies, was appointed governor of Newfoundland in 1852; *ENL*, 2: 786.

7 CO 194/140, 83–6, Hamilton to Newcastle, 19 Nov. 1853, encl.: Hamilton to Bridge, 7 March 1853.

8 *Ledger*, 23 April 1851; *Courier*, 23 Sept. 1854, 10 March 1855.

9 Archives of the Anglican Diocese of Eastern Newfoundland and Labrador, "A Charge Delivered to the Clergy of the Diocese of Newfoundland by the Bishop, at His Second Visitation, on the Feast of St. Matthew, 1847."

10 *Post*, Assembly debate, 4 Feb. 1850.

11 Ibid., 26 Feb. 1850; see also *Courier*, 18 April 1850.

12 *Post*, Assembly debate, 26 Feb. 1850.

13 Ibid., 29 Jan. 1851.

14 Ibid., 18 March 1851.

15 George Henry Emerson (1798–1889) was born in Nova Scotia and came to Newfoundland in 1831 to practise law; Baker and Pitt, *Dictionary*, 98–9.

16 *Post*, Assembly debate, 17 March 1851.

17 On the Education Bill, 1852, see *Express*, Assembly debates, 19, 26 Feb., 12, 19, 23, 26 March, 13, 14, 19, 21, 26, 27 May, 9, 10, 11 June 1852.

18 Ibid., 12 March 1852.

19 *Post*, Assembly debate, 18 March 1851.

20 *Express*, Assembly debate, 12 March 1852.

21 Ibid.

22 *Express*, Council debate, 14 April 1852.

23 Ibid.

24 Ibid., 17 May 1852.

25 *Express*, Assembly debate, 19 May 1852.

26 Ibid., Council debate, 9 June 1852.

27 Ibid., Assembly debate, 9 June 1852.

28 Under this bill, the education grant, which had to date been granted to general protestant boards in St John's and Conception Bay, was subdivided on a per-capita, denominational basis and distributed to separate, denominational boards in those regions.

29 *Pilot*, 27 March 1852.

30 Ibid., 26 June 1852.

31 *Newfoundlander*, 30 Aug. 1852.

32 *Patriot*, 23 Aug. 1852.

33 *Pilot*, 13 Nov. 1852.

34 Ibid., 2 Oct. 1852.

35 *Courier*, 3 Jan. 1852.

36 Ibid., 31 Jan., 7, 11, 21 Feb., 3, 10, 13, 17, 20 March 1852.

37 *Patriot*, 19 Jan. 1852.

38 *Courier*, 3 April 1852.

39 Ibid., 22 May, 19 June, 3 July, 25 Sept. 1852.

40 *Pilot*, 2 Oct. 1852.

41 *Courier*, 1 Sept. 1852. Benning (1785–1865) was born in the British Isles, probably England, and in 1804 emigrated to Newfoundland as agent for an English firm in Placentia Bay; *DCB*, 9: 46–7.

42 William Talbot (*c.* 1792–1873) was an ex-patriate Irishman who taught school in Carbonear; *Courier*, 7 May 1873; *Telegraph*, 14 May 1873.

43 John Hayward (1819–85) was born in Harbour Grace and admitted to the bar in 1841; *ENL*, 2: 863.

44 *Pilot*, 13 Nov. 1852.

45 CO 194/136, 23, LeMarchant to Pakington, 15 June 1852.

46 *Ledger,* 22 June 1852.

47 Ibid., 10 Sept. 1852.

48 Ibid., 1 Oct. 1852.

49 *Newfoundland Express,* 6 March, 5 Aug. 1852.

50 *Pilot,* 9 Oct. 1852.

51 Ibid., 23 Oct. 1852.

52 Emerson defected to the Liberals early in the session of 1853.

53 Appendix, table 4.

54 *Express,* Assembly debate, 21 March 1853.

55 Appendix, table 5.

56 *Express,* Assembly debate, 21 May 1853.

57 *Journal, Assembly,* 1853, 278–9: message from the Council to the
   Assembly.

58 CO 194/139, 27, Hamilton to Newcastle, 21 Feb. 1853.

59 Ibid.

60 Ibid., Hamilton to Newcastle, 4 May 1853.

61 CO 194/139, 124, Hamilton to Newcastle, 4 May 1853: marginal notes
   by Newcastle.

62 The British government had awarded responsible government to the
   colony with a suggestion that there be an increase of representatives
   and a geographical subdivision of districts.

63 *Express,* Assembly debate, 24 March 1854.

64 Appendix, table 6.

65 *Express,* Assembly debate, 6 April 1854.

66 John Bemister (1815–92) was born in Carbonear, where he eventually
   established a mercantile operation in the fishery; ENL, 1: 174.

67 Stephen March was born in Old Perlican and founded there a substantial fishery operation; ENL, 3: 452.

68 *Express,* Assembly debate, 6, 7, 10 April 1854.

69 *Courier,* 18 March, 15 April 1854.

70 Council, *Journal,* 8, 9 May 1854.

71 *Express,* Assembly debate, 19 May 1854.

72 Ibid., 7, 8 June 1854.

73 CO 194/143, 253–62, Hamilton to Grey, 8 July 1854.

74 Ibid., encl.: "Case of the Protestant Inhabitants of Newfoundland
   Against the Unconditional Concession of Responsible Government as
   set forth in A Letter to the Rt. Hon. Sir George Grey, secretary of state
   for the Colonies, from H.W. Hoyles, Member of the House of Assembly, Newfoundland."

75 Ibid., 440, Hoyles to Peel, 14 Aug. 1854, marginal notes by Peel. (All
   signatures and X's are in the same handwriting.)

76 Ibid., 141, 65, Hamilton to Newcastle, 23 March 1854.

77 Ibid., f.137, 14 June 1854.

78 Ibid., marginal note by Newcastle.
79 Ibid., f.153, Newcastle to Hamilton, 6 July 1854.
80 Ibid., ff.155–64, 1 Aug. 1854.
81 Council, *Journal*, 20, 24, 27, 28, 29, 30 Oct. 1854.
82 CO 194/142, 33, Hamilton to Grey, 3 Oct. 1854, encl.: Archibald, Crowdy and Noad to Hamilton 3 Oct. 1854.
83 Ibid., Hamilton to Grey, 23 Nov. 1854, encl.: Joseph Hume to Captain Hamilton (brother of governor), 25 Oct. 1854.
84 Appendix, table 8.

CHAPTER TEN

1 *Courier*, Assembly debate, 22 Nov. 1854. As with the legislative debates cited above for 1851–52, the dates cited below for debates published in the *Courier* in 1854–55 refer to the dates of the debates themselves.
2 Appendix, table 8.
3 CO 194/142, 24, Hamilton to Grey, 19 Sept. 1854.
4 Ibid., 65, Hamilton to Grey, 14 Nov. 1854.
5 *Courier*, Assembly debate, 22 Nov. 1854.
6 Ibid., 24 Nov. 1854, Hamilton to Philip Little and Ambrose Shea, 24 Nov. 1854.
7 Ibid., 27 Nov. 1854.
8 CO 194/142, 82, Hamilton to Grey, 23 Nov. 1854.
9 Ibid., 100, Hamilton to Grey, 29 Nov. 1854.
10 Ibid.
11 Ibid., 167, Hamilton to Grey, 30 Nov. 1854.
12 Ibid., 144, 38, Grey to Hamilton 16 March 1855.
13 *Express*, Assembly debates, 2, 15 March, 6, 7, 13, 30 April 1852; *Ledger*, 24 Feb. 1852, report of a meeting of the Commercial Society; *Ledger*, 4 March 1853.
14 *Express*, Assembly debate, 31 January 1853, speech form the throne.
15 *Express*, 31 January 1854; also, *Courier*, 10 Sept. 1853.
16 *Courier*, 10 Oct. 1854; *Express*, 2 March 1854, and *Courier*, 2 Sept. 1854.
17 *Patriot*, 29 July, 19 Aug. 1854.
18 *Ledger*, 11 March, *Times*, 12 March, *Courier*, 16 March, *Newfoundlander*, 17 March 1853.
19 *Express*, 23 Nov. 1853.
20 *Ledger*, 23 May 1854.
21 Ibid., 20 Oct. 1854.
22 *Express*, Assembly debate, 1 May 1854.
23 *Patriot*, 12 March 1855.
24 *Express*, Assembly debates, 23 Feb., 7 March 1853; *Courier*, Assembly debates, 30, 31 May 1855.
25 Ibid., 10 April 1854.

26 AASJs, Morris, *Diaries*, 17 Feb. 1855.

27 Mullock Papers, 104/1/6, Kent to Mullock, 20 Feb. 1855.

28 Little was in England as a delegate from the House of Assembly seeking removal of Governor Hamilton.

29 *Courier*, 10 Feb. 1855.

30 *Patriot*, 19 Feb. 1855.

31 AASJs, Morris, *Diaries*, 20 Feb. 1855.

32 Ibid. The events surrounding the nomination of candidates for St John's were hidden from public view while Edward Morris recounted them in his secret diary. It is to that diary that the author is indebted for the following account. My account is supplemented by a careful and detailed study of all surviving files of the various newspapers of that period.

33 George Emerson was the incumbent member for Twillingate-Fogo.

34 Peter Winser was the incumbent member for Ferryland.

35 Thomas Glen was a St. John's, Presbyterian merchant who had represented Ferryland in the House of Assembly, 1842–48.

36 George Hogsett was a Roman Catholic lawyer later chosen to represent Placentia–St Mary's.

37 William Talbot was one of the incumbent members for Conception Bay and was later chosen to represent Harbour Main.

38 James Tobin was extensively engaged in the transatlantic trade with John B. Bland of St John's under the company name of Bland and Tobin.

39 Although Parsons may well have been considered for the two ridings, yet Morris must have made a careless error for John Fox, a St John's, Roman Catholic merchant, became the sixth Liberal candidate for St John's.

40 Morris, Diary, 24 Feb. 1855.

41 CO 194/143, Robinson to Grey, 28 Dec. 1854; *Courier*, Assembly debate, 22 June 1855.

42 *Courier*, 21, 25 April 1855.

43 *Ledger*, 27 Feb. 1855.

44 *Patriot*, 19 March 1855.

45 *Courier*, 3 March 1855.

46 Ibid., 24 Feb. 1855.

47 *Newfoundlander*, 21 May 1855.

48 *Express*, 5 June 1855.

49 *Courier*, 23 May 1855.

50 PANL, Papers of Phillip F. Little, 1840–1890, MG 212, B–1–1, Cummin to Little, 17 March 1854.

Index